DATE DUE

WOMEN'S STATUS
AND FERTILITY
IN THE
MUSLIM WORLD

WOMEN'S STATUS AND FERTILITY IN THE MUSLIM WORLD

edited by

James Allman

 Praeger Publishers New York • London

Library of Congress Cataloging in Publication Data
Main entry under title:

Women's status and fertility in the Muslim world.

  Bibliography: p.
  1. Family size—Near East—Case studies.
2. Fertility, Human—Near East.   3. Women, Muslim.
4. Women—Near East—Social conditions.   I. Allman,
James, 1943–
HQ760.W65   1978   301.32′1   78–5897
ISBN 0-03-042926-9

PRAEGER SPECIAL STUDIES
383 Madison Avenue, New York, N.Y. 10017, U.S.A.

Published in the United States of America in 1978
by Praeger Publishers,
A Division of Holt, Rinehart and Winston, CBS, Inc.

89 038 987654321

Preface

During the last few years, the importance of the Middle East and North Africa in the world's economic and political affairs has dramatically increased. The region is in the midst of rapid transformation, and events that occur in the area have far-reaching, global implications. While studies dealing with the political and economic situation within the countries of this region have increased, information and analysis of social and cultural change are much less abundant. This is particularly true in the interrelated areas of population dynamics, changing family patterns, and women's roles and status. We know relatively little about the often substantial changes taking place throughout the region in these areas and, therefore, are rarely able to point to determinants that policy makers and planners might attempt to influence.

This collection of essays attempts to remedy partially the dearth of information on demographic change and to provide the reader with some recent approaches to the study of changing family patterns and women's status. The range of the contributions covers the entire Middle East and North Africa, including the non-Arab countries of Turkey and Iran. The general overviews (on recent research in the social sciences dealing with family patterns and women's role in the Introduction, on demographic change in Chapter 1 and on family planning in Chapter 2) provide information on all the countries of the region. The individual case studies of demographic change include Algeria, Tunisia, Egypt, Kuwait, Jordan, and Turkey. The social science approaches to family patterns and women's status, which all have direct or at least indirect implications for population dynamics, deal with Turkey, Iran, Lebanon, North Yemen, Tunisia, and Morocco. Several excellent additional papers were considered for publication in the volume; however, we were not able to include all the worthwhile material submitted due to the need to keep the volume within a reasonable size.

This collection is primarily the work of researchers who have lived and worked in the region for many years. Many are from the region, and Turkey, Egypt, Tunisia, Morocco, and Lebanon are represented. Their research attests to the fact that social sciences adapted and applied to the region's problems are in the making. The American, British, and French contributors have been permanent residents of the Middle East or have worked there for long periods of time.

Readers will find three levels of guidance in approaching this volume and the themes contained within. First, the Introduction summarizes the general implications of the issues surveyed in each of the two parts. In addition, Chapter 1 on the demographic transition provides an overview of the demographic parameters and dynamics throughout the region. Finally, a general, comprehensive bibliography appears at the end of the volume and is intended as a source for further reading.

The material included in the volume has been altered only for editorial consistency and ease of reference. The studies are all based on recent empirical research conducted in the countries of the region and both published and unpublished statistical data that have become available within the last few years.

Acknowledgments

The editor wishes to thank all those who assisted him in this enterprise, both in and out of the Middle East and North Africa. Special thanks go to Pertil Mathsson at UNESCO, Paris, who first encouraged the editor to pursue the idea of interdisciplinary research (using demographers and other social scientists) on population dynamics in developing countries. During work under his direction at UNESCO from September 1973 to December 1974, we were able to organize several field projects (in Iran, Morocco, and Jordan), hold a conference on population dynamics and changing family patterns in Beirut in July 1974, and prepare documentation in the form of bibliographies and research papers. This background and the opportunities UNESCO provided me with to travel extensively throughout the region contributed considerably to developing the material appearing in this volume. Serim Timur continued work in demography and the social sciences at UNESCO when she joined the Population Division in fall 1974. She deserves thanks for supporting some of the research presented here, as well as for contributing Chapters 3 and 11.

Many of the contributors to this volume and much of the research on the determinants of population dynamics in the region in general have benefited from the assistance of international organizations. For example, several of the contributors are currently or were resident advisors for the Population Council, the UN Population Division, or UNESCO. The research projects were supported by the Pathfinder Fund, the Ford Foundation, the UN Fund for Population Activities, the Population Council, the U.S. Agency for International Development, and the International Planned Parenthood Federation. The early efforts of these organizations, which were often of an innovative nature, have gradually been supported and extended by universities both in and outside the region, as well as by national statistical, research, and family planning institutions.

I would also like to thank the Faculty Research Committee of the American University of Beirut (AUB) and Terry Prothro, director of AUB's Center for Behavior Research, for financial support and encouragement while I completed the volume in academic year 1975-76. Colleagues at AUB--Samir Khalaf, Peter Dodd, Gerry Obermeyer, Fuad Khouri, Huda Zurayk, Iliya Harik, and Allan Hill--provided suggestions and comments that proved very helpful. In addition, I benefited from the reactions, comments, and critiques of students from the Middle East when I was teaching at AUB and leading a seminar on changing family patterns in the region.

My main thanks go to the contributors represented in these pages and, also, to those who submitted papers that I was unable to include. Travels during 1974-76, from France to Lebanon in the midst of civil war and, finally, to Haiti, made coordinating this collective undertaking at times rather difficult.

Toby Stone at UNESCO, Paris, Seteny Shami at AUB, and Kettly Laguerre at the Institut Haitien de Statistique provided exceptional secretarial and bibliographical help and deserve thanks for their patience and perseverance.

Finally, I must thank my wife, Suzanne Nedjati, for putting up with the infringement on our family life that this project entailed.

Contents

LIST OF TABLES AND FIGURES

Introduction:
Family Life, Women's Status, and Fertility: Middle East and North African Perspectives

JAMES ALLMAN

This volume focuses both on fertility trends and differentials in the Middle East and North Africa as well as on changes in family life and women's status that lie behind the demographic statistics. The first of these themes falls generally within the purview of demography, the second of anthropology, sociology, psychology, and, in certain respects, political science, history, economics, law, and the medical sciences. Changing demographic trends in the region have long been neglected, partially because of a dearth of data. However, in recent years, progress in data collection has been rapid. Considerable information is currently available; a major effort by statisticians, demographers, economic and social planners, and policy makers in the region is needed to analyze, interpret, and use this new information.

The task confronting social scientists is more complex. In addition to the relatively little research data available, current theoretical and methodological approaches need to be critically examined in these disciplines. Later, after reviewing the state of social science research on family patterns and women's status in the region, we will discuss some promising approaches that are presented in this volume, as well as consider future research needs in general.

The eight chapters that make up Part I show clearly that the countries of the Middle East and North Africa are currently in the process of a demographic transition--from high to low mortality and fertility. As in other regions of the world, demographic modernization appears related to socioeconomic development; the variables traditionally associated with the development of differential fertility and decline (levels of education, occupational status, urban experience, income and standard of living, exposure to mass media, and so forth) are indeed important factors in determining population dynamics in the Middle East and North Africa. Further, there is some evidence that the demographic transition may be moving at an accelerated pace in this region in comparison with the time it took to complete the transition in currently developed countries. However, the situation is far from clear, since fertility appears to have increased in certain countries.

After an introductory chapter, which provides an overview of demographic parameters in 1975, Chapters 3 to 8 present case studies of fertility trends and differentials in Turkey, Egypt, Jordan, Kuwait, Algeria, and Tunisia. While the overall trend toward lower rates of fertility and mortality is probably inevitable, evidence shows that fertility is rising in some of the countries; this could be associated with the early stages of socioeconomic development found in some of the countries of the region. In recent years, in Algeria and Kuwait, increases have pushed the birth rates to some of the highest in the world. In both countries, however, economic development, the spread of literacy through formal education, improvement in health care, and greater access to social services seem likely to lead to declines in fertility in the decades ahead.

In the past, some observers of the Middle East have argued that social customs and ideological factors prevented Muslim natality from declining, as has been the case in developed countries. This view is not supported by current evidence. We see clear indications of fertility decline in Tunisia, Egypt, and Turkey. In addition, as Chapter 2 demonstrates, knowledge and interest in family planning is growing increasingly throughout the region. Although declines in fertility directly related to family planning programs are not yet as dramatic in this part of the world as in some of the Asian nations, governmental population policies and popular acceptance of the idea of planning births are likely to be of major importance in determining demographic trends in the future.

Although the changing demographic reality of the region has begun to draw the attention of demographers, statisticians, planners, and policy makers, social scientists have yet to respond actively to the challenge the changes in population dynamics pose to their respective disciplines. This is not surprising, since, in general, social science research in developing countries has played a rather limited role in population research. Until recently, little attention was given to the socioeconomic prerequisites to demographic change. Social science research, although important from the beginning (and throughout the expansion) of family planning programs, has had little to say about these fundamental problems.[1] Foreign missions to developing countries were usually followed by field surveys to show the low knowledge of modern contraceptives, the positive attitudes toward birth control, and the practices, often labeled traditional, leading to more children than the parents interviewed considered ideal. Social scientists then became involved in the development, monitoring, and evaluation of family planning programs. However, by the early 1970s, an awareness of the somewhat shaky assumptions, supposedly based on social science research, which laid the basis for family planning activities began to appear.[2]

The 1974 World Population Conference marked a turning point, since it placed an emphasis on policies beyond family planning and fertility, namely, on the indirect socioeconomic means of population policy. Major conclusions of the conference included the ideas that population policy objectives cannot properly be isolated from other social and economic objectives and that population policy should not be restricted to the control of population growth and the reduction of fertility but rather should deal with a large variety of variables. In this approach, family planning is not viewed exclusively as a direct means of affecting fertility; it is a human right that must be respected and promoted irrespective of the demographic consequences.[3]

Around this time, social scientists began to realize the need for studies of population dynamics and family planning that would take into account changes in family patterns and the roles and status of women within the context of socioeconomic development. For example, the UN 1973 Symposium on Population and the Family in Honolulu and the Committee on Population and the Family at the 1974 World Population Conference in Bucharest concluded that the interrelationships between family structure and demographic change were poorly understood and that connections between family structure and fertility were obscure. They further concluded that "in the respective disciplines there had been insufficient attention to the role of the family in population change," and that many "governments frequently lacked the factual bases for establishing national policies concerning populations and family relationships." Similarly, the 1975 International Women's Year Conference in Mexico emphasized the importance of "population-oriented research upon which to base policies relevant to women and development" and recommended research on the "interrelationship between types of marital status and union status and the participation of women in economic activities outside the home and patterns of reproduction."[4]

What is needed, then, is research linking population dynamics with changes in family patterns and the status of women. This research, which should take into account the processes of socioeconomic development and cultural change, would have to draw on the theoretical approaches and methodological tools of several disciplines. Cross-cultural, interdisciplinary studies would lead to the type of scientific knowledge with practical policy implications currently being called for.

All this, of course, is easier said than done. Interdisciplinary research linking various social science approaches to family patterns and women's status with demographic change in the process of development presupposes a demographic data base and substantial research in such fields as anthropology, sociology, psychology, political science, and, probably, economics, history, law, and the medical sciences. At this point, before further discussing social science approaches to population dynamics in the Middle East and North Africa, it might be useful to review the current state of social science research on family patterns and women's status in the region. Sources of documentation have been drawn primarily from several bibliographies on these and related topics that have appeared during the last few years.[5]

SOCIAL SCIENCE RESEARCH ON FAMILY PATTERNS AND WOMEN'S STATUS IN THE MIDDLE EAST AND NORTH AFRICA

After an extensive and thorough review of the social science literature available around 1960 on women, the family, and certain aspects of the demographic situation in the Middle East and North Africa, Goode concluded that "there has been far more systematic field research among the Bantoid peoples of Africa" than in this region of the world. He went on to say that "it seems likely that a flood of sociological studies in the major Arab countries will appear in the next decade," and "many of the present gaps in our knowledge of the Arab family will probably be filled." We must note now that this flood of research has turned out to be little more than a "trickle."[6] In many areas covered in Goode's presentation, we cannot meet his challenge to "build on these findings or correct them where necessary."[7] The needed data simply are not available, or if they have been collected in recent censuses, surveys, and field studies, they have yet to be analyzed, interpreted, and disseminated.

Let us look more closely at the topics Goode covered in his study of changing family patterns in Arabic Islam in order to see if more recent data modify his conclusions. He considered the following topics: choice of mate, polygamy, age at marriage, fertility and contraception, illegitimacy, infanticide, the extended family, larger kinship structures, relations internal to the family, the position of women in the larger society, and, finally, divorce, widowhood, and remarriage.

Goode correctly predicted that "in the next decade . . . efforts at controlling fertility will begin to show results in at least the more advanced Arab countries, and possibly others as well."[8] However, the oversimplified view that Islam was primarily responsible for the high fertility rates in the region and offered an insurmountable barrier to fertility decline[9] has been challenged by more thorough analysis.[10] (Recent fertility trends and the development of population policies and family planning are reported in detail in Chapters 1 and 2 and elsewhere.)

Infanticide will not be considered, since as Goode concluded, "the available data do not suggest infanticide, nor even any perceptible neglect of females which might cause their mortality to be higher than of males."[11] Polygamy will only be discussed briefly, since it is increasingly a marginal practice throughout the region. (A review of recent research in the 1960s concluded that "polygamy is not studied frequently," since "the decreasing number of polygamous families has removed it from the level of serious problems."[12]) Also, little will be said about illegitimacy, since data on this phenomenon are not available.

Choice of Mate

For many of the topics Goode discussed, data are still very inadequate--often, little more is available than when he did his review (around 1960). Generally, in those cases, we have to go along with his conclusions (without being entirely satisfied that they accurately portray the situation). For example, in his section on choice of mate, it would be difficult to deny, based on recent studies, that there are moves in the direction of freer mate choice. But how much of a free choice is there? How important are background factors, such as social class, wealth, education? In marriage choice, what role do parents and relatives play in arranging marriage and so forth? For more easily measurable factors related to mate choice, such as the preference for marrying father's brother's daughter, recent evidence is by no means conclusive in regard to whether, as Goode concludes, "the likelihood of cousin marriage has declined."[13] There really are no representative data to substantiate this claim for a particular society, much less for the whole region; however, we do have some recent studies that help to illuminate the meaning of the practice in Muslim society.[14]

We could review the most recent studies dealing with parallel cousin marriage and such topics as bride-price patterns and student attitudes toward mate choice. However, what would emerge would be pretty much a general impression of somewhat of a decline in "traditional" practices, with greater "modernization." This does not take us very far in understanding change in the region in a scientific way, nor does it provide us with useful information that has relevance for social policy.

Similarly, remaining at the level of an analysis of ideological positions, as Goode frequently does, is not particularly illuminating and can lead to wrong predictions. For example, in the section on mate choice, Goode noted that "without any question the revolutionary fervor in Arab countries over the past fifteen years has been a prime

mover in the changing position of the woman and the changing structure of the family."[15] He cited Algeria as a case in point. In that
country, he stated that the woman, because of her participation in
the revolution and because of the regime's revolutionary socialist
ideology, "now, instead of being passive and compliant and denying
her part in the marriage process . . . actually takes part in the
contract, signing it herself, and generally feels much freer in her
relations with men in her own family."[16] However, a study done in
1966 concluded that the involvement of Algerian women in the war
against France and the government's socialist ideology did not result in a substantial uplift in women's status. According to Gordon,
"Women soon found that, whatever the law might say or however
fervent Ben Bella might be in insisting on their rights, Algeria was
still a man's world, and that they were still, for all practical purposes, second-class citizens."[17] More recent research suggests
that women's status in Algeria has not improved greatly in the last
ten years.[18]

    Similarly, in the other more "progressive" countries of the
region, such as Iraq and Syria, women's status has not apparently
improved dramatically. The People's Democratic Republic of
Yemen may be an exception.[19] Here, as in the Muslim republics
of Soviet Central Asia, women appear to be more fully integrated
into all aspects of national life and to play more of a major role in
national development than in other Middle Eastern countries.[20]
Although more research needs to be done on this question, it does
seem that countries which have undergone ostensibly bourgeois
revolutions aiming at national liberation and independence and/or
the replacement of a traditional ruling class by a more dynamic
middle class (for instance, Turkey, Tunisia, Egypt, and Iran)
have so far gone farther than the socialist Arab states in promoting
women's rights. Indeed, women appear to have the greatest freedom
in Lebanon, where the government has played little role in socioeconomic change, except by standing back and letting local entrepreneurs and international market forces operate. In addition, in
Lebanon, some of the most archaic laws remain on the books, and
the political system has yet to modernize. Although currently, we
are far from a clear understanding of the determinants of women's
roles and status in the Middle East and North Africa, a consideration of "persistent Arab propaganda in favor of the emancipation of
women and their fuller participation in social and occupation
realms"[21] may not lead us too far in this task. A much closer look
at the new institutions being created and opening up to women, the
process by which women enter new roles, as well as the conflicts
engendered by the clash of demands made by old and new roles seems
called for. One can hardly talk of women's freedom to choose with

regard to jobs, nonfamilial roles, or even mate choice if there are no or very few opportunities available that differ from those found in traditional life.

Some have argued that even if the opportunities were available for education, employment, extrafamilial roles, and so forth, women might not take advantage of them because of traditional values.[22] This is questionable. In the few examples offered, it might be argued that supposed "opportunities" entail giving up substantial advantages. This could be the case in women's reluctance in this region to become airline stewardesses or to work in factories. The regimentation of factory life and the disruption of social and family life entailed by being a stewardess may not be compensated for sufficiently. If women can avoid employment, especially that which is monotonous and unrewarding, it is not surprising that they do so. However, we know so little about actual women's experiences in the labor force in this region that it is difficult to go beyond speculation.

Age at Marriage

The situation in the region appears to be more complex than Goode suggested when he concluded that "without doubt, the age of marriage is rising in all Arab countries."[23] Recent data, which are probably more accurate than Goode's sources, suggest, for example, that average age at marriage for females has decreased in Algeria since World War II[24] and declined in Tunisia between 1965 and 1970.[25] In Kuwait, the mean age at first marriage has not changed with the extension of health services and overall prosperity during the last 25 years,[26] nor has it declined with increasing women's liberation and declining fertility in Turkey.[27] Recent data also suggest that the age at marriage declined in Iran between the mid-1950s and the mid-1960s. This downward trend has not continued however; in 1972, the mean age at marriage was not as low as it was in the 1950s.[28] While some research supports Goode's conclusion, it is perhaps premature to state, as do Prothro and Diab, that "the days of child brides seem definitely in the past, and the overall trend toward later age at marriage is unmistakable";[29] while their data do indicate an increase in age at marriage in some areas of Lebanon, Syria, and Jordan, the overall picture, even in these countries, is not clear. Before reaching general conclusions about trends in age at marriage for the region, we need analysis based on data that are representative of whole societies and provide a broad sample, rather than just looking at a few communities or urban areas.

The Extended Family

Subsequent research has confirmed Goode's belief that the extended patriarchal family is more an ideal than a reality. Demographic analysis shows that with the conditions of mortality, life
expectancy, and age at marriage that prevail in traditional societies,
the majority of families have, in fact, to be nuclear rather than extended, in spite of people's preferences. In addition, data from
Egypt and Turkey suggest that economic considerations play an important role in determining to what extent the patriarch keeps his
family together.[30]

Goode also appears correct in stressing the fact that "the intensity of family ties . . . remains strong."[31] Additional research
supports the continued social and psychological reality of the extended family. This is manifested by the support family members
find during periods of crisis (by frequent visits or, in urban areas,
by telephone calls), by the development of family associations, and
by the importance of family ties in economic, political, and cultural
areas.

It also appears true that with young people's desire to choose
their mates, there also comes the "move both to establish such
conjugal units and to defend them ideologically."[32] These two possibly conflicting tendencies appear to co-exist, although we do not
have a great deal of information on how this process actually takes
place.

Larger Kinship Structures

Goode's discussion of the extension and linking of kin ties into
larger groups draws primarily on previous publications, including
some anthropological studies based on adequate field work but, also,
on material, such as accounts by travelers and political advisers,
which even he considered far from satisfactory. Since 1960, anthropologists, political scientists, and sociologists have completed additional studies of nomadic-pastoral groups, village communities,
and urban areas that shed some light on the role of larger kinship
structure in the political, economic, and social life of the region.
These studies, which have been reviewed elsewhere, considerably
deepen our understanding of the importance of kinship ties in the
region.[33] They generally point to the existence of persistent, important roles for the extended family.

Goode's conclusion that in the city, the larger kinship structure disintegrates has not been confirmed in more recent research.
Gulick, for example, believes that in spite of the "unsupported

stereotype" that "allege[s] that pastoral nomads are enmeshed in very large, widely ramified corporate tribes, and (at the other extreme) that urban people are only involved in nuclear families . . . there are indications that all of the organizational variations of kinship . . . probably . . . occur in Middle Eastern cities."[34] He cites, as examples, the continuance of tribal organization among the squatters in and around Baghdad and the legal incorporation of large, but hitherto unorganized, patrilineal kin groups into the social structure in Lebanon during the past 40 years. Khalaif similarly notes that in Lebanon, the increasing efforts of both governmental and nongovernmental agencies in the fields of social welfare and community development have not been accompanied by a decline in the incidence of family associations.[35]

In those countries of the region where centralized state authority is a relatively recent phenomenon and what social scientists would consider a national, bureaucratic structure only beginning to function, a knowledge of kinship relations is essential to understanding economic, political, social, and cultural dynamics. In general, an in-depth analysis of political or other elites in most countries of the region will soon lead one to relationships based on kinship, common geographical origin, or particular sects and communal groups. Yet, although it is fairly common knowledge that kinship continues to play a role in social change in the region, we do not have available systematic studies dealing with this question.

It should not be surprising that in countries where monarchies still prevail--Morocco, Saudi Arabia, Jordan, Qatar, Bahrain, Kuwait, Oman, and Iran--belonging to the royal family or having ties with members of this family is important. Similarly, in countries that have only (relatively) recently abolished regimes with monarchs and noble families--Tunisia, Libya, Iraq, North Yemen, Egypt, and, to some extent, Turkey--it is understandable that familism continues to exist.

Women's Status

Goode's major conclusions on women's status in the region have been confirmed by more recent data. For example, he believed that "the improvement of the position of Arab women in a larger society both grows from and contributes to her position within the family and kinship network itself . . . the great changes of the past decade cannot be reversed, and the immediate future should see changes equally important."[36] Since there was not a great deal of research available on women's status in the region when he was writing, he looked primarily at some of the new laws

concerning women and the family, information on women's movements, and available data on women's education and employment.

A review on the literature on women's status suggests that in
general, the question of women's roles in Arab Muslim societies
was first presented from a religious perspective--woman in Islam.
Western observers usually lamented what they saw as Muslim's
women subservient, submissive, powerless position. Muslim
authors, from about 1950, adopted a similar perspective but generally with an apologetic aim, especially focusing on how Islam
improved women's status and the fact that many of the practices
denounced by Westerners were corruptions of "true" Islam. The
activities of the feminist movement, especially in Egypt, and the
various laws passed to improve women's status also received
attention.

After 1960, the topic of women in the region begins to be approached from both a cultural and socioeconomic point of view. For
example, the Gulick's bibliography of 137 studies, referred to previously, cites about 10 works dealing with women's employment,
19 dealing with women's movements and status, 14 with family
planning, and about 25 concerned with honor, sexuality, and Islamic
values affecting women. From a geographic point of view, they
indicate 18 village studies, 5 tribal nomadic studies, and only 6
urban studies.

The general theme of the studies since 1960 dealing with
women's employment is that women are underrepresented in the
labor forces of Muslim countries and, because of Islamic values,
confined to certain professions, where their contact with men is
limited.[37] This is probably still true, although most of the studies
rely on data that go back to 1960 or before, and they tell us little
about the problems and successes of the increasing numbers of
women in the region who are, nevertheless, in spite of obstacles
and cultural barriers, finding places in the labor force. Considerable unanalyzed data from censuses and surveys could be usefully
studied to shed light on these questions. On the other hand, the
numerous studies of the honor code and Islamic restrictions of
women's freedom perhaps tell us as much as we need to know about
the background and setting of the obstacles to women's emancipation. Perhaps what is more important now in the 1970s is the fact
that women are overcoming these ideological barriers. It is important to quantitatively document this and to study the impact of,
say, postschool socioeconomic roles or female employment on
family life, child rearing, husband-wife interaction, fertility behavior, divorce, and so forth. In other words, the numerous studies
of religious texts and Koranic injunctions should give way to a focus
on women's actual behavior, based on quantitative data rather than

on subjective opinions, particularly as it affects family life and demographic variables.

A recent study on women's education in the Arab states covering the period up to 1970 notes dramatic improvement in access to education by women, but disparities of educational opportunities still exist for girls in the 16 Arab states studied.[38] These include unbalanced enrollments, with fewer girls than boys in all levels and types of education; higher absenteeism and dropout rates among girls; concentration of girls in the humanities in secondary and higher education and their limited access to vocational and technical training; and, finally, a greater allocation of funds to boys' education due to the preceding disparities. The author of the study believes that these differences are partially explainable by "the existence of a Muslim cultural barrier to girls' education which lies not in the legal status of women as delineated in Islamic texts, but in women's actual status as it evolved since the Middle Ages, and in certain traditional attitudes towards girls and women and their role in society." However, this was true much more in the past than today, since the dramatic postcolonial "expansion in girls' education has narrowed the gap between the educational opportunities for the two sexes." Further, "Today, the existing disparities of educational opportunities for girls and the differences among the Arab states in this regard is attributed to differences in the level of economic development."[39]

An additional recent theme in social science research on women in the region is an attempt to clarify interpretations of women's roles and power, biased previously insofar as the analysis had access only to the man's world; consequently, only Middle Eastern male interpretations of women's status were reported. (These biased interpretations were sometimes clouded by inappropriate Western conceptual categories, which tended to present a false picture of complex social phenomena.) While scientific studies by women social scientists from the region may provide insight and understanding into the role of women in traditional society and the impact of current forces of change on women's status, they are not necessarily a guarantee that social scientists will go beyond stereotypes. The questions involved are complex; as recent reviews suggest, a great deal more research grounded in empirical reality will be necessary for both adequate description and conceptual clarification.[40]

Relations Internal to the Family

Goode's observation that "there are no contemporary studies of the changes in the relations among the various members of the

Arab family" is still largely true today.[41] During the last 15 years, there has been some work on husband-wife communication, particularly as this relates to decisions on use of family planning. In addition, a few social scientists, inspired by Bott's Family and Social Network, considered complementary and segregation role relationships within the family.[42] But in-depth studies drawing both on quantitative data and qualitative information gathered by participant observation, such as Bott's work and Rainwater's Family Design, are not available for this region.[43]

Because of the paucity of data, it is still "not possible . . . to chart the changes now going on among the various relationships within the Arab family."[44] This is a major gap, and we can do little more than offer "anecdotal impressions" until it is filled.

Divorce, Widowhood, and Remarriage

With the exception of Prothro and Diab's research, reported in Changing Family Patterns in the Arab East, there has been little systematic study of empirical data from the region on divorce, widowhood, and remarriage since Goode reviewed available findings. He noted that "we would expect the Arab countries to exhibit a declining divorce rate as they move toward industrialization."[45] Prothro and Diab's survey data, their examination of religious court records, and their review of national statistical data from Jordan, Syria, and Lebanon support Goode's conclusion.[46] Additional studies done during the last 15 years discuss changes in laws affecting divorce, particularly in North Africa, but there is apparently little attention to the empirical data--court records, censuses, surveys, and so forth--which would allow us to determine more precisely trends and patterns and offer hypotheses concerning possible changes due to various modifications in socioeconomic conditions.

Cultural or Ideological Bias in Research
on Family Patterns and Social Change

One of the major shortcomings of Goode's approach, as well as in much of the research on family patterns in the region, is the lack of concern for the impact of basic structural changes on the economic and social organization of the countries of the region. Goode concludes, for example, that what he sees as striking changes in the position of women and family life "occurred first of all as a political and ideological revolution, in anticipation of, or perhaps in preparation for, the changes that are beginning in the economic sphere."[47]

Similarly, Prothro and Diab conclude that in the Middle East, "industrialization is too slight to be looked upon as an important causative factor. Urbanization has long characterized the Middle East and was for centuries compatible with traditional family ways." They suggest two factors "which contribute to the continuing evolution of the family . . . first . . . a continuing Western influence" and "second . . . the spread of an egalitarian ideology in the pursuit of political objectives."[48] While these approaches, which stress values and ideological or cultural factors, do provide justification for new patterns of behavior and participation in new institutions and roles, it should not be forgotten that in spite of relatively little industrialization, all the countries of the region have been profoundly affected by (often drastic) economic change. Issawi sums up how some of these changes influenced urban life in the Middle East:

> In the course of the nineteenth century the various parts of the Middle East were drawn, to a greater or lesser extent, into the international network of trade and finance. This entailed the immigration of European businessmen and technicians, the investment of foreign capital, the development of mechanical transport, and the shift from a subsistence to a cash crop agriculture. The introduction of modern hygiene led to a sharp population growth, and foreign competition resulted in the ruin of handicrafts.
>   All these trends had marked effects on the location, size and structure of Middle Eastern towns. Perhaps the simplest way to put it is that the economy began to be oriented outwards, toward the export of its primary products, that transport was developed accordingly. . . .[49]

Thus, although it is true that the Middle East is a region which has been urbanized for many centuries, the diverse political, economic, and social transformations of the nineteenth century had a drastic impact on the traditional structure of Middle Eastern cities. Baghdad, Tunis, or Cairo in the twelfth, thirteenth, or fourteenth centuries were certainly not the same kinds of cities as they were in the early twentieth century. In addition, since the 1920s, several important trends have been at work to accelerate changes in the structure and functions of urban centers. These included

> population growth, the discovery and exploitation of oil, the impact of the Second World War, the exodus of foreigners and minority groups from certain countries, the decline in foreign trade of some countries relative to their gross national products, foreign aid, and following

independence, the use of state power to promote industrialization and other forms of economic development.
The results have been a marked acceleration in urbanization and a reversal of the shift of population concentra-
tions from inland cities to the coast.[50]

We note similar profound changes during the past two centuries
throughout the Middle East when we go outside the cities as well. In
discussing rural-urban relations in historical perspective, Harik
identifies three phases in the modern development of Middle Eastern
societies:

> The first phase is characterized by a noncompetitive sub-
> sistence system of agriculture and by international trade;
> these co-exist with a minimal degree of interaction. The
> second phase is characterized by the growth of a domes-
> tic market bound to an export sector and state centraliza-
> tion, starting roughly at the beginning of the nineteenth
> century. This may be considered as the first phase of
> modernization in the Middle East. The third phase per-
> tains to the contemporary scene, starting by and large
> in the post-World War II era. It is basically character-
> ized by the modification of the domestic market in cer-
> tain Middle Eastern countries in such a way as to limit
> the political and economic roles of large landlords and
> money lenders and at the same time reduce the size of
> the subsistence sector of agriculture. National leaders
> are generally oriented toward a welfare, though still an
> authoritarian, social policy.[51]

The social transformations involved in each of these phases
were profound and extensive. In many cases, economic and social
conditions improved quite dramatically. Population growth, which
was related to improved rural conditions, generally triggered migration to the cities and the development of a proletariat or sub-
proletariat, which, of course, was not without implications for the
political movements that lead to independence and national liberation in many countries of the region. Harik argues that "if rural
people in some Middle Eastern countries are presently the benefi-
ciaries of reform-minded regimes, it is due largely to the fact that
they have become part of national life, and out of their stock many
an influential national leader has appeared."[52]

The last two centuries have been marked by substantial, far-
reaching, and often profound changes. One could discuss at great
length the development of new political organizations, unions,

associations, the experience of military service and training, the impact of experience abroad, and numerous other aspects of involvement in suprafamilial institutions during the nineteenth and twentieth centuries in the Middle East. Indeed, these changes can and must be examined in detail if we are to understand the determinants of changing family patterns, women's status, and demographic patterns. It simply is not adequate to ignore these factors in favor of pointing to "Western influence," "egalitarian ideology," or "ideological revolution."

While it is not our concern to evaluate the positive and negative consequences of the changes mentioned above, it is essential to do away with the stereotype of traditional, unchanging Middle Eastern societies. Rosenfeld formulates the challenge well in regard to rural areas:

> Those who believe in the Immovable East with an unchanged peasantry existing in some places for five to six thousand years must prove their thesis. They must prove that there have been no population movements; no interchange of nomadic, village, and urban peoples; no intercontinental commercialism; no creation of new peasantry out of tribal elements or out of declassed urban elements; and no creation of tens of empires and hundreds of petty states which based themselves on the peasantry.[53]

Except for a few countries, such as the two Yemens, Saudi Arabia, and Oman, which remained relatively isolated and outside the world economy and the colonial empires of the nineteenth century, most of the countries of the Middle East have had their economies, social and political structures, and demographic structures radically and profoundly transformed in the course of the last two centuries. Even those countries that have only recently begun movements toward development must be viewed within the context of international geopolitics. Further, it can be argued that colonialism was an important factor blocking movements that would have led to structural reforms in the countries of the region that remain the most underdeveloped today.[54]

The following comment by Geertz about community studies in the Middle East and North Africa applies equally well to an overly cultural approach in studies dealing with the family, women's status, and demographic patterns: the "genre as it now exists tends in fact to be inherently antitheoretical and powerfully inhibitory of analytic progress in almost any direction."[55] We are definitely in need of new approaches and directions in this important area, which has both theoretical and practical importance.

FAMILY STRUCTURE, WOMEN'S STATUS,
AND POPULATION DYNAMICS

The chapters included in Part II are recent efforts by anthropologists, sociologists, psychologists, and political scientists that focus on various aspects of family structure, women's status, and population dynamics, often with attention to changes in fertility patterns or the impact of family planning. Although the interconnections between social science research on family patterns and women's status, on the one hand, and demographic studies of population dynamics, on the other, can no longer be overlooked in the study of the developing nations, the interest of social scientists and demographers in doing research linking these areas in the Middle East and North Africa has not been pronounced. Consequently, it is an opportune moment to present some recent efforts that move in this direction. Of course, no one book can cover all aspects of these related fields in an area as large as the Middle East and North Africa. Gaps left in coverage are readily apparent; among these are studies dealing with family planning programs, historical studies, research on tribal nomadic groups, and so forth. But comprehensiveness of coverage is not, however, our main goal; rather, we seek to present both promising methodological and theoretical approaches to the family, women's status, and fertility, as well as information about countries often neglected but clearly undergoing important changes. The material presented will, we hope, serve both as a stimulus and an example for further research.

The studies in Part II were undertaken during the last ten years--most in the first half of the 1970s. They all present newly gathered data; generally, they are case studies of how various aspects of development are influencing family patterns and women's roles. As with fertility trends and differentials, the countries of the region show wide variation in regard to their movement toward women's emancipation and the development of "modern" family patterns. For example, in Turkey, Lebanon, and Tunisia, there have been very substantial changes in the importance of the extended family, the role of parents, and access of women to education and employment. Changes in these areas, though real and important, are much more recent and less widespread in countries such as North Yemen and in certain parts of Iran. In these areas, we have sought to present material drawn from sectors of society where change is apparent, that is, among the urbanized, educated, working middle and upper classes. In these groups, even in countries that have been relatively closed to outside influences, change is taking place. One reflection is in regard to fertility patterns. It is generally among these groups that the small family

norm develops, nutrition and maternal health improves, interest
and access to contraceptives develops, and family planning begins
to become a part of life.

We believe that more research should be undertaken in rural
areas of the Middle East in order to provide data that could be used
for economic, health, and social programs and policies to improve
the difficult conditions of the least-favored inhabitants of those
areas. Yet, in this first effort to bring together research linking
social science studies with demographic change, it was felt particularly important to emphasize change, especially in those areas
that old stereotypes still stigmatize as being in the Middle Ages.
This may lead the reader to develop an overly optimistic view of
the rapidity of change in the region. However, many of the contributors deal with this question and help put the situation in a
proper perspective.

For example, in Chapter 9, John and Margaret E. Gulick
focus on a sample of working-class families in the rapidly growing
city of Isfahan. They consider the readiness of their sample, a
group composed of both migrants and longtime residents of the
city, for family planning. They find that many of the traditional
patterns of sex segregation, female seclusion, and high fertility are
indeed changing, but these changes are far from being a radical,
total transformation leading rapidly to a modern, Western-style,
professional middle-class value system. Change, though real and
significant, is slow, and attitudes toward family planning and the
successful use of modern contraceptives are still influenced by a
host of factors related to traditional behavior patterns and values.
While the social reality they depict is complex, education seems to
be a key differentiating factor; it is also related to successful use of
family planning. Their chapter also looks closely at the household
within the urban setting and finds that family structure is complex.
Although there is a preponderance of nuclear families, most of
these are immersed in complex networks of close-living relatives
rather than being isolated.

Mary-Jo Delvecchio Good's findings tend to support the
Gulicks' conclusions. Her chapter is based on fieldwork in 1972-74
in the provincial town of Maragheh among primarily lower- and
middle-class families. She focuses on the relationship between
social stratification, parental aspirations for children, and family
planning. Change in the community is clearly in evidence due to
governmental efforts at development, which have transformed the
social structure in important ways during the twentieth century.
Good views the individual's place in the new system of social stratification and the opportunities for mobility as the background against
which governmental policies and programs in family planning are

xl

received by the people to whom they are directed. She argues that further vast changes in the occupational and educational distribution of the population are necessary before positive attitudes toward small families and successful use of modern contraceptives will characterize the major part of the population of cities like Maragheh. The process will necessarily be a slow one. Like the Gulicks, she gives high priority to educational expansion, but also stresses the importance of providing access to upward mobility to those in the lower classes.

Social stratification and the economic conditions in a developing country are also given attention by Serim Timur in Chapter 11. She analyzes the socioeconomic factors that underlie Turkish family patterns. Her data are drawn from a nationally representative demographic survey carried out in the late 1960s. She finds that the creation and maintenance of family types (patriarchally extended, independent nuclear, or transient extended) are closely related to the property and work relations that prevail in Turkey. She argues that when income and occupation come to depend on factors beyond the power of the extended family, a change in family structure occurs, even without urbanization, industrialization, or modernization. Further, once certain family types are formed, they influence individual behavior and intrafamily interaction in regard to age at marriage and choice of spouse, authority patterns, and the husband-wife relationship. Although the existence of certain family types and the fertility declines clearly taking place in countries such as Turkey are both linked to the process of socioeconomic development, the causal mechanisms involved are still not clear. In order to link family structure and formation with fertility patterns, Timur calls for more research in the area where the family is thought to be acting as an intermediate agent.

The value of bringing to bear sociological and psychological approaches to areas that have traditionally been the concern of formal demography is illustrated in Chapter 12 by Greer Litton Fox. She deals with age at marriage, a topic that has been extensively treated in the demographic literature, but rarely from an interdisciplinary perspective and only recently with a view toward social policy. Using Turkish data from the Ankara family study, her chapter explores the mechanism through which age at marriage influences fertility. It considers both theoretical and policy-relevant questions. The data suggest the need to consider community context and the availability of nonfamilial roles as determinants of age at marriage. These, in turn, influence fertility through marital behavior. After discussing a policy model based on demographic research and her own modifications based on the Turkish data, she urges caution to those who believe that legislation raising the age of marriage could have important effects in fertility reduction in the developing countries.

Cynthia L. Myntti's study of changing roles in Beirut (Chapter 13) uses an anthropological approach--participant observation--to provide one of the rare considerations of internal family dynamics. She examines cultural patterns, such as visiting, which, she notes, serves as a transmission of gossip, an important means of social control. Her discussion of child-parent and husband-wife relationships, the role of the extended kin, extrahousehold roles, the influence of women in the home, and behavior controls on women help explain why even in Beirut, which was the most cosmopolitan city in the region before the 1975-76 civil war, family organization and the roles of women have been one of the slowest aspects to change.

Tunisia and Morocco, two countries that won independence from France in the mid-1950s, enacted very different policies with regard to women's emancipation and the family. Tunisia, as Mark A. Tessler, Janet M. Rogers, and Daniel R. Schneider point out in Chapter 14, had a vigorous program of planned social transformation, which placed important emphasis on women's liberation from traditional roles since independence in 1956. After briefly discussing the changing political context of social change in independent Tunisia, the authors present survey data gathered in 1967 and 1973, which are drawn from a wide range of social categories. Their sample reflects the diversity of the Tunisian middle and working classes. Although they find that total support for reform appears to have declined during the six-year period under study, support for female emancipation and liberal child-rearing practices was still fairly strong in 1973. They see a movement away from cultural controversy and an increasing agreement that some, but not radical, change in the traditional status of women and in child-rearing practices is desirable.

The situation in Morocco is different in regard to governmental policies on women and the family. Fatima Mernissi argues in Chapter 15 that after independence, national leaders attempted to reenact traditional approaches to women and the family. But because profound economic changes had taken place, which continued to accelerate between the 1960 and 1971 censuses, the traditional role of the patriarch could no longer be sustained. New roles and status for women, especially in regard to contact with the social welfare functions of the developing nation-state, are an irreversible feature of contemporary Moroccan society. In spite of traditional ideology, the new realities are forcing changes that policy makers disregard to their own and their nation's detriment.

Carla Makhlouf and G. J. Obermeyer's chapter on women in urban North Yemen (Chapter 16) suggests that even in the most traditional areas of the region, social change is under way and is gradually playing a role in the daily lives of women. They look particularly at the institutional and ideological sources of change and, based on participant observation, attempt to assess the positive and negative impact of these changes on the attitudes and aspirations of the women they studied.

SOME FINAL CONSIDERATIONS ON RESEARCH APPROACHES TO CHANGING FAMILY PATTERNS, WOMEN'S STATUS, AND POPULATION DYNAMICS

We have already mentioned some of the gaps and weaknesses in social science research on the Middle East and North Africa, particularly with respect to the changing demographic realities of the region. A major problem is still lack of data in important areas, but orientation of studies should also be considered. For example, an overemphasis on values, norms, and belief system, should, we believe, give way to more attention to empirical indicators of the impact of new institutions, the participation of people of the region in new roles, and the problems faced in the development of new behavior patterns. Similarly, the vision of a past "unchanging, traditional society" should give way to historical studies that help explain the rise of new economic, social, and political institutions and the processes that have brought about and continue to support social change.

An additional consideration in developing research on the family, women, and population dynamics is the need to look at problems that are the real concern of people in the region. Thus, the preoccupation with Muslim-Christian differences, which was an aspect of colonial and Orientalist scholarship, now has given way to a concern with themes that are perhaps relevant to Western industrial societies but appear to have less importance in the Middle East. For example, studies of "authoritarianism," "need for achievement," "attitudinal modernity," and the impact of the "communications revolution" clearly have their origin in Western social science traditions, but their value to understanding social change in the Middle East is not always apparent. These concepts tend to place responsibility for underdevelopment on the culture or psyche of individuals; they tend to ignore the fact that social structure is a totality and that political, economic, and social factors must be viewed historically and holistically.

A related question is that of the focus of research. For example, virtually the only studies we have of youth in the region concern secondary and university students. While one may argue that

xliii

they are nascent elites, whose current attitudes provide an idea of the actions of the region's future leaders, it is regrettable that the overwhleming majority of the youth of the region--the uneducated, the dropouts, the rural farm youngsters--receive no attention from social scientists. There is also a tendency to continue stressing research on the village community and tribal nomadic groups. Urban slums, suburban communities, and working-class and middle-class urban communities, particularly in provincial centers, receive little attention. Since these areas are the major centers of change, a compelling case can be made for their receiving particular attention.

The elucidation of possibly interesting and unusual practices, such as cousin marriage, should be viewed in light of the fact that some vitally important areas of research have been practically unexplored. For example, migration, both inter- and intraregional, is extremely important, yet our knowledge of the processes involved in the Middle East is very limited. There are practically no studies linking this phenomenon, with multiple implications for economic, political, and social life, with changing family patterns, women's status, and other demographic variables, such as fertility.

Efforts are clearly needed to improve the value and relevance of social science research in the region. Two suggestions might be proposed. First, a large number of censuses and nationally representative surveys have recently begun to appear throughout the countries of the region. Now and in the decades ahead, a major task for social scientists interested in changing family patterns, women's status, and other areas that have implications for development is to avail themselves of these data and, in conjunction with their students, begin to analyze them. This information could be used to test hypotheses about changes in family patterns, relationships between various aspects of development and demographic change, as well as providing descriptive data on social reality that are at present lacking. It should be obvious that empirical knowledge is a necessary prerequisite to building theory and to developing even preliminary formulations of hypotheses. As Wargon notes: "It is significant that some of the most fruitful contributions to family research and theory in recent decades have been made by analysts--who include sociologists, historians and demographers--using population data and demographic techniques."[56]

A second step that should be taken by social scientists working in the region in the years ahead is to work in closer cooperation with national planning and statistical institutes; ministries of health, education, labor, cooperatives, and social development; and international organizations concerned with development. An exposure to the needs and points of view of these agencies and institutions, which are attempting to deal with the problems of development, albeit with varying success, could be very salutory in regard to encouraging social scientists to confront the most pressing and urgent problems facing their nations. The often ambitious national development efforts that characterize most countires of the region could, and probably should, benefit from the support of social scientists, particularly in areas such as planning and evaluation.

In concluding, we might recall a question posed in the early 1960s by Berger in his classic study The Arab World Today. "Considering the variety of Arabic life . . . can we speak of the Arab family," he asked. At that time, he answered in the affirmative, because he believed that "one can profitably discuss the Moslem family in general, despite . . . differences, because it displays certain patterns. This is a result of the strength of tradition in the Arab world, the confinement thus far of profound social change to the wealthier and more educated classes in the cities, and pervading influence of Islam and its prescription for family life."[57] Now, in the last quarter of the twentieth century, the strength of tradition is breaking down, and Islam is adapting to new institutions, roles, and behavior patterns. The challenge to social scientists should be to leave the discussion of what is happening "in general" and to analyze what is happening, specifically and in detail, to different social groups, in different areas, as they participate in new experiences. It is only after this kind of information becomes available that we will be able to develop complex, explanatory models of social change.

NOTES

1. For critical approaches to overstressing the potential impact of family planning programs, see Davis, K., 1967, and Tabbarah, R. B., 1964.

2. See Allman, J., and Mathsson, B., 1975. For a recent evaluation of the impact of family planning programs, see Freedman, R., and Berelson, B., 1976.

3. Tabbarah, R. B., 1974.

4. See United Nations Economic, Cultural and Scientific Organization (UNESCO) Project Proposal to UNFPA, 1975, for a proposed attempt to fulfill some of these research needs on a worldwide scale. Quotations in the text are from this document.

5. For recent material on family patterns, women's status, and children and youth in the Middle East and North Africa, we have relied primarily on the following bibliographies: Allman, J., Ben Achour, C., and Stone, T., 1974; Gulick, J. and Gulick, M. E., 1974; Arab Culture and Society in Change, 1973, especially chaps. 4-6; Gray, A. W., 1973; Nedjati, S., 1974; Al-Qazzaz, A., 1975.

6. Goode, W. J., 1963, p. 87.

7. Ibid., p. 88.

8. Ibid., p. 120.

9. Seklani, M., 1960; Kirk, D., 1966.

10. Arowolo, O., 1973; Chamie, J., 1976; Musallam, B. F., 1974.

11. Ibid., p. 123.

12. Arab Culture and Society in Change, op. cit., p. 15.

13. Goode, op. cit., p. 101.

14. Khuri, F. I., 1970.

15. Goode, op. cit., p. 99.

16. Ibid.

17. Gordon, D., 1968, p. 82.

18. Arab Women, 1975.

19. Ibid.

20. Zeyoms, S., 1971, Heer, D. M. and Youssef, N., 1977.

21. Goode, op. cit., p. 100.

22. Dodd, P. C., 1973, p. 54.

23. Goode, op. cit., p. 107.

24. Vallin, J., 1973.

25. Behar, L., 1975.

26. Hill, A., chap. 5 of this volume.

27. Berksan, S. in Shorter, F. C., and Guvenc, B., eds., 1969.

28. Momeni, D., 1975.

29. Prothro, E. T., and Diab, L. N., 1974.

30. Peterson, K. K., 1968; Timur, S., 1971, chap. 3 of this volume.

31. Goode, op. cit., p. 129.

32. Ibid.

33. Gulick, J., in Lapidus, I. M., ed., 1969.

34. Ibid., p. 125.

35. Khalaf, S., 1971.

36. Goode, op. cit., p. 154.

37. Youssef, N., 1974.

38. El-Sanabary, N. M., 1974.

39. Ibid., pp. 1-2.

40. For a discussion of research priorities in women's studies, see Van Dusen, R. A., 1976, and Fernea, E., and Joseph, S., 1976.

41. Goode, op. cit., p. 139.

42. Bott, E., 1971.

43. Rainwater, L., 1965.

44. Goode, op. cit., p. 144.

45. Ibid., p. 158.

46. Prothro and Diab, op. cit.
47. Goode, op. cit., p. 162.
48. Prothro and Diab, op. cit.
49. Issawi, C., in Lapidus, I. M., ed., op. cit., p. 108.
50. Ibid.
51. Antoun, R., and Harik, I., eds., 1972, p. 338.
52. Ibid., p. 362.
53. Ibid., p. 55.
54. For a development of this theme in regard to the countries of the Arabian peninsula, see Halliday, F., 1974.
55. Antoun and Harik, op. cit., p. 461.
56. Wargon, S., 1974, p. 560.
57. Berger, M., 1964, p. 99.

PART I

Changing Fertility Patterns

1

The Demographic Transition in the Middle East and North Africa

JAMES ALLMAN

Is there indeed a new or renewed demographic transition? The evidence suggests that there is. A rapidly
growing number of countries of diverse cultural background have entered the natality transition since World
War II and after a 25-year lapse in such entries. In
these countries the transition is moving much faster
than it did in Europe. This is probably related to the
fact that progress in general is moving much faster in
such matters as urbanization, education, health, communication, and often per capita income.

> Dudley Kirk, A New
> Demographic Transition?
> Rapid Population Growth

Recent data from the Middle East and North Africa suggest
that Kirk's generalization about an accelerated demographic transition may apply to the Middle East and North Africa, as well as to
those regions where more information was available when he wrote
his article. While fertility rates for the region generally remain
very high, there have been important declines in Egypt, Turkey,
Tunisia, and Lebanon. Differential fertility patterns, based generally on urbanization, occupation, social class, income, and levels
of education, have developed in Algeria, Morocco, Jordan, and Iran.
These patterns may be forerunners of fertility declines, as has been
the case in other regions of the world. On the other hand, there are

---

A version of this chapter will appear in the International
Journal of Middle East Studies.

some indications that fertility is increasing in some countries, possibly in Saudi Arabia and the lower Gulf states. This chapter provides an analysis of recent fluctuations in fertility throughout the
Middle East and North Africa, including a discussion of some of the
factors associated with fertility changes.*

CURRENT DEMOGRAPHIC SITUATION IN THE
MIDDLE EAST AND NORTH AFRICA

The quality and quantity of information about the demographic
situation in the Middle East and North Africa has improved substantially in the last decade.[1] Census results, vital registration, and
numerous surveys increasingly provide data needed for the analysis
of population dynamics. However, one must still agree with Clarke
that "population data for the region are far from comprehensive and
statistics available often have a low level of reliability."[2] Nevertheless, without waiting for the 1980 round of censuses, the achievement of fully comprehensive vital registration, or the results of
numerous surveys planned or in progress, we can get an acceptably
accurate idea of the major demographic parameters for the region.
Of the several estimates available, we will use those provided in
the 1975 World Population Data Sheet of the Population Reference
Bureau. These data (see Table 1.1) are based on unpublished UN
Population Division estimates. It should be noted that birth, death,
and infant mortality rates refer to the average of the 1970-75 period.[†]
In further analysis, it will become clear that "presumably because of
recent fertility declines, current birth rates for many countries . . .
are appreciably lower than those given . . . for the average of the
1970-75 period."[3] This appears to be the case for Egypt, Tunisia,
Turkey, and Lebanon, as we shall see when we examine historical
trends.

For countries such as the two Yemens, Saudi Arabia, and the
lower Gulf states, excluding Bahrain, the vital rates are estimated
from a very slender factual base: this is particularly true when we
turn to more detailed demographic parameters, such as the infant

----

*The countries discussed in this chapter are listed in Table
1.1. Generally, the area under consideration, which we refer to
as the Middle East and North Africa, corresponds to the geographical area from Morocco in the west to Iran in the east.

†The crude death rate (CDR), the crude birth rate (CBR), and
infant mortality rates are given per 1,000 throughout the text.

TABLE 1.1: Population Size, Vital Rates, Infant Mortality, Rate of Population Growth, and Per Capita Gross National Product[a] for Countries of the Middle East and North Africa, 1975

Country	Population Estimate Mid-1975 (millions)	Birth Rate Average 1970-75 (thousands)	Death Rate Average 1970-75	Infant Mortality Rate	Rate of Population Growth (annual, percent)	Per Capita GNP[a]
North Africa						
Algeria	16.8	48.7	15.4	128	3.2	430
Egypt	37.5	37.8	14.0	103	2.4	240
Libya	2.3	45.0	14.8	130	3.0	1,830
Morocco	17.5	46.2	15.7	149	2.9	270
Sudan	18.3	47.8	17.5	141	3.0	120
Tunisia	5.7	40.0	13.8	128	2.2	380
Southwest Asia						
Bahrain	0.3	49.6[b]	18.7[b]	138[b]	3.1	640
Iran	32.9	45.3	15.6	139	3.0	490
Iraq	11.1	48.1	14.6	99	3.4	370
Israel[c]	3.4	26.5	6.7	21	2.9	2,610
Jordan[c]	2.7	47.6	14.7	99	3.3	270
Kuwait	1.1	47.1	5.3	44	7.1	4,090
Lebanon	2.9	39.8[b]	9.9[b]	49[b]	3.0	700
Oman	0.8	49.6[b]	18.7[b]	138[b]	3.1	530
Qatar	0.1	49.6[b]	18.7[b]	138[b]	3.1	530
Saudi Arabia[d]	7.2	49.5[b]	20.2[b]	152[b]	2.9	520
Syria	7.3	45.4	15.4	93	3.0	310
Turkey	39.9	39.5	12.5	119	2.5	370
United Arab Emirates[e]	0.7	49.6[b]	18.7[b]	138[b]	3.1	3,220
North Yemen Arab Republic[f]	5.2	49.6[b]	20.6[b]	152[b]	2.9	90
South Yemen, People's Republic of	1.7	49.6[b]	20.6[b]	152[b]	2.9	120

[a]U.S. dollars.

[b]Estimates are subject to wide margins of error.

[c]These estimates apparently refer to the pre-1967 borders of Jordan and Israel. The Jordanian government estimated the population of the East Bank at 1.8 million in 1975.

[d]The estimated 7.2 million population of Saudi Arabia for 1975 is based on the official census results of September 1974, which put the Saudi population at 7.0. (See Economic Commission for Western Asia, Regional Seminar, Amman E/ECWA/POP WF 5/14). The Population Reference Bureau estimate is 9 million.

[e]Preliminary figure from the first UAE census, end of 1975, reported in Jordan Times, February 8, 1976. The Population Reference Bureau estimate is 0.2 million.

[f]This estimate is based on the February 1975 census. An additional 1.2 million Yemenis are estimated to be living outside the country. The Population Reference Bureau estimate is 6.7 million for the total population of North Yemen.

Source: World Population Data Sheet 1975 (Washington, D.C.: Population Reference Bureau, 1975).

mortality rates. (Table 1.1 indicates the rates that are liable to wide margins of error.) In addition, changes were made where more recent and reliable data were available. These are noted at the bottom of the table and apply to demographic estimates for Jordan, Israel, North Yemen, and Saudi Arabia.

Two aspects of the demographic situation in the region that must be mentioned but which will not be treated here are the often large migrant populations temporarily out of their countries for varying periods and the Palestinian population. For Morocco, Algeria, Tunisia, and Turkey, the migrant populations working in Europe are substantial. In Kuwait, Bahrain, the United Arab Emirates (UAE), and Qatar, recent migrants make up a large percentage of the population (and a significant percentage in Saudi Arabia). North and South Yemen export generally unskilled workers; Lebanon and Jordan send out skilled and well-educated professional workers. There has been some discussion of the "brain drain," particularly in regard to Iran and Egypt, but this problem, like the others mentioned above, has been given very little systematic study.[4]

The Palestinian population can be divided into those living in refugee camps (in Syria, Lebanon, Jordan, and Gaza), some of whom are receiving support from the UN Relief and Works Agency (UNRWA); those with generally higher levels of education who have settled in Saudi Arabia, Kuwait, the Gulf states and, to a lesser extent, in other countries of the region and the world; and those living outside camps in Syria, Lebanon, and Jordan. Some surveys and statistical data exist on the Palestinians who have received assistance from UNRWA. The Population Division of the UN Economic Commission for Western Asia is currently planning a census of the Palestinian population, which should provide much useful information.[5]

APPLYING DEMOGRAPHIC TRANSITION MODEL
TO THE MIDDLE EAST AND NORTH AFRICA

The demographic transition model states that during modernization, mortality passes from a high, unstable level to a low, relatively stable level and fertility passes from a high, noncontraceptive level, to a low, controlled level. The fertility decline lags behind the mortality decline, thus giving rise to a transitional period of rapid population growth. This process of transition is usually divided into three (sometimes four) periods: (1) high mortality, high fertility, no or slow population growth; (2) declining mortality, high fertility, rapid population growth; and (3) low mortality, declining fertility, declining growth. The third stage, or the posttransitional period, is seen as a period of low mortality and fertility, with fluctuations in fertility within a relatively narrow range due to political, social, and economic conditions.[6]

This model of demographic change during the course of modernization is very general. However, it has proven useful as an overall approach to population dynamics, particularly for social scientists interested in various aspects of social change.[7] Demographers continue to embrace it; sorting out and explaining the exceptions and contradictions to it continues to be a concern in demographic research. For example, Coale notes that

> in spite of . . . objections, qualifications, and doubts concerning particular parts of the demographic transition, there remains an overall generalization that can hardly be denied. In Paul Demeny's words, "In traditional societies fertility and mortality are high. In modern societies fertility and mortality are low. In between, there is demographic transition."[8]

Similarly, Teitelbaum finds that "at high levels of generality the basic causal structure of transition theory appears sound." Furthermore, "when the available data on the 19th century decline in European fertility are analyzed on a systematic basis, some major propositions of transition theory are empirically supported." Research in Latin America suggests that "transition theory can achieve a similar moderate level of success . . . especially when the traditional theory is substantially modified and additional causal variables including cultural factors are introduced."[9]

A consideration of the demographic transition should be an essential component in any analysis of development. In fact, such a consideration underlies much of the current debate on human population phenomena. But in spite of the need to consider progress toward the final stage of the transition to low mortality and fertility in developing countries, we should bear in mind the fact that "the weakness of the concept is associated with the difficulty of defining a precise threshold (a checklist of essential characteristics, or a combined score on some socio-economic scale) of modernization that will reliably identify a population in which fertility is ready to fall."[10] Or put in more practical and policy-relevant terms, Tabbarah cautions that

> with regard to future trends of the birth rate in presently under-developed countries . . . the theory does not indicate when these rates will begin to fall or the fundamental reasons why they should fall. Obviously, the "when" is of utmost importance for population projections,

and the "why" is of equal importance to the formation
of rational and effective population policy. [11]

One might add that the "why" is also an essential ingredient for a
scientific explanation of demographic phenomena; a strict interpretation of scientific theory would not consider the transition model a
scientific explanation, since it tells us so little about the causal
mechanisms that trigger change.

Early efforts at applying the demographic transition model to
the Middle East and North Africa suffered from a lack of data. However, the inevitability of fertility decline along lines predicted by
past experience and knowledge of differential fertility patterns that
accompanied modernization was hypothesized by some observers. [12]
In an attempt to apply the model to the region, we are now able to
draw on data that have substantially improved during the last decade.
A classification of the countries of the region is provided in Table 1.2.

Instead of three periods or phases, five are provided. This
allows us to take into account a possible increase in fertility in the
process of modernization (stages 2 and 3) due to changes in reproductive behavior and increases in fecundability related to improved
health conditions, nutrition, and changes in breast-feeding practices.
In addition, this classification takes into account differential fertility
and the use of contraception. The need to consider fertility differentials in studying fertility trends has been cogently argued by Cho
and his colleagues, who note that

> a major weakness in all theories of fertility change is
> the almost complete absence of attention to the phe-
> nomenon of differential fertility. This is paralleled, in
> the field of differential fertility research, by another
> weakness; students of differential fertility have been
> almost completely descriptive and have shunned the
> task of developing a general theory concerning the
> subject. [13]

Reference to contraception is made in our classification of the transition in the region, because it is likely that modern contraceptive
technology has potentially a very important role to play in the rapid
transition to low fertility that has been evident in many developing
countries during the last decade. [14]

None of the countries of the region are in stages one or five.
All are currently undergoing mortality declines, which are likely to
continue in varying degrees in the years ahead. The major variations are in regard to fertility--high and possibly rising (CBR: 45-51);
high but probably at a peak; and declining though still relatively high

TABLE 1.2: Stages of the Demographic Transition in the Middle East and North Africa*

Stage	Mortality	Fertility	Growth Rate	Fertility Differentials	Modern Contraception	Countries of the Region in This Stage
One	High	High	Low	None	None	None
Two	Declining	High and possibly increasing	High	None or slight	None or little	Saudi Arabia, United Arab Emirates, Qatar, Oman, Libya, Iraq, Sudan, North Yemen
Three	Declining	High, but probably at maximum	High	Some	Beginning, but generally very little	Morocco, Algeria, Jordan, Bahrain, Kuwait, Iran, South Yemen, Syria
Four	Declining	Declining	Decreasing	Marked	Increasing use	Turkey, Tunisia, Egypt, Lebanon
Five	Low	Low	Low	Slight	Widespread use	None

*Excludes Israel, since most of its Jewish population is of European extraction and exhibits European demographic traits.

Source: Compiled by the author.

9

(CRB: 35-40) in comparison with developed, industrialized nations. Fertility differentials range from differences to marked differences. Those countries that exhibit differential fertility patterns generally have social groups whose life-styles and standards of living are similar to the middle classes in industrial nations. These groups exhibit distinctly modern demographic behavior. There are also the countries in stage three that may have very high fertility rates but where differentials by urban residence and experience in large cities, occupational category, and education nevertheless are clear. Moreover, contraceptive use similarly varies--from increasing use in countries like Tunisia and Egypt (stage four), where over 10 percent of the women in the childbearing groups are covered, to practically none at all in countries where the government has an explicit or de facto pronatalist policy or which are still insufficiently developed to elicit demands for methods of modern family planning.

The classification of countries is approximate. We caution the reader at the outset that our approach is preliminary and tentative rather than final and definitive. But before discussing the shortcomings of the classification, let us first consider in detail the demographic situation of the countries grouped in stages four, three, and two. This order allows us generally to move from a discussion of countries with substantial demographic data to those with less information. [15]

Stage Four: Countries Undergoing Mortality and Fertility
Declines, Marked Fertility Differentials,
Decreasing Growth Rates, and Increasing
Use of Modern Contraceptives

Turkey, Egypt, Tunisia, and Lebanon all fall in stage four of the demographic transition, as we have characterized it for the Middle East and North Africa. Before discussing demographic trends, we should briefly consider the comprehensiveness and reliability of demographic data in each of the four countries. This varies considerably but is generally sufficient for reasonably accurate estimates of demographic parameters. [16]

Turkey has perhaps the most comprehensive data. The first Turkish census conducted on a scientific basis was held in 1927. Since 1935, there has been a census every five years. Vital registration is still incomplete. However, a series of demographic surveys done during the last 15 years permit estimates of vital rates, as well as providing valuable sources of socioeconomic as well as demographic information. [17] Egypt also has extensive demographic data. Vital statistics, when viewed with suitable caution in regard to coverage and reliability, can be of considerable use. The last full census was held in 1961; the next is scheduled for March 1976. Several surveys done since the late 1950s are also of use in analyzing population dynamics.

Results of the Tunisian census of 1975 are not yet available, but the results of the 1956 and 1966 censuses are of help in establishing demographic parameters. In addition, vital registration is good in this small country of less than 6 million--it has been estimated to be 95 percent complete. Surveys conducted in Tunisia during the last ten years help fill in gaps in our knowledge.

Lebanon has not held a census since 1932 due to the sensitivity concerning the size of Christian and Muslim populations. In addition, those controlling the Lebanese economy have not required demographic data for economic planning and national development, since the economy is largely oriented to economic interests outside the country. Further, the provision of social services, which would also require demographic data, has never been a high priority for the Lebanese government. However, the 1970 Lebanese Labor Survey, the 1971 Knowledge, Attitude and Practice Survey sponsored by the Lebanese Family Planning Association, and a number of microstudies do provide substantial data from which demographic parameters and some indications of change can be derived. Vital registration, though incomplete, is also of some use if considerable caution is exercised and a certain amount of ingenuity used in interpretation.

Those studying Egyptian demographic trends generally express considerable reserve, if not skepticism, at the accuracy of official statistics. However, much data is available from censuses, surveys, and various microstudies. These provide sufficient information to measure demographic parameters and detect trends during the most recent decades.[18]

Mortality Trends

The CDRs in each of the four countries range between approximately 10 and 15. Infant mortality rates are between 100 and 130, with the exception of Lebanon, with a lower rate of 59. It seems clear that mortality in Turkey "increased during the years of World War II and underwent a rapid decline in a decade and a half following the War. The decline continued through the 1960s, at a pace much slower than before."[19] The CDR is estimated at 34.6 for the 1935-40 period, whereas it declined to 12.7 between 1965 and 1970.[20] Further, Macura notes that "the decline in mortality among adults was accompanied by a decline in infant and early child mortality. It is certain that some decline took place prior to the mid-1950s," but it is not possible to determine when it started or how it progressed.

He provides estimates of infant mortality of 187 for the 1955-60 period, 152 for 1966-67, and 145 for 1968.[21]

Similar mortality trends are found in Egypt. CDRs are estimated at 24.9 in 1930, 28.3 in 1942, over 20 in 1949, and 15.1 in 1970.[22] Declines in infant mortality followed the same pattern over time as declines in CDR. Khalifa estimates the Egyptian infant mortality at 116 in 1970. He believes that at the beginning of the twentieth century, infant mortality may have reached 400, decreased to around 150 in 1930, and then declined to about 120 for the 1965-70 period.[23]

In Tunisia, as well, mortality was high (CDR: 27-28) during the World War II period; it rapidly decreased thereafter, reaching 18 in 1960. The CDR in 1973 was estimated at 13.[24] Infant mortality rates for the city of Tunis are likely to be reasonably accurate, according to Seklani, who gave 110.9 as an estimate for 1971.[25]

We have much less information on Lebanon. The CDR appears to have been around 9 in 1970, according to Courbage and Fargues. They estimate infant mortality at 68.6 for males and 61.4 for females in 1970.[26]

Fertility Trends and Differentials

Turkish fertility, as well as mortality, has gradually declined over the last 35 years. From a high of 51.0 in the 1935-40 census period, the CBR dropped to 47.8 in 1945-50, 45.0 in 1955-60, and 38.4 in 1965-70. Declines in the CBR in 1960-65 can be largely attributed to changes in the age structure of the population. During this period, the arrival of the relatively small World War II cohort to childbearing years meant that the proportion of the reproductive population was relatively low. This tended to depress fertility until 1970, when normal size cohorts came to childbearing age.[27] Only very preliminary results are available for the 1975 census. They suggest that the downward trend in Turkish fertility continued in the 1970-75 period; the current CBR is between 32 and 35.

Differential fertility has been studied in detail, based on the censuses and the Turkish Demographic surveys (TDSs). Presenting data from the 1966-67 TDS and the 1968 Hacettepe Institute of Population Studies survey on "Family Structure and Population Problems in Turkey," Timur summarizes the findings by noting that

> almost all the traditional (or historical) fertility differ-
> ential in industrially advanced countries have been ob-
> served in Turkey. In the three metropolitan centers
> (Ankara, Istanbul and Izmir) that have gone farthest
> in fertility decline there were extremely wide fertility
> differentials by social class. The differentials were

less pronounced in other urban areas where fertility
levels were also high. In rural areas where fertility
was highest, there were no differentials among socioeconomic groups. In fact, high levels of income and
large landownership were positively associated with
fertility.[28]

In Egypt, the CBR has generally varied between 40 and 45
since 1930. It was below 40 several times during or after periods
of crisis, such as during World War II, in 1956, and in 1967. Recent estimates based on census data suggest that it increased from
42 in 1947 to 45.1 in 1960.[29] Official estimates point to a steady
decline in CBR since 1966. The CBR was estimated at 34.3 in 1972,
17 percent less than the 1966 figure. The declines are similar when
we look at general fertility rates (GFRs): there has been a 14.5 percent decrease between the 177.77 GFR in 1966 and the 152 GFR of
1972. Age-specific fertility rates also show declines in all age
groups, ranging between 24 percent to 33 percent of the 1966 level
for age groups 25-29, 35-39, and 45-49.[30] However, the official
estimate for 1973 puts the CBR at 35, a slight increase.[31]
        Urban-rural fertility differentials in Egypt were initially slow
to develop. This surprised several demographers who looked at
1947 and 1960 census data.[32] More recent data support the idea that
Egypt went through three phases of urban-rural fertility differentials:
(1) where rural fertility was higher than urban (up to the end of
World War II); (2) where urban fertility surpassed the rural level
(the 20 years following World War II); and (3) a phase beginning in
the early 1960s, in which rural fertility began to surpass urban fertility.[33]
        Differentials based on education and occupational status were
detected earlier than urban-rural differentials. From these, Abu-
Lughod predicted that in spite of the fact that

the Egyptian birth rate has shown no signs of decrease
. . . we may anticipate a gradual decline in fertility as
education becomes more widespread and as norms alter
in conformity with those already well established within
the better-educated and upper-occupational urban
classes.[34]

Recent studies show her reasoning to have been correct. In addition, Khalifa, examining survey data, found a clear inverse relationship between fertility behavior and various indicators of modernization. He noted that "all variables, namely wife's and husband's education, family income, husband's occupation, wife's

status, ownership of modern durables and access to mass-media, all contributed significantly to fertility differentials."[35]

Tunisia has undergone rapid fertility declines in a much shorter period of time than either Turkey or Egypt. The CBR went from 45.7 in 1960 to 35.7 in 1974, a decline of 22 percent. General fertility (for the age group 15-49) has similarly declined--from 210 in 1966 to 160 in 1974. There is general agreement that these trends reflect real declines. Vital registration is about 95 percent complete for births and has been verified with the 1968-69 Demographic Survey.

Differential fertility in Tunisia is marked: in 1974, CBRs varied from 29 in the urbanized governorate of Tunis-Nord to 42 in the rural, underdeveloped interior province of Kasserine. The 1968-69 Demographic Survey, which provides data on general fertility rates by age group, found rural rates consistently higher than urban. Completed fertility averaged 6.1 for urban areas and 7.6 in rural settings. Differentials by education, occupation, and standard of living are also pronounced in Tunisia, although most of the available data on this question are based on microstudies in limited areas of the country rather than on nationally representative surveys.[36]

Courbage and Fargues, drawing on the 1970 Lebanese Labor Survey and vital registration, found that fertility declined in Lebanon between 1959 and 1971. They estimate the CBR at 34.6 in 1970, 8.9 percent to lower than the CBR during the 1959-62 period. The authors believe that this reduction is not due simply to changes in the size of cohorts of women in the peak reproductive years during this period but, rather, to real declines in fertility brought about by use of contraceptives, as well as by possible changes in age at marriage. They provide estimates of completed family size, which they believe also consistently declined since 1964. The estimated number of children born per marriage has decreased by almost one child between the 1958-63 period and 1973. This represents a decrease of 18 percent from 5.70 children per marriage in the 1958-63 period to 4.66 in 1973.[37]

Distinct urban-rural fertility differences in Lebanon were first reported in a study conducted by Yaukey in 1959.[38] The 1970 Lebanese Labor Survey shows that differences are still important. Courbage and Fargues used the survey data (uncorrected) and calculated the CBR at 21.8 for Beirut, 32.2 for its suburbs, 32.2 for other cities, and 29.1 for rural areas. The low CBR for rural areas is a function of the relatively small number of women in the 15-44 age group in rural areas. General fertility rates better reflect the situation: they are estimated at 187 for Beirut, 256 in the suburbs of Beirut, 273 in other cities of Lebanon, and 279 in rural areas.[39]

Yaukey believed that there were significant differences between Muslim and Christian fertility in Lebanon. However, due to
methodological problems, such as insufficient controls for socioeconomic background, he probably overestimated the importance of
the religious factor.[40] Courbage and Fargues argue that in Lebanon
attitudes toward childbearing are determined more by class origin
than by religion. Religion appears important because social classes
are not represented in the two major communities in the same proportions.[41] Recent data support this argument. For example, a
study done by the UN Demographic Division in Beirut at a public
maternity clinic, which served primarily low-class families, found
no significant Christian-Muslim differences in regard to average
number of children classified by age group of mother. Similarly,
two recent studies of Lebanese rural villages failed to indicate religious differences in fertility when social class was taken into account.[42] In addition, data based on a subsample of the 1971 Lebanese Knowledge, Attitude, and Practise (KAP) survey (250 nonusers
of contraceptives and 250 users of nonmedical methods of contraception) plus data from a survey of users of medical methods of contraception were used to test the hypothesis that Christians tend to use
medical methods of contraception more than Muslims. The author
found the "religious hypothesis . . . unsupported . . . Muslims by
a large majority make up the medical user sample and Christians
are largely non-medical users of contraceptives."[43] Factors such
as urban residence, education, and literacy were found to be related
to contraceptive use and family size. Unfortunately, controls for
socioeconomic status and income could not be done, since the study
followed the coding of the 1971 Lebanese KAP survey. The survey
results were presented in a way that limits what it tells us about
fertility differentials. A reanalysis based on recoding and multivariate analysis should be of more interest than the first presentation of the survey results.[44]

Additional support for the idea that Islam is not a major barrier to contraceptive use in Lebanon is found in a survey of 156
married men in the largely Shi'a Muslim city of Tyre. Over 70 percent of the sample group approved of, and were using, contraceptives.
The study found that "all of the respondents have heard of contraception. Lack of information is apparently not a major problem for
them."[45]

Based on the 1970 Labor Survey, vital statistics, and various
estimates of community size and births, Courbage and Fargues estimated a CBR of 25 for the Maronite and Christian community and a
CBR of 42 for the combined other groups in Lebanese society (mostly Sunni and Shi'a Muslims), indicating that Muslims are mainly in
low socioeconomic classes.[46]

The growth rate of the four countries in stage four probably ranges from 2.2 to 2.5. The estimated 3.0 growth rate of Lebanon provided in Table 1.1 is likely to be too high, as is the estimation of fertility at 39.8 for the 1970-75 period. Courbage and Fargues found fertility rates clearly on the decline during the 1960s. They estimated the CBR in 1970 at 34.6. One might reasonably expect a continued decline since them, so a growth rate of around 2.5 might be a more reasonable estimate for Lebanon in 1975. [47]

Population Policies and Family Planning[48]

All of the four countries in this stage of the demographic transition have active family planning associations, and all but Lebanon have national population policies that include substantial support for family planning. In Turkey, official policy advocates voluntary planning for the desired number of children a family wishes to have. This policy was stated in the 1965 family planning law. In Egypt, the 1965 presidential decree established a national policy to reduce population growth. In 1969, the target was specified--the CBR should be reduced by one point per year for ten years. The Tunisian government issued a population policy in 1964. According to the Fourth National Development Plan (1973-76), the minimum objective was to diminish the general fertility rate (175 births per 1,000 women aged 15 to 49 in 1971) by 2.5 points each year. Lebanon has no official population policy, but a family planning association has been active since 1969.

The Population Council estimated that between 14 percent and 21 percent of married women of reproductive age were currently using modern methods of contraception in Egypt in 1974. [49] In Tunisia, an estimated 10 percent of the same age group were protected by the national family planning program (up from 7 percent in 1972) and a further 2 percent through the private sector. [50] Preliminary results from the 1973 Hacettepe survey reported 47 percent of the Turkish women as users (ever) of modern methods of contraception and 38 percent as current users. The 1968 results gave 41 percent as users (ever) and 32 percent as current users. [51] Measures of current contraceptive use by percentage of married women in reproductive years are not available for Lebanon. However, several studies suggest that knowledge of contraceptives is widespread in Lebanon. [52] Contraceptives are generally available in most cities in the country.

The determinants of fertility trends in the four countries are not well understood. Consequently, it is difficult to measure the impact of family planning on recent fertility declines. Ayad, updating the analysis made by Lapham on the determinants of fertility declines in Tunisia, recently estimated that almost 40 percent of the current decline in fertility is due to the national family planning program.[53] Unfortunately, estimates are not available for the other three countries. The small family norm seems to be increasingly widespread. It seems clear that with family planning known and contraceptives available, the possibilities of acting on the desire to limit family size will increase in these four countries.

Future Trends

Fertility rates are likely to continue their steady downward trend in Tunisia, Lebanon, and Turkey. Their experience, and especially Tunisia's rather rapid recent fertility declines between 1966 and 1974, supports Kirk's idea of a possibly accelerated demographic transition in some of the developing countries. Fertility control in Tunisia appears to be due to a combination of governmental initiatives, particularly in regard to social development. There has been relatively little economic development, so this is not a major factor in the Tunisian case. Turkey and Tunisia merit further study, since they support the idea that demographic phenomena can be dealt with through conscious governmental efforts at social and economic development, even without the wealth of their oil-rich neighbors.

It remains to be seen whether fertility will continue to decline in Egypt. Part of the decline between 1966 and 1972 could be due to the state of mobilization caused by war with Israel. There is some evidence that the number of users of modern contraceptives has leveled off during 1972-74.[54] While an increase in fertility rates in Egypt is a possibility, especially in the short run, the emergence of differential fertility along lines similar to those that accompanied fertility declines in other countries and the efforts made by the government to further social development and support family planning are grounds for hope that Egypt has embarked upon the irreversible path of demographic modernization.

Stage Three: Countries with Declining Mortality, High
Fertility Rates, Rapid Growth Rates, Emerging
Fertility Differentials, and Little
Contraceptive Use

The eight countries in this stage--Morocco, Algeria, Jordan, Syria, Bahrain, Kuwait, Iran, and South Yemen--vary considerably in the quality and quantity of their demographic data. Demographic surveys and census data from Morocco, Algeria, and Jordan provide valuable insights into demographic parameters in these countries, especially fertility rates. Kuwait has virtually complete vital registration and a series of good censuses. We will have to rely on the

1970 Syrian census for data on population dynamics there. Bahrain
has a series of five censuses, but the most recent 1971 census appears inaccurate, and "current information on mortality, natality
and migration in Bahrain is still insufficient."[55] Iran has census
data for 1956 and 1966, but "with the exception of the 1966 census,
the accuracy and completeness of much of the now prolific Iranian
data is doubtful."[56] The demographic situation in South Yemen is
virtually unknown, but we do have some data on the capital, Aden,
which was formerly a British colony. In all the countries, with the
exception of Kuwait, vital registration is very poor and of limited
use for demographic analysis.

Mortality

CDRs for the countries in this group generally range between
15 to 20. This is the case for Syria, where the CDR is estimated at
15.4 in 1975. Estimates for Algeria put the CDR at 32.2 for 1946-50,
dropping to 14.9 for the 1966-69 period.[57] Longitudinal data are un-
available for Morocco, although the CDR of 19 according to the 1961-
63 Moroccan Demographic Survey may be compared with the 15.7
CDR estimated for 1975.[58] Surveys carried out in Iran in 1956,
1966, and 1971 place the CDR at 20.1, 16.2, and 15.2, respectively.[59] Improvement in medical facilities in the 1960s supports the
idea that the Jordanian CDR has moderately declined during this
period, and 14.7 might not be an unrealistic estimate for 1975.[60]
Rizk estimates the CDR at 13.7 for the 1970-75 period.[61] Similar
downward trends in infant mortality in Jordan have been estimated
by Fisher.[62] The CDR is estimated at 18.7 in Bahrain for 1975 and
20.6 in South Yemen. Data are scarce for both countries. Infant
mortality is estimated at 138 in Bahrain and 152 in South Yemen. A
recent study of 45 midwives over age 54 in three rural provinces of
South Yemen found infant mortality rates of 398 in two of the provinces and 364 in the third.[63]

The low CDR and infant mortality rates of Kuwait (5.3 and 44,
respectively, in 1975) reflect the substantial investment in medical
facilities and the fact that people in this small, almost completely
urban country have free and easy access to hospitals and clinics.[64]

Fertility Trends and Differentials

Fertility rates appear to have increased in some stage three
countries in recent years. Krotki and Beaujot, using census data
and stable population models, estimate that the CBR rose from 44.0
to 49.5 between the 1960 and 1971 Moroccan censuses.[65] Vallin
found that the Algerian CBR increased from 35 to 50 during a period
of 50 years and perceptibly increased between 1955 and 1965 for all

age groups.[66] He estimated the Algerian CBR at over 50 between
1957 and 1965. The CBR increased from 44 in 1957 to 50 in 1969-71
and rose to a high of 51 in 1965. Total fertility has, however, been
almost constant (7.3-7.5) since 1957.[67] Rizk provides data that
suggest that the CBR in Jordan rose from 45.3 between 1950 and
1955 to a maximum of 49.1 between 1965 and 1970. He estimates
the 1970-75 CBR at 48.2.[68] This indicates a slight fertility decline,
but given the limited data and the short period of time, it is perhaps
premature to speak of a downward trend. There are some indications of fertility declines in Bahrain. Kjurciev and Courbage, using
indirect methods, estimate the GFR in Bahrain at 187 between 1966
and 1971, about 25 percent lower than their estimates of 249 for
1961-66 and 254 for 1956-61.[69] Unfortunately, vital registration is
very incomplete in Bahrain, and the census data are unsatisfactory.
Consequently, we can say little about the apparent decline in fertility
in Bahrain, except that it is plausible in view of the extent and pace
of industrialization and the long-established educational system on
the islands, and it certainly deserves further study.

There is a dearth of recent data on fertility rates in Iran. A
comparison of the 1956 and 1966 censuses shows no change in completed fertility for married women: it averaged 8.46 in 1956 and
8.42 in 1966. However, the 1965 demographic survey carried out by
the University of Tehran indicated completed fertility rates of 6.0
for Tehran and 7.6 for rural areas.[70]

Data on fertility is limited in Syria as well. However, an
adjustment of the 1970 Syrian Census made by the UNESCO-Syrian
project suggests that the CBR is over 50.[71]

In spite of high national fertility rates, which appear to have
risen substantially in the last two decades in some of the countries,
there are nevertheless clear-cut fertility differentials in stage three
countries along the lines one might suspect, based on knowledge of
past patterns of fertility change in developed countries. Where sufficient data are available, fertility is generally found to vary by
urban-rural residence, social class (measured by occupational
category and status, income, and standard of living, or an index
based on a combination of these variables), and, especially, level
of education. For example, Vallin found differentials according to
these variables in analyzing the 1970 Algerian Demographic Survey.
Initial analysis of urban-rural fertility found no differences until
refinements in analysis were made. These consisted of studying the
fertility of large rather than small cities, and within the large urban
centers, analyzing fertility behavior of women born or settled there
before their marriage, that is, the only true "urban women." When
these controls were made, fertility rates were generally found to be
lower in all age groups of the urban women. Wife's education was

associated with lower fertility rates. Vallin also found differentials based on husband's education and occupation. He concluded that when "we examine fertility differences between different social groups we can see that family planning exists" in Algeria. Even though these groups "only form a marginal fringe of society . . . they point to a new evolution in Algerian society. The least fertile women, mainly urban, are generally educated, married to men in the professional or managerial group, and sometimes have an economic activity."[72]

Rizk found similar fertility differentials in Jordan. However, as in the case of Algeria, there were no significant differences in fertility among women living in rural, urban, and semiurban areas. Unfortunately, controls were not made for the amount of time women actually resided in these areas, nor was it clear whether a more restricted definition of "urban" might not have indicated fertility differentials. Socioeconomic background was associated with fertility in Jordan. Rizk devised a socioeconomic index based on income, education of husband and wife, occupation, house rental, home facilities, and cultural activities. He found that toward the end of reproductive life (duration 25 to 29 years), the average fertility per woman was 6.4 live births for class one, the more privileged group, 8.7 for class two, and 9.0 for class three. Both husband's and wife's education were inversely related to fertility, although wife's education was much more important. Cumulative fertility ranged from around 2.9 for the wives of men in highly technical jobs to 6.3 for men in agriculture.[73]

Fertility differentials in Morocco have not been studied in detail, but from the information available, urban-rural differences appear to be developing. For example, the Population Growth Estimation study carried out by the Centre de Recherches et d'Etudes Démographiques reported CBRs of 48.65 for the urban population.[74] It calculated that a Moroccan woman who had been married for 15 years gave birth to an average of 6.0 children. This varied between an average of 4.5 in urban areas and 7.0 in rural areas.[75] Similarly, Lapham's research, the 1966 urban KAP study and the 1967 rural KAP study all found urban and rural differences between the ideal number of children, desire for more children, knowledge and use of contraceptives, ideal age at marriage, and so forth. However, these measures are all attitudinal and not behavioral; they are limited in what they can tell us about what people actually do. Lapham dealt with this issue and concluded that

> for the Sais Plain, the rural/urban differential is substantial. The style of life in the city is quite different from that of the Douars, and knowledge and attitudes

vary considerably, although until now at least total fertility is only slightly lower in the city than in the surrounding rural areas. [76]

Similarly, based on a 1962 multipurpose survey, Sabagh found that
in families where husband and wife had some modern education,
fertility was generally lower. [77] Other findings from the survey are
rather surprising: for example, it estimated the Moroccan CBR at
46.1 in 1962, with urban rates averaging 47.2, with a maximum of
50.0 in Casablanca, and rural rates averaging 45.6. [78] These estimates do not coincide with current estimates, which place rural fertility rates above the urban rates. The reason for the discrepancy
deserves further study; unfortunately, we cannot go into it here due
to lack of the necessary data.

Paydarfar recently interviewed women in 1,384 tribal, rural,
and urban households in a southern province of Iran. He found that
"in regard to the indices of fertility practice, the tribal families had
the largest number of children ever-born per household; urban families the smallest. The high tribal death rate, however, reduced
tribal, rural, and urban differences with respect to living children"
so that there were almost equal numbers of living children per household in all these groups. [79] His study also provided evidence for the
hypothesis that "the improvement of socio-economic conditions
among non-urban sectors of developing countries will improve the
nutritional conditions of the rural populations and this will reduce
child mortality and raise the mean number of living children. "[80]

The Amani study, restricted to the cities of Tehran and Isphan,
found positive relationships between education and knowledge and use
of contraceptives and awareness of population issues. There was a
much less clear relationship between education and age-specific fertility. Unfortunately, controls were not made for social class. [81]

Fertility rates and trends are not clear for South Yemen. Statistics issued by the Aden government in 1965 put the Aden CBR at
36.3. The Arab population of the city that remained after the British
withdrew in 1967 probably benefited from the social and medical infrastructure established during the colonial period. Consequently,
the birth rates may be still relatively low for the city. We have
little data on the interior but, as Khalil points out, "while Aden, as
a British colony, experienced urban growth and modernization, the
rural parts known as Aden Protectorates, retained their old modes
of life, socially, economically and culturally. "[82] Her sample of 45
midwives over age 54 had between 7.2 and 8.1 children ever-born. [83]
It seems likely that rural rates of fertility are much higher than
urban rates in South Yemen, although we can say little else about
fertility differentials in this country.

Only slight rural-urban fertility differentials were found in Syria based on the 1970 census.[84] However, there were very marked differences in regard to the average number of children born alive per woman for all age groups when level of education was taken into account.[85]

Population growth rates in stage three countries are among the highest in the world, ranging from 2.9 for Morocco and South Yemen to 5.9 for Kuwait between 1970 and 1975, due in the latter case to rapid immigration, as well as to a high rate of natural increase. Jordan, Iran, and Bahrain have growth rates varying between 3.0 and 3.3. As in the case of the countries in stage four, the high percentage of the total population below age 20 means that these countries will continue to grow rapidly in the immediate future.

Population Policies and Family Planning

Morocco and Iran both have national population policies and active, though not always completely effective, government family planning programs. Morocco's policy aims at reducing the CBR from an estimated 49 in 1972 to 43 in 1977. One of the objectives of the Five-Year Plan (1973-77) is to inform, educate, and motivate the population to practice voluntary family planning. The number of contraceptive users as a percentage of the women aged 15 to 44 was estimated at 6.2 percent in Morocco in 1973. Iran similarly has an official policy to reduce the population growth rate from 3.2 percent to 1.6 percent over 20 years in order to facilitate socioeconomic growth. In 1974, an estimated 14 percent of all the eligible women in the 15-44 group were using contraceptives.

Both Algeria and South Yemen are countries with official involvement in health and social welfare-oriented family planning activities. Algeria believes that rapid economic and social development will lead to long-term declines in fertility. Consequently, Algeria believes that a population policy aimed at reducing population growth is not needed. However, the government also believes that maternal and child health could benefit from child spacing; assistance for this from international agencies, such as the World Health Organization (WHO) and the UN Fund for Population Activities (UNFPA), has been sought. This is also true of South Yemen, where there is neither a population policy nor a family planning association; however, the government is interested in improving maternal and child health through child spacing.

Syria founded a family planning association in 1974, and in spite of legal restrictions, contraceptives are becoming available. The government is very interested in furthering demographic research; in addition to the ministries concerned with planning, development, and statistics, the universities in Damascus and Aleppo are developing population studies programs.

Jordan has had a Family Planning and Protection Association since 1963. There is close cooperation with government agencies, especially in the health field, but the Jordanian government does not have a population policy and is not officially involved in family planning. Many of the activities in the area of family planning in Jordan were centered in the now-occupied West Bank. Since 1972, activities have been growing in the East Bank. The 1971 fertility survey of 4,811 East Bank married women found that 32.4 percent of the total respondents used contraceptives at one point in their married life. [86]

Contraceptives are widely available from government hospitals and clinics and from private practitioners and pharmacies in Kuwait and Bahrain. There are indications that they are being increasingly used by higher-parity women, over 30, in Kuwait. [87] This may be happening in Bahrain as well. Neither country has an explicit population policy, although Bahrain established a family planning association in 1975, and both countries have very clear policies on immigration, mortality, and other demographic phenomena.

Future Trends

Because of governmental efforts to improve socioeconomic and health conditions, as well as because of the resources available, one may reasonably expect fertility declines in Bahrain, Kuwait, and Iran in the immediate future. There is some evidence that these may already be taking place in Kuwait and Bahrain, but more research is needed to clarify the situation. It is much more difficult to predict when Morocco, Algeria, Jordan, Syria, and South Yemen will begin the transition from high to declining fertility. The rapid increases in fertility in these countries to CBRs of over 50 during the last decade may mark peaks; rapid declines in fertility may occur in the next decade as socioeconomic development takes place.

Stage Two: Declining Mortality, High Fertility, Rapid
Growth Rate, Minor Fertility Differentials, Virtually
No Modern Contraception

Our discussion of the demographic parameters of the eight countries in stage two--Saudi Arabia, Qatar, Oman, UAE, North Yemen, Iraq, Sudan, and Libya--will be more brief, since few reliable data are available. Some countries have no official census data; the vital registration in all the countries is very incomplete,

and there are few surveys to allow estimations. In some of the
countries, political considerations prevent the objective depiction
of demographic phenomena.

Mortality

Estimates of the CDRs in each of the countries in stage two
generally put the rates at between 15 to 20. Iraq and Libya tend to
be toward the lower end of the range; the other countries are still
close to, or slightly over, 20. Infant mortality in all the countries
is high--generally between 130 and 150 in 1975. In the oil-rich countries, which have all begun ambitious development programs, mortality may decline rapidly in the years ahead. However, in Sudan
"it seems most likely that . . . in the next 10 or 20 years mortality
will decline very moderately."[88] The same may be true of North
Yemen, which, like Sudan, has a relatively large, dispersed rural
population and few resources.[89] Iraq has been pursuing an ambitious program of national economic and social development. In
spite of numerous obstacles, major achievements have been accomplished in the last 15 years. It is likely that the CDR and the infant
mortality rate (around 100), which are already lowest in this group,
will continue to decline.

Fertility

The CBRs in each of the countries appear to be around 50.
One survey in Libya and estimates presented by the Sudanese delegate to the 1972 UN-sponsored Working Group on fertility levels and
differentials in Africa suggest that the CBR estimates in Table 1.1
for these two countries may be below actual rates.[90]

Perhaps primarily because of the paucity of data, few of the
countries in this group exhibit fertility differentials. The only exceptions we found were differentials in Sudan based on urban and
rural residence, socioeconomic grouping, and "mode of living."[91]
In addition, Henin found that in the Sudan, "nomads have a lower fertility at almost every age, when compared with the rain cultivators"
in his survey.[92] A household survey in the Libyan cities of Tripoli
and Benghazi found CBRs of 49.6 percent in Tripoli and 57.9 percent
in Benghazi, as well as substantial variation by monthly income in
both cities. Fertility tended to be lower for higher income groups;
for example, in Tripoli, the CBR of the low-income group was 62.8,
for the middle group 42.8, and 29.6 for the high-income group.[93]

Population Policy

Both Saudi Arabia and Iraq have recently taken strong pronatalist positions. The Saudis prohibited the sale and distribution

of contraceptives in spring 1975. Iraq officially stated at the 1974
World Population Conference in Bucharest that its 3.4 percent average annual population increase rate should be maintained at least
until 1980. Further, the government did not request the renewal of
the three-year WHO /UNFPA population project, which originally
envisaged substantial extension of family planning services beyond
1974.[94] Libya, Oman, Qatar, and the UAE are also pronatalist;
modern contraceptives are generally not available and in use in
these countries. The Sudan has had a Family Planning Association
since 1965, but availability of modern contraceptives is limited to
urban areas. North Yemen also created a family planning association in 1974; in spring 1976, it launched a maternal and child health
services program, which will include family planning. In general,
all the countries in this group are pronatalist or have no explicit
population policy. Modern contraceptives are rare and not readily
available. However, awareness that demographic factors must be
taken into account in economic, social, and, especially, health planning is rapidly increasing in these countries. Consequently, the
potential for dramatic change in the demographic parameters (especially decreasing mortality and eventually fertility) in this group
of countries is great.

Future Trends

        In each of these countries, there are two broad social groups
whose fertility behavior may begin to change relatively soon. First,
nomadic and seminomadic rural people are gradually becoming seden-
tary and detribalized. Evidence from Iran and the Sudan suggests
that among tribal nomadic groups, as the socioeconomic conditions
improve, especially in regard to nutrition, infant and child mortality
can be expected to rapidly decrease, and the mean number of living
children will rise.[95] If this hypothesis is confirmed, the countries
in stage two, which all contain substantial tribal or recently detribalized nomadic populations, may experience very rapid growth due to
high fertility and reduced mortality. More research should focus on
the demographic, as well as the social, economic, and political behavior of tribal nomadic groups, since large segments of many countries in the region originate from these groups.
        A second group that deserves particular attention in regard to
demographic behavior in stage two countries is the small, but rapidly growing, middle class. Although the nature of the new middle
class in the Middle East has generated some controversy among
social scientists,[96] the experience of countries in stages three and
four suggests that in countries like Saudi Arabia, Iraq, and Sudan,
fertility differentials and declines can be expected to appear. These
groups may already be experiencing differences in actual and desired

family size related to their occupational category, level of education, social mobility, urban experience, life-style, and so forth.

EXPLAINING FERTILITY PATTERNS AND THEIR
DETERMINANTS IN THE MIDDLE EAST
AND NORTH AFRICA

In discussing some of the findings of the Princeton study of the decline of fertility in each of the provinces of Europe, Coale concluded that

> only an optimist would still expect a simple account of
> why fertility fell . . . perhaps we shall through a stroke
> of insight or good fortune discover a grand generaliza-
> tion that will provide a compact and widely valid ex-
> planation of the decline in marital fertility in Europe.
> But at the moment it appears that the process was more
> complex, subtle, and diverse than anticipated. [97]

This cautious and modest approach to a scientific understanding of fertility patterns in Europe, where substantial data are available, might be usefully kept in mind when considering the possibility of studying the determinants of fertility patterns in the Middle East and North Africa. As is clear from the preceding discussion of the demographic transition in the region, we are frequently at a loss because data needed to test hypotheses are lacking. While laudable efforts are currently underway to improve the situation, it will be some time before demographic data in the region are both comprehensive and reliable. Indeed, the next decade will continue to require substantial efforts in the area of estimation from incomplete data, as well as concerted efforts to improve vital registration, coordinate census taking, and develop survey research as a source of data for socioeconomic and health planning. These activities will require more training of local people in demography and population studies and will strain the current supply of statisticians, demographers, planners, and social scientists working in the region.

Some efforts have been made to explain fertility patterns and their determinants in the Middle East and North Africa. Attention to ideological factors and values was at one time considered a key to understanding the high rates of fertility in the region. For example, not so long ago, Islam was considered by some as a major obstacle to the diffusion of family planning, fertility control, and modern demographic behavior. Kirk noted that "empirically Islam has been a more effective barrier to the diffusion of family planning than

Catholicism." He saw a "persistent resistance of Moslems to change," which differed from many traditional societies in "the tenacity with which old beliefs and practices are maintained by Moslems and influence life today."[98] Similarly, Seklani argued that the Muslim ethical system appears explicitly to contain teachings which even to this day resist Malthusian, or antinatalist, ideas.[99] Both authors, as well as other observers, gave particular importance to the role of family patterns in supporting Muslim natality, as well as to Islamic values and beliefs.

Based on recent data and research, we know that religious support of pronatalist behavior is much less important among Muslims than was at one time supposed.[100] In fact, it can be argued that Islam is more favorable to family planning than other religions and that the obstacles to economic and social development which many Islamic countries face are the major determinants of their "traditional" demographic behavior.[101] Furthermore, it seems reasonable to suppose that as development progresses, Muslim natality will probably differ little from natality levels in other developing countries. Muslims are likely to behave much like other peoples of the world experiencing profound social, economic, and cultural change.

Other attempts to explain fertility trends and their determinants in the Middle East and North Africa have used empirical data and multivariate techniques of statistical analysis. Because of the thin data base, the conclusions of these studies are rather general and limited in their policy implications. For example, Kirk correlated various national socioeconomic characteristics with birthrates in 15 Islamic countries and found that "in the Islamic world measures of education clearly stand out as variables most related to natality levels."[102] Similarly, Audroing and his colleagues did a correlation study of 40 demographic, sociological, and economic variables in 12 Arab countries. The authors considered standard of living, cultural level, years of schooling, urban experience, and the rate of social change in an attempt to analyze the interrelations among demographic, social, and economic factors in the Arab countries.[103]

Schultz used a more sophisticated multivariate statistical analysis in studying the determinants of fertility in the Arab Middle East. However, since he relied almost exclusively on the 1960 Egyptian census as a source of data, his generalizations about demographic phenomena throughout the region are questionable. This is especially true in regard to his ideas on population policy, which he views very narrowly as "involving two fundamental elements: subsidizing the provision of birth control information, services and supplies, and influencing family size goals."[104] This view does not correspond to the approach of the leaders of most of the states in the region in regard to population policy. Some states are pronatalist and favor policies that increase their native populations; most give more importance to demographic factors as elements in the planning of social and economic development than to influencing family size; and all stress family planning rather than birth control.[105]

In general, it seems likely that a great deal more basic research will be needed before we will be able to go beyond very general comparative analyses of fertility trends and their determinants in the Middle East and North Africa.

CONCLUSION

Characterizing the countries of the Middle East and North Africa according to their place in the demographic transition has hopefully provided the reader with a clearer understanding of the demographic reality in the region. It is clear that in 1975, some countries have already entered a phase of fertility decline, which appears to be moving considerably more rapidly than was the case in the developed nations. In addition, most of the countries of the region, especially the large nations, are increasingly aware of the importance of demographic factors. This is likely to mean continued positive action in the fields of public health and social and economic development, which will have important implications for demographic changes, including eventual declines in fertility. It should be noted, however, that much more demographic data collection and analysis is necessary before we will satisfactorily understand the changes taking place in the populations of the region. In addition, it should be emphasized that all the countries of the region, including those currently undergoing fertility declines, will have to deal with populations at least twice as large as those of 1975 before or around the year 2000.[106]

NOTES

1. For a review of the situation in the region only a few years ago, see El Shafi, A. M. N., 1969, pp. 286-93. See also Sabagh, G., 1970, pp. 1-9, and United Nations Economic and Social Office in Beirut, 1972, pp. 13-19.

2. Clarke, J. I., and Fisher, W. B., eds., 1972, p. 15.

3. World Population Data Sheet 1975, notes 2 and 3.

4. For a discussion of migration in the region, see the essays in Clarke and Fisher, op. cit., and Courbage, Y., and Fargues, P., 1975, pp. 111-41.

5. For a discussion of the demography of the Palestinians, see Courbage and Fargues, op. cit., and Hill, A. G., 1976.

6. For recent discussions of the demographic transition, see Coale, A. J., 1973, pp. 53-72; Teitelbaum, M. S., 1975, pp. 420-25; and Beaver, S. E., 1975.

7. See, for example, Riesman, D., 1961, chap. 1.

8. Coale, op. cit., p. 64.

9. Teitelbaum, op. cit., p. 424.

10. Coale, op. cit., p. 65.

11. Tabbarah, R. B., 1971, p. 258.

12. See Abu-Lughod, J., 1965 and 1964, and Shorter, F. C., 1966, pp. 340-54.

13. Cho, L.-J. et al., 1970, p. 296.

14. Some of the problems involved in measuring this impact are discussed in Watson, W. B., and Lapham, R. J., eds., 1975, pp. 215-19.

15. Several demographic factors, such as age structure and life expectancy, which have effects on CBR, CDR, and growth rate, will generally not be dealt with in this chapter, since satisfactory data are unavilable for most of the countries of the region. For a discussion of these factors, see Frejka, T., 1973, chap. 1, and Coale, A. J., in Sheps, M. C., and Ridley, J. C., eds., 1965, pp. 242-65.

16. For a recent review of the demographic situation with emphasis on family planning, see Montague, J. G., ed., 1975, pp. 302-19. Also of great interest in regard to demographic data are the country monographs sponsored by the Committee for International Coordination of National Research in Demography (CICRED) based at the National Institute of Demography in Paris. We have used extensively the studies prepared on Morocco, Algeria, Tunisia, Egypt, Lebanon, Iran, and Turkey in this chapter.

17. CICRED, The Population of Turkey, 1974, p. 12.

18. See Khalifa, A. M., 1973a, for more details.

19. CICRED, The Population of Turkey, 1974, p. 39.

20. Ibid., p. 17.

21. Ibid., p. 40.

22. CICRED, The Population of the Arab Republic of Egypt, p. 5.

23. Ibid., pp. 13-14.

24. CICRED, La Population de la Tunisie, 1974, p. 59.

25. Ibid., p. 67.

26. CICRED, La Population du Liban, 1974, p. 37.

27. CICRED, The Population of Turkey, 1974, p. 17.

28. Ibid., p. 38.

29. See Coale, A. J., Hill, A. G., and Trussell, T. J., 1975, pp. 207-08.

30. See El-Biblawi, H. A. , 1974, pp. 14-15.

31. Montague, op. cit. , p. 306.

32. See Abu-Lughod, 1964, and El-Badry, M. A. , 1965, pp. 140-86.

33. See Khalifa, op. cit. , chap. 4 of this volume.

34. Abu-Lughod, 1964, p. 251.

35. CICRED, The Population of the Arab Republic of Egypt, 1974, p. 11.

36. See Ayad, M. , and Jemiai, Y. , chap. 8 of this volume.

37. CICRED, La Population du Liban, 1974, pp. 28-29.

38. Yaukey, D. , 1961.

39. CICRED, La Population du Liban, 1974, p. 31.

40. See the critique of his study in CICRED, La Population du Liban, 1974, pp. 32-35.

41. Ibid. , p. 35.

42. Ibid.

43. Ahmad, R. , 1974, p. 26.

44. This has been recently completed by Joseph Chamie in his Ph.D. dissertation, Population Studies Center, University of Michigan. Part of his findings were presented in a paper read at the annual meeting of the Population Association of America, Montreal, April 1976, entitled "Religious Differentials in Fertility: Lebanon 1971."

45. Tanas, R. S. , 1974, p. vi.

46. CICRED, La Population du Liban, 1974, p. 32.

47. Ibid. , p. 27.

48. The data in the section on population and family planning are drawn primarily from Montague, op. cit. , and Nortman, D. , 1974.

49. Montague, op. cit. , p. 307.

50. Ibid. , p. 309.

51. Personal communication from Serim Timur, Population Division, UNESCO, Paris, April 1976.

52. See Tanas, op. cit. , Ahmad, op. cit. , and CICRED, La Population du Liban.

53. See Ayad, and Jemiai, op. cit.

54. Montague, op. cit. , p. 307.

55. Kjurciev, A. , and Courbage, Y. , 1974, p. 39.

56. Clarke and Fisher, op. cit. , p. 71.

57. CICRED, La Population de l'Algérie, 1974, p. 19.

58. CICRED, La Population du Maroc, 1974, p. 17.

59. CICRED, La Population de l'Iran, 1974, p. 13.

60. Cairo Demographic Center, Demographic Measures and Population Growth in the Arab Countries, 1970, p. 69.

61. Rizk, H. , chap. 6 of this volume.

62. Clarke and Fisher, op. cit., p. 215.

63. Khalil, F., 1972, p. 169.

64. See Hill, A., chap. 5 of this volume.

65. Krotki, K. J., and Beaujot, R., 1975, p. 367.

66. See Vallin, J., chap. 7 of this volume.

67. Hill, op. cit.

68. Rizk, op. cit.

69. Kjurciev and Courbage, op. cit., p. 45.

70. CICRED, La Population de l'Iran, 1974, p. 10.

71. UNESCO Regional Office for Education in the Arab States, Population Dynamics and Educational Development in Syria, 1974.

72. Vallin, op. cit.

73. Rizk, op. cit.

74. Centre de Recherches et d'Etudes Démographiques, "La Fécondité Marocaine," 1974, pp. 10-11.

75. CICRED, La Population du Maroc, 1974, p. 20.

76. See Lapham, R. J., 1970, p. 22.

77. Sabagh, G., 1969, p. 263.

78. CICRED, La Population du Maroc, 1974, p. 14.

79. Paydarfar, A. A., 1975, pp. 156-57.

80. Ibid., p. 166.

81. Amani, M., 1971.

82. Khalil, op. cit., p. 233.

83. Ibid., p. 169.

84. UNESCO, Regional Office for Education in the Arab States, op. cit., p. 16.

85. Kjurciev, A., et al., 1976, p. 50.

86. Rizk, op. cit.

87. Hill, op. cit.

88. Cairo Demographic Center, op. cit., p. 186.

89. For a discussion of demographic parameters in the Yemen Arab Republic and a presentation of recent survey data, see Allman, J., and Hill, A. G., 1977.

90. Noureldin, S. S., 1971 and El Tay, O. A., 1972.

91. Ibid.

92. Henin, R. A., 1969, p. 796.

93. Noureldin, op. cit., pp. 48, 51.

94. Montague, op. cit., p. 314.

95. See Henin, op. cit., and Paydarfar, op. cit.

96. For a recent review of this controversy, see Harik, I., 1974, pp. 13-27, and van Nieuwenhuijze, C. A. O., ed., 1977.

97. Coale, A. J., 1969, p. 19.

98. Kirk, D., 1966, p. 561.

99. Seklani, M., 1960, p. 832.

100. See Nazer, I. R., et al., 1974. Originally published in Arabic, the two volumes provide the papers and proceedings of a meeting of Muslim religious leaders in Rabat, Morocco, in 1971. See also Musallam, B. F., in Parry, H. B., ed., 1974, pp. 300-10.

101. See, for example, Arowolo, O., 1973.

102. Kirk, op. cit., p. 144.

103. Audroing, J. F., et al., 1975, p. 75.

104. Schultz, T. P., in Cooper, C. A., and Alexander, S. S., eds., 1972, p. 442.

105. See the discussion in Watson and Lapham, op. cit., pp. 207-20.

106. For population projections for the region, see Hill, 1976.

2

Family Planning and Population Policies in the Middle East and North Africa

*INTERNATIONAL
PLANNED PARENTHOOD FEDERATION—
MIDDLE EAST AND NORTH AFRICA REGION*

HISTORICAL BACKGROUND

The concepts of family planning and population policy arose in the Middle East, North Africa, and their neighboring countries. The oldest written records concerning contraceptives were found in Egypt, and the oldest considerations on population policies appeared in the texts of the Greek philosophers. Family planning, that is, conscious attempts to limit fertility, were discussed in great detail in the famous Petri, or Kahun, papyrus, found in Egypt in 1899, which dates back more than 4,000 years. Some of the methods described are totally ineffectual, while others are known to have had effective contraceptive properties. Many later documents from ancient Egypt repeat and expand on the methods given in this papyrus. There are also many references to fertility, family planning, and, more often, problems of infertility in the Old Testament and in Talmudic texts, while the Greek schools of medicine devoted much space and effort to family planning methods, again a mixture of totally ineffectual and more or less useful means.[1]

Family planning is far from alien to the Islamic world. Most of the great medical books of Islamic science, particularly during its most flourishing period (ninth to eleventh centuries), contained

This chapter was originally presented at the First Regional Population Conference, sponsored by the UN Economic Commission for Western Asia and the Lebanese government, Beirut, Lebanon, February 18–March 1, 1974. Slight changes were made for presentation in this volume.

long lists of contraceptive compounds and instructions for their use.
(The texts and researches of the Greek scientists were preserved
and further developed by the great Islamic scholars.) The writings
of such men as Abu-Bakr al Razi (Rhazes), Ali Ibn-Abbas Al-Majusi,
Ibn Sina (Avicena), and Ibn Al Jami remained standard works of
reference for centuries.

References to population policy may also be found. We find
that the lawmakers and scholars concerned themselves with the size
of the population. Given the social and political conditions of the
day and the need for conquest and the propagation of faith, it is not
surprising that the majority of such references were frankly pronatalistic. However, the Greek philosophers Plato and Aristotle
believed that the city-state had an optimum population and that
rulers should attempt to keep the population at this level by popularizing fertility regulation when the population rose and by encouraging births when it fell below this level.

The great emphasis on contraception in antiquity, and especially in Islamic medicine and jurisprudence, seems to prove two
things: (1) that there must have been considerable interest in the
topic, as well as a significant demand for contraceptives; and
(2) that contraception was a completely legitimate concern of the
public and the professions. With the passing of the first Islamic
empire, Islamic scholarship began to wane. This occurred at the
same time as the writings of its most eminent scholars were being
eagerly translated into Latin, to serve as standard texts for centuries in the medical schools of medieval Europe.

MODERN FAMILY PLANNING MOVEMENT

During the eighteenth and nineteenth centuries, the focus of
development in family planning shifted to the industrialized societies
in northwestern Europe and North America, where the organized
family planning movement started to take form. This movement
was inspired by individuals and groups concerned with the social
effects of large family size in the new industrialized society, the
appalling living conditions of the poor, the status of women in society, and the increasingly clear evidence that uncontrolled fertility,
particularly with the increasing incidence of illegal abortion, presented serious health hazards.

Most of the people and groups advocating family planning did
so at the risk of incurring the displeasure of the authorities. Indeed, many went to court on one or more occasions, and several
were jailed for their advocacy of family planning. However, the
social changes of nineteenth-century Europe and North America,

and later of twentieth-century Japan, helped to make family planning
an established way of life in these countries. Two or three children
per family is now the accepted norm, whereas one or two generations earlier, it had been six or seven. No force or inducement
was involved in this basic change of family pattern. It was the result of individual decisions of millions of couples, who wished, and
were often pressed by socioeconomic changes, to shape their own
lives.

A new outlook toward family planning has come to the fore-
front over the last three decades. Many countries have become
seriously concerned about the implications of population growth resulting from the continuation of the old pattern of high birth rates
and steadily declining death rates. An enormous expansion of
production would be necessary just to maintain the existing standards
of living, although the goal is to increase these standards. Thus,
many countries have adopted family planning as an official policy in
order to lower their birth rates, the first major country to do so
being India, in the early 1950s. Now about 40 countries have joined
India in such policies. In the Middle East and North Africa, Iran,
Egypt, Turkey, Tunisia, and Morocco have national family planning
programs that aim to reduce birth rates and, consequently, the
annual net population increase.

FAMILY PLANNING AND POPULATION POLICY

At this stage, it is necessary to make the distinction between
family planning and population policy quite clear. Family planning
may be defined as the conscious actions taken by individual couples
to regulate the number and spacing of their children in accordance
with their personal preferences. A family planning policy will thus
consist of a series of actions designed to facilitate, as far as possible, the realization of these preferences by the individual families.
Such actions would form part of the overall health and social poli-
cies--in accordance with the concept of family planning not only as
a human right but, also, as a valuable component of social and
health policies. The family planner views the problems of human
fertility at the microlevel, that is, the family units, where decisions about the outcome of their reproductive activities are made.

Population policy has the explicit or implicit goal of bringing
the demographic parameters under control and, in planning ter-
minology, would be to bring them from the exogenous to the endoge-
nous sphere. Apart from questions of spatial distribution of population, most of these policies today aim at reducing birth rates,
which are regarded as excessively high. Rapid population growth

is considered to be an impediment to raising per capita incomes and a factor that slows the rate of social and economic development. Ultimately, the goal, of course, is also to improve the welfare of the individual and the family, but the problem is viewed at the macrolevel in this case.

RELATIONSHIP BETWEEN FAMILY PLANNING
AND POPULATION POLICY

Although there is this real difference in the basic philosophy of family planning and population control, both of them share and depend upon the use of contraceptives. The difference in philosophy leads to differences in priorities, emphasis, programming, and action. However, the fact that a family planning program is usually the first step in the implementation of a population policy has led to confusion between the two. To bring this difference into perspective, what happens in a pronatalistic country might be discussed. There, the family planners would argue that access to, and availability of, family planning sciences should be made for health and social reasons and as a human right. The fact that this will ultimately lower fertility levels is, to them, incidental.

Furthermore, an official policy to increase the birth rate or to keep it at a high level cannot be built on the withholding of contraceptive services, as this would not be humane and would most probably also lead to an increased incidence level of induced abortion. Other social policies would have to be used to further the pronatalistic aims. This type of situation is in no way theoretical; thus, when Hungary wanted to increase its crude birth rate (CBR) from 12 to 16, it subsidized family planning services and compulsory premarriage, postpartum, and postabortum contraceptive instruction, besides instituting a system of maternity benefits, which exceeded average wages, for women.

Thus, population policy and family planning policy are two distinct types of approaches, and although they are aimed at achieving different goals, their means to achieve these goals and the outcome are the same. In practical programs of population control, the distinction tends to dissolve, because irrespective of the policy intent, people will only adopt family planning if convinced of its benefits at the level of the individual and of the family.

DEVELOPMENT OF FAMILY PLANNING AND
POPULATION POLICIES IN THE MIDDLE
EAST AND NORTH AFRICA

In spite of the fact that the Islamic Middle East and North Africa were among the pioneers of family planning, the modern planned parenthood movement came late to this area, as compared to other parts of the world. The situation of each country in the region will be covered in a later section, but it seems useful to give a brief chronology of some of the major events related to family planning and population policies in the region. (See Table 2.1.)

Family Planning and Population Policies
in the Individual Countries

In this section, the position with respect to family planning and population policy in the countries of the region will be discussed. It is possible to group them under four separate headings:

Official Family Planning Policy
Intended to Reduce the Rate
of Population Growth

The four countries with official population policies--Egypt, Iran, Morocco, and Tunisia--have all explicitly adopted this policy as part of their overall efforts to speed up social and economic development. The reasons are well stated in the Second Moroccan Five-Year Plan:

> At the present day, the rate of natural increase in the
> population is about 3.2 per cent; this rate, which is one
> of the highest in the world, gives rise to an unfavourable
> demographic situation, not only because of the rate of
> increase, but also because it brings about an age pyra-
> mid in which the dependant population (those under
> fifteen and over sixty-four years of age) constitutes a
> large proportion of the total population. Realizing the
> importance of this question, the Government set up a
> pilot program of family planning in 1966. The national
> program of family planning proposes, within the

TABLE 2.1: Chronology of Family Planning Events in the Middle East and North Africa

Years	Events
1930-37	Family planning interest starts in Egypt with seminars and public discussions.
1937	International Birth Control Conference is held in Cairo, Egypt, under sponsorship of the Egyptian Medical Association. Mufti of Egypt issues fatwa favorable to modern family planning.
1952	Egypt establishes a National Population Commission, and the first clinical services in the region are established.
1953	The Fatwa Committee of Al Azhar University, Egypt, re-endorses the legality of family planning.
1958	Family Planning Association of Iran is founded in Teheran and begins the provision of clinical services. The National Population Commission in Egypt is changed to the Egyptian Association for Population Studies. Clinical services are expanded. First attempts to form a family planning association in Jordan fail, due in part to confusion between family planning and population policy in the public mind.
Early 1960s	Increasing concern among the medical profession over sociomedical effects of uncontrolled fertility leads to a beginning debate on family planning in many countries.
1962	President Nasser promulgates the new National Charter of Egypt, which emphasizes the problem of rapid population growth and endorses a national family planning program.
1963-64	Formation of the Jordan Family Planning and Protection Association in Jerusalem. Opening of clinical services in Jerusalem and some other towns. Pan Arab Medical Union endorses family planning as an integral part of preventive medicine during its meeting in Jerusalem.
1964	Grand Mufti of Jerusalem issues a fatwa favoring responsible planned parenthood. Tunisia embarks on a national pilot program of family planning.
1965	Family Planning Association founded in Sudan, and clinical services started with support from the Pathfinder Fund. Tunisia liberalizes laws governing induced abortion to allow abortion on social grounds for women with more than five living children.
1966	Morocco embarks on a National Family Planning Program, creates a High Council for Family Planning, and holds the first National Seminar on Family Planning. All official family planning activities in Egypt reorganized under a Supreme Council for Family Planning. All private and voluntary efforts are put under the sponsorship of the Egyptian Family Planning Association. Services are rapidly expanded. The National Family Planning Program in Tunisia is placed on a permanent footing.
1967	Iran embarks on a National Family Planning Program. First clinical services introduced to the University hospitals of Algiers, Constantine, and Oran in Algeria.

38

1968	Family planning association—Afghan Family Guidance Association—formed in Afghanistan. Creation of the Tunisian Family Planning Association (Association Tunisienne de Planning Familial). International Conference on Human Rights convened by the UN in Teheran. The Declaration of Teheran endorses as a fundamental human right that "parents have a right to freely and responsibly determine the number and spacing of their children."
1969	Founding of Family Planning Association in Lebanon. King Hassan II, President Nasser, and President Bourgiba are among the 12 original signatories to the world leaders' declaration on population. Creation of the Population Unit, UN Economic and Social Office in Beirut (UNESOB).
1970	Family Planning Section of the Iraqi medical association created. UNESOB Expert Group meeting on the application of demographic data and studies to development planning. IPPF Middle East and North Africa regional office created.
1971	Family Planning Association created in Cyprus, Iraq, and Morocco. Family planning as discussion topic at the WHO Eastern Mediterranean Region Conference in Monastir, Tunisia. Iraq requests WHO/UNFPA assistance for a pilot project under the maternity-centered approach to family planning. IPPF Middle East and North Africa region arranges two conferences: "Induced Abortion—A Hazard to Public Health?" and "Islam and Planned Parenthood." UNESOB Expert Group meeting on traditional and new techniques of demographic data collecting.
1972	UNESOB Expert Group meeting on mortality in cooperation with WHO. National Seminar on Population Policy as related to development strategy in Jordan.
1972-73	National Population Commission formed in Iraq, Jordan, Lebanon, Saudi Arabia, Sudan, and Syria in preparation for World Population Year.
1973	Afghanistan, Sudan, and People's Republic of Yemen request WHO/UNFPA assistance for pilot project under the maternity-centered approach to family planning. UNESOB Expert Group meeting on fertility. Family Planning Week in ten countries to celebrate IPPF twenty-first anniversary year.
1973	Tunisia liberalizes abortion laws.
1974	First Regional Population Conference, Beirut, Lebanon.

Sources: G. F. Brown, "Moroccan Family Planning Program: Progress and Problems," Demography 5, no. 2 (1968); W. G. Povey and G. F. Brown, "Tunisia's Experience in Family Planning," in ibid.; O. Schieffelin, Muslim Attitudes to Family Planning (New York: Population Council, 1972); H. A. Shanawany, "Family Planning: An Equilibrium Response to Demographic Conditions in the UAR," Ph.D. diss., Cornell University, 1967; and reports from international organizations, International Planned Parenthood Federation, and national associations.

> framework of the cultural and religious foundations of
> our society, to make all the necessary means available
> to families to enable them to choose the number of chil-
> dren they want and to have them when they so desire.
> For this purpose, a programme of education and informa-
> tion will be put into effect, side by side with the medical
> program. . . .
>   The longer-term objective of this policy of family
> planning is to reduce the birth rate to 35 per thousand
> towards 1980-85; this will help towards providing a solu-
> tion to the problems of nutrition, schooling, housing, and
> employment, by rendering them less acute. [2]

This emphasizes a number of important points also underlying the
policies of the other three countries. First, the problems are posed
by population growth rates, not population densities. Second, the
problem is related both to the influences of population growth and to
population structure. Third, the main policy instrument is a nationwide family planning program, including the necessary educational
backup. Fourth, the policies are voluntary, based on the decisions
of individual families. This does not preclude introducing socioeconomic changes that alter the reproductive plans of the families.
Fifth and last, a population policy is considered neither an end in
itself nor a panacea for development. It is one factor only.
    Iran's development plan emphasizes the dual nature of a family
planning program--as a social welfare measure in its own right and
as an instrument in that country's population policy.

> With abundant unskilled labour, and the declining death
> rate, the likelihood of a higher population growth rate
> will reduce the pace of increase in per capita income.
> Thus, for both economic and general welfare considera-
> tions, in the next decade or two, family planning should
> be popularized and it should constitute one of our im-
> portant welfare programs in the future plans. [3]

All four countries would probably agree to the Moroccan statement as a rationale for their population policy. However, there
are differences between each of them in the relative priorities given
to the policy and in the structure of its execution. This will appear
in the description of each of the four programs.

Egypt. Egypt is the country of the region with the largest family
planning program, in the official as well as the private sector. The
national program has more than 3,000 clinics in operation, 450 of

which are under the auspices of the Egyptian Family Planning Association. The policy dates back to 1962 with the promulgation of the National Charter, which included the following statement:

> Population increase constitutes the most dangerous obstacle that faces the Egyptian people in their drive towards raising the standard of production in their country in an effective and efficient way. Attempts at family planning deserve the most sincere efforts by modern scientific means.

Although expansion of Family Planning Services followed this policy statement, real large-scale and coordinated action started in 1966. In that year, all official family planning activities were brought under the coordination of a Supreme Council for Family Planning, while private sector activities were consolidated under the Egyptian Family Planning Association, which traces its history back to the establishment of the first National Population Commission in 1952 (and the subsequent Egyptian Association for Population Studies).

The program is based on the so-called cafeteria-approach, which entails the provision of all types of contraceptives, although in fact, oral contraceptives and the intrauterine device (IUD) are predominant. Supplies of oral contraceptives are locally manufactured.

Since the inception of the intensive program in 1966, the CBR has declined from an average of about 42 to 35 per 1,000, or about 17 percent. This is, in fact, a larger fall than can be ascribed to the actual achievements of the family planning program, even on the most optimistic evaluation. Other factors must have played a role as well, especially a change in the age structure and a gradual rise in the age at the first marriage. It is felt possible that there will be a rebound effect once peace has been achieved in the region. Unfortunately, the available statistics do not, as yet, allow for a definitive analysis of the contributing causes and pattern of the decline.

It is currently believed by the Supreme Council for Family Planning that the program will reach a plateau level unless a process of social change to support the fertility decline is initiated. Among the chief considerations, considering the high priority of the program, will be systematic improvement of status and job opportunities for women, as well as active intervention in certain established social patterns favoring high fertility.[4]

Iran. A Family Planning Association was formed in Iran in 1958, and clinical services on a small scale were initiated. Gradually,

interest in family planning as a part of maternal and child health
(MCH) services began manifesting itself in the Ministry of Health,
and during the preparation of the Third Five-Year Plan, the Plan
Organization expressed concern over the rapid population increase.

In 1967, a formal population policy and a national family planning program were announced, emphasizing both developmental and
MCH aspects of the planned activities. The program is under the
direction of an undersecretary for family planning in the Ministry
of Health. However, the private sector is heavily engaged in the
program. This includes the Family Planning Association, the
medical services of the National Industries, and many other bodies,
including the Sun and Lion, the Iranian Red Cross Society. The
level of clinical services in Iran is somewhat lower than that of
Egypt.

Although the two countries have roughly the same population,
the provision of services in Iran tends to be more difficult because
of the dispersed pattern of population settlements. Iran is currently
expanding its information and education services, partly through the
use of personnel seconded to family planning activities from the
various corps of young people serving in lieu of military service.

Morocco. The National Family Planning Program in Morocco was
initiated in 1966 and is even more closely integrated in the Ministry
of Health than is the case in Iran. Family planning services were
quietly integrated into the basic health services with no supportive
motivational work and little training of the personnel. The quantitative achievements of the Moroccan program so far have not been
considerable; they represent only a fraction of what would have been
necessary to achieve in order to attain the stated demographic goal,
namely, lowering of the birth rate by 10 percent before 1973.[5]

In 1971, a Family Planning Association was formed with the
basic aim of assisting the national program in information and education and to run model clinics. Morocco has recently been re-
evaluating the program and upgrading its priority. New plans for
strengthening clinical services and for information and education
backup have been developed, and a request has been submitted to
the UN Fund for Population Activities (UNFPA) for partial funding
of this expansion. The information and education components have
been planned in cooperation with the Family Planning Association.
The total request was nearly $1 million for 1973 and 1974. In all
probability, the coming few years will witness a marked expansion
in the number of clients.

Tunisia. The Tunisian Family Planning Program was started on a
pilot basis in 1964 and placed on a permanent footing in 1966. From

the outset, emphasis on use of the IUD was very strong. Initial reaction was good, but lack of proper information concerning foreseeable side effects, coupled with insufficiently trained personnel, led to serious setbacks. The result was that a real fear of the IUD developed (which persisted for several years). Political and administrative support was lost at a time when an effective educational program was most needed.[6]

It was in this situation that the Tunisian Family Planning Association was formed, to assist in generating popular and political support for the national program. A large number of the most influential private bodies in Tunisia were affiliated with the association. By 1971, the momentum and acceptance of the program had, once again, been assured. (Overall coordination of the program during the past few years has been vested with the Office of Population, a statutory board with wide membership and its own secretariat.)

A unique feature in this region is that the Tunisian program uses tubal ligation as one of its methods. About 2,500 of these operations are performed annually. Another unique feature is that abortion is now available to women who do not wish to give birth, provided that the pregnancy interruption takes place in the first trimester. The previous law, which allowed abortion only to mothers with five living children, was liberalized in September 1973. Although this is expected to lead to an important rise in the number of abortions, it has been emphasized that large-scale abortion is not a satisfactory long-term solution and that family planning advisory services must be considerably strengthened. During 1972 and 1973, the service statistics indicated a substantial increase in almost all the methods used.

There has been a definitive decline in the CBR along the same general lines as in Egypt. The reasons seem to be partly family planning usage and partly a rise in the age of marriage, coupled with the emancipation of women and the general modernization taking place in Tunisia.

Official Involvement in Health and Social Welfare-Oriented Family Planning Activities

This group of countries--Afghanistan, Algeria, Iraq, Sudan, and the People's Republic of Yemen--normally participates in family planning activities out of a mixture of concern with MCH and out of appreciation of family planning as a basic human right, as emphasized

in the <u>Declaration of Teheran.</u>* The health aspects are probably the
most important consideration. There is certainly sufficient evidence to link nutritional deficiencies of mother and child, as well
as maternal and infantile morbidity and mortality in general, to excess fertility. While lack of adequate spacing of births may be the
more important factor, high parity and age of the mother carries
its own risks.[7] Such direct health effects are probably overshad-
owed by more general effects on family welfare, which are, however, very difficult to quantify.

<u>Afghanistan</u>. Family planning activity in Afghanistan started in 1968
with the establishment of the Afghan Family Guidance Association.
From the outset, the association was seen as supplementary to the
overall MCH program of the Ministry of Health. The constitution
of the association specifically states that "where possibilities exist
the Ministry of Health should make available to the Association
buildings and necessary technical personnel for the purpose of the
full operation of the clinics."[8]
    The association is now running 19 clinics all over the country.
All but a few of these have been put at their disposal by the Ministry
of Health. Recently, the government has approached the UNFPA
for funds for the expansion of MCH services, including family planning, which will be coordinated with the work of the association.

<u>Algeria</u>. The first family planning clinic was opened in Algeria in
1967 at the University Hospital of Algiers, followed shortly afterward by clinics at the universities of Oran and Constantine. The
government has been discussing the inclusion of family planning in
the MCH services, and the attitude toward family planning as a
social welfare measure is positive. The government has also requested World Health Organization (WHO) assistance in formulating
recommendations in this respect. Some voluntary bodies in Algeria
provide family planning services as part of their clinical activities,
but there is no family planning association.
    Algeria has taken a firm stand on the question of a population
policy--it is regarded as unnecessary. It is thought that rapid economic and social development will, in itself, lead to a long-term
decline in fertility. In any case, Algeria can support a much
larger population than it does today.

---

*The <u>Declaration of Teheran</u> was promulgated at the Interna-
tional Conference on Human Rights, convened by the UN in Tehran
in 1968.

Iraq. Interest in family planning started in medical circles in the
1960s. In 1970, a family planning section of the Iraqi Medical Association was formed, which was formally incorporated as an autonomous Family Planning Association the following year. Later, the
government asked for WHO/UNFPA assistance to implement a program under the WHO concept of the maternity-centered approach to
family planning, a program now under implementation in cooperation with the Family Planning Association. Both the association and
the government regard family planning purely as a necessary ingredient in MCH care. The phrasing of the draft request to the
UNFPA illustrates this purpose clearly: "To provide the Iraqi population with an integrated MCH/Family Planning Service for the promotion of health of mothers, children and the family."

Three large hospital clinics are now operating in Baghdad in
cooperation with the association and the Ministry of Health, while
two other clinics are run by the association in Baghdad. During
1973, activities were also started in Basra and Mosul. So far, a
policy of decreasing the birth rate has not been considered necessary. Iraq has many natural resources, including a great potential
for irrigating more land, which could absorb an increasing population.

Sudan. Family planning activities in the Sudan date back to 1965,
when a group of professional personnel formed the Sudan Family
Planning Association. Services, initially on a small scale, were
limited to the area of Khartoum and Omdurman, but they are now
spreading to the provinces. From the outset, good relations were
established with the Ministry of Health. All clinical services were
run in government health centers, and in the provinces, the chief
medical officer supervised the family planning activity. Results
were encouraging, and in 1973, the government requested the cooperation of WHO and UNFPA in a broader pilot program--to integrate
family planning in the MCH services, initially in the area around
the capital.[9] Close cooperation with the family planning association
will be maintained.

People's Republic of Yemen. In 1973, the government requested
WHO to assist in drawing up plans for a maternity-centered family
planning program.[10] There is no family planning association in the
country.

These five countries--Afghanistan, Algeria, Iraq, Sudan, and
the People's Republic of Yemen--have chosen to implement family
planning in the interest of their mothers, children, and families. It
must not be forgotten that such considerations have also played a
major part in the countries with formal population activities. This
shows a responsibility of attitude toward the health needs of the population, which in many of the developed countries is not forthcoming.

Family Planning Associations
but No Official Involvement
in Family Planning

In all three cases--Cyprus, Jordan, and Lebanon--there are
close links and cooperation with associations and relevant government departments.

Cyprus. A Family Planning Association was established in late
1971, and a pilot clinic was opened in Nicosia, followed by one in
Famagusta. There is no government policy toward family planning,
but the creation of the association was officially welcomed. In fact,
the low birth rate in Cyprus (about 25 per 1,000) seems to indicate
that fertility control is already well established. The association
is thus more concerned with popularizing the most efficient methods
of contraception, especially as it is believed that Cyprus has a
serious abortion problem. (Greece, with a comparable birth rate
and similar cultural and socioeconomic background, is estimated to
have as many abortions as live births.)[11] In order to attain this
goal, the association plans to focus its attention on information and
education programs rather than on the provision of clinical services.

Jordan. Interest in family planning in Jordan dates back to the late
1950s, when attempts to form a family planning association were
made. Although clearly motivated by sociomedical interests, including the wish to combat illegal abortions, the initial attempt was
stymied--in part because of confusion in the public's mind between
family planning and population control. The Jordan Family Planning
and Protection Association was eventually formed in 1963. A changing climate of opinion and the endorsement of family planning as an
integral part of preventive medicine by the Pan Arab Medical Union
helped to make this development possible. At the same time, religious attitudes were changing, culminating in a fatwa (pronouncement) from the Grand Mufti of Jerusalem approving family planning.[12]
Until the 1967 war, the association received an annual subsidy
from the Ministry of Social Affairs. However, virtually all activity
had been on the West Bank, and the subsidy ceased in 1967. In spite
of many difficulties, the association has continued to expand on the
West Bank and now runs about 20 family planning centers in all of
the larger towns. In 1972, a branch of the association was established in Amman, and clinics were opened in Irbid and Amman.
These developments coincided with the holding of a conference in
Amman, "Population Policy in Relation to Development Strategy,"
organized by the Department of Statistics. Among its resolutions
were that in order to "help families determine their number of

off-spring," family planning services should be attainable from the
Ministry of Health clinics, that other branches of government should
assist with information, and that voluntary bodies in the field should
be given support. [13]

Lebanon. Individual physicians had long been prescribing contraceptives in Lebanon, although the penal code forbade any propaganda for,
or sales of, contraceptive methods under any circumstances. In
1969, following a Children's Week, sponsored by the Child Welfare
Association, it was decided to form a Family Planning Association.

Though the principal aims and objectives of the association are
contrary to existing legislation, the association was formally registered and gained the support of most relevant ministries. It was
later made a Public Utility Agency by presidential decree, which
confers tax exempt and consultative status on the association.
About ten clinics are now in operation in Beirut, Saida, Tripoli,
and Baalbek, some of which are housed in the facilities of the
government-sponsored Social Development Office.

The association has been represented on a committee that was
charged with preparing a draft for legislative change of the laws
governing contraception; so far, however, no legislative action has
been taken. Most types of contraception are available from commercial sources and private practitioners, in addition to the Family
Planning Association. However, the degree of information and education about contraception appears low, and there is evidence that
induced abortion is becoming a steadily more serious problem.

No Formal Family Planning Activities

The remaining countries in the region--Bahrain, Kuwait,
Libya, Oman, Qatar, Saudi Arabia, Syria, United Arab Emirates,
and the Yemen Arab Republic--have no official policy with respect
to family planning, nor have they any family planning associations.
However, with the partial exception of Syria, where the legal situation is identical to that of Lebanon, there are no legal restrictions
on family planning, and most types of contraceptives are available
from private practitioners and pharmacies. In several countries,
private, benevolent hospitals have small-scale family planning
activities.

In a number of these countries, governments and/or groups
of private citizens are considering the establishment of pilot family
planning activities, and in general, the attitude toward family planning in the context of MCH is quite positive. This is in contrast to
the widespread skepticism that prevailed even a few years ago. In
all likelihood, the coming few years will see the emergence of
further family planning programs in the region. It is hoped that

they may fully utilize the significant body of experience available from other countries of the region with similar backgrounds.

OBSTACLES AND BARRIERS TO FAMILY PLANNING

Family planning may be viewed at three different levels:

1. Family planning as a basic human right is, at the same time, the simplest and the most fundamental concept. It implies that no one should be denied access to family planning.

2. Family planning for maternal and child welfare implies the encouragement of family planning in the interest of public health in general, and the health and welfare of mothers and children in particular.

3. Family planning as a component of a population policy implies the attainment of specific goals in terms of a change in the birth rate and, consequently, in the number of contraceptive accepters as well.

The basic problems of organizing a family planning program are the same in all three cases, but some important differences will become apparent in the following section, which deals with some real and imagined obstacles to family planning.

Among the reasons given for lack of program success are that religious attitudes impede the use of family planning. The fact that the Catholic Church, alone among the larger religious groups, forbids the use of all contraceptives (allowing the "natural" method of rhythm to be used) has especially stimulated the interest in religious attitudes. In fact, most religions have pronatalist sentiments, which is not surprising, considering they were born in competition with other religions and at a time when mortality was high. Most studies show that the religious beliefs generally play a small part in fertility. France, an almost wholly Catholic country, has had low fertility levels longer than any other country, and the fertility of Catholics and non-Catholics in the United States is roughly equal. Islam has been believed by some to be especially pronatalist. It is certainly true that the levels of fertility in Islamic countries are among the highest in the world, but this is ascribable to the overall socioeconomic conditions rather than to religious beliefs as such. This is evidenced by the fact that standardized for socioeconomic conditions, there are hardly any differentials between Christians and Muslims in the Middle East.[14]

Furthermore, it is now clear that virtually all Muslim scholars and religious leaders actively endorse responsible planned parenthood within marriage and accept the modern methods of contraception. The 1974 conference in Rabat has summarized the Islamic position in all parts of the world. [15]

The real problems confronting a family planning program are basically of the same nature as those confronting other public health programs. It is necessary to have a proper management and field structure, as well as a system of reporting, which will enable a smooth supply system and program evaluation. Without a well-trained staff who have a sympathetic outlook toward the clients, a family planning program must expect to run into problems that may later be very difficult to surmount. An effective information and education program will help both in overall implementation and in surmounting specific problems. For reasons of economy and efficiency, the introduction of family planning services should be closely integrated into existing health and social development programs. This will allow for the maximum impact on the many interrelated factors governing fertility behavior. The provision of services in rural areas, where existing structures are already weak, poses special problems.

An extensive, and not very conclusive, literature on the organization and management of family programs is available (details will not be cited here). The exact structures will, in any case, depend upon the local conditions. It should be stressed, however, that in many respects, family planning is a more difficult proposition than other public health programs, since success depends on the continued motivation and use of contraceptives by a large number of individuals.

The definition of success in a family planning program is not easy. Looked at in the light of the Declaration of Teheran, which states that "parents have a right to freely and responsibly determine the number and spacing of their children," it is at least necessary to ensure that the population has access to information and contraceptive supplies. This may not be enough from a public health and social welfare point of view. It may be necessary to supplement the mere availability of supplies with information and education programs, as well as with free or subsidized services to stimulate the use of contraceptives.

When a family planning program forms part of a policy designed to reduce the birth rate, such problems are compounded. Although there is a significant body of evidence that couples in developing countries would wish to regulate fertility, it is also true that they want to have a relatively large number of children. This is certainly so in countries of this region. Thus, even if a family planning program were to be successfully implemented, it might be impossible to achieve the desired reduction in fertility. Under such circumstances, other measures would have to be taken--especially, attempts to induce selective change in some of the socioeconomic conditions that govern fertility attitudes and behavior. Egypt and Tunisia are cautiously taking such steps at the moment, with the status of women in society as one of the important issues. This clearly illustrates the difference between a family planning and a population policy.[16]

FUTURE PROSPECTS

Governmental Involvement

It seems safe to assume that governmental involvement in family planning programs throughout the world, including this region, will increase in the coming years. The social and health hazards of uncontrolled fertility are more clearly recognized, and the governmental responsibilities for aiding in their solution accepted. It is vital that the data already gathered are made available to any new family planning programs; this, fortunately, has usually been the case. In the interest of efficiency and cost, it is also desirable that family planning activities should utilize fully the existing framework for socioeconomic development. The most obvious is the already existing MCH services, but family planning also lends itself to integration into adult literacy programs, family welfare services, social work, and rural extension, to mention only a few. Some such services may have wider coverage than the present MCH services.

The role of the government is crucial in any family planning program. Even with the active support of a government, a nongovernmental organization would not (and probably should not) be in a position to provide family planning services for an entire population.

Nongovernmental Organizations

The main (though by no means the only) nongovernmental agencies involved in family planning activities are the more than 80 Family Planning associations that are members of the International Planned Parenthood Federation (IPPF). The role of such associations may differ considerably according to circumstances, but it becomes possible to discern a certain pattern:

1. In countries with no governmental family planning program, the association works to generate support for the concept of family planning, and establishes a network of pilot clinics.

2. In countries with recent governmental family planning programs, the association cooperates with the government in the provision and expansion of family planning services and the necessary information and education programs.

3. When the governmental program develops, the Family Planning Association generally dissociates itself from providing routine clinical services and concentrates on developing new methods and structures, as well as on disseminating information and education. The aim at this stage is to complement and assist the governmental program.

Local circumstances may lead to departures from this pattern, however. In this region, the associations in Morocco and Tunisia were created specifically to assist in obtaining popular support for already existing national programs, while the Egyptian Family Planning Association still has the responsibility for 400 clinics, performing about one-quarter of all clinical services in the country.

However, it is important to note that whatever the governmental policy, a voluntary family planning association can play a useful, complementary role and that all ten associations in this region can act in close cooperation with their respective governments. A family planning association may also be a useful focal point for the coordination of all nongovernmental efforts in the field.

CONCLUSION

The last ten years, and especially the last five, have seen widespread developments in the field of family planning in the region. Since 1964--when only a few modest pilot clinics were in operation and the concept of planned parenthood was new--the point has been reached where the bulk of the population live in countries where formal family planning services are available, as can be seen from Table 2.2.

About 85 percent of the total population of this region now live in countries where family planning services are available through organized governmental or private programs. This does not mean, however, that services are available to the entire population of those countries, since few of the programs have achieved nationwide coverage. It is virtually impossible to estimate the actual degree of coverage of the programs, but an estimate that about 25 percent to 30 percent of the population in the region have easy access to planned parenthood services is probably close to the truth.

There is a great need, therefore, for a continued expansion of family planning programs in the region, as well as for improving the quality of existing services. There is also a great need to integrate family planning into other programs for social and economic development, as well as into the educational systems. Moreover, there will be an increasing need for all countries to consider the implications of continued rapid population growth in relation to their development planning, which may again lead to a greater urgency in the expansion of family planning services.

TABLE 2.2: Status of Family Planning in the Middle East
and North Africa, January 1974

Group of Countries	Number of Countries in Group	Percent of Total Population in the Region*
Countries with an official family planning policy intended to reduce the rate of population growth	4	49
Countries with official involvement in health and social welfare-oriented family planning programs	5	34
Countries with family planning associations but no official involvement in family planning	3	3
Countries with no formal family planning activities	9	14
Total	21	100

*Total population of the region, mid-1971: 174,529,000.
Source: Compiled by International Planned Parenthood Federation.

Finally, it is necessary to reemphasize that family planning services are no panacea for developmental problems or social welfare. Family planning is one component of the overall strategy and should always be viewed in this light. There is a strong interrelationship between family planning and progress in overall socioeconomic development. Gains in either of the two will reinforce progress in the other, and to some extent, they may be dependent on each other. It is, for example, very unlikely that large-scale adoption of family planning in the rural areas of the region will take place without concomitant large socioeconomic changes.

The likely future of family planning in this region would appear to be one of gradual expansion and consolidation of services. This will not be in the form of large-scale crash programs, such as have been seen in other parts of the world. It will, rather, be through the less spectacular inclusion of family planning in health services, education, and other developmental programs. This may yield results too slowly for countries that wish a rapid decrease of population over a short time, but in the long run, it presents the best possibility of changing fertility patterns in the interests of MCH, social welfare, and socioeconomic development.

NOTES

1. International Planned Parenthood Federation, 1967.
2. Morocco, Plan Quinquennal, 1968-72.
3. Iran, Planning Division, 1963.
4. Bindary, A., 1972.
5. Brown, G. F., 1968.
6. Povey, W. G., and Brown, G. F., 1968.
7. World Health Organization, 1970.
8. Afghan Family Guidance Association, 1969.
9. United Nations Fund for Population Activities, 1973.
10. Ibid.
11. Valaoras, V., 1970.
12. Schieffelin, O., 1972.
13. Jordan, Department of Statistics, 1972.
14. Rizk, H., 1973; Yaukey, D., 1961.
15. Nazer, I. R., Karmi, H. S., and Zayid, M. Y., eds., 1974.
16. See Davis, K., 1967, pp. 730-39, for a summary of the problems.

3

Socioeconomic Determinants of Differential Fertility in Turkey

SERIM TIMUR

INTRODUCTION

Several studies have emphasized the lessening of class differences in relation to fertility in Europe in recent years. Within the economically advanced countries, there now appears to be a narrowing of previously wide fertility differentials by urban-rural residence, educational attainment, and socioeconomic status.[1] The character of socioeconomic development seems to have prescribed a uniform modern fertility pattern within narrow limits.[2] Furthermore, there appears to have been a considerable shift in the previous pattern of socioeconomic differentials. Some empirical studies have indicated the reversal of the negative relation between socioeconomic status and fertility, at least among the upper strata, in some European countries.[3] The evidence indicates, however, a weaker association than the previous negative associations, arising possibly from a much narrower range in the number of children born per woman in different social strata.

Despite some variations in the historical patterns of fertility decline in Europe,[4] it is accepted that a high level of social and economic development has generally led to a reduction in fertility. In the view of most demographers and sociologists, fertility decline in already developed countries usually follows a period of social and economic development and radical changes in the traditional role of the family, as well as of women and children.[5]

Differentials in fertility decline seem to be related to socioeconomic differences. The classical pattern of fertility differentials in the world involves three distinguishable phases. Starting from a situation of uniformity of birth rate among social classes, or possibly a weak direct correlation with class position, fertility decline intro-

duces a second phase, where the influences producing the reduction
in fertility operate first and most effectively on the highest socioeconomic groups. Thus, in this second phase, fertility tends to be
lower among urban families than among the uneducated, among high-
income families than among low-income families, and so forth.
This inverse association between fertility and socioeconomic groups
seems, however, to be a transitional phase in the general decline of
the birth rate. It is expected that in the third phase, the association
of fertility to socioeconomic status may again be positive and that
this correlation will arise when low-income families have accepted
fertility control and have decided that they can afford to have only a
few children.[6] It is expected, therefore, that the negative association of fertility with socioeconomic status may be characteristic
only of periods of demographic transition from high to low fertility,
or from uncontrolled to controlled family size.[7] In every developed
country, fertility differences by socioeconomic status are especially
marked when the birth rate begins to fall.[8]

The largest differentials in the world today are observed between developed and underdeveloped countries, since these two
groups of countries differ with regard to which stage of the cycle of
fertility differentials they occupy. The developed countries seem to
be somewhere in the transition between stages two and three, whereas most underdeveloped countries have reached some point between
stages one and two.

In view of the controversy centering around the questions of
how the so-called demographic transition has been completed in developed countries and whether the presently underdeveloped countries will repeat the same pattern, it should be of interest to investigate fertility differentials in a country characterized by very high
fertility in general. It is of further interest to investigate fertility
differentials in a country where 99 percent of the population adhere
to the Islamic religion, since studies carried out in other countries
have generally found consistently higher fertility rates for Muslims,
as compared to those of other religions.[9]

TURKISH CASE

Turkey, with its 37 million inhabitants, is a predominantly
agricultural country with an underdeveloped economy. The majority (66 percent) of its population live in rural communities of less
than 5,000 people, and among these, 85 percent live in villages of
less than 2,000 people. Seventy-two percent of all the economically
active population, and 58 percent of the active male population are
engaged in agriculture. The annual per capita income is about

U.S.$250. About half the population over ten years of age is illiterate (51 percent). The illiteracy rate by sex is 68 percent for females and 33 percent for males. It is not surprising then that the crude birth rate (CBR) is as high as 40 per 1,000, or using more refined measures, the total fertility rate is 5.7 and the gross reproduction rate (GRR) is 2.6. The corresponding mortality rates are 15 per 1,000 crude death rate (CDR) and 153 per 1,000 infant mortality rate.[10]

The aggregate national indicators, however, do not reveal the striking rural-urban and regional differentials. Although Turkey is in the process of development, economic growth and capital expenditures are (visibly) inequitably distributed throughout the country. This is reflected in marked urban-rural and regional fertility differences. Fertility is lowest in the metropolitan centers of Istanbul and Izmir, at the western end of the country, where economic and social development is highest. (CBRs are 24 and 25 per 1,000, respectively). Fertility in rural areas of the more developed west is also low (CBR: 36 per 1,000), as compared to the less developed central and eastern parts of the country (with rural CBR over 50 per 1,000).[11]

Some Hypotheses

The level of socioeconomic development indicates that metropolitan cities may be in the second phase of fertility transition while the more backward rural areas may be in the initial phase. Hence, in light of the foregoing theoretical considerations, we expect a strong inverse relation between fertility and socioeconomic variables in metropolitan cities and a weak inverse, or even a direct, relation in rural areas. To test this hypothesis, this chapter analyzes differentials in fertility behavior and family planning knowledge and practice by urban-rural residence and by salient socioeconomic characteristics, such as income, education, husband's occupation, and woman's employment status.

The impact of certain individual socioeconomic characteristics on fertility without regard to the structure of the society in which the individual lives, however, does not adequately explain differentials in fertility. For it is often seen that certain socioeconomic traits are more significant in some societies than in others. Thus, one should be concerned not only with the individual socioeconomic traits but, also, with the relative importance these traits have in different social structures. In this chapter, an attempt will be made to determine the extent to which individual socioeconomic traits influence fertility behavior in different community structures. For this reason, we roughly categorize community structure into four types: metropolitan, cities, towns, and villages. Though the classification is by size of population of settlements, it is still felt that the community structure in each category is distinct. The differences in these social structures are empirically reflected by our survey data on the differential distributions of the populations by occupation, income, education, and so forth in each settlement.

Methodology

The data for this chapter are taken from a nationwide multistage probability sample survey on "Family Structure and Population Problems in Turkey," conducted by the staff of the Hacettepe Institute of Population Studies in the summer of 1968. The estimates presented in this chapter are based on data relating to 3,200 currently married women under 45 years of age and their husbands.[12]

Fertility Measure Used

The basic measure of fertility used in this chapter is the average number of live-born children of currently married women of reproductive age (44 years old and younger). This measure has the advantage of summarizing the entire fertility history of women, but since it includes children born some years ago, it is not very informative about recent trends. In order to minimize the difficulties that may arise in comparing groups with different compositions of marital duration, data on children ever-born have been standardized for duration of marriage, using as a standard the marriage duration distribution of all women in the sample. Since female age at marriage in Turkey is low (mean age at marriage is 17.1), and since 90 percent of all women in the sample were married before age 20, further control of age at marriage was not necessary.

In comparing the standardized means of live-born children, in general, a difference of 0.5 may be taken to be statistically significant at the level of 5 percent.

Findings

Urban-Rural Residence

The earliest and most rapid declines in the birth rates in the Western countries are in the largest cities. The latest and slowest are in rural areas, with the smaller towns between the two extremes.[13] The same pattern is observed in Turkey when the mean number of live-born children is compared by community size. The

average number of live-born children for all Turkish women in reproductive ages is 3.9. This figure is higher (4.2) in rural areas
with less than 2,000 population and considerably lower in metropolitan areas (2.7). Small towns and other urban areas are in between,
with an average live births of 3.8 and 3.4, respectively (see Table
3.1).

TABLE 3.1: Number of Live-Born Children to Currently
           Married Women of Reproductive Age, by
           Community Size, in Turkey, 1968

Community Size (Population)	Standardized Mean Number of Live-Born Children	Currently Married Women Aged 15 to 44	
		Percent Distribution	Number of Women in Sample
Less than 2,000	4.2	60.8	1,423
2,000-14,999	3.8	13.2	337
15,000 and over	3.4	15.7	1,189
Metropolitan (Ankara, Istanbul, Izmir)	2.7	10.4	318
Turkey	3.9	100.0	3,267

Source: "Family Structure and Population Problems in
Turkey," survey conducted by the Hacettepe Institute of Population
Studies in 1968.

As shown in Table 3.2, among women who have been married
15 to 19 years, village women have twice as many children as metropolitan women. Metropolitan women have few live births after 14
years of marriage, while the other women take a longer duration to
complete their families. The comparison of older women in our
sample also indicates that these fertility differentials have possibly
existed in the recent past. Since our sample was confined to women
younger than 45, it is not possible to trace these differentials farther
back.

Parallel to fertility differentials, there are basic differences
between village, town, city, and metropolitan centers in regard to
their economic, social, and cultural development. (However, fertility rates are not uniform within each residential stratum.)

TABLE 3.2: Number of Live-Born Children per Currently
Married Women of Reproductive Age, by
Duration of Marriage (10-14 and 15-19 Years)
and by Community Size, in Turkey, 1968

Community	10-14 Years		15-19 Years	
	Mean Number of Live-Born Children	Number of Women	Mean Number of Live-Born Children	Number of Women
Metropolitan	3.26	12	3.34	39
Other urban	4.55	227	5.32	190
Town	5.14	80	5.71	51
Village	5.78	295	6.34	235
Turkey	5.23	674	5.88	515

Source: "Family Structure and Population Problems in
Turkey," survey conducted by the Hacettepe Institute of Population
Studies in 1968.

In self-supporting communities, where the family is the principal producing unit, the family's main source of power lies in its
numbers. Children are an economic asset. Advanced agricultural
techniques and mechanization of farming activities raise the standards of living and diminish the economic utility of offspring as pro-
ducers. This tends to reduce fertility and is reflected in regional
fertility differentials. In the more developed western villages, the
mean number of live-born children, standardized by duration of
marriage, is 3.5; it goes up to 4.9 in the primitive agricultural
setting of eastern Turkey.

In urban areas, fertility is significantly related to the respondent's birth place irrespective of current residence. Although
urbanization is certainly important in reducing fertility rates, the
migration of peasants to the cities is not accompanied by an immediate decline in their fertility. This relation between migration
to the city and fertility can best be shown by comparing the mean
number of live births of women born in the village but who are now
living in urban or metropolitan areas with those born in the village
and still living in the village.

As shown in Table 3.3, one-fourth of the metropolitan women
and one-third of the women in other urban areas are of rural origin.
The fertility of these village-born women in urban areas, however,
is virtually the same as for those in rural areas. The mean number

of live-born children to women of peasant origin in metropolitan centers is about four, that is, twice as high as that of city-born metropolitan women and equal to the average in rural areas. Apparently, migration to the cities, primarily the result of a push from poor rural areas, does not induce lower fertility in itself, unless it is a move toward higher socioeconomic status.

TABLE 3.3: Mean Number and Percent Distribution of Live-Born Children, by Place of Birth and by Current Residence, in Turkey, 1968[a]

| Place of Birth | Current Residence | | | | |
	Metropolitan	City	Town	Village	Turkey
Village	3.9	3.6	4.0	4.2	4.1
Percent distribution	23	33	34	96	71
Town	2.7	3.0	3.9	5.0	3.5
Percent distribution	28	17	62	3	15
City	2.2	3.4	b	b	2.9
Percent distribution	49	50	4	1	14
Total live-born children	2.7	3.4	3.8	4.2	3.9
Total percent	100	100	100	100	100
Number	310	1,162	332	1,413	3,217

[a]Standardized by duration of marriage of currently married women between the ages of 14 to 44.

[b]Less than 20 cases were excluded.

Source: "Family Structure and Population Problems in Turkey," survey conducted by the Hacettepe Institute of Population Studies in 1968.

Education of Women

It is usually believed that one of the reasons for fertility decline in developed countries is the educational advancement of the general population. As the level of education rises, fertility usually declines in both economically developed and underdeveloped countries. Furthermore, numerous studies have shown that the education of the wife is more strongly associated with fertility than the education of the husband.

In Turkey, where only about one-third of the women are literate, educated women form a highly select group, and declines in fertility are expected even at very moderate levels of education. Although illiterate women have almost three times as many births as
women university graduates, a marked reduction in fertility is also
observed with as low as five years of education. As shown in Table
3.4, the average number of live births is 4.2 for illiterate women,
3.2 for merely literate women, 2.8 for those with primary school
education, 2.0 for those who have completed secondary school or
lycée, and 1.4 for university graduates. In other words, mere literacy reduces fertility by 24 percent; 5 years of education reduces
it by 33 percent; both 8 and 12 years of education, by 50 percent;
and 16 years of education, by 67 percent.

However, rather than a regular accelerating effect of education on fertility, we can distinguish three turning points where fertility is reduced by one-fourth from the preceding educational category. These three points are mere literacy, secondary school, and
university education. As with other socioeconomic characteristics,
there is a marked relation between urban-rural residence and female
education. Although 80 percent of the metropolitan women are literate, this proportion is 43 percent in other urban areas, 39 percent
in small towns, and only 17 percent in the villages. Does a specific
educational level affect fertility at the same rate both in urban and
rural areas? Since there are few women with higher education when
we control for community type, the effect of educational level on fertility by urban-rural residence will be shown by combining educational categories (see Table 3.5). The data by community type reveal that illiterate women have virtually the same high level of fertility in metropolitan, urban, and rural areas. When we look at the
degree of change in fertility associated with educational level, we
see that mere literacy reduces fertility by almost 40 percent in
metropolitan centers, whereas this proportion is 20 percent in other
urban areas, 30 percent in towns, and only 12 percent in the villages.

Primary school education, likewise, reduces fertility by 40
percent in metropolitan centers but by only 25 percent in rural areas.
Among literate and primary school-educated peasant women, fertility is much higher than among women of the same educational level
in urban areas. Thus, both urban-rural residence and education (in
interaction) affect fertility. Although education produces a reduction in fertility irrespective of community type, a specific level of
education does not produce the same level of fertility in both urban
and rural areas. In other words, educational level and fertility are
highly interrelated, but most of the effects of education operate
through residence, metropolitan residence being especially influential.

TABLE 3.4: Mean Number of Live-Born Children, by Woman's Education, and Percentage of Reductions in Fertility, by Educational Level, in Turkey, 1968*

Educational Level	Mean Number of Live-Born Children	Percent Reduction in Fertility from Preceding Category	Percent Reduction in Fertility from the Category of Illiterates	Percent Distribution of Women in Each Category
Illiterate	4.2	--	--	68.2
Did not complete primary school	3.2	24	24	12.0
Completed primary school (5 years)	2.8	13	33	15.9
Completed secondary school (8 years)	2.1	25	50	2.1
Completed lycée (12 years)	2.0	5	52	1.3
University graduate (16 years)	1.4	30	67	0.5
Total	3.9	--	--	100
Number	3,267	3,267	3,267	3,267

*Standardized by duration of marriage of currently married women between the ages of 14 to 44.
Source: "Family Structure and Population Problems in Turkey," survey conducted by the Hacettepe Institute of Population Studies in 1968.

TABLE 3.5: Mean Number and Percent Distribution of
Live-Born Children, by Education of Women
and by Community Type, in Turkey, 1968[a]

Education of Women	Live-Born Children				
	Metropolitan	City	Town	Village	Turkey
Illiterate	4.1	3.8	4.3	4.3	4.2
Percent distribution	20	51	61	83	68
Did not complete primary school	2.5	3.1	3.1	3.8	3.2
Percent distribution	23	18	15	8	12
Completed primary school (5 years)	2.6	2.7	2.6	3.2	2.8
Percent distribution	33	26	21	9	16
Secondary and over	1.9	2.9	b	--	2.1
Percent distribution	24	5	--	--	4
Total live-born children	2.7	3.2	3.8	4.2	3.9
Total percent	100	100	100	100	100
Number	318	1,189	337	1,423	3,267
Ratio of highest to lowest[c]	2.60	1.41	1.65	1.34	2.00

[a]Standardized by duration of marriage of currently married
women between the ages of 14 to 44.
[b]Less than 20 cases were excluded.
[c]Lowest = 1.
Source: "Family Structure and Population Problems in
Turkey," survey conducted by the Hacettepe Institute of Population
Studies in 1968.

Husband's Education

Men in Turkey are considerably more educated than women.
The influence of men's education on fertility, however, is less at
each educational level. A break in fertility occurs only at the secondary school level. Sixteen years of education reduces fertility by
less than half (47 percent). The fact that mere literacy or five years
of education do not affect the fertility pattern is observed both in
urban and rural areas. The very few women in higher educational
groups in rural areas prevent us from making more conclusive
statements on urban-rural differences.

However, as will be seen in Table 3.6, urban-rural residence seems to affect fertility independent of education. Within each broad educational category, metropolitan and other urban men have fewer children than those residing in towns and villages.

TABLE 3.6: Mean Number and Percent Distribution of Live-Born Children, by Education of Husband and by Community Type, in Turkey, 1968[a]

Education of Husband	Live-Born Children				
	Metropolitan	City	Town	Village	Turkey
Illiterate	b	3.8	4.2	4.5	4.3
Percent distribution	4	13	14	31	23
Did not complete primary school	3.6	3.6	4.6	4.4	4.2
Percent distribution	8	20	21	32	25
Completed primary school (5 years)	3.1	3.2	3.7	4.1	3.7
Percent distribution	45	48	51	37	42
Secondary school and over	2.5	2.8	3.1	--	2.8
Percent distribution	43	19	14	--	11
Total live-born children	2.8	3.3	3.8	4.3	3.9
Total percent	100	100	100	100	100
Number	259	960	254	957	2,430
Ratio of highest to lowest[c]	1.44	1.37	1.35	1.10	1.50

[a]Standardized by duration of marriage of currently married women between the ages of 14 to 44.
[b]Less than 20 cases were excluded.
[c]Lowest = 1.
Source: "Family Structure and Population Problems in Turkey," survey conducted by the Hacettepe Institute of Population Studies in 1968.

Husband's Occupation

Similar to the historical trends of developed countries during the demographic transition, the relationship between occupation and fertility is most pronounced among the professionals and farmers: while the former have an average of 2.3 live-born children, the latter have an average of 4.4. (See Table 3.7.) It should be noted that farmers constitute the largest occupational category (51 percent), whereas professionals constitute the smallest (2 percent). Men in commerce and businessmen occupy the second-lowest fertility category, followed by clerks and junior civil servants. After farmers, workers and artisans are the next two high-fertility categories.

TABLE 3.7: Mean Number and Percent Distribution of Live-Born Children, by Husband's Occupation and by Community Type, in Turkey, 1968[a]

Husband's Occupation	Live-Born Children				
	Metropolitan	City	Town	Village	Turkey
Commerce and businessmen	2.4	3.7	b	--	2.8
Percent distribution	6	3	2	--	2
Professionals	1.9	3.0	b	--	2.3
Percent distribution	8	2	1	--	2
Clerks and junior civil servants	2.9	3.0	3.8	--	3.1
Percent distribution	31	22	13	1	10
Artisans and small-scale retailers	2.4	3.4	4.0	3.9	3.5
Percent distribution	32	39	33	8	20
Workers	4.0	3.3	3.3	4.4	4.4
Percent distribution	23	29	25	6	15
Farmers and farm workers	--	3.5	4.8	4.4	4.4
Percent distribution	--	5	25	85	51
Total live-born children	2.8	3.3	3.8	4.3	3.9
Total percent	100	100	100	100	100
Number	238	250	937	251	949
Ratio of highest to lowest[c]	2.11	1.23	1.26	1.13	1.91

[a]Standardized by duration of marriage of currently married women between the ages of 14 to 44.
[b]Less than 20 cases were excluded.
[c]Lowest = 1.

Source: "Family Structure and Population Problems in Turkey," survey conducted by the Hacettepe Institute of Population Studies in 1968.

The same general pattern is observed in metropolitan centers, but fertility is lower than the national average in every category, except for workers. In other urban areas, once again, professionals and civil servants have the lowest fertility, whereas men in commerce and businessmen, as well as farmers (absentee), have the highest fertility. In all existing categories, towns have a higher fertility than metropolitan and urban areas. In rural areas, where businessmen and professionals are nonexistent, fertility is highest for all the remaining categories, and no differentials are observed.

Income

A classification of families by income shows a regular decline in fertility with rising levels of income. In order to maximize the accuracy of reporting of income, questions were asked about the income of each member of the household, as well as each possible source of income in cash or in kind. In this context, per capita income is a more accurate measure than total household income. It controls for the total number of family members and earners. Otherwise, some of the extended families may be included in the highest income bracket, in spite of the fact that their standard of living may not be high.

The number of children ever-born is 4.6 in the lowest income bracket, whereas it is 2.7 in the highest income group (see Table 3.8). Although regular but slight decreases in fertility are observed among the three lowest categories within each community type, a break in fertility occurs only in the fourth income group. Among the three lowest categories, comprising 72 percent of the total population, there are virtually no differentials by community type. In other words, 25 percent of the metropolitan population, 60 percent of the urbanites, 68 percent of the town population, and 83 percent of the villagers earning less than 2,000 Turkish liras per capita have the same high fertility (about four live births).

The most interesting finding in Table 3.8, however, is that fertility exhibits a u-shaped curve in towns and villages; the highest fertility is found in the lowest income bracket and gradually decreases to the highest group, where it increases slightly. Thus, rural fertility seems to be positively related to income in the highest group.

This pattern corresponds perfectly with the situation we would hypothesize based on data from developed countries. There is a well-defined transition from inverse association of economic status to fertility in urban areas to direct relation among the upper strata in rural areas.

TABLE 3.8: Mean Number and Percent Distribution of
Live-Born Children, by per Capita Income
and by Community Type, in Turkey, 1968[a]

Annual per Capita Family Income in Turkey[b]	Live-Born Children				
	Metropolitan	City	Town	Village	Turkey
1-499	--	4.4	5.3	4.6	4.6
Percent distribution	--	6	16	38	26
500-999	4.7	4.2	4.2	4.3	4.3
Percent distribution	3	18	22	29	24
1,000-1,999	4.1	3.5	3.7	4.0	3.8
Percent distribution	22	36	30	16	22
2,000-3,999	2.7	2.8	2.8	3.4	3.0
Percent distribution	34	28	20	11	17
4,000+	2.2	2.3	3.1	3.7	2.7
Percent distribution	40	12	13	6	12
Total live-born children	2.8	3.4	3.8	4.2	3.8
Total percent	100	100	100	100	100
Number	249	919	248	1,005	2,421
Ratio of highest to lowest[c]	2.14	1.91	1.89	1.35	1.70

[a]Standardized by duration of marriage of currently married
women between the ages of 14 to 44.

[b]U.S. $1 = 14 Turkish liras.

[c]Lowest = 1.

Source: "Family Structure and Population Problems in
Turkey," survey conducted by the Hacettepe Institute of Population
Studies in 1968.

Besides income, the amount of land owned, another indicator
of rural wealth, also reveals the same positive association of fertility with size of large landholdings, (see Table 3.9). In a widely cited
article, Stys has also found a positive association of fertility with the
size of family farms in southern Poland among women born prior to
1900.[14] He cites in his explanation the earlier marriage of wealthier
girls, who bear children sooner, more frequently, and over a longer
period.

TABLE 3.9: Mean Number and Percent Distribution of Live-Born Children, by Size of Land Owned and by Rural Residence, in Turkey, 1968[a]

Size of Land Owned (in decares)[b]	Town Mean Number	Town Percent Distribution	Village Mean Number	Village Percent Distribution	Rural Turkey Mean Number	Rural Turkey Percent Distribution
0–10	4.9	35	4.8	24	4.8	25
11–25	5.5	18	4.4	24	4.4	23
26–50	4.4	27	4.1	28	4.2	28
51–100	5.7	13[c]	4.1	15	4.2	15
101 and over	6.1	8[c]	5.3	9	5.4	9
Total	5.1	100	4.4	100	4.5	100
Number	82	--	739	--	821	--

[a]Standardized by duration of marriage of currently married women between the ages of 14 to 44.

[b]One decare = 1,000 square meters.

[c]Less than 20 cases were included in this table to show the consistency of the trend.

Source: "Family Structure and Population Problems in Turkey," survey conducted by the Hacettepe Institute of Population Studies in 1968.

In Turkey, where both the mean and median age at marriage for village women is about 16, no consistent variation is observed at marriage. One plausible explanation could be that in rural areas, which are highly conducive to a large number of children, very few people are sufficiently motivated to limit their fertility successfully. Those who feel this need somewhat more are the middle-income farmers. Thus, holding other things constant, middle-income farmers may feel themselves to be under more economic pressure than the wealthy and more concerned than the poor, who understandably do not have realistic expectations of bettering their lot, with or without high fertility. A recent study in rural areas also found that among the rich farmers, who control the economic and political life of the village, a large family with many sons carries a good deal more prestige than a smaller-sized family of equal wealth.[15]

Employment Status of Women

In all developed countries, where socioeconomic differences in fertility tend to diminish, the strongest and most persistent type of differential is found to relate to women's employment status. In Turkey, where gainful employment for females is relatively rare (11 percent of all married women aged 44 and younger are employed), the fertility differentials related to women's working status is the least pronounced. In urban areas, currently employed women have, on the average, 2.9 live births, and women who have never worked have 3.5 live births. In fact, there are almost no differentials among metropolitan women: currently employed women have 2.7 live births, whereas women who never worked have 2.8 live births (see Table 3.10). This overall comparison, however, might be a spurious one.

TABLE 3.10: Mean Number and Percent Distribution of Live-Born Children, by Woman's Employment Status and by Community Type, in Turkey, 1968[a]

| Working Status | Live-Born Children | | | | |
	Metropolitan	City	Town	Village	Turkey
Currently employed (nonagricultural)	2.7	2.7	3.2	--	2.9
Percent distribution	12	10	7	--	4
Previously employed (nonagricultural)	2.5	3.0	b	--	3.1
Percent distribution	14	11	2	--	4
Never worked (urban women)	2.8	3.4	3.8	--	3.5
Percent distribution	74	79	76	--	32
Currently employed (agricultural)	--	--	3.7	3.9	3.9
Percent distribution	--	--	4	11	7
Never worked (rural women)	--	--	4.6	4.2	4.2
Percent distribution	--	--	11	89	54
Total live-born children	2.7	3.3	3.8	4.2	3.9
Total percent	100	100	100	100	100
Number	317	1,177	335	1,415	3,244
Ratio of highest to lowest[c]	1.04	1.26	1.43	1.08	1.44

[a]Standardized by duration of marriage of currently married women between the ages of 14 to 44.
[b]Less than 20 cases.
[c]Lowest = 1.
Source: "Family Structure and Population Problems in Turkey," survey conducted by the Hacettepe Institute of Population Studies in 1968.

In Turkey, as in most underdeveloped countries, the majority of the "few" women who work are either unskilled workers or professionals. In metropolitan areas, where the proportion of gainfully employed women is 12 percent, these proportions are 16 percent in the highest-income bracket and 25 percent in the lowest, whereas the proportion of working women is below the average for Turkey in the middle-income groups. The same pattern is also observed by educational level: 16 percent of the illiterate women and 21 percent of the women with secondary school education and over are employed in metropolitan areas. In contrast to most of the developed countries, where female employment is concentrated in middle-level jobs,[16] the Turkish female employment pattern seems somewhat bipolarized at the lowest and highest categories. Thus, the weight of these two extreme categories (the uneducated low-income high-fertility group and the educated high-income low-fertility group) may attenuate the overall average fertility measure of employed women.

When the fertility of employed women and those who never worked is compared within each educational level and income group, however, fertility is consistently lower among employed women. (See Table 3.11.)

When urban-rural residence and literacy status are held constant, both currently employed and previously employed women have somewhat lower fertility rates than urban women who never worked (see Table 3.11). Gainfully employed women in each income bracket also exhibit lower fertility rates (see Table 3.12). As would be expected, the relation is most apparent in urban areas.

Based on the aforementioned bipolarized female employment pattern in Turkey, the negative relation between employment and fertility is most pronounced for the lowest- and higher-income categories, where women are more likely to be employed, and disappears among the middle-income group. That is, although employed women of low and high incomes have lower fertility than housewives with equal family incomes, there were no differentials among the employed and never-employed women in the middle-income group.

With respect to the question of whether low fertility encourages women to work or whether working women deliberately control their fertility, our data on contraceptive use suggest that lower fertility among married employed women is due to conscious control of fertility. Data on contraceptive use among employed and never-employed urban women show that a higher proportion of employed women use contraceptives. The difference is statistically significant at the level of 1 percent.

Our data suggest that female employment depresses fertility. However, it is also clear that in Turkey, the relationship between women's working status and fertility is weaker than the relation of other socioeconomic variables with fertility.

TABLE 3.11: Mean Number of Live-Born Children, by Woman's Employment Status and by Woman's Literacy Status, in Turkey, 1968*

Literacy Status	Nonagricultural				Agricultural		
	Currently Employed	Previously Employed	Never Worked	Total Urban Women	Currently Employed	Never Worked	Total Rural Women
Illiterate	3.2	3.4	4.0	3.9	4.0	4.3	4.3
Literate	2.2	2.5	2.7	2.6	3.6	3.8	3.8
Total live-born children	2.9	3.1	3.5	3.3	4.0	4.2	4.2
Number	172	146	1,430	1,748	183	1,309	1,492

*Standardized by duration of marriage of currently married women between the ages of 14 to 44.

Source: "Family Structure and Population Problems in Turkey," survey conducted by the Hacettepe Institute of Population Studies in 1968.

TABLE 3.12: Mean Number of Live-Born Children, by Woman's Employment Status and by per Capita Family Income, in Turkey, 1968[a]

Per Capita Family Income in Turkey[b]	Nonagricultural				Agricultural		
	Currently Employed	Previously Employed	Never Worked	Total Urban Women	Currently Employed	Never Worked	Total Rural Women
1-499	c	c	4.4	4.4	4.4	4.6	4.6
500-999	3.7	c	4.4	4.3	4.1	4.3	4.3
1,000-1,999	3.7	3.6	3.6	3.6	3.7	4.1	4.1
2,000-3,999	2.2	3.1	2.8	2.8	c	3.5	3.4
4,000+	1.9	1.9	2.4	2.3	c	3.8	3.8
Total live-born children	2.9	3.1	3.4	3.3	4.0	4.2	4.2
Number	136	113	1,093	1,342	124	929	1,053

[a]Standardized by duration of marriage of currently married women between the ages of 14 to 44.
[b]U.S. $1 = 14 Turkish liras.
[c]Less than 20 cases.

Source: "Family Structure and Population Problems in Turkey," survey conducted by the Hacettepe Institute of Population Studies in 1968.

CONTRACEPTIVE USE IN TURKEY

Differential marital fertility can be explained largely by differences in the extent and effectiveness of contraceptive use. A detailed discussion of contraceptive knowledge and practice of different groups in Turkey is beyond the scope of this chapter, for it is necessary not only to know the extent to which couples use some form of birth control but, also, such factors as the time at which contraceptive use is initiated, the effectiveness of the methods used, and the efficiency of the users.

About 40 percent of the currently married couples in Turkey have used at least one contraceptive method sometime during their marital life. As expected, this proportion shows large variations by type of community. The proportion of the ever-used category was 81 percent in metropolitan areas, 57 percent in cities and towns (combined), and 27 percent in the villages. (See Table 3.13.)

TABLE 3.13: Distribution of Couples, by Contraceptive Use and by Community Type, in Turkey, 1968

	Ever-Used	Never Used or Unknown	Total
Metropolitan			
Percent	80.7	19.3	100.0
Number	250	69	319
Cities and towns			
Percent	56.7	43.3	100.0
Number	887	642	1,529
Villages			
Percent	27.2	72.8	100.0
Number	380	1,044	1,424
Turkey			
Percent	41.5	58.5	100.0
Number	1,517	1,755	3,272

Note: Chi-square = 494, significant at .001 level; couples who have ever used at least one of the following methods: coitus interruptus, condom, oral pill, IUD, foam, diaphragm, douche, or pessary.

Source: "Family Structure and Population Problems in Turkey," survey conducted by the Hacettepe Institute of Population Studies in 1968.

Similarly, statistically significant relationships (chi-square significant at .01 level) for Turkey as a whole are found between contraceptives ever-used and both husband's and wife's educational level, husband's occupation, urban working status of women, and family income.[17] Demographic variables, such as the number of children ever-born, children surviving, woman's age, and duration of marriage have also yielded the expected statistically significant relationships with contraceptive use (chi-square significant at .01 level). That is, in general, the older and high-parity women were more likely to have used contraceptives.

Various methods of contraception, and especially coitus interruptus, were used by Turkish couples to limit fertility. As indicated in Table 3.14, both the extent of knowledge and use of contraceptives are considerably less in rural areas. However, Table 3.14 gives no evidence that lack of knowledge is the reason for nonuse in rural areas. For instance, coitus interruptus was known by 88 percent of the metropolitan women and by 50 percent of the village women. But, although 63 percent of the metropolitan women who knew this method used it, only 36 percent of the peasant women who knew this method used it. The same differences are observed in the use of other methods, with the exception of the new intrauterine devices (IUDs) used by a small minority in urban areas. Furthermore, lack of knowledge may well reflect lack of motivation, since both knowledge and use increase by parity and age in rural areas.

DISCUSSION

In this presentation of the socioeconomic determinants of Turkish fertility differentials, an attempt is made to combine the aggregate and individual levels of analysis. Based on data from a nationwide sample of Turkish couples, community structural implications for differentials at the individual level were investigated, in addition to the impact of individual socioeconomic characteristics.

Although socioeconomic variables were negatively associated with fertility at the individual level, the degree of this association, and sometimes even the direction, was found to be different between urban and rural communities. Thus, our findings (so far) clearly reveal that fertility varies with specific or different conditions of socioeconomic structure.

The birth rate in Turkey is effected essentially by the same causes acting toward its decline in developed countries. Almost all the traditional (or historic) fertility differentials in industrially advanced countries have been observed in Turkey. The three metropolitan centers of Ankara, Istanbul, and Izmir have gone farthest in

TABLE 3.14: Contraceptive Knowledge and Use, by Community Type, in Turkey, 1968 (percent)

Community Type and Method of Contraception	Heard of It	Ever-Used	Currently Using	Current and Consistent Users	Ever-Used of Those Who Heard about the Method
Coitus interruptus:					
Metropolitan	88.0	55.1	40.7	25.8	62.6
City	72.3	34.6	22.7	15.3	47.8
Town	58.9	30.0	21.8	12.9	50.9
Village	50.0	17.8	5.2	0.9	35.6
Total	58.8	26.1	18.5	12.4	44.4
Condom:					
Metropolitan	85.5	39.5	17.6	11.3	46.2
City	70.6	19.1	7.0	5.0	27.0
Town	57.3	17.9	8.2	5.0	31.3
Village	25.3	2.1	1.0	0.7	8.2
Total	43.0	10.8	4.7	3.1	25.1
Oral pill:					
Metropolitan	86.9	14.9	5.8	4.5	17.2
City	74.0	15.6	6.1	5.5	21.7
Town	59.2	11.6	2.6	2.2	19.6
Village	41.6	2.2	0.05	0.05	5.3
Total	53.9	6.9	2.2	2.0	12.8
IUD:					
Metropolitan	82.0	4.5	1.9	1.9	5.5
City	74.4	5.0	3.2	3.2	6.5
Town	52.2	1.9	1.8	1.8	3.6
Village	28.6	1.4	0.9	0.9	5.0
Total	44.8	2.5	1.6	1.6	5.5

Note: Total number = 3,169 (currently married women 15-44).

Source: "Family Structure and Population Problems in Turkey," survey conducted by the Hacettepe Institute of Population Studies in 1968.

fertility decline, but there are extremely wide fertility differentials by social class. The differentials were less pronounced in other urban areas, where fertility levels were high. In rural areas, where fertility was highest, there were no differentials among socioeconomic groups. In fact, high levels of income and large landownership were positively associated with fertility.

Differences in fertility rates are the result of a network of socioeconomic and psychological factors. Only the socioeconomic aspects of differential fertility in Turkey were discussed in this chapter. Residential influences and socioeconomic factors usually affect fertility indirectly. However, in considering the direct cultural and sociopsychological causes of fertility, it should be recalled that all those factors, and even the sociodemographic "intermediate variables,"[18] are deeply embedded in the social and economic structure of the society.

Given the extremely marked fertility differentials by urban-rural residence and socioeconomic factors in our nationwide survey, the importance of other factors in determining fertility levels seems to be negligible. Once one controls for position in the social structure, values and norms about fertility, family type, religiosity, and knowledge about contraceptive methods, such factors as communication between spouses, family authority patterns, and other social psychological variables will probably add very little to the explanation of fertility differentials in Turkey.

In our analysis, the effect of each socioeconomic variable was investigated independently. Here I should like to point to the danger of the "particularistic fallacy," to use Blake's term (which occurs when one turns one's attention entirely to the associations between particular variables--education, income, urbanization, and so forth--instead of utilizing the association to trace out the basic and more general mechanism involved),[19] for it is known that the relevant importance of all variables associated with declines in fertility greatly differ both in time and space. Most socioeconomic variables are highly interrelated, and the impact of each is much less important than the effect of their joint interaction.

For instance, among the socioeconomic variables that were investigated in this chapter, that of woman's educational level was most highly associated with fertility and that of female employment status the least. However, based on this finding, it would be misleading to conclude that more widespread female education in the future will decrease fertility at its present rate. Everything else being equal, a disproportionate rise in Turkish female education would most probably result solely in decreasing the explanatory power of this variable. By the same token, economic advancement and corresponding changes in female economic participation will increase the impact of female employment on fertility.

This study suggests that fertility is largely determined by the socioeconomic structure of the society and by the position the individual holds within the given social structure. Our findings also lead us to conclude that in Turkey, where massive structural differences exist between urban-rural communities, as well as immense inequalities among social classes, further important reductions in fertility are unlikely unless profound and rapid changes in the economic and social structure are attained.

NOTES

1. Kiser, C. V., 1967.
2. Ryder, N. B., 1967.
3. Johnson, G. Z., 1960; Glass, D. V., 1969.
4. Coale, A. J., 1969.
5. Freedman, R., 1963.
6. Hawley, A. H., 1950; Petersen, W., 1970; Freedman, op. cit., pp. 115-18.
7. Johnson, op. cit.
8. Notestein, cited in Hawley, op. cit., p. 117; Wrong, D. H., 1958.
9. Davis, K., 1951; Yaukey, D., 1961; Breznik, D., 1968.
10. Turkey, Ministry of Health and Social Welfare, School of Public Health, 1970.
11. Ibid.
12. For more information on sampling and questionnaire design, see Timur, S., 1971.
13. Johnson, op. cit.
14. Stys, W., 1957.
15. Ozankaya, O., 1970.
16. Glass, op. cit.; Roux, C., 1970.
17. For social class differences in the efficiency of contraceptive use, see Rainwater, I., 1965; Yurtören, S., 1965.
18. Davis, K., and Blake, J., 1956.
19. Ibid.

4

Rural-Urban Fertility Differences and Trends in Egypt, 1930-70

ATEF M. KHALIFA

Modern population growth occurs through a decline in the death rate while the birth rate remains relatively high. The widening excess of births over deaths that results produces an accelerating increase in population. This phase of the demographic transition is followed by a decline in fertility, to a point where it once again approaches the level of mortality. Population growth decelerates and, presumably, tends to end in an equilibrium state. Egypt, like most developing countries, is still lingering in an intermediate phase of transition, that is, low mortality and high fertility, thus producing rapid population growth.

The main assumption underlying an investigation of rural-urban fertility differences is that fertility behavior is a function of the social structure. Hence, changes in that social structure or changes in the distribution of individuals within that structure are the principal causes of changes in fertility. Urbanization is one of these structural shifts. The process and implications of urbanization are broad. It certainly is not just numbers of people living or residing in places labeled urban that is important for fertility behavior; rather, it is the process of transforming types of social organizations and individuals' psychological characteristics. It involves a transformation in the nature of man himself. Although we recognize the importance of these factors, this chapter will have the more limited aim of describing changes in rural fertility patterns in Egypt between 1930 and 1970.

We assume that major changes in fertility attitudes and behavior normally begin in certain sectors of the population and subsequently filter outward to other sectors of the population. Based on past research, we expect that fertility changes will occur first among urban population, then through diffusion to other areas of the society.

The hypothesis dealing with differences between urban and rural
fertility is one of the most widely investigated. As commonly
asserted, fertility level is higher in rural than urban areas. Explanations are usually connected to different ways of living, economic activities, social norms, and so forth. In Western European
countries, the rural-urban fertility differences became progressively
larger during the period of fertility decline, but narrowed during
the period of recovery following World War II.[1] The situation appears to be different in developing countries:

> The process of urbanization in developing countries has
> not been quite similar to the corresponding process in
> the currently developed countries. One major difference
> is in the way of life of the new urban population. It has
> been suggested that in developing countries, geographic
> mobility from the rural to the urban does not bring
> about any appreciable social mobility and the way of
> life of the new arrivals in the city remains "rural" for
> a long time. If this is true we need not expect any sig-
> nificant decrease in the urban fertility level compared
> with the rural rate.[2]

Before dealing with rural-urban fertility differentials in
Egypt, we shall first discuss sources of data and some points of
caution that should be taken into consideration before further analysis. Then, the trends and stages of fertility differences between
each area will be discussed. Finally, age-specific fertility differences will be investigated.

SOURCES OF DATA: SOME POINTS OF CAUTION

In Egypt, census and vital statistics data provide a relatively
long series of rural-urban fertility indices. However, before analyzing these data, we should note that there are three areas where
caution should be exercised when studying rural-urban fertility
trends and differentials.

Underregistration of Births

The problem of underregistration of births is expected to be
higher in rural than urban areas. Therefore, "the fertility level in
rural areas may actually be higher than the reported data indicate."[3]
This is due to several factors. For example, many rural areas

(though decreasing in number over time) do not have a health bureau that is accessible in order to report a vital event. This is true for both deaths and births. Table 4.1 provides some evidence of this phenomenon.

TABLE 4.1: Comparison between Vital Rates
            in Areas with and without Health
            Bureaus, in Egypt, 1956-60*

Regions	CBR	CDR	Infant Mortality Rate
Total Egypt	41.44	16.81	117.13
Areas with health bureaus	45.69	19.30	149.32
Areas without health bureaus	37.56	14.83	86.25

*The rates are given per 1,000.
Source: V. G. Valaoras, Population Analysis of Egypt (1935-1970) Occasional Paper no. 1 (Cairo: Cairo Demographic Center, 1972), p. 22.

It is clear that areas of the country within the network served by the various governmental health bureaus have higher figures. This suggests more complete registration in these areas. According to Valaoras: "In 1960 about 48% of the total population was covered by these institutions. If it is assumed that the registration there was virtually complete, or 100%, the rates pertaining to total Egypt would represent 90% completeness of registration for the births."[4]

Examining data from both urban and rural regions with or without health bureaus since 1939, it can be noticed that the registration has improved remarkably.[5] This led Omran to the observation that "the substantial improvements in rural birth reporting . . . may actually conceal genuine changes in the trend of rural fertility."[6]

There is still a tendency to underreport females, as compared to males; therefore, female registration is less complete. This is clear when we review sex ratio at birth in both rural and urban areas. Sex ratio at birth (males per 100 females) is (remarkably) higher in rural than urban areas.

Table 4.2 offers some evidence of more underregistration in rural than urban areas. Due to more underreporting of females than males, particularly in rural areas, sex ratios at birth (as reported) are higher than in urban areas. In addition, the data in Table 4.2 support the assertion that there has been an improvement in reporting, since the sex ratios at birth continued to decline from 1950 to 1969.

TABLE 4.2: Sex Ratio at Birth for Rural and Urban Areas of Egypt, 1950-69 (four-year average)

Period	All Egypt	Urban	Rural
1966-69	106.4	105.3	107.1
1962-65	108.3	107.1	109.2
1958-61	113.7	106.0	119.0
1954-57	110.3	106.8	113.7
1950-53	109.5	105.3	112.2

Source: Central Agency for Public Mobilization and Statistics (Cairo), Population: Researches and Studies 1, no. 1 (October 1971) 1971): 31.

A final problem in rural birth underregistration is a tendency not to report as a live birth neonatal or even sometimes postneonatal deaths. They are not reported either as live births or as infant mortality. This phenomenon is expected to be more prevalent in rural than urban areas. Valaoras examined this problem for neonatal infants (less than 28 days of age) and for older infants. He concluded that a sizable number of neonatal deaths escaped registration and that the age of the dead children was not always correctly reported. Furthermore, he noted that "omissions were larger in the rural than the urban population, as expected."[7] In addition, vital rates derived from registered data for the period 1950-69 also show that postnatal death rates were higher in urban than rural areas.[8] This suggests higher underregistration in rural areas.

Differences in Age-Sex Composition
Due to Rural Migration

Especially due to the considerable rural to urban migration (increasing in recent years), some differences in the demographic characteristics between each of the areas have emerged. The major "pulling" or "receiving" areas are the metropolitan areas, in particular, Cairo and Alexandria, and the Canal Zone prior to 1967.

The urbanization in Egypt has been rapid. In 1882, the urban population did not exceed 19 percent of the total population, and it continued at that level until 1917.* Since then, the urban population has increased rapidly. In 1947, the percentage jumped to 31, then to 38 in 1960. The population of the city of Cairo alone has almost doubled in the 15 years since 1960 (from about 3.5 million to 7 million).[9]

This rapid process of urbanization complicates the analysis of rural-urban differences in many ways. For example, due to the differences in demographic rates and migration streams from rural to urban areas, the age-sex composition is different, though the magnitude of the observed differences is relatively small. Table 4.3 shows the percentage distribution of the rural and urban populations according to broad age groups, along with the sex ratios, in Egypt in 1960.

The age composition of the rural and urban populations differs slightly. The proportion of the group under 15 is less in rural than in urban areas, which may be due to the underenumeration of females of that age in rural areas. It may also be due to migration of females to the cities. The proportion of the 15 to 44 age group is likewise less in rural than in urban areas. This is probably due to emigration of males of working age from rural to urban areas.[10] According to Abu-Lughod, who examined 1947 census data, "Only the very largest cities deviate significantly, a fact that must be attributed to the Egyptian pattern of migration which tends to bypass smaller cities and towns and be directed almost exclusively toward the largest cities."[11]

Furthermore, differences in sex ratios must be traced always to selective migration: "Rural to urban migration, concentrated after fifteen years of age, produces a major dislocation noticeable particularly in the middle years of life, with the sex ratios highest in the large, fast-growing communities."[12]

---

*Urban populations are those that live in areas defined as urban. Urban places, according to the 1960 census (all other figures were adjusted accordingly), included two types of areas: all metropolitan areas (five in number), and capitals of other governorates (20,000 inhabitants or more). This is the definition adopted in this chapter.

TABLE 4.3: Percentage Distribution of Population of Egypt and
            Sex Ratios in Rural and Urban Areas, according
            to Broad Age Groups, 1960 (1960 census)

	Age Groups			
	Less than 15	15-44	45-64	65 and Over
Rural				
Percent population	42.3	39.9	14.0	3.8
Sex ratio	109	96	91	82
Urban				
Percent population	43.6	41.5	12.1	2.8
Sex ratio	104	102	111	96
All Egypt				
Percent population	42.8	40.5	13.3	3.5
Sex ratio	107	98	97	86

Source: A. M. Khalifa, The Population of the Arab Republic
of Egypt (Committee for International Coordination of National Research in Demography series, World Population Year) (Cairo:
CICRED, 1973), pp. 25-27.

     In general, both age and sex composition differ only slightly
and will have only a relatively small effect on measures of fertility.
However, adjusted rates will be used in the analysis.
     Though urbanization is a way of life, the definition we adopted
for this chapter is based on residence only. The problem here, as
Abu-Lughod puts its, is that "there are vast quarters within the
mosaic of Cairo where, physically and socially, the way of life and
characteristics of residents resemble rural Egypt."[13] This factor
explains why some sociologists consider migration to Cairo as the
process of ruralization of the city. This phenomenon is important
when dealing with rural-urban fertility differences. According to
Omran:

          Rural fertility behavior is not necessarily restricted to
          the 60 percent or so of Egyptians classified as rural by
          census definition, nor only to those living in villages
          where the main industry is agriculture. Rather, rural
          or traditional fertility performance extends to a sizable
          proportion of the remaining 40 per cent of the population
          which lives in towns and cities.[14]

Therefore, the hypothesis that urban fertility is not pure and is contaminated by rural fertility behavior due to sizable migration to the cities is certainly applicable to the Egyptian case.

Return to Rural Areas for Birth of Children

A final point of caution in regard to available data is the fact that there is a fairly widespread practice among urban women (from rural origin) of returning to their family of orientation for childbirth. Most of them then register their births where delivery took place rather than at their place of residence. This practice would inflate the rural births. Omran asserts that this factor may be counteracted, since "infants delivered in hospitals or maternity centers located in Cairo, Alexandria, provincial capitals, or other cities . . . even if they are born by rural women . . . may be recorded as urban births."[15]

In the analysis of rural-urban fertility differences and trends, which follows, all the above points of caution must be taken into consideration. When possible, we shall attempt to avoid some of their effects; otherwise, we must bear in mind their possible complications and be wary of the results.

PHASES OF RURAL-URBAN FERTILITY TRENDS

Vital statistics in Egypt have a relatively long history. "Registration of births and deaths in rural as well as urban areas dates back to 1839; it was made obligatory toward the end of the last century."[16] Our analysis considers data since 1930. Table 4.4 presents the crude birth rates (CBRs) in rural (with and without health bureaus) and urban areas of Egypt, in addition to general fertility rates from 1930 to 1970.

Three phases of rural-urban fertility differences can be identified. The first is where urban fertility is lower than rural fertility; the second phase is where urban fertility surpasses the rural fertility; and finally, in recent years, the normal pattern of excess rural fertility is repeated.

Phase One: Early Period of Lower Urban Fertility

Cleland, using data from 1906 to the early 1930s, concluded that there was probably no rural-urban fertility differential in Egypt during that period.[17]

TABLE 4.4: Crude Birth Rates and General Fertility Rates for Rural
and Urban Areas of Egypt, 1930-70 (per 1,000)

Year	Urban Areas		Rural Areas			All Egypt	
	CBR	GFR	CBR with Health Bureaus	CBR without Health Bureaus	GFR	CBR Reported	GFR
1930	32.2	142.0	n.a.*	n.a.*	237.0	45.4	201.9
1934	44.4	n.a.*	49.1	41.0	n.a.*	42.2	n.a.*
1935	42.5	n.a.*	47.0	40.5	220.9	41.3	183.5
1936	45.1	n.a.*	50.9	43.4	n.a.*	44.2	n.a.*
1937	46.9	180.0	47.2	42.1	203.3	43.4	196.1
1938	44.7	n.a.*	46.3	42.4	n.a.*	43.2	n.a.*
1939	44.4	n.a.*	47.0	40.6	n.a.*	42.0	n.a.*
1940	42.5	179.0	47.5	40.8	220.3	41.3	207.7
1941	40.0	170.5	46.8	39.9	217.8	40.4	203.7
1942	40.7	175.7	41.1	36.0	195.0	37.6	189.0
1943	44.5	194.1	41.3	36.1	194.9	38.7	194.6
1944	48.0	211.3	42.5	36.0	194.8	39.8	200.1
1945	49.8	222.5	47.1	39.0	210.7	42.7	214.5
1946	49.1	221.1	43.9	37.3	200.0	41.2	207.9
1947	49.9	233.0	48.7	40.2	216.3	43.8	221.8
1948	49.5	249.0	45.0	39.2	202.3	42.7	216.8
1949	49.0	265.0	43.6	37.9	190.4	41.8	212.4
1950	51.0	281.2	45.2	40.6	202.7	44.4	225.7
1951	51.8	282.1	46.1	40.8	206.3	44.8	229.3
1952	51.2	275.6	46.7	41.6	214.0	45.1	233.3
1953	50.9	272.6	43.4	37.5	196.4	42.5	220.9
1954	50.7	269.9	43.4	37.6	198.5	42.4	222.1
1955	50.0	263.6	43.7	33.5	183.1	40.2	210.3
1956	48.1	252.7	39.2	36.0	192.8	40.6	213.6
1957	41.1	214.6	39.4	35.4	190.2	37.8	199.1
1958	43.9	229.7	42.2	39.0	209.5	41.1	216.8
1959	44.1	229.7	45.2	41.1	222.7	42.6	225.3
1960	47.5	226.5	40.6		227.9	42.6	227.3
1961	46.5	226.5	42.3		207.7	43.7	215.0
1962	43.8	215.3	39.7		198.6	41.5	205.1
1963	44.8	217.3	41.9		209.3	43.0	212.5
1964	40.1	197.2	43.4		216.8	42.3	208.9
1965	38.3	188.2	43.7		218.2	41.7	206.1
1966	38.3	188.0	42.8		213.9	41.2	203.3
1967	35.5	174.0	41.7		208.1	39.2	194.3
1968	35.2	173.1	40.1		200.3	38.2	189.0
1969	33.3	163.8	39.3		196.4	37.0	182.7
1970	18.8	141.8	39.2		195.8	35.1	172.9

*Not available.

Sources: For the years 1934-59, the crude rates are from M. A.
El-Badry, "Trends in the Components of Population Growth in the Arab Countries of the Middle East: A Survey of Present Information," Demography 2
(1965): 144; for the years 1930-60, GFRs are from Central Agency for Public
Mobilization and Statistics (CAPMAS), "Vital Statistics since 1930," mimeographed (Cairo: CAPMAS), Tables 18 and 19. All rates since 1962 were computed from published data of CAPMAS for those years.

According to Table 4.4, it appears that the period ending in the early 1940s was characterized by excess rural fertility over that of urban areas. (Rural rates were computed only for areas that had health bureaus.) Therefore, based on CBRs and general fertility rates (GFRs), the period from the early 1930s to approximately the end of World War II was the period of higher rural than urban fertility. This is the "typical," or usual, case.[18] During the war, fertility behavior in both rural and urban areas showed a decline and became approximately equal by the end of the war.

El-Badry noticed excess rural fertility during this period. He asserted that "the crude birth rates of all urban areas, where birth registration can be assumed to be nearly complete, were definitely lower than those of rural areas and equal to about 45 up to 1939."[19]

In general, rates for both areas were relatively high, fluctuating around 44 and 47 per 1,000 for rural and urban areas, respectively, except during the period of World War II, when rates showed a slight, temporary decrease.

Phase Two: Period of Excess Urban over Rural Fertility

After World War II, urban fertility increased gradually, until it reached its peak in the period 1950-55; afterward, a general downward trend began, until the CBR reached an average of 44 per 1,000 and the GFR reached about 220 per 1,000 in the early 1960s. Rural fertility retained the same prewar level, and the CBR fluctuated in the 40-45 per 1,000 range during the 20-year period following the war. The result of this situation was a clear excess in urban fertility.

This helps to explain the findings of many demographers who studied the rural-urban fertility differentials in Egypt during this period. The 1947 population census was the first to include data on fertility by age of mother and duration of marriage. El-Badry utilized these results, as well as vital statistics, to investigate whether fertility differentials existed between the rural and urban population. One of his major findings was that there was no evidence to support the hypothesis of lower fertility in urban than in rural Egypt. In a later study, he utilized 1960 population census data and found that "regional fertility differences in 1960 are strikingly similar to those of 1947."[20] Abu-Lughod, analyzing data of the 1950s, was similarly unable to support the excess rural fertility hypothesis.[21] The results of the 1960 population census suggest the same conclusion. This situation was due mainly to the fact that a large proportion of the urban population had rural roots, and the urban milieu had had little effect upon them.

Figure 4.1 shows the differences between urban and rural CBR for the whole period. The peak of excess urban fertility can be noticed in the period immediately following the war and the early 1950s. After 1955, the excess urban fertility started to decline, until the early 1960s. The difference became negative in 1964.

These differences may be due partially to the factors explained in the previous section dealing with sources of data. However, the decline in urban rates beginning in the mid-1950s seems to be persistent and steady (1956 was the year of the Suez War). This pattern of differences was due mainly to the urban fluctuations, for the rural rates were more stable. According to Omran, the increase of the urban rates in the early 1940s assumed an "epidemic pattern which reached a peak of 51.9 births per thousand population in 1952 and then leveled off somewhat."[22]

Phase Three: Modern Period of Lower and More Rapidly Declining Urban Fertility Rates

Starting in the early 1960s, a gradual but significant and steady decline can be observed in the urban fertility rates. And for the first time since the early 1940s, rural fertility exceeds that of the urban areas. The gap increases over time (since 1963).

The metropolitan areas (Cairo and Alexandria) have been more sensitive to change and faster in their decline. The same may be said of a comparison between Lower and Upper Egypt (that is, Lower Egypt is faster in decline). Table 4.5 presents CBRs and GFRs for the period 1962-70 according to different geographic areas.

Figure 4.2 presents the GFRs for rural, urban, and metropolitan areas of Egypt for the period 1962-70. From Table 4.5 and Figure 4.2, we can conclude the following:

1. Metropolitan areas (Cairo and Alexandria) always show the lowest CBRs and GFRs. Rural rates are generally the highest; urban rates are intermediate.

2. Both metropolitan and urban rates are constantly declining, though the decline began earlier in the metropolitan areas and was then followed by the urban areas. Decline in fertility level of rural areas began even later, and at a slower rate.

3. Due to the above factors, the difference between urban and rural fertility levels is widening over time.

4. Taking into consideration the differences between Lower and Upper Egypt: the urban Upper Egypt fertility level is higher than that of urban Lower Egypt in any given year, and the rural Upper Egypt fertility level is lower than that of rural Lower Egypt for each corresponding year.

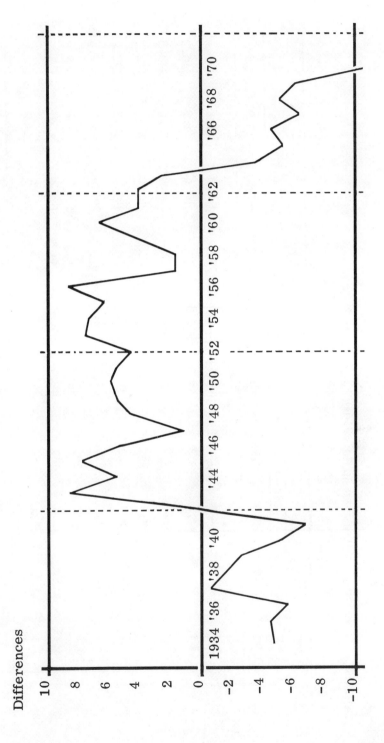

FIGURE 4.1: Differences between the Crude Birth Rates in Rural
and Urban Areas of Egypt, 1934–70

Differences

87

TABLE 4.5: Crude Birth Rates and General Fertility Rates in Different Geographical Areas of Egypt, 1962–70 (per 1,000)

Year	Lower Egypt Urban		Rural		Upper Egypt Urban		Rural		Metropolitan	
	CBR	GFR	CBR	GFR	CBR	GFR	CBR	GFR	CBR	GFR
1962	42.7	213.0	42.6	214.0	44.3	216.0	38.3	184.0	41.8	200.3
1963	44.1	221.0	44.5	223.0	45.5	222.0	40.9	194.0	41.1	197.3
1964	39.3	197.0	45.3	227.0	41.4	202.0	42.5	205.0	38.6	184.9
1965	37.7	189.0	45.9	230.0	37.5	183.0	42.6	205.0	36.6	175.7
1966	37.3	187.0	43.8	220.0	41.4	201.0	43.6	207.0	36.0	173.2
1967	36.1	181.0	41.8	214.0	40.7	198.0	43.0	207.0	33.1	158.6
1968	36.0	180.0	40.3	202.0	43.0	209.0	41.2	199.0	33.1	158.8
1969	35.5	178.0	40.3	202.0	41.8	204.0	39.5	191.0	31.0	148.8
1970	27.1	136.0	40.4	204.0	34.9	171.0	39.2	189.0	29.2	140.1

Source: Computed from Central Agency for Public Mobilization and Statistics, "Births and Deaths, Statistics," mimeographed (Cairo: CAPMAS, 1962–70).

FIGURE 4.2:   General Fertility Rates in Rural, Urban,
                        and Metropolitan Areas of Egypt, 1962-70

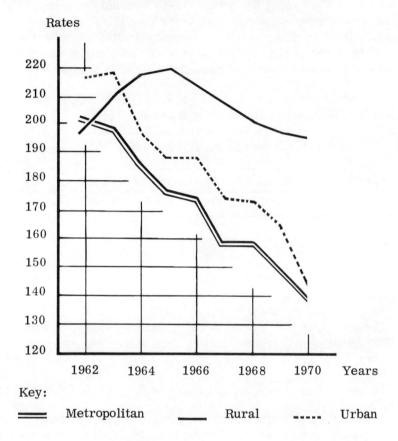

Key:

═══   Metropolitan   ▬▬   Rural   ....   Urban

The causes for these fertility declines have yet to be adequately analyzed. Changes in population policy and family planning
are probably partially responsible for the trends observed in the
1960s. Furthermore, the socioeconomic changes since 1961,
coupled with the 1967 war, are also responsible to a great extent
for those trends. [23]

RURAL-URBAN DIFFERENCES IN AGE
PATTERN OF FERTILITY

An analysis of age-specific fertility rates leads us to some
important conclusions regarding fertility behavior. Table 4.6

represents the differences between fertility rates by age of mother. It is clear that rural rates are always higher than urban rates, except for the very young age group--15-19. In this age group, both rates were approximately similar in the year 1970. In general, fertility level in all age groups has clearly declined, whether in rural or urban areas. Urban fertility reaches its peak in the age group 25-29, whereas it peaks in the age group 30-34 in the rural areas.

TABLE 4.6: Age-Specific Fertility Rates and Their
            Percentage Distribution, in Rural and
            Urban Areas of Egypt, 1966 and 1970

	Age Groups of Mother						
	15-19	20-24	25-29	30-34	35-39	40-44	45-49
1966							
Urban							
Rates	48.1	229.8	267.4	260.9	194.3	91.3	37.9
Percent	4.3	20.3	23.6	23.1	17.2	8.1	3.4
Rural							
Rates	38.3	238.8	281.8	309.7	228.8	133.2	58.5
Percent	3.0	18.5	21.9	24.0	17.8	10.3	4.5
1970							
Urban							
Rates	32.1	185.8	214.6	188.0	129.2	60.5	21.9
Percent	3.9	22.3	25.8	22.6	15.5	7.3	2.6
Rural							
Rates	31.6	219.4	251.1	276.1	205.4	124.0	56.9
Percent	2.7	18.8	21.6	23.7	17.6	10.7	4.9

Source: Computed from Central Agency for Public Mobilization and Statistics, "Births and Deaths, Statistics," mimeographed (Cairo: CAPMAS, 1962-70).

In 1970, while both rural and urban age-specific fertility rates started approximately from the same rate in the age group 15-19, rural women tended to have more children during the remainder of the reproductive period. The highest difference was for the age group 30-34. As for fertility rates for women in the older age groups of 40-44 and 45-49, rural women clearly had higher rates. For these two age groups, the age-specific fertility rates were approximately double for the rural areas, as compared to urban areas. We find that whereas only 7.3 percent of the births were born in the age group 40-44 in urban areas, it reached 10.7 percent in rural areas. Similarly, the age group 45-49 contributes only 2.6 percent in urban areas and 4.9 percent in the rural areas.

One of the explanations that may be given to these differences is the difference in age at marriage in rural and urban populations. The mean age at first marriage for females (an average for the four years 1965-68) was 21 years in urban areas but less than 20 years for the rural areas. However, the difference is not great enough to provide a satisfactory explanation for fertility differences.

To further examine the rural-urban fertility differences, we can use total fertility rate. Table 4.7 presents total fertility rates (TFRs), gross reproduction rates (GRRs), and net reproduction rates (NRRs) in both rural and urban areas for selected years.

TABLE 4.7: Total Fertility Rates, Gross Reproduction Rates, and Net Reproduction Rates for Rural and Urban Egypt, 1966 and 1970 (per women 15-49)

	1966	1970
Urban		
TFR	5.65	4.16
GRR	2.76	2.03
NRR	1.93	1.47
Rural		
TFR	6.45	5.82
GRR	3.11	2.80
NRR	2.17	2.03
All Egypt		
TFR	6.14	5.15
GRR	2.98	2.49
NRR	2.08	1.80

Source: Computed from Central Agency for Public Mobilization and Statistics, "Births and Deaths, Statistics," mimeographed (Cairo: CAPMAS, 1966, 1970).

From Table 4.7 we notice that TFRs, GRRs, and NRRs are all higher in rural than in urban areas in both 1966 and 1970. The TFR dropped in both rural and urban areas during the four-year period 1966-70, though the urban decline was greater.

CONCLUSION

This chapter discussed rural-urban fertility differences and trends in Egypt based on data covering the 1930-70 period. Three phases were clearly distinguished.

The first phase covers the period up to the mid-1940s (approximately the end of World War II). During that period, rural fertility level was reported to be higher than that of urban areas, though both areas had relatively high rates. This period, however, was highly affected by deficiencies of data (reviewed in this chapter).

The second phase, which extended for the 20 years following World War II up to the early 1960s, shows urban fertility surpassing the rural level. Urban fertility gradually increased to a peak in the period 1950-55, then began to decline. Even using the higher rate of rural areas with health bureaus, the same trend exists.

Starting in the early 1960s, a third phase began to take place, where rural fertility levels began to surpass those of the urban areas. This happened while rates in both rural and urban areas were gradually declining. The urban rate declined to its lowest level ever--about 29 per 1,000 population--in 1970; the rural rate declined to about 39 per 1,000 population at that time. Several factors are probably responsible for the decline; some are related to structural changes during the period and others to the initiation and implementation of the population control program that began in 1962.

The differences in the age pattern of fertility were also dealt with (based on data from the third, post-1960, phase). It was found that for all age groups of the mother, rural fertility rates were always higher than the corresponding urban ones. In particular, starting with the age group 20-25, the differences increased, and it was largest for the age group 30-34. Thereafter, though differences decreased, the rural fertility rates were still relatively higher than the urban ones.

Many points of caution were expressed regarding the accuracy of the data for comparison purposes. The three most important were the following:

1. The problem of underregistration of births is expected to be higher in rural than urban areas. Some explanations for this include: (1) the nonexistence of health bureaus in many rural areas;

(2) the tendency to underreport females as compared to males, particularly more so in the rural areas; and (3) a greater tendency in rural areas not to report some infant mortality either as births or deaths.

2. There are differences in some demographic characteristics in rural as compared to urban areas, such as differences in age-sex composition. This is due to selective migration from the rural to urban areas.

3. Other aspects, such as the practice of women residing in urban areas to return to their rural family of orientation for delivery of births, complicate comparisons.

Generally speaking, it seems safe to conclude that the urban population in Egypt in the long run has been undergoing a reduction in fertility. Obviously, it is not just the mere residence in cities that is responsible for the lower urban fertility rates but, rather, the "urban mentality" resulting from the different socioeconomic structure in the urban areas.[24] Therefore, due to the rapid rate of urbanization in Egypt, plus the high rate of rural migrants in the cities, this urban mentality, which is believed to reduce fertility, is observed to be spreading, though still rather slowly.

NOTES

1. United Nations, 1973b.
2. Zachariah, K. C., in Cairo Demographic Center, 1970.
3. Omran, A. R., ed., 1973, p. 88.
4. Valaoras, V. G., 1972, p. 22.
5. El-Sayegh, M. A., in Cairo Demographic Center, op. cit.
6. Omran, op. cit., p. 88.
7. Valaoras, op. cit., p. 22.
8. Central Agency for Public Mobilization and Statistics, 1971, p. 26.
9. Khalifa, A., and Khalifa, A. M., 1973, p. 71.
10. Central Agency for Public Mobilization and Statistics, 1971, pp. 32-33.
11. Abu-Lughod, J., 1964, p. 481.
12. Ibid., p. 482.
13. Abu-Lughod, J., 1961, p. 25.
14. Omran, op. cit., p. 101.
15. Ibid., p. 88.
16. El-Badry, M. A., 1965, p. 144.
17. Cleland, W. W., 1936.
18. Abu-Lughod, 1961, p. 476.

19. El-Badry, op. cit., p. 148.

20. Ibid.

21. Abu-Lughod, 1961, p. 477.

22. Omran, op. cit., p. 90.

23. For additional background on population policy and family planning in Egypt, see Cleland, op. cit., Khalifa and Khalifa, op. cit., and Omran, op. cit., p. 189.

24. These questions are dealt with in Khalifa, A. M., 1973b.

5

Fertility Trends and Differentials in Kuwait*

ALLAN G. HILL

For the Kuwaiti population of Kuwait, we have some of the most comprehensive and reliable statistics on fertility currently available in the Middle East. These data are contained in a series of five censuses (1957, 1961, 1965, 1970, and 1975) and in a set of annual publications on vital events (which have been enlarged and improved by the Central Statistical Office since 1967, when it took over responsibility from the Ministry of Health for checking and publishing the vital statistics). For the non-Kuwaiti population, the data are probably less reliable, and checking this information is more difficult, as the immigrant population is not stable, turns over very rapidly, and consists of a kaleidoscope of over 30 different nationalities, each with distinctive demographic characteristics. The growth of both components of Kuwait's population is shown in Table 5.1.

It seems from the demographic data and examination of the methods for collection of these data that the distinction between the Kuwaiti and the non-Kuwaiti populations has been successfully maintained in the statistical series on fertility. It is almost impossible to become a Kuwaiti by naturalization, except for a few favored individuals and for the foreign-born wives of Kuwaiti husbands. The Kuwaiti population, however, even allowing for some naturalization by the above methods, is not entirely "closed," for between 1965 and 1970, its annual growth rate was 8.8 percent, and between 1970 and 1975, it was 6.1 percent (see Table 5.1). The source of these additions in excess of the natural increase rate indicated by the reported births and deaths (which was about 4.3 percent per annum between 1970 and 1975) appears to be the population living in shacks in the desert. The majority of these people (82 percent) claimed Kuwaiti nationality in 1970, but if the strict standards applied elsewhere in Kuwait (which require proof--preferably written--of continued residence in Kuwait or descent from a Kuwaiti) are applied to the shanty

TABLE 5.1: Population of Kuwait, 1957-75

Date	Kuwaitis			Non-Kuwaitis			Total	
	Number	Sex Ratio	Annual Intercensal Growth Rate (percent)	Number	Sex Ratio	Annual Intercensal Growth Rate (percent)	Number	Annual Intercensal Growth Rate (percent)
February 1957	113,622	109		92,851	365		206,473	
May 1961	161,909	109	8.18	159,712	267	12.52	321,621	10.24
April 1965	220,059	105	7.83	247,280	--	11.16	467,339	9.54
April 1970	347,396	102	9.14 (8.83)*	391,266	166	9.17	738,662	9.15
April 1975	472,088	100	6.13	522,749	142	5.79	994,837	5.95

*Excludes the 5,195 Kuwaiti residents of the northern half of the former Neutral Zone.

Sources: Kuwait, Ministry of Social Affairs and Labor, Census of Population (in Arabic) (1957); and Kuwait, Planning Board, Central Statistical Office, Census of Population (in Arabic) (1961, 1965, 1970), and Preliminary Results of the 1975 Census (in Arabic) (1976).

dwellers, the Planning Board estimates that only 8.5 percent would be classed as true Kuwaitis (that is, those carrying the blue citizen's identity card).[1] For our purposes, the important thing is that the shanty dwellers, who think of themselves as Kuwaitis, appear to report their vital events as Kuwaitis. In addition, the age structure of these people seems balanced or approximately stable, and we can treat them as Kuwaiti citizens, despite the effect they have (more of these people are found at each census) on the intercensal growth rate of the Kuwaiti population. They may be in a kind of twilight zone as far as legal citizenship is concerned (defined as persons carrying brown Kuwaiti identity cards), but for all practical purposes, we can consider them part of the Kuwaiti population.[2]

FERTILITY OF THE KUWAITIS

Age Pattern of Fertility

Around 1965, the level of fertility of the Kuwaitis was a little above that in a number of Arab countries (see Table 5.2). Between 1965 and 1975, little change took place in the fertility of most of the Arab countries, and rather surprisingly, in view of the significant economic and social changes that have occurred in Kuwait, the crude birth rate (CBR) of the Kuwaitis has remained almost constant since 1965. Let us begin a close examination of the situation in 1970 (when the data are most reliable) and work backward and forward from this date.

TABLE 5.2: Fertility in Selected Arab Countries, around 1965

Country	CBR	GRR
Kuwait:	.	
Kuwaitis	51.3	3.6
Non-Kuwaitis	39.8	3.5
Algeria	45.5	3.5
Egypt	44.5	3.0
Iraq	49.5	3.5
Jordan	49.2	3.5
Libya	46.4	3.3
Morocco	49.6	3.4
Sudan	49.0	3.4
Syria	47.9	3.5
Tunisia	46.4	3.4

Source: Cairo Demographic Center, Fertility Trends and Differentials in Arab Countries (Cairo: Cairo Demographic Center, 1971), p. 16, Table 2.

Comparison of the pattern of Kuwaiti fertility with that constructed from a number of populations known to be experiencing "natural fertility"[3] reveals that the Kuwaitis, in 1970, were close to the model pattern, although the departures from the model become more pronounced above age 35 (Table 5.3). One plausible explanation for this tendency is that the Kuwaitis were beginning to control their fertility in 1970 and that the women most involved were older women, probably those with high parities. There is some direct evidence for this trend, since the demand for contraceptives (mostly pills and coils) is rising steadily. Contraceptives are freely available in Kuwait through the widely scattered health clinics or through the maternity hospital. Detailed records of the number and the characteristics of the accepters are unfortunately not maintained, but they will be available when the community health plan, run with the cooperation of the neighborhood clinics, becomes fully operational in 1976. In the meantime, only the crudest calculations can be made on the basis of the number of intrauterine devices (IUDs) and pill cycles that are imported. Assuming that two-thirds of these contraceptives are being used by Kuwaiti women, who we would expect to constitute the majority of those attending the government clinics, and that all the users are aged 35–49, then it would seem that at least one-third of the married Kuwaiti women aged 35 to 49 are using a modern method of contraception. This would certainly be enough to reduce significantly the marital age-specific fertility rate in those age groups to the levels shown in Table 5.3, but of course these calculations are highly speculative. More direct evidence of contraceptive use will be available shortly if a proposed fertility survey is completed. Although the level of fertility is high, especially in the age range 20-24, the age-specific rates are not as high as those for some populations of European extraction (Table 5.4). It seems that as with the synthetic model schedule shown in Table 5.3, the departure of the Kuwaiti schedule from the mean of the rates shown on Table 5.4 becomes more pronounced with age (the figure for Kuwaitis aged 45 to 49 is inflated due to age misreporting).

There are, however, a large number of factors that can affect the level and age pattern of fertility, even in populations not using methods of contraception. We know that poor nutrition and extended lactation both reduce fecundability,[4] that separation of spouses for any reason reduces the probability of a conception, and that certain cultural norms concerning proper and improper times for intercourse tend to bias fertility downward. While our information on the beliefs and practices of the Kuwaitis is incomplete, we have enough circumstantial evidence to suggest that, for example, the net effect of the high rate of divorce, some polygamy, and required waiting periods between divorce and remarriage is to reduce fertility below the high

TABLE 5.3: Fertility of the Kuwaitis, 1965 and 1969-71 (marital age-specific fertility per 1,000 women)

Age	Rates		Proportions (percent)		Model Schedule[a]		Proportions of Model Rates	
	1965	1969-71	1965	1969-71	Percent	Rates	1965	1969-71
15-19	370	366	19.9	18.9	18.4	411	.90	.89
20-24	429	453	22.1	23.3	21.0	469	.91	.97
25-29	440	419	22.7	21.6	19.8	442	.99	.95
30-34	341	349	17.6	18.0	17.8	399	.85	.87
35-39	261	253	13.4	13.0	14.4	323	.81	.78
40-44	93	75	4.8	3.9	7.5	167	.56	.45
45-49	--	23	--	1.2	1.1	25	--	.92
Total	--	--	100[b]	100[b]	100	--	--	--
Total fertility	9.7	9.7	--	--	--	11.2	--	--
CBR (per 1,000)	51.3	49.7	--	--	--	--	--	--
GRR	3.6	3.5	--	--	--	--	--	--
NRR	3.3	3.3	--	--	--	--	--	--

[a]The model schedule is the average of a number of observed schedules known to be experiencing natural fertility. See A. J. Coale, A. G. Hill, and T. J. Trussell, "A New Method of Estimating Standard Fertility Measures from Incomplete Data," Population Index 41, no. 2 (April 1975): 186-87 for details.

[b]Totals are slightly different from 100 due to rounding.

Sources: Kuwait, Planning Board, Central Statistical Office, Census of Population (in Arabic) (1965, 1970), and Annual Bulletin of Vital Statistics (1962-present).

MUSLIM WOMEN'S STATUS AND FERTILITY

levels recorded for the European populations (shown in Table 5.4),
which generally had more stable marriage systems. In addition,
some of these effects can be age selective; it could be that older
women breast-feed longer than younger women, who are probably
more receptive to new ideas on child care, including early weaning
with cow's milk and baby foods. Further, it seems that the probability of divorce increases as women approach the menopause and
that older women may be less fecund than younger ones, since the
latter have been exposed to much better health care and nutrition
throughout their childbearing lifespan. These are all important factors in shaping the level and age pattern of fertility; until the fertility survey is complete, it is impossible to attach any precise weights
to each of the factors.

TABLE 5.4: Some Marital Fertility Schedules Compared, 1674-1971
            (rate per 1,000 women)

Groups	Age						
	15-19	20-24	25-29	30-34	35-39	40-44	45-49
Hutterites married 1921-30	--	550	502	447	406	222	61
Families of Geneva, husbands born 1906-49	419	525	485	429	287	141	5
Marriages in Crulai of 1674-1742	320	419	429	355	292	142	10
Canada, marriages of 1700-1929	493	509	496	484	410	231	30
Marriages in Mesnil and Beaumont, 1740-99	452	524	487	422	329	135	17
Tunis, marriages 1847-1925	408	488	434	380	303	169	11
Mean	418	499	472	419	338	173	22
Kuwaitis 1969-71	366	453	419	349	253	75	23
Ratio of Kuwaitis to the mean	.87	.91	.89	.83	.75	.43	1.04

Source: J. Ganiage, Trois villages d'Ile-de-France au XIIIe siècle
(Travaux et Documents, no. 40) (Paris: Institut national d'études démographiques
[INED], 1963), Table 17.

Parity Measures

The parities reported in the 1970 census by age and duration of marriage (Table 5.5) are particularly valuable, since they allow us to obtain a good estimate of current fertility that is independent of the vital statistics.[5] Three more sophisticated measures of fertility have been calculated in the second part of Table 5.5.

First, the parity progression ratios strongly suggest a population that to a large extent does not use contraceptive methods. Second, the long delay (2.9 years) between marriage and the first birth is, in fact, a statistical error, since Kuwaitis, like other Middle Eastern populations, have a two-stage marriage system. The first stage, known as writing the book, is equivalent to engagement in European terms, but the woman reports her marital status as "married" after the ceremony. Cohabitation follows after an average delay of about seven months in Kuwait (four months in 1957), although this delay appears to be a fairly new introduction. In the past, it seems that the ceremonial marriage and cohabitation were almost simultaneous. Thus, subtracting these seven months from the first mean interbirth interval produces a consistent series of intervals that suggest that fecundability is nearly constant up to parity 5. Unfortunately, the data do not allow us to make any assessment of trends in fertility, but the parity progression ratios are one of the more sensitive measures of changing fertility norms. So far, it seems that there is no clear preference for families of a certain size, although this may change in the near future.

Nuptiality and Fertility

One factor that is partly responsible for the high level of fertility of the Kuwaitis is the pattern of early and almost universal marriage (see Tables 5.6, 5.7, and 5.8). Although the singulate mean age of marriage rose slightly between 1965 and 1970, the proportions of females ever-married remained close to 0.98. However, the increase in the proportion that was single in the age range 15-24 is a significant indicator of social change, since the opportunities for single women to pursue an independent career are still very restricted in Kuwait. There are some problems in comparing the proportions married in 1965 and 1970, since the degree of age misreporting altered slightly between the censuses, and we know that the shift across an age-group boundary is selective with reference to marital status. Nevertheless, if we simply accept the two nuptiality patterns at face value, it appears that the change in the marriage pattern between 1965 and 1970 was too small to affect fertility to any

TABLE 5.5: Average Parities* for Kuwaiti Women, by Marriage Duration, 1970

Item	0-4	5-9	10-14	15-19	20-24	25+
Years P_i	.93	3.12	4.99	6.44	8.51	8.11

*P_i.
Sources: Kuwait, Planning Board, Central Statistical Office, Annual Bulletin of Vital Statistics and Census of Population (1970).

TABLE 5.6: Average Parities* for Kuwaiti Women, by Age, 1970

Item	15-19	20-24	25-29	30-34	35-39	40-49	50+
Years P_i	.83	2.23	4.09	4.09	5.22	6.17	5.72

*P_i.
Sources: Kuwait, Planning Board, Central Statistical Office, Annual Bulletin of Vital Statistics, and Census of Population (in Arabic) (1970).

TABLE 5.7: Parity Progression Ratios for Kuwaiti Women, 1970

Item	Parity								
	0	1	2	3	4	5	6	7	8
Probability of women with parity (x) reaching parity (x + 1)	.962	.985	.948	.901	.885	.825	.719	.665	--
Mean age at parity (x)	--	21.9	24.8	26.5	28.5	30.5	32.5	36.9	40.5
Mean interbirth interval in years between parity (x) and (x + 1)	2.9	1.7	2.0	2.0	2.0	4.4	3.6	5.1	4.2

Sources: Kuwait, Planning Board, Central Statistical Office, Annual Bulletin of Vital Statistics, and Census of Population (in Arabic) (1970).

great extent, since the 1970 marital age-specific fertility schedule multiplied by the 1965 proportion married would raise total fertility by only 3 percent. As Coale and Tye[6] and Lesthaege[7] have indicated, fertility in the countries characterized by early and universal marriage is unlikely to alter dramatically without some significant change in the intensity of nuptiality, but the present trends under way in Kuwait, if greatly extended, could make a significant contribution to lower fertility in the near future.

TABLE 5.8: Kuwaiti Women, by Age and Marital
Status, 1965 and 1970

Age	Percent Single		Percent Married		Percent Divorced		Percent Widowed	
	1965	1970	1965	1970	1965	1970	1965	1970
15–19	58.1	66.1	40.5	33.0	1.0	0.7	0.3	0.2
20–24	16.1	23.8	80.8	73.7	2.2	2.0	0.8	0.5
25–29	5.2	6.6	90.7	89.7	2.4	2.4	1.6	1.2
30–34	3.2	3.3	90.3	90.6	3.2	3.2	3.3	2.9
35–39	2.0	1.8	88.0	89.0	3.7	3.7	6.1	5.5
40–44	2.3	2.7	76.0	97.1	4.3	6.1	17.3	18.9
45–49	2.2	1.6	65.4	68.0	4.5	4.1	27.7	26.2

Sources: Kuwait, Planning Board, Central Statistical Office, Census of Population (in Arabic) (1965), Table 44a, and (1970), Table 6.

An interesting feature is that although the legal age for marriage according to Islamic law is the age at menarche, the decline in the age of menarche in Kuwait has not been accompanied by a fall in the age of marriage. A recent survey of schoolgirls showed that their mean age at menarche was just 12.7 years,[8] while the mean age for their teachers was 12.9 years. The principal reason for this low age at menarche is undoubtedly the excellent nutritional status of the Kuwaitis, who now have a very high per capita daily consumption of calories and an adequate intake of protein.[9] In view of this diet, it is likely that the mean age at menopause has also risen, so that the length of the childbearing period is much longer than it ever was in the past. Both these changes tend to inflate the level of fertility, other things being equal.

Fertility Trends

It appears from the evidence shown in Table 5.9 that fertility
has been virtually constant since 1957. The birth rates for individual
years vary considerably, especially in the late 1960s (for example,
55.7 for 1969 and 46.7 for 1970), probably because the Central Bureau
of Statistics was making special efforts to improve registration about
this time, as well as because of the small size of the total population.
From 1970 onward, the series is more consistent and indicates a
birth rate close to 51 per 1,000. Total fertility calculated for census
years, using direct and indirect methods, has fluctuated very little
over almost 20 years.

TABLE 5.9: Fertility of Kuwaiti Women, 1957-74

Age	1957	1965	1969-71	1974
15-19	220	150	121	133
20-24	312	347	334	340
25-29	319	399	376	377
30-34	279	308	316	301
35-39	219	230	225	215
40-44	101	71	73	58
45-49	13	--	16	23
Total fertility rate	7.3	7.5	7.3	7.2
CBR (per 1,000)	44	51	50	51

Sources: The 1957 figures were derived from a table of average parities by duration of marriage; see A. J. Coale, A. G. Hill,
and T. J. Trussell, "A New Method of Estimation, Standard Fertility Measures from Incomplete Data," Population Index 41, no. 2
(April 1975: 182-210), for details. The 1965, 1969-71, and 1974
figures are based on reported births by age and the census age distributions of women.

This finding, when set beside the evidence from the age-
specific fertility schedules, which suggest that some form of control
is being practiced by older women, is rather surprising. The explanation could be that there are some factors at work that contribute
to a high level of secondary infertility. Another factor could be the
established use of traditional methods of birth control. The evidence
of the age-specific fertility schedules, however, is inadequate

evidence from which to decide that contraception is becoming more widespread; in fact, total fertility shows no downward trend over 20 years, although we must be alert to the possibility of a higher pregnancy rate (higher levels of fecundability) and lower levels of foetal wastage being exactly offset by increased contraceptive use, thus giving us a nearly constant level of fertility from 1957 to 1974.

The conclusion that fertility is apparently not changing despite greatly improved health conditions and substantial changes in the welfare of Kuwaiti families (Table 5.10) is itself notable, but we should be aware that unchanging fertility does not mean that all the fertility determinants have been fixed since 1957. Some shreds of evidence indicate that in fact the true situation is very much more complex, but much more cannot be said until the fertility survey of 1977 is completed.

TABLE 5.10: Selected Indexes of Social Change in Kuwait, 1957-70*

Index	1957	1970
Percentage aged 10 and over illiterates:		
Male	23.8	32.0
Female	74.1	62.7
Percentage women 15-60 at work	1.6	2.5
Percentage women 20-24 with at least		
a primary school education	1.6	26.7
Percentage women 15-19 ever-married	70.0	33.8

*Kuwaitis only.

Source: Kuwait, Planning Board, Central Statistical Office, Census of Population (in Arabic) (1957, 1970).

FERTILITY OF THE NON-KUWAITIS

Composition and Growth

While a substantial proportion of the total population of Kuwait has traditionally consisted of immigrants or transients, mostly from Iran, Iraq, and the lower Gulf states,[10] the main influx of migrants took place after 1946, when the demands for labor of all grades were growing rapidly. At the time of the first census (February 1957), the immigrant population totaled nearly 93,000 persons, 78 percent of whom were males, mostly in the 15-50 age range. Gradually, the

structure of this immigrant population has matured as a result of
natural increase and changes in the demographic composition of the
migrant stream, but the features that are characteristic of immigrant populations throughout the world were still recognizable in
1970 (see Table 5.11). One of the reasons for the change in the
structure of the non-Kuwaiti population has been the proportional
increase in the Jordanian and Palestinian populations compared to
almost all other nationalities (see Table 5.12).

TABLE 5.11: Immigrant Population of Kuwait, 1957-75

Date	Total Non-Kuwaitis Male	Female	Sex Ratio	Percent under Age Five	Percent Illiterate (males ten+)	Percent of Total Population
February 1957	72,904	19,947	365	7	43	45.0
May 1961	116,246	43,466	267	--	--	49.7
April 1965	173,743	73,547	236	15	33	52.9
April 1970	244,368	14,898	166	17	32	53.0
April 1975	307,168	215,581	142	17	*	52.5

*Not available.

Sources: Kuwait, Department of Social Affairs and Labor, Census of Population (in Arabic) (1957, 1961) (only a limited number of tabulations were produced
from the 1961 census); and Kuwait, Planning Board, Central Statistical Office,
Census of Population (in Arabic) (1965, 1970), and Preliminary Results of the 1975
Census (in Arabic) (1976).

Several factors are responsible for the changes in the nationality composition of the immigrants. Kuwait's labor laws make it compulsory for employers to offer any vacancy first to a suitable quali-
fied Kuwaiti, second to an Arab of another nationality, and finally to
any other suitable person. The groups most vulnerable to this kind
of discrimination have been the Indians and the Pakistanis, who filled
many of the clerical grade jobs, initially in the oil companies and
subsequently in the civil service, when levels of literacy in the Arab
world were much lower than they are today. Another reason is that
manual labor is less in demand in Kuwait than it was during the construction boom of the late 1950s and 1960s. As a result, those groups
who specialize in this kind of work, such as the Iranians and the
Omanis, are leaving, some of them to take up better paid employment in the lower Gulf states, still in the middle of their "construction boom" phase of development. Finally, the periodic wars and
uncertain political conditions in the Levant have encouraged more
northern area Arabs, and especially the Palestinians (who find

considerable support for their nationalistic struggle in Kuwait), to migrate to Kuwait.

TABLE 5.12: Nationality Composition of the Non-Kuwaitis
             in Kuwait, 1957-70 (percent)

Non-Kuwaitis	1957	1961	1965	1970
Palestinians and Jordanians	16	23	31	37
Iranis	21	11	12	10
Iraqis	28	17	10	10
Egyptians	2	10	4	8
Syrians	2		7	7
Lebanese	7	10	8	6
Indians	4	5	5	4
Omanis	7	9	8	4
Pakistanis	3	4	5	4
Saudis	2	1	2	2
Others	8	10	8	8
Total	100	100	100	100

Sources: Kuwait, Department of Social Affairs and Labor, Census of Population (in Arabic) (1957, 1961) (only a limited number of tabulations were produced from the 1961 census); and Kuwait, Planning Board, Central Statistical Office, Census of Population (in Arabic) (1965, 1970), and Preliminary Results of the 1975 Census (1976).

The nationality composition of the non-Kuwaiti population has a direct bearing on the natural increase rate of the immigrants because of the very different demographic attributes of the separate national groups.[11]

The proportion of the total population who are non-Kuwaitis has been held at around 53 percent for the last ten years or so by controlling the number of work permits and visas issued. Nevertheless, a substantial proportion of the annual growth of the non-Kuwaiti population is currently due to natural increase, since the freely available health, education, and welfare services have been extensively used by the immigrants (with some relatively minor restrictions in the past). The natural increase of the immigrants is very close to that for the Kuwaitis (see below), largely because of greatly reduced mortality and an unchanging fertility regime.

Marital Fertility

From the vital registration data, it seems that the level of
non-Kuwaiti fertility, although high, was slightly below that for the
Kuwaitis in both 1965 and 1969-71 (compare Tables 5.3 and 5.13).
Judging from the level of marital fertility in the 20-29 age range,
the principal reason for the non-Kuwaitis' smaller total fertility is
apparently their lower fecundability and not their increased use of
contraception. As with the Kuwaitis, the age pattern of fertility is
consistent with a small amount of control, increasing in significance
with age. The two age patterns are virtually indistinguishable: the
mean age of childbearing was just over 27 years in both cases, and
approximately the same proportions (18 percent) of the average
women's fertility experience still remained at age 35.

The similarities between the age pattern of the two fertility
schedules is less surprising when we bear in mind that the great
bulk of migrants are from the Arab world, in which fertility patterns
are broadly similar. There are sure to be some contrasting schedules among the varied national groups comprising the non-Kuwaiti
population, but we lack the detailed data to examine these differences.
It is worth remembering that the Jordanians and Palestinians alone
constituted 37 percent of the immigrant population in 1970 and, on
the average, were responsible for about half of all non-Kuwaiti
births. This group is one of the most permanent immigrant groups
in Kuwait and, as a result, has a well-balanced age structure. The
influence of this single and fairly homogeneous group on the demography of the immigrants is very large and may account for the sim-
ilarity of the non-Kuwaitis' fertility schedule as a whole to the patterns observed in neighboring Arab countries and among Kuwaitis in
Kuwait.

Variations in Fertility by Nationality

The quality of the vital registration data for the different immigrant nationalities is unlikely to be as good as for the Kuwaitis,
but this is difficult to check because of the mobility of the immigrants. Using a combination of census data and some vital registration data for individual nationalities, it is possible to calculate some
crude fertility indexes (Table 5.14), which, among other things,
show that the quality of the fertility and census data varies from
nationality to nationality. For groups such as the Yemenis, the
Iranians, and the Omanis, it seems that the census data on married
women is an erroneous denominator to use in calculating fertility
indexes, either because some women were not counted in the census

TABLE 5.13: Fertility of Non-Kuwaitis in Kuwait, 1957-70

Age	Marital Fertility (per 1,000 women)			Ratio of Observed Schedule to Model Schedule*			Proportions (percent)		
	1957	1965	1969–71	1957	1965	1969–71	1957	1965	1969–71
15–19	274	381	372	.66	.93	.90	18.4	21.1	21.5
20–24	312	419	394	.66	.89	.84	20.9	23.2	22.8
25–29	294	379	370	.66	.86	.84	19.7	21.0	21.4
30–34	266	308	284	.66	.77	.71	17.9	17.0	16.4
35–39	215	242	216	.66	.75	.67	14.4	13.4	12.5
40–44	111	79	71	.66	.47	.42	7.4	4.4	4.1
45–49	17	--	22	.66	--	.88	1.1	--	1.3
Total fertility (married women only)	7.4	9.0	8.6	--	--	--	100	100	100
CBR (per 1,000)	14.6	39.8	44.9	--	--	--	--	--	--

*The model schedule is the average number of observed schedules known to be experiencing natural fertility--see A. J. Coale, A. G. Hill, and T. J. Trussell, "A New Method of Estimating Standard Fertility Measures from Incomplete Data," Population Index 41, no. 2 (April 1975): 182–210, for details.

Sources: Kuwait, Planning Board, Central Statistical Office, Census of Population (in Arabic) (1965, 1970), and Annual Bulletin of Vital Statistics.

TABLE 5.14: Estimated Fertility of the Non-Kuwaitis in Kuwait, by Nationality, 1969-71

Nationality	Births per Year	Children per 1,000 Women, 15-44, 1970	Births per 1,000 Women, 15-44, 1969-71	Births per 1,000 Married Women, 1969-71
Jordanian and Palestinian	8,673	1,308	299	342
Syrian	1,565	974	318	352
Iraqi	1,370	784	209	234
Egyptian	962	366	114	166
Iranian	860	1,240	567	561
Lebanese	808	1,006	155	172
Saudi	780	1,220	411	462
Pakistani	744	1,081	335	356
Omani	562	1,380	674	750
Indian	529	529	129	145
Yemen Republic	342	1,294	2,342	2,552
Kuwaiti	17,184	1,000	253	312

Sources: Kuwait, Department of Social Affairs and Labor, Census of Population (in Arabic) (1957, 1961) (only a limited number of tabulations were produced from the 1961 census); and Kuwait, Planning Board, Central Statistical Office, Census of Population (1965, 1970), and Preliminary Results of the 1975 Census (in Arabic) (1976).

or because the women had their children in Kuwait, where the birth
was recorded, but left soon after, so that only a fraction of the
women were enumerated in the 1970 census. It is worth noting that
these nationals are frequently illegal entrants and might have good
reason to conceal the birth of their children, which would usually
take place in a hospital or clinic--one of the reasons why the non-
Kuwaitis came to Kuwait in the first place.

Although the overall picture is confusing, it seems that the
fertility of the Jordanians and the Palestinians, the Saudis, and
probably the Syrians is higher than that of the Kuwaitis. The Indian
and the Egyptian immigrant groups display the lowest fertility, while
the Lebanese and the Iraqis occupy an intermediate position. Unfortunately, further details that might help to explain these significant
variations in fertility by nationality are not available either in the
census or in the vital statistics. The one firm conclusion seems to
be that the Jordanians and the Palestinians have a fertility level perhaps 20 percent higher than that of the Kuwaitis, corresponding to a
fertility rate close to 9.

In conclusion, it seems that the fertility of the non-Kuwaiti
population as a whole is very similar to that of the Kuwaitis. Both
are early marrying populations, in which over 90 percent of all
women marry. Assuming that the mortality level of the two populations is also comparable, it seems that the decisive factor in determining the relative rates of natural increase of the two components of the population of Kuwait is the nationality composition of
the immigrants. Further increase in the proportion of high fertility
components among the immigrant population is sure to life the fertility of the immigrant population as a whole, but of course, it is
impossible to say how quickly contraceptive use will be spread in
the Kuwaiti and non-Kuwaiti populations in the future.

NOTES

*The generous assistance of the Planning Board, especially
Mr. Fuad Mulla Hussein and Mrs. Wasmia al-Ghuneim, is grate-
fully acknowledged.

1. For details, Buchanan, C., 1976.
2. The Government of Kuwait appears to have reached the
same conclusion since the National Housing Authority, which can
assist Kuwaitis only with their housing problems, has been instructed
to cater for the needs of the shanty dwellers.
3. The definition of natural fertility is that used by Henry, L.,
1961, pp. 81-89. In practice, natural fertility levels vary consid-

erably from place but the distinguishing characteristic of a natural fertility regime is that fertility behavior does not alter with parity.

4. There is a large literature on these topics; see Rosa, F., 1976, for a recent summary and Slaber, E. J., Feinlieb, M., and MacMahon, B., 1966, for the classic reference on breast feeding and amenorrhoea. The effects of nutrition are dealt with in Frisch, R., 1974.

5. Coale, A. J., Hill, A. G., and Trussell, T. J., 1975.

6. Coale, A. J., and Tye, C. Y., 1961.

7. Lestaeghe, R., 1971.

8. Hathout, H. H., and el Din Selim, M. M., 1972.

9. This statement is based on the data collected by the periodic family budget surveys conducted and published by the Planning Board, Kuwait.

10. Some historical information on the population of Kuwait is contained in Lorimer, J. G., 1908 and 1915, and also Wilson, A. T., 1928.

11. French, G. E. and Hill, A. G., 1971.

6

Fertility Trends and Differentials in Jordan

HANNA RIZK

When the unity of the East and West banks of the Jordan River was established in 1950 under the rule of King Abdalla, the total population of the kingdom was estimated at 1,237,000,[1] in an area of 97,740 square kilometers, 90 percent of which was barren desert. Due to marked efforts at modernization, mortality rates declined sharply; however, fertility levels remained practically unchanged. This has led to a rapid increase in the population in the last 22 years. The military occupation of the West Bank territory in 1967 resulted in a massive population movement to the East Bank (38,000 from Ghaza and 123,000 from the West Bank).* This phenomenal population growth in Jordan due to immigration was intensified by a high rate of natural population growth (excess of births over deaths), as we can see in Table 6.1. The current population of Jordan is estimated at 2.6 million.[2]

The unfavorable consequences of rapid population growth were deeply felt in cities and rural areas, and the leaders of the government saw that Jordan needed accurate information about changes occurring in the number, structure, and distribution of the population,

---

This chapter draws on "Trends in Family Size, Attitudes and Practice of Family Planning in Jordan," an unpublished report prepared by the author in 1975, based on the 1972 National Fertility Sample Survey of Jordan.

*In 1972, the United Nations Relief and Welfare Agency (UNRWA) and the Jordanian government reported 494,000 registered refugees (moved in during 1947–48) and 246,000 displaced persons (moved in during 1967) in the East Bank.

and to determine the factors and consequences of these changes.* Consequently, in 1969, the government requested the UN to advise and assist in conducting a national fertility survey. The request was accepted, and field work began early in 1972.

TABLE 6.1: Estimated Crude Birth Rates, Crude Death
            Rates, and Rates of Natural Growth (Medium
            Variant), in Jordan, 1950-75

Period	Average CRB (per 1,000)	Average CDR (per 1,000)	Average Rate of Natural Growth
1950-55	45.3	21.0	24.3
1955-60	46.8	21.1	25.7
1960-65	49.0	18.3	30.7
1965-70	49.1	16.0	33.1
1970-75	48.2	13.7	34.5

Source: 1972 National Fertility Sample Survey of Jordan (Amman, Jordan: Department of Statistics).

METHODOLOGY

The survey was limited to ever-married women in the reproductive ages (15-49), although nonmarried women were also interviewed if they were part of a household that contained an ever-married woman.[3] The questionnaire used for the study followed closely the recommendations made by the UN and the International Union for the Scientific Study of Population (IUSSP) in their publication Variables and Questionnaire for Comparative Fertility Survey.[4] Slight adaptations were made to meet the conditions of life in Jordan. The main purpose of the study was to investigate the fertility history of women in the sample, their attitudes toward the size of their families, the extent and effect of knowledge and use of contraceptives, if any, on fertility levels, and socioeconomic status of husbands and wives in the sample.

----

*The only census taken in Jordan was in 1961. The political situation following the conflict in 1967 made it impossible for Jordan to take another census.

Data were collected by women interviewers from 4,811 households. This number included 232 substitutes for households where women were not eligible (49), households not located (185), women who had been away from home (17), unoccupied households (7), and household with foreign residents (1). In this analysis, all the household substitutes were eliminated. Another set of 24 households were eliminated due to inaccurate information or refusal to be interviewed, leaving a total of 4,555 households. One other adjustment was made, namely, that the number of ever-married women in the rural area of the Governorate of Amman was weighted so that the ratio of the sample to the population in the area, as estimated in 1971, was equal to the ratio in other areas. Therefore, the number of women, referred to as respondents hereafter, included in the analysis is 5,214 ever-married women, whose ages at the time of interview were under 50 years.

COMPOSITION OF THE SAMPLE

The educational, socioeconomic, residential, and religious composition of the 5,214 respondents and their present husbands (if married once and living with husband) or last husbands (if married more than once or divorced, widowed, or separated) varied considerably. The educational composition shows, as expected, a pronounced difference between educational attainment of husbands and wives. The university wives, at the top of the educational ladder, constituted only 1.0 percent. At the bottom, the illiterate husbands constituted 25.4 percent, while the illiterate wives constituted 60.1 percent. For residential distribution, three types of areas were distinguished: (1) "urban," where inhabitants were over 10,000; (2) "semiurban," where inhabitants were not less than 5,000 but not more than 10,000, and (3) "rural," where the population was less than 5,000. The residential distribution of the respondents was 46.3 percent urban, 9.2 percent semiurban, and 44.6 percent rural. These percentages correspond to the general distribution in the East Bank of Jordan. According to a socioeconomic scale,* the respondents

---

*A scale of points was set up that included 12 items (income, education of husband and of wife, occupation, house rental, home facilities, and cultural activities). Points were accorded to each respondent, according to her status or achievement on the 12 items. The total number of points was 51. Class one included those who scored 36+; class two, 21–35; and class three included those who scored 20 points or less.

in class one were 4.2 percent; class two included 32.7 percent, and class three constituted 63.1 percent. As the attitude of any people may be influenced by their religious affiliation, the respondents were classified also into the two major religions prevailing in the area: 93.1 percent of the respondents were Muslims, 6.8 percent were Christians, and 0.2 percent were others or unknown.

MARRIAGE CUSTOMS AND AGE AT FIRST MARRIAGE

Jordanian society sets a high value on marriage, particularly for females. Therefore, about one-third of the females in the age group 15-19 were already married, as were 73 percent of the age group 20-24. In the age group 25-29, only 7 percent remained unmarried. Less than 3 percent were unmarried by age 40-44. Marriage at an early age and the high percentage of total marriage are important factors leading to high fertility due to the lengthy period of exposure to the risk of pregnancy. (See Table 6.2.)

TABLE 6.2: Age at Marriage of Women, in Jordan, 1972

Age Group	Total Number of Women	Ever-Married Women	
		Number	Percent of Total
15-19	1,740	530	30.4
20-24	1,303	951	73.0
25-29	1,206	1,120	92.9
30-34	991	955	96.4
35-39	803	782	97.4
40-44	627	616	98.2
45-49	388	370	95.4

Source: 1972 National Fertility Sample Survey of Jordan (Amman, Jordan: Department of Statistics).

Most of ever-married women in the sample were living with their husbands (94.3 percent) and thus exposed to the risk of pregnancy. Only 0.7 percent were found divorced, and 3.3 percent were widows. In addition, there were 86 respondents (1.6 percent)

separated from their husbands,* mostly due to migration or temporary conflict between husband and wife. The small percentage of
divorce is due to the fact that most divorced women remarry. The
percentage of widowhood was highest among respondents in the late
years of their reproductive life.

FERTILITY PATTERNS OF RESPONDENTS

Cumulative fertility (children ever-born) will be related to
all women in the fertility survey, ever-married respondents, and
ever-married mothers. These will be referred to as the cumulative
maternal fertility and the cumulative marital fertility, respectively.

Table 6.3 shows the cumulative number of live births per
1,000 women in each of the three categories. It is obvious from the
table that there is a marked difference between the fertility of the
three groups in the early age groups; the difference diminishes gradually at higher age groups. The difference in the age group 40-44
is one-half child per woman between the groups "all women in the
sample" and "ever-married women," and the same difference exists
between the groups "ever-married women" and "ever-married
mothers." The following conclusions may be drawn from the table:
(1) the women who do not marry at an early age do get married soon
after and make up for their relatively late marriage in reproduction; (2) childlessness is negligible, particularly after the age group
20-24; the fertility difference between ever-married women and
ever-married mothers in the age group 40-44 being 176 children
per 1,000 women, or a difference of 2 percent; (3) the average fertility of the Jordanian woman is one of the highest in the world. The
cumulative fertility of ever-married women is six live births per
woman by the time they are in the middle of their reproductive life.
As they approach the end of their reproductive life (40-44), a woman
would have had an average of over 8.3.

The fertility of the Jordanian woman becomes more apparent
when ever-married women are classified by duration of marriage
(see Table 6.4). A woman delivers an average of 5.4 children by
the time she has been married for 10 to 14 years. She continues the
process of reproduction; the average number of live births per
woman rises to 8.8 by the time her duration of marriage is 25 to 29
years and rises again to 9.2 children for those married 30 years
or over.

---

*Any woman who had been living away from her husband for a
period of three or more months was considered "separated."

TABLE 6.3: Cumulative Fertility (Ever–Born Children) of All Women, Ever–Married Women, and Ever–Married Mothers in the Sample, Classified by Age Groups, in Jordan, 1972

Age Group	Number of Live Births	All Women in the Sample		Ever-Married Women		Ever-Married Mothers	
		Number	Live Births (per 1,000)	Number	Live Births (per 1,000)	Number	Live Births (per 1,000)
15–19	407	1,740	234	508	801	292	1.394
20–24	2,252	1,303	1,728	936	2,406	830	2,713
25–29	4,816	1,206	3,993	1,104	4,362	1,068	4,509
30–34	5,795	991	5,848	953	6,081	942	6,152
35–39	5,752	803	7,163	771	7,460	751	7,659
40–44	4,789	627	7,638	578	8,285	566	8,461
45–49	2,799	388	7,214	343	8,160	332	8,431
Total	26,610	7,058	3,770	5,198	5,124	4,781	5,506
Standardized rate for age distribution	--	--	3.6	--	4.0	--	4.6

Source: 1972 National Fertility Sample Survey of Jordan (Amman, Jordan: Department of Statistics).

TABLE 6.4: Live Births per 1,000 Ever-Married Women,
Classified by Duration of Marriage,
in Jordan, 1972

Duration of Marriage in Years	Total Number of		Average Live Births per 1,000 Respondents
	Respondents	Live Births	
0-5	1,054	1,102	1,046
5-9	1,039	3,408	3,280
10-14	1,040	5,594	5,379
15-19	867	6,022	6,946
20-24	593	4,920	8,297
25-29	424	3,751	8,847
30+	197	1,813	9,203
Total	5,214	26,610	5,104

Source: 1972 National Fertility Sample Survey of Jordan
(Amman, Jordan: Department of Statistics).

In Jordan, it is no longer true that high death rates and high
fertility rates counterbalance each other. Due to the availability
of effective medicines, advancement in sanitary systems, and
modernizing efforts in different areas, mortality rates have declined sharply in a short time without a major reorganization of
social and economic conditions, which might reduce fertility. Thus,
the number of living children for women in the survey is high.
Over two-thirds of the Jordanian respondents have a large family
(six or more living children) by the end of their child-bearing age,
and about one-third of that age group have an extremely large
family (nine or more living children).

DIFFERENTIAL FERTILITY: RURAL, URBAN, AND SEMIURBAN FERTILITY

Contrary to the experience in many other countries, the difference in fertility of respondents classified by geographical areas
was insignificant and did not show definite trends when respondents
were classified by age. The number of live births per 1,000 respondents in these areas are compared in Table 6.5. In the age
group 20-24, the semiurban respondents had an excess of 96 live
births per 1,000 urban women. In the age group 15-19, the

TABLE 6.5: Children Ever-Born per 1,000 Respondents, Classified by Age and Residence, in Jordan, 1972

Age	All Respondents		Urban		Semiurban		Rural	
	Wives	Live Births (per 1,000)	Wives	Live Births (per 1,000)	Wives	Live Births (per 1,000)	Wives	Live Births (per 1,000)
0-15	21	0	5	0	1	0	15	0
15-19	508	407	164	848	49	633	295	803
20-24	936	2,252	379	2,311	76	2,553	481	2,457
25-29	1,104	4,816	488	4,225	108	4,528	508	4,459
30-34	953	5,795	437	5,915	78	6,372	438	6,194
35-39	771	5,752	417	7,518	78	7,577	276	7,341
40-49	921	7,588	522	8,132	88	8,727	311	8,280
Total	5,214	26,610	2,412	5,407	478	5,377	2,324	4,732

Source: 1972 National Fertility Sample Survey of Jordan (Amman, Jordan: Department of Statistics).

semiurban women had 170 fewer live births per 1,000 women than the rural women and 215 fewer live births per 1,000 women than the urban women. However, the cumulative ever-born children shows that live births per 1,000 women were least among rural women and most among urban women: the difference between the least and the most was 675 per 1,000 women.

Undoubtedly, Jordan's large cities are changing, but it seems that the changes are not deep enough to affect a change in values (and in the marriage system) that would produce a decline in fertility.

SOCIOECONOMIC STATUS

The socioeconomic status of respondents was determined by a scale, and three classes were distinguished--class one being the highest and class three, the lowest. A comparison of the number of live births per 1,000 women classified by socioeconomic status and duration of marriage is provided in Table 6.6.

Following the first duration of marriage, the data show a definite inverse relation between the average number of live births and the status of women. This relation is pronounced between class one and the other two classes, but unimportant between class two and class three. Toward the end of reproductive life (duration 25 to 29 years), the average fertility per woman is 6.4 live births for class one, 8.7 for class two, and 9.0 for class three.

EDUCATIONAL ATTAINMENT OF WIFE

The study shows that education is the strongest factor affecting fertility levels. There is an inverse relation between the level of educational attainment of wives and the average number of live births. When respondents are classified by four educational levels (university, secondary, primary, and illiterate) and age, we find that at age 20-24, the cumulative fertility per woman is 1.2 for the university-educated group, 1.6 for secondary educated, 2.4 for primary, and 2.6 for illiterates. By age 30-34, the fertility per woman in these four educational levels is 2.7, 4.0, 5.9, and 6.4, respectively (see Table 6.7).

The same inverse relation between education and fertility was found when the respondents' fertility was classified by the education of their husbands. However, differential fertility was much less for women classified by education of husband than when classified by education of respondents.

TABLE 6.6: Live Births per 1,000 Respondents, Classified by Socioeconomic Class and Duration of Marriage, in Jordan, 1972

Duration of Marriage in Years	Total		Class One		Class Two		Class Three	
	Respondents	Live Births (per 1,000)	Respondents	Live Births (per 1,000)	Respondents	Live Births (per 1,000)	Respondents	Live Births (per 1,000)
0-5	1,054	1,102	50	1,100	362	1,028	642	1,051
5-9	1,039	3,408	53	2,396	342	3,240	644	3,374
10-14	1,040	5,594	37	3,432	310	5,277	693	5,528
15-19	867	6,022	37	4,703	243	6,798	587	7,148
20-24	593	4,920	27	5,074	202	8,030	364	8,684
25-29	424	3,751	12	6,417	166	8,717	246	9,053
30+	197	1,813	3	7,333	81	8,951	113	9,434
Total	5,214	26,610	219	3,283	1,706	5,019	3,289	5,269

Source: 1972 National Fertility Sample Survey of Jordan (Amman, Jordan: Department of Statistics.

TABLE 6.7: Live Births per 1,000 Respondents, Classified by Their Educational Attainment and Age, in Jordan, 1972

Age	University		Secondary Education		Primary Education		Illiterate	
	Respondents	Live Births (per 1,000)	Respondents	Live Births (per 1,000)	Respondents	Live Births (per 1,000)	Respondents	Live Births (per 1,000)
0-15	0	0	0	0	13	0	8	0
15-19	0	0	26	577	295	803	187	829
20-24	10	1,200	94	1,617	424	2,420	408	2,603
25-29	18	1,833	68	2,809	388	4,247	630	4,673
30-34	19	2,737	51	4,020	198	5,894	685	6,381
35-39	4	4,750	30	4,300	203	6,502	534	8,022
40-49	1	5,000	19	4,737	218	7,335	683	8,630
Total	52	2,327	288	2,715	1,739	4,024	3,135	5,968

Source: 1972 National Fertility Sample Survey of Jordan (Amman, Jordan: Department of Statistics).

RELIGION

The limited number of Christians in the sample (353) did not allow us to divide them into the three or four Christian denominations in Jordan. Therefore, the fertility of Christian respondents was compared, as one group, with that of Muslim respondents.

In socioeconomic classes one and two, the fertility of Muslim respondents was higher than that of the Christians in almost all marriage durations after the first five years. In class three, there was no definite trend between the fertility of the two groups. The cumulative fertility per woman standardized for marriage duration, shows the following rates: (1) class one: Muslims 3.9 live births and Christians 3.1; (2) class two: Muslims 5.1 and Christians 4.4; and (3) class three: Muslims 5.3 and Christians 5.0. Table 6.8 refers to the trend of mean age at first marriage among Muslims and Christians in the four educational levels during the last three decades. It is noticed that (1) the Muslims generally marry at earlier ages than the Christians; (2) the higher the level of education--in the last two decades--the higher the age at marriage; and (3) age at marriage has been rising for both groups, even though the average age at marriage is still low.

TABLE 6.8: Mean Age at First Marriage of Wives in Urban Sample, Classified by Education, Religion, and Decade of Marriage, in Jordan, 1972

| | Level of Education | | | | |
	Illiterate	Primary	Secondary	University	Total
1940-49					
Muslims	15.5	15.9	15.0	--	15.6
Christians	16.6	17.2	18.8	--	17.6
1950-59					
Muslims	16.9	17.6	19.0	20.7	17.3
Christians	19.7	19.3	20.6	21.0	19.8
1960-71					
Muslims	18.4	17.6	19.9	22.2	18.2
Christians	26.8	21.7	20.7	23.3	21.0

Source: 1972 National Fertility Sample Survey of Jordan (Amman, Jordan: Department of Statistics).

EFFECT OF OCCUPATION OF HUSBANDS
ON FERTILITY

The occupational classification of husbands shows that 24 percent were in military service, 15.2 percent were in government service, 13.7 percent were skilled laborers, 13.1 percent were in agricultural activities, 11.0 percent were in private business, 5.7 percent were in commerce, 5.5 percent were in industry, 4.9 percent were nonagricultural day laborers, and 1.1 percent worked in highly technical fields.

The fertility of wives classified by occupation of husbands and duration of marriage indicates that in the last two marriage durations (25–29 and 30+), the live births per 1,000 wives was highest where husbands worked in agricultural activities. The unskilled laborers group was next. The overall fertility was found highest (6.3) among landowners and land tenants. It was lowest (2.8) among wives of highly skilled technicians. The next lowest fertility was among wives of military men (4.3) and wives of men in government service (4.5). The fertility of the rest of the occupational categories fluctuated, as can be seen in Table 6.9.

KNOWLEDGE AND USE OF CONTRACEPTIVES

Almost all respondents knew one or more of the conventional methods of birth control. The women who said that they had no knowledge of any contraceptives were 1.3 percent of respondents in urban areas, 1.8 percent in semiurban areas, and 11.0 percent in rural areas. At the other extreme, 50 percent of respondents in urban areas, 44 percent in semiurban areas, and 17 percent in rural areas knew between 7 and 11 methods.

An analysis was made of the knowledge of respondents of each contraceptive separately and the percentage of its users. The pill seemed to be the best-known and most-used method. It was known by 100 percent of class one, 98 percent of class two, and 89 percent of class three. However, it was used in the past by 54.0 percent of class one, 35.0 percent of class two, and 10.4 percent of class three. It is presently used by 38 percent, 24 percent, and 6 percent of the three classes, respectively. The next most widely known contraceptive was suppositories. Two of the most widely known methods but the least used were the intrauterine device (IUD) and the diaphragm.

Knowledge does not necessarily lead to action; while 94 percent of total women in the sample knew of one or more methods of

TABLE 6.9: Live Births per 1,000 Respondents, Classified by Occupation of Husband and Marriage Duration, in Jordan, 1972 (per 1,000 women)

Occupation	Number of Women	Duration of Marriage					
		0-5		5-9		10-14	
		Live Births	Number of Women	Live Births	Number of Women	Live Births	Number of Women
Agriculture:							
Pay by day	177	1,053	19	3,435	23	5,447	38
Land tenant	168	1,450	20	3,000	13	5,905	42
Landowner	376	1,188	32	3,298	57	5,343	70
Monthly pay	36	1,000	6	4,000	11	6,200	5
Industrial	269	1,213	61	3,122	49	5,404	52
Government service	772	1,122	197	3,188	176	5,054	147
Commercial	294	1,022	45	3,277	47	5,453	53
Military	1,342	825	348	3,226	327	5,229	306
Private companies	18	1,333	3	2,000	4	--	--
Nonagricultural day worker	238	1,222	36	3,167	36	5,212	52
Skilled laborer	674	1,146	144	3,549	142	5,763	114
Highly technical	49	1,000	18	2,400	15	4,000	6
Private activities	556	1,241	79	3,467	90	5,610	105
Not classified	245	1,130	46	3,286	49	5,600	50
Total	5,214	1,046	1,054	3,280	1,039	5,379	1,040

Duration of Marriage								Cumulative Fertility	
15-19		20-24		25-29		30+			
Live Births	Number of Women	Live Births	Number of Women	Live Births	Number of Women	Live Births	Number of Women	Live Births	Number of Women
7,083	36	8,958	24	9,154	26	8,000	11	6,226	177
6,543	35	8,375	24	9,440	25	8,444	9	6,298	188
6,714	84	9,022	46	8,455	55	9,781	32	6,269	376
8,000	4	8,889	9	9,000	1	--	--	5,611	36
6,047	43	7,641	39	7,778	18	8,143	7	4,695	269
6,933	119	7,879	66	8,025	40	9,704	27	4,473	772
6,981	54	7,971	35	9,514	37	10,000	23	5,874	294
7,024	169	7,889	117	8,698	56	8,895	19	4,253	1,342
5,000	4	7,000	4	8,000	1	12,500	2	5,167	18
7,268	56	8,229	35	8,789	19	11,250	4	5,613	238
7,355	124	8,447	76	8,692	52	8,864	22	5,233	674
5,200	5	7,333	3	10,000	1	4,000	1	2,857	49
7,011	93	8,867	83	9,273	77	8,379	29	6,014	556
6,732	4	8,531	32	9,500	16	9,636	11	5,306	245
6,946	867	8,297	593	8,847	424	9,203	197	5,104	5,214

Source: 1972 National Fertility Sample Survey of Jordan (Amman, Jordan: Department of Statistics).

family planning, only 28.3 percent of all respondents had used any
of the contraceptives in the past, and only 21.1 percent of wives
living with husbands were using contraceptives at the time of interview. We found a direct relationship between socioeconomic status,
on the one hand, and knowledge and use of contraceptives, on the
other. There was a vast difference between knowledge and practice
between the three socioeconomic classes. The negligible percentage
of women who used contraceptives in class three and the low percentage of women who controlled their fertility found in class two
may help explain the high rate of population growth in Jordan.

The motivation for use or nonuse of contraceptives varied
markedly by educational levels of respondents. Of all the respondents, 32 percent expressed disapproval of family planning, 55
percent expressed conditional approval, 12.5 percent expressed
unconditional approval, and 0.3 percent had no opinion. Out of the
total women in the sample, 44 percent of the illiterates, 21 percent
of the primary educated, 3.6 percent of the secondary educated,
and 1.6 percent of the university educated disapproved of family
planning.

About one-third (1,631) of the respondents attempted to control their fertility. These constituted 79 percent of the university-
educated women, 69 percent of the secondary-educated women,
44 percent of the preparatory and primary-educated women, and
20 percent of the illiterates.

ATTITUDES TOWARD ABORTION

The respondents were asked whether they approved of abortion and if so, for what reason. The answers indicate that 56.5
percent of total respondents approved of abortion, 42.6 percent
disapproved, and 0.9 percent did not have a definite opinion. The
most important reasons for approval of abortion, according to the
2,947 approving women were (1) to save mother's life (55.0 percent); (2) "if pregnant woman was not married" (27.0 percent);
(3) "for fear of a defective child" (10.0 percent); (4) "if husband and
wife don't want to have more children" (4.0 percent); and (5) "to
give good care to children" (3.0 percent). When respondents were
classified by religion, abortion was approved by 54 percent of the
Muslims and by 78 percent of the Christians. Of the 2,947 respondents who approved of abortion, only 10 percent (298) had attempted an abortion; 122 had succeeded and 176 had failed in their
attempts.

ATTITUDE TOWARD SIZE OF FAMILY
AND SEX PREFERENCE

The respondents living with husbands were asked whether they wished to have additional children and how many, by sex. They were also asked about the ideal number of children they would like to have if they could start life all over again.

The answer to the first question indicated that 46 percent of respondents did not wish to have additional children, 2 percent did not know, and 52 percent wanted additional children. It was clear that the desire for additional children was due mainly to son preference, as Table 6.10 indicates. The motivation for male preference declines with both increased education and total number of children.

TABLE 6.10: Average Additional Number of Male and Female Children Desired by Respondents, Classified by Education and Average Number of Living Children, in Jordan, 1972

Educational Attainment	Number of Respondents	Living Children	Addition Desired		Total Children
			Male	Female	
Illiterate	1,533	3.8	3.9	0.6	8.3
Primary	605	2.5	2.8	0.7	6.0
Preparatory	295	1.6	2.4	0.9	4.8
Secondary	155	1.6	1.6	0.8	4.0
Higher institutes	12	2.0	1.3	0.8	4.0
University	18	1.3	1.5	0.8	3.6
Total	2,618	3.1	3.3	0.7	7.1

Source: 1972 National Fertility Sample Survey of Jordan (Amman, Jordan: Department of Statistics).

CONCLUSION

Differences in fertility were found in the study between levels of educational attainment, socioeconomic status, and religious groups. The data were examined for direct evidence of factors that shape the pattern of high fertility in general and differential fertility in particular. Two factors of particular importance were the high rate of marriage and the pattern of marriage at an early age.

The findings of the study show that 32.4 percent of the total respondents admitted using contraceptives. Of this group, 2.4 percent made preventive attempts before first pregnancy, 12.4 percent before the second, and 13.0 percent before the third; 31 percent were distributed among women who had from four to six pregnancies, and 31 percent were among women who had seven or more pregnancies. These findings are clear evidence that wives of all ages, regardless of the number of live births they have had, do attempt to postpone one or more pregnancies.

NOTES

1. United Nations, 1973a, p. 115.
2. These data are from Population Reference Bureau, 1973.
3. For details of sample design, see Rizk, H., 1975 and 1973.
4. International Union for the Scientific Study of Population, n.d.

7

Fertility in Algeria:
Trends and Differentials

JACQUES VALLIN

With a crude birth rate of over 50 per 1,000 women and an average of eight children per woman, Algeria has one of the highest fertility rates in the world. Over the last few decades, fertility in Algeria has increased and has probably reached its maximum. By measuring the influence of various economic and social factors, this chapter will analyze current movements and will suggest probable future fertility trends.

FERTILITY INCREASES IN ALGERIA
OVER THE PAST FEW DECADES

The registration of vital statistics for Algeria since the French colonization in the early nineteenth century gives a far from perfect image of fertility trends (although all of Algeria since the turn of the century has been covered). Underregistration of births, currently estimated at around 10 percent,[1] has existed for a long time. However, the works of Briel and Biraben, based among other things on analysis of the masculinity ratio of registered births and the results of specific surveys, make it possible to draw up a more or less acceptable series of the annual number of births in Algeria since 1891.[2] According to this estimation, crude birth rates since 1910 would be:

This chapter is a revision of a paper presented to the Population Division, UNESCO, Paris, 1975.

131

Years	Percent
1911–15	35.3
1916–20	34.9
1921–25	37.2
1926–30	42.3
1931–35	43.4
1936–40	42.1
1941–45	42.9
1946–50	42.2
1951–55	47.4
1956–60	45.6
1961–65	48.5
1966–69	47.8

Over a period of roughly 50 years, the crude birth rate (CBR) went from 35 to about 50 per 1,000 women. Even if the adjustment of vital statistics is imperfect, and allowing for a certain observational bias due to improved registration, we can nonetheless consider that this movement corresponds at least partially to a slow but constant fertility increase.

The 1970 Fertility Survey of Algerian Women confirms this phenomenon for recent years.[3] By cumulating age-specific fertility rates corresponding to a given period, we can, through this survey, measure the total fertility rate around 1955, 1960, and 1965.[4] The mean number of children per woman thus obtained increases perceptibly between 1955 and 1965 for all age groups at marriage (see Table 7.1). There is an increase of approximately 10 percent in ten years.

TABLE 7.1: Total Fertility Rate from 20 Years of Age (or from 25 Years of Age for Women Married at 20 to 24), in Algeria, 1955, 1960, and 1965

	Women Married at		
Year	Under 17	17 to 19	20 to 24
1955	7.6	8.3	6.0
1960	7.8	8.7	6.4
1965	8.1	9.0	6.8

Source: Republique Algerienne Democratique et Populaire, Secrétariat d'Etat au Plan, Direction des Statistiques, Etude statistique nationale de la population, résultats de l'enquete fécondité, ser. 2, vol. 2 (Oran: Centre Nationale de Recherches Economiques et Sociales [CNRES], 1972).

TABLE 7.2: Marital Fertility Rates, According to Age of Woman at Childbirth and at Marriage (Women Still in First Marriage), in Algeria, 1970

Age at Childbirth	Present Age Group						
	20-24 (1945-49)*	25-29 (1940-44)*	30-34 (1935-39)*	35-39 (1930-34)*	40-44 (1925-29)*	45-49 (1920-24)*	50-54 (1915-19)*
Age at Marriage: Under 17							
20-24	398.4	425.5	403.1	372.8	376.7	376.8	325.9
25-29	--	387.0	400.0	353.4	369.8	349.4	321.7
30-34	--	--	366.2	343.8	358.9	329.5	290.9
35-39	--	--	--	279.1	275.2	283.8	271.3
40-44	--	--	--	--	183.2	161.0	139.9
45-49	--	--	--	--	--	29.2	16.8
Number	986	800	651	566	404	241	143
Age at Marriage: 17-19							
20-24	443.3	439.1	440.1	526.1	378.8	376.6	341.6
25-29	--	404.9	406.0	393.3	352.2	356.4	340.1
30-34	--	--	324.1	395.8	346.8	350.0	313.2
35-39	--	--	--	315.8	322.2	326.6	292.0
40-44	--	--	--	--	173.4	209.6	198.5
45-49	--	--	--	--	--	68.1	39.4
Number	730	654	564	475	293	188	137
Age at Marriage: 20-24							
25-29	--	464.9	410.6	386.9	384.8	355.4	361.8
30-34	--	--	344.2	365.9	382.7	378.6	350.6
35-39	--	--	--	307.4	345.2	307.1	242.7
40-44	--	--	--	--	211.2	189.3	161.8
45-49	--	--	--	--	--	46.4	51.7
Number	--	271	301	229	197	112	89

*Generation groups correspond to current age groups.

Source: Republique Algerienne Democratique et Populaire, Secrétariat d'Etat au Plan, Direction des Statistiques, Etude statistique nationale de la population, résultats de l'enquete fécondité, ser. 2, vol. 2 (Oran: CNRES, 1972).

Here again, the movement may have been amplified by an observational bias, the most recent births being the best reported. But we have sufficient indications confirming the quality of the Algerian survey[5] to suppose that this phenomenon is due largely to a rise in fertility. Moreover, the rise only concerns the most fertile age groups, 20-24 and 25-29 years, as we can see from the evolution by cohort of age-specific fertility rates presented in Table 7.2.

This evolution may be explained by three basic factors. First, there has been a general improvement in health conditions, which is evident if one considers the evolution of infant mortality.[6] This has reduced the number of infant deaths and, perhaps, even sterility. Second, age at first marriage for Algerian women, a decisive factor for fertility in a country where there is no valid family planning, has dropped considerably since World War II.[7] It passed from an average of 20.1 years in 1948 to 18.4 years in 1966 (see Table 7.3). Finally, changes in breast-feeding behavior have probably had an important effect on the interval between birth and the next conception, since prolonged breast-feeding delays return to a normal ovular cycle. In Algeria, young women breast-feed less frequently and for shorter lengths of time than their elders.[8] The women aged 20 to 24 at the time of the survey had breast-fed their next to last live-born child for an average of 11 months, as against 15 months for those aged 50 to 54 (see Table 7.4). This phenomenon is more pronounced in urban areas. The combined effect of these different factors explains the rise in fertility in Algeria and its present very high level.

TABLE 7.3: Recent Trends in Female Nuptiality,
in Algeria, 1948, 1954, and 1966

Elements	1948	1954	1966
Mean age at first marriage	20.1	19.7	18.4
Percentage unmarried at age 20 to 24	23	21	11
Percentage unmarried at age 50 to 54	2	2	1

Source: Republique Algerienne Democratique et Populaire, Secrétariat d'Etat au Plan, Direction des Statistiques, Etude statistique nationale de la population, résultats de l'enquete fécondité, ser. 2, vol. 2 (Oran: CNRES, 1972).

TABLE 7.4: Mean Length of Breast-Feeding for Next-to-Last
Live-Born Child, According to Age of Mother,
in Algeria, 1970 (months)

Age	Town	Country	Total
20-24	8.6	12.2	11.1
25-29	10.3	13.8	12.7
30-34	11.1	14.8	13.7
35-39	12.0	14.7	13.8
40-44	12.5	15.4	14.5
45-49	12.2	16.1	14.7
50-54	14.4	15.2	14.9

Source: Republique Algerienne Democratique et Populaire,
Secrétariat d'Etat au Plan, Direction des Statistiques, Etude statistique nationale de la population, résultats de l'enquete fécondité,
ser. 2, vol. 2 (Oran: CNRES, 1972).

VERY HIGH RATES OF FERTILITY IN ALGERIA

The 1970 fertility survey was a probability sample of ever-
married women of childbearing age (under 55). The mean number
of children per informant (4.73) therefore measures mean cumulative fertility at a given time. This mean cumulative fertility of 4.73
is the result of two elements: a very high fertility and the youth of
the ever-married women of reproductive age (this element is determined by the age structure of the female population and its marriage
history). Mean age of informants was 33 years: 42.2 percent were
under 30 at the time of the survey.

The mean number of children per woman increases rapidly
with age (see Table 7.5). Though nonmarried women were excluded
from the survey, we can get an idea of the mean cumulative fertility
per woman, regardless of marital status, by computing the mean
number of children observed with the proportion of nonmarried
women in each age group. As illegitimate fertility rates are negligible in Algeria, only the denominator (number of women) need be
modified. The percentages used are those drawn from the first pro-
visional results of the population survey.[9] The populations concerned do not tally exactly, since the sampling procedure used for
the fertility survey replaced households where women of childbearing
age who were never-married were found. But approximate figures
are sufficient here. Table 7.5 also gives the cumulative fertility of
women still in their first marriage.

TABLE 7.5: Mean Number of Children per Woman, According
to Current Age Group of Mother, for Different
Groups of Women, in Algeria, 1970

Age Group	Women Still in First Marriage		All Ever-Married Informants		All Women
	Mean Number of Children	Number of Women	Mean Number of Children	Number of Women	
15–19	0.6	1,008	0.6	1,103	0.2
20–24	2.1	1,921	2.0	2,210	1.7
25–29	4.1	1,757	3.8	2,155	3.7
30–34	5.6	1,587	5.2	2,140	5.1
35–39	7.1	1,340	6.3	2,016	6.2
40–44	8.0	946	7.2	1,510	7.2
45–49	8.5	571	7.5	1,020	7.4
50–54	7.7	396	6.9	814	6.8

Note: In rural areas, observed figures were doubled before
calculation.

Source: Republique Algerienne Democratique et Populaire,
ENSP, Premiers résultats provisoires de l'enquete démographique
(Algiers: Secrétariat d'Etat au Plan, 1971).

At ages 50 to 54, fertility for all groups is seen to be lower
than for ages 45 to 49. Unless there is a behavior difference between the 1915-19 cohort (women aged 50 to 54 in 1970) and the
1920-24 cohort (women aged 45 to 49 in 1970), which seems highly
improbable, this drop can only be explained by an error in observation. Moreover, certain difficulties were encountered concerning
the age limit of women in the fertility survey sample; it is therefore
preferable to leave this age group aside in our analysis.

Apart from the very young ages, there is little difference between ever-married women and all women. Women who do not
marry young are fairly rare, and if not completely negligible at age
15 to 19, or even 20 to 24, they are after that. Conversely, the
difference between women still in first marriage and all ever-
married women is slight at the beginning, then increases regularly
with age, reaching an average of one child at age 45 to 49. This
means that dissolved marriages (divorce or widowhood) definitely
reduce fertility.

The most important characteristic, we believe, is the very
high level of completed fertility: 7.4 children at age 45 to 49 for

all women, regardless of marital status, and 8.5 children for women
still in their first marriage.

The results obtained for some other African countries are
much lower. For example, the mean number of children per woman
in the Tunisian and Moroccan surveys was 6.9 and 6.6, respectively.[10] For surveys in tropical Africa (where the data are calculated
for women in all marital statuses rather than for ever-married
women, as in the cases of Tunisia and Morocco), the numbers range
between 5.7 and 4.1.[11] Fertility in Algeria appears, therefore, to
be one of the highest in African countries.

We should bear in mind the fact that the fertility observed
characterizes cohorts of women no longer in childbearing age. However, the Algerian population survey allows us to measure current
fertility for the different cohorts of childbearing age. By cumulating
the age-specific fertility rates, we obtain a "current" index, which
is comparable with the mean number of children per woman. It is
slightly higher than the fertility survey figure: 8.0 instead of 7.5 at
age 45 to 49.[12] The difference is perhaps partly due to retrospec-
tive observation errors for women aged 45 to 49, but it also reflects
the rise in fertility over the last few decades.

With a gross reproduction rate (GRR) of 3.9, Algeria has one
of the highest fertility rates in the world. Practically no other country with reliable fertility figures reaches a higher level than this.
Other Muslim or tropical African countries may reach this figure,
but there is not sufficient data for comparison.

SOCIAL AND ECONOMIC FACTORS AND
FERTILITY IN ALGERIA

In countries with very high fertility rates, variations in fertility can only be slight or concern only small groups of the population.
The Algerian fertility survey does, however, bring out certain differences in behavior. These suggest hypotheses for changes in fertility patterns that will take place in the future.

We have already mentioned the influence of age at first marriage. But we must come back to this, before going any further, as
it throws light on the influence of urbanization, education, and some
economic characteristics.

Influence of Age at First Marriage

We must distinguish between two effects of age at first marriage on fertility. On the one hand, early marriage may impair a
woman's reproductive capacity, causing lower fertility. But more

importantly, the earlier a woman marries, the more time she has to produce a large family.

The first phenomenon, which can only be studied in a nonplanning population, is seen in Algeria. Table 7.2 shows that fertility rates for the same age group vary according to whether or not women married young. The difference is very clear between women married under age 17 and those married at age 17 to 19. Fertility rates are consistently higher for the latter group. Women who are married when they are very young are more open to the risk of becoming less fecund due to a higher number of childbirths and to childbirths that are often more difficult than if the woman were more mature.

Cumulated into a current index, these differences in fertility by age group are fairly important (see Table 7.1). With the fertility conditions observed around 1960 or 1965, a woman married at age 17 to 19 would have had a total of one child more between ages 20 and 50 than a woman married before age 17.

However, the difference is less evident between women married at age 17 to 19 and those married at age 20 to 24. By cumulating current fertility rates, from the age of 25 to 50, for the 17 to 19 and 20 to 24 age groups at marriage, we obtain the indexes shown in Table 7.6.

TABLE 7.6: Indexes of Fertility for Women Married between 17 and 19 and 20 and 24 Years of Age, in Algeria, 1955, 1960, and 1965

| Period Centered | Women Married at Age | |
Around	17 to 19	20 to 24
1955	6.2	6.0
1960	6.5	6.4
1965	6.8	6.8

Source: Republique Algerienne Democratique et Populaire, Secrétariat d'Etat au Plan, Direction des Statistiques, Etude statistique nationale de la population, résultats de l'enquete fécondité, ser. 2, vol. 2 (Oran: CNRES, 1972).

Considered from the same age on, women married at age 20 to 24 have a slightly lower total fertility than those married at age 17 to 19. Much smaller in number (1,404 out of 9,527), this group has, on the average, sociological characteristics that are fairly different from those of the rest of the population. The women are better educated, more likely to be living in urban areas, their marriages are less endogamous, and their husbands are also more educated and generally do some sort of skilled work.[13] These findings suggest that in this particular group of women, there exists a beginning of family planning, which previous analyses could not detect.[14]

The most important effect of age at marriage is a reduction of mean completed fertility with a rise in age at marriage (see Table 7.7). Whereas a woman aged 45 to 49, married at 17, has had an average of 9.2 live births, a woman of the same age married at over 25 years of age has had only 5.0. The difference seems due much more to duration of marriage than to different fertility behavior. Women married at a very young age do not seem to have children at a faster pace than others. A woman married at age 20 to 24 has an average of 1.1 children at 20 to 24 years, and would have 2.7 children (1.6 children more) at the same age if she had married before age 17. The difference between completed fertility of women married at age 20 to 24 (7.6 children) and that of women married before age 17 (9.2 children) is also 1.6. A rise in age at marriage seems, therefore, to have a direct effect on completed fertility.

The most we can say is that if women married at age 20 to 24 did not have a slight tendency toward birth control, there would be less difference in completed fertility, insofar as the effect of duration of marriage would be partially offset by the increase of fertility with age at marriage, as previously mentioned. As fertility is linked with nuptiality, comparisons between different socioeconomic groups must take the nuptiality variable into consideration.

Urban-Rural Differences

There is little difference in completed fertility between urban and rural women.* Women aged 45 to 49 at the time of the fertility survey had an average of 7.2 children in urban areas and 7.7 in rural areas. The difference remains slight if we examine data on women still in their first marriage at the time of the survey: 8.2 children for urban women and 8.7 children for rural women. Moreover, this

———————————————

*The survey defined "urban" as women living in communes, where the capital city contained more than 1,000 nonagricultural workers and in which these 1,000 workers formed over 75 percent of the working population. All the rest were considered "rural."

TABLE 7.7: Mean Number of Children per Woman Still in First Marriage, According to Current Age Group of Mother and Age at Marriage, in Algeria, 1970

Age Group	Women Married at								
	-17		17 to 19		20 to 24		25 or Over		Total
	Mean Number of Children	Number of Women	Mean Number of Children	Number of Women	Mean Number of Children	Number of Women	Mean Number of Children	Number of Women	
15-19	0.7	667	0.3	341	--	--	--	--	0.6
20-24	2.7	986	1.7	730	1.1	205	--	--	2.1
25-29	4.7	800	3.9	654	2.8	271	0.7	32	4.1
30-34	6.6	651	5.6	564	4.3	301	2.2	71	5.6
35-39	7.6	566	7.5	475	5.5	229	3.7	70	7.1
40-44	8.9	404	7.9	293	7.4	197	4.2	52	8.0
45-49	9.2	241	8.7	188	7.6	112	5.6	30	8.5

Source: Republique Algerienne Democratique et Populaire, Secrétariat d'Etat au Plan, Direction des Statistiques, Etude statistique nationale de la population, résultats de l'enquete fécondité, ser. 2, vol. 2 (Oran: CNRES, 1972).

difference is only reached at the end of the reproductive period. Up to age 35 to 39, there is practically no difference in fertility between urban and rural women, and it is even slightly higher in town for the younger ages.

If we group women by age at first marriage, as in Table 7.8, the difference between urban and rural women increases as age at marriage becomes higher. It is simpler to consider only women still in first marriage at the time of the survey.

TABLE 7.8: Mean Number of Children per Woman Still in First
Marriage, According to Current Age and Age at
Marriage, in Algeria, 1970

Current Age	Age at Marriage							
	-17		17 to 19		20 to 24		25 and Over	
	Urban	Rural	Urban	Rural	Urban	Rural	Urban	Rural
15-19	0.8	0.7	0.3	0.4				
20-24	3.0	2.6	2.0	1.6	0.7	0.6		
25-29	5.2	4.6	4.2	3.7	2.8	2.8	0.8	0.7
30-34	6.4	6.7	5.7	5.6	5.0	4.1	2.0	2.3
35-39	8.1	7.4	7.6	7.5	5.9	5.7	3.5	4.0
40-44	8.8	8.9	7.9	8.0	7.0	7.6	4.1	4.2
45-49	9.1	9.2	8.6	8.8	7.4	7.7	4.9	6.4

Source: Republique Algerienne Democratique et Populaire, Secrétariat d'Etat au Plan, Direction des Statistiques, Etude statistique nationale de la population, résultats de l'enquete fécondité, ser. 2, vol. 2 (Oran: CNRES, 1972).

For women married before age 17 or between 17 to 19, fertility is higher in urban areas until age 30; then, there is apparently no difference between urban and rural areas. For women married between the age of 20 to 24, on the other hand, fertility in urban areas is scarcely any higher than in rural areas for the younger ages, and completed fertility is lower among urban women. Finally, the fertility of women married at age 25 or over is constantly lower in urban than rural areas, in particular at age 45 to 49 (4.9 children in urban as against 6.4 in rural).

Therefore, women who marry very young--and they are the majority--have the same completed fertility in urban as in rural areas. In both cases, social pressure forces most women to marry young and to have large families (an average of 9.2 children per woman married before age 17). The reasons for later marriage, on the other hand, seem to vary with place of residence, and they result in different total fertility patterns. In town, "late" marriage is due above all to social change--for instance, age at marriage increases with a woman's education or her husband's social status category--which can, in itself, cause a drop in fertility. In the rural areas, on the other hand, late marriage is certainly more fortuitous, and much less associated with family planning.

The age-at-marriage classification also shows that lower rural fertility for the younger ages is characteristic of women who married very young (before 17 or at age 17 to 19) but disappears completely for women married at age 25 or over. Thus, with the same marriage and fertility behavior, urban women would be slightly more fertile. This may be explained by better health conditions, which reduce causes of sterility and lower the infant death rate. Moreover, the mean length of breast-feeding is shorter in urban areas, whatever the woman's social status.

This urban "excess fertility" at the younger ages drops or disappears completely for urban women practicing some sort of birth control. Even here, however, it is only at the end of the childbearing period that the mean number of children becomes perceptibly lower for urban women, indicating a still timid and belated use of family planning.

REFINEMENTS IN FERTILITY ANALYSIS BY
URBAN AND RURAL CLASSIFICATION

There are two ways of refining the urban-rural differences observed above: (1) choose only the largest cities and (2) distinguish between urban women born in town or living there before their marriage and women who settled there after marriage. In choosing only large cities for analysis, we find that the mean number of children per woman is perceptibly lower in other towns (see Table 7.9). Urban-rural differences, therefore, are due mainly to the situation in large towns. Within the large urban centers, women born there or settled there before their marriage--that is, the only true "urban women"--have a lower fertility than the others for almost every age group. Within the "small towns," on the other hand, the same distinction reveals no perceptible difference between women living there for a long time and those newly arrived.

Thus, the social group affected by lowered fertility is reduced; it corresponds to socioeconomic characteristics limited to a privileged fringe of Algerian society.

TABLE 7.9: Mean Number of Children per Woman, According to Current Age and Place of Residence, in Algeria, 1970

Current Age	Large Urban Centers			Other Urban Areas (Small Towns)			Rural
	Women Born in Large Urban Centers or Living There before Marriage	Women Settled in Large Urban Centers since Marriage	Total	Women Born in Small Towns or Living There before Marriage	Women Settled in Small Towns since Marriage	Total	Rural
15–19	0.4	0.7	0.5	0.6	0.7	0.7	0.7
20–24	1.9	2.4	2.2	1.9	2.5	2.1	2.1
25–29	3.6	4.0	3.8	3.8	4.0	3.9	3.9
30–34	4.9	4.9	4.9	5.4	4.9	5.2	5.2
35–39	5.7	6.3	6.2	6.4	6.3	6.1	6.1
40–44	5.8	7.1	6.8	7.5	6.8	7.1	7.1
45–49	6.6	6.8	6.8	7.1	7.7	7.4	7.4

Source: Republique Algerienne Democratique et Populaire, Secrétariat d'Etat au Plan, Direction des Statistiques, Etude statistique nationale de la population, résultats de l'enquete fécondité, ser. 2, vol. 2 (Oran: CNRES, 1972).

143

INFLUENCE OF EDUCATIONAL STATUS

The mean number of children per woman still in her first marriage varies a great deal according to the level of education of the
mother (see Table 9.10). At age 30 to 34, an illiterate woman has
had an average of 5.7 children, a woman who attended primary or
traditional Koranic schools (medersa) 4.7, and 3.5 if she attended
secondary or higher educational institutions. At age 40 to 44, a
woman who has received primary education has, on the average,
almost two children less than an illiterate one.

Education appears to play a very important role in fertility.
It also influences age at marriage: mean age at first marriage is
17.8 for illiterate women, 20.7 for those with primary or Koranic
education, and 22.0 for those with secondary or higher education.[15]
Thus, the fertility difference can be partially explained by a shorter
total duration of marriage. But variations in fertility are too strong
to be accounted for by this factor alone. Moreover, fertility at ages
20 to 24 and 25 to 29 is the same for illiterate women as for those
who have had primary school or medersa education; the difference
only appears later on, at 30 to 34 years of age. It is, therefore,
the result of a rather late use of family planning. For women with
secondary or higher education, on the other hand, the difference
appears at age 20 to 24. Higher age at marriage has its effect, but
these women may also adopt family planning earlier.

Thus, a woman's education, even an elementary one, is a
highly significant factor. Primary education constitutes an important threshold in fertility behavior. Education of the husband plays
a less dominant role. Only women whose husbands have received
high school or university education have lower fertility, and the
difference is only half as great as for the woman's education (0.9
as against 2.0 children at age 35 to 39).

INFLUENCE OF CERTAIN ECONOMIC VARIABLES
ON FERTILITY

The relationship between fertility and economic activity is not
obvious. Algerian women participating in economic activities are
very rare and are found almost exclusively in cities. In our analysis,
we were only able to make the distinction between employed and unemployed women (see Table 7.11). Nevertheless, fairly clear-cut
differences appear in the number of children. Thus, a woman's
economic status, like her education, is probably a decisive element
in fertility. However, whereas for education, the differences continue to increase with age, here, they reach a maximum at age 35

TABLE 7.10: Mean Number of Children per Woman Still in First Marriage, According to Current Age and Educational Status of the Woman and Her Husband, in Algeria, 1970

Age	Education of Woman				Education of Husband			
	None	Medersa or Primary	Secondary or Higher	Total	None	Medersa or Primary	Secondary or Higher	Total
15-19	0.6	0.5	0.5	0.6	0.6	0.5	0.5	0.6
20-24	2.2	2.0	1.5	2.1	2.1	2.1	2.0	2.1
25-29	4.1	4.1	2.7	4.1	4.0	4.3	3.4	4.1
30-34	5.7	4.7	3.5	5.6	5.7	5.6	4.6	5.6
35-39	7.1	6.1	--	7.1	7.1	7.0	6.2	7.1
40-44	8.1	6.3	--	8.0	8.0	8.2	7.1	8.0
45-49	8.6	--	--	8.5	8.5	8.5	--	8.5

Source: Republique Algerienne Democratique et Populaire, Secrétariat d'Etat au Plan, Direction des Statistiques, Etude statistique nationale de la population, résultats de l'enquete fécondité, ser. 2, vol. 2 (Oran: CNRES, 1972).

to 44. At age 35 to 39, a working woman has only 3.9 children, as
against 6.4 for an unemployed woman. But the difference decreases
afterward, and at age 45 to 49, it is only 0.6 children (6.6 as
against 7.2).

TABLE 7.11: Mean Number of Children per Woman, in Urban
            Areas, According to Current Age and Economic
            Activity of the Woman, in Algeria, 1970

Age Group	Employed	Unemployed	Total
15-19	--	0.6	0.6
20-24	1.2	2.3	2.2
25-29	2.3	4.0	3.9
30-34	3.7	5.1	5.0
35-39	3.9	6.4	6.2
40-44	4.9	7.1	6.9
45-49	6.6	7.2	7.2

Source: Republique Algerienne Democratique et Populaire,
Secrétariat d'Etat au Plan, Direction des Statistiques, Etude statistique nationale de la population, résultats de l'enquete fécondité,
ser. 2, vol. 2 (Oran: CNRES, 1972).

Working women who are now aged 45 to 49 do not belong to the
same social category as those under 35 years. The older women
probably started working late in life to provide for the needs of a
large family. The younger women, if they have worked since the
beginning of their marriage, can be expected to have fewer children
at the end of their childbearing years than the working women who
are currently aged 45 to 49.

The branch of economic activity of the husband appears to play
a small role in determining fertility behavior. The differences between broad occupational categories are slight, as can be seen from
Table 7.12. The slightly higher fertility of women whose husbands
are in agriculture is perhaps not significant.

The husband's occupational status plays a slightly more important role, but as seen in Table 7.13, only wives of the "professional and managerial" group have a really lower fertility rate.

If we examine the husband's type of work for employees only,
we discover a basic split similar to that observed for education (see
Table 7.14). Only women married to managerial or executive staff

have a fertility really different from the rest. Between skilled and nonskilled workers, on the other hand, the difference is insignificant.

TABLE 7.12: Mean Number of Children per Currently Married Woman, According to Husband's Field of Activity and Current Age Group of Woman, in Algeria, 1970

| Woman's Present Age Group | Field of Activity | | |
	Agriculture and Mining	Industry	Transport, Trade, and Civil Service
15-19	0.6	0.6	0.5
20-24	2.1	2.0	2.0
25-29	3.8	3.9	3.9
30-34	5.4	5.1	5.2
35-39	6.3	6.0	6.4
40-44	7.4	7.1	7.2
45-49	7.9	7.8	6.8

Source: Republique Algerienne Democratique et Populaire, Secrétariat d'Etat au Plan, Direction des Statistiques, Etude statistique nationale de la population, résultats de l'enquete fécondité, ser. 2, vol. 2 (Oran: CNRES, 1972).

ADDITIONAL ANALYSIS OF FERTILITY BY SOCIAL STATUS

A survey on attitudes toward contraception carried out by the Association Algerienne pour la Recherche Demographique Economique et Sociale[16] in 1968 gives figures on fertility by social status category. The most interesting analysis is on the mean number of children per "woman-year," measured in terms of effective married life* (see Table 7.15). Starting at the bottom of the social ladder, we find first a zone of "lower fertility," corresponding to the poorest social groups (in

---

*This is the ratio of number of live births to total number of years of effective married life (excluding the years when the husband was "absent" and years of dissolved marriage) lived by the total number of women who were studied.

TABLE 7.13: Mean Number of Children per Currently Married Woman, According to Husband's Occupational Status and Current Age Group of Woman, in Algeria, 1970

Occupational Status	Current Age Group of Woman						
	15-19	20-24	25-29	30-34	35-39	40-44	45-49
Unoccupied	0.5	1.5	3.1	4.6	5.4	6.1	7.1
Professional and managerial	0.4	1.7	3.7	4.0	5.8	6.4	7.6
Clerical	0.6	1.9	3.7	5.2	7.3	7.2	6.7
Sales	0.7	2.1	4.1	5.4	6.2	7.1	6.2
Farmers, fishermen	0.6	2.1	3.8	5.4	6.3	7.5	7.9
Transport, communications	0.4	2.2	3.7	5.1	6.2	6.8	7.1
Craftsmen, manual workers, and miners	0.6	2.0	3.9	5.1	6.1	7.3	8.0
Service, sports, and so forth	0.5	2.2	4.1	5.3	6.5	7.0	6.8
Subtotal "working men"	0.6	2.0	3.8	5.2	6.3	7.3	7.6
Total	0.6	2.0	3.8	5.2	6.3	7.3	7.5

Source: Republique Algerienne Democratique et Populaire, Secrétariat d'Etat au Plan, Direction des Statistiques, Etude statistique nationale de la population, résultats de l'enquete fécondité, ser. 2, vol. 2 (Oran: CNRES, 1972).

TABLE 7.14: Mean Number of Live-Born Children per Woman,
According to Husband's Type of Work and Current
Age of Woman, in Algeria, 1970

| | Type of Work | | |
Current Age	Nonskilled	Skilled	Managerial and Executive Staff
15-19	0.6	0.5	0.3
20-24	2.1	2.1	1.7
25-29	3.9	3.9	3.6
30-34	5.2	5.1	3.5
35-39	6.4	6.4	6.0
40-44	7.2	7.3	7.9
45-49	8.0	7.4	5.8
50-54	6.6	5.7	--

Source: Republique Algerienne Democratique et Populaire, Secrétariat
d'Etat au Plan, Direction des Statistiques, Etude statistique nationale de la
population, résultats de l'enquete fécondité, ser. 2, vol. 2 (Oran: CNRES,
1972).

TABLE 7.15: Ratio of Live Births to Total Number of Years of Effective
Married Life Lived by Total Number of Women in Each
Social Status Category, in Algeria, 1968

Social Status Category	Number of Births per "Woman-Year"	Total Number of Women Informants
Unemployed	0.435	289
Irregular agricultural employees	0.427	194
Permanent agricultural employees	0.412	105
Khames ("sharecroppers")	0.377	72
Fellahs	0.429	221
Irregular unskilled workers	0.405	126
Regular unskilled workers	0.480	255
Skilled workers	0.505	182
Small independent trades	0.399	70
Craft and Tradesmen	0.453	293
Small nonmanual workers without qualification	0.466	92
Clerical	0.491	135
Executive staff	0.433	82
Managerial and professional	0.402	29
Pensioners, independently wealthy	0.455	55
Not stated		48
Total	0.442	2,138

Source: Association Algerienne pour la Recherche Démographique,
Economique et Sociale, Enquete socio-démographique (Algiers: Secrétariat
au Plan, 1972).

particular sharecroppers [khames], small traders, and people ir-
regularly employed); then, a zone of "excess fertility," corresponding to intermediate categories (in particular, regular wage earners,
skilled workers, and office workers); and, finally, another zone of
"lower fertility" for the professional and managerial group.

In the first zone, lower fertility is probably "involuntary,"
due to health conditions and longer periods of breast-feeding. Lower
fertility in the third group is voluntary due to family planning.

CONCLUSION

Following a slow but steady progression over the years, the
very high fertility of Algerian women bears all the signs of a "natural"
fertility, that is, of couples who do not practice contraception. In
spite of the absence of a certain number of men working in Europe,
completed fertility for a woman married before age 18 (which is very
often the case, as mean age at first marriage is 17.9 years) and remaining married until the age of 45 to 49 is, on the average, 9.2
children. This is very near the figure generally taken to characterize natural fertility.[17] The only apparent limits are those of fecun-
dity, infant survival, and duration of marriage. When there is no
voluntary birth control, the evolution of fertility depends on these
limits.

Sterility may decrease with improved health conditions, but its
incidence is not high enough for its reduction to cause an important
rise in fertility. We cannot say the same thing of the infant death
rate, however, which with better protection during pregnancy will
certainly drop. Likewise, temporary infecundity due to prolonged
breast-feeding may well decrease in the future, since length of
breast-feeding seems to be becoming shorter among the younger
generations.[18]

Duration of marriage may also change. Age at marriage has
recently dropped, but it is unlikely that this trend will continue for
long, and we may even hope that it will be reversed due to greater
educational access for women.[19] The place reserved for women in
Algerian society in the future is of critical importance. Duration of
marriage or marriages) also depends on the number of dissolved
marriages, another important influence on fertility. It is difficult
to say whether or not these will decrease in the future, but an improvement in woman's social status would, in time, certainly bring
about the disappearance of "repudiation" or family desertion, which
is still currently practiced, though banned by law.

If we examine fertility differences between different social
groups, we can see that family planning exists in certain groups.

Although they only form a marginal fringe of society, and although differences are only slight, these groups may point to a new evolution in Algerian society. The least fertile women, mainly urban, are generally educated, married to men in the professional or managerial group, and sometimes have an economic activity.

Increasing age at marriage, broadening educational possibilities, and greater participation in paid economic activity may bring about a decrease in fertility or, at least, increase the number of less fertile women. A certain number of policies may, therefore, have a considerable effect on fertility. However, education, employment of women, and age at marriage are only elements of a whole. The key issue is the social status of the Algerian woman, the real heart of the problem, and this may be far from changing in the near future.

NOTES

1. Republique Algerienne Democratique et Populaire, Secrétariat au Plan, Direction des Statistiques, 1974.

2. Breil, J., 1954, pp. 795-808; Biraben, J. N., 1969.

3. Republique Algerienne Democratique et Populaire, Secrétariat au Plan, Direction des Statistiques, 1972.

4. Negadi, G., and Vallin, J., 1974.

5. Vallin, J., 1973a.

6. Tabutin, D., 1974.

7. Vallin, J., 1970.

8. Tabutin, D., 1973.

9. Republique Algerienne Democratique et Populaire, 1971.

10. Vallin, J., 1971; Sabagh, G., 1969.

11. Nadot, R., 1966; Gondreau, F. and Volle, M., 1967.

12. Republique Algerienne Democratique et Populaire, Secrétariat d'Etat au Plan, Direction des Statistiques, 1974.

13. Vallin, J., 1973c.

14. A more detailed analysis of these behavior differences is found in a previous article: Vallin, J., 1973b.

15. Vallin, J., 1973c.

16. Association Algerienne pour la Recherche Demographique, Economique et Sociale, 1972.

17. Sauvy, A., 1966 (vol. 2, p. 113) gives ten children for a couple united at puberty and still together by the menopause. Certain others give an estimate of 11 children.

18. Tabutin, op. cit.

19. Vallin, 1973c. Moreover, the results of the population survey seem to confirm this hypothesis (see Vallin, J., 1974).

8

Fertility Declines in Tunisia: Factors Affecting Recent Trends

MOHAMED AYAD
YOLANDE JEMAI

Tunisia is a country in which vigorous governmental efforts and investments in social change have contributed to rapid fertility decline in spite of relatively modest economic development. This chapter will first present data on Tunisian population growth and fertility trends and differentials. Then, it will consider the impact of socioeconomic changes and will provide measures of the effect of various factors on the decline in fertility since 1966.

POPULATION GROWTH AND FERTILITY TRENDS

The Tunisian censuses of 1891 and 1911 were limited to the French colonial population. Beginning with the census of 1921, when the total population of the country was enumerated, the population has evolved as follows:[1]

Date of Census	Total Population
1921	2,093,939
1926	2,159,708
1931	2,410,692
1936	2,608,313
1946	3,230,952
1956	3,783,169
1966	4,533,351
1975	5,572,229

In half a century, the population of Tunisia increased two and one-half times. Demographic growth remained low until 1946, scarcely surpassing 20 per 1,000. Just after World War II, and particularly beginning in 1956, the year of Tunisia's independence, the mortality rate witnessed a rapid decline due to improvement in the health infrastructure in the country. This led to an increase in the natural growth rate, especially since the overall birth rate had not greatly changed. Beginning around 1967, the natural growth rate began to waver; this decline was due to the effect of several factors that we will consider in this chapter.

EVOLUTION OF BIRTHS AND THE
CRUDE BIRTH RATE

According to Table 8.1 registered births only surpassed the peak of 200,000 for the two years 1964 and 1966. This was partly because of the very large number of marriages contracted in 1963 and 1964, on the eve of, and immediately following, the law of February 20, 1964, raising the legal age at marriage for both men and women. The adjusted crude birth rate (CBR) became lower than 40 per 1,000 in the 1970s, reaching 35.7 per 1,000 for the first time in Tunisia in 1974. (See Table 8.1.)

The general fertility rate (GFR) went from 193 per 1,000 in 1966, to 157 per 1,000 in 1971, and to 149 per 1,000 in 1974 for women between 15 and 54 years of age. For women between 15 and 49, the GFR rate (per 1,000) was 210 in 1966, 169 in 1971, and 160 in 1974. In the space of eight years, the general fertility rate was reduced by 44 per 1,000, which represents a considerable decline. This decline is seen at all age levels and, especially, in the youngest age groups: 15-19 and 20-24. (See Table 8.2.) It is greatest in the most fertile age group, namely, 25-29.

Marital fertility has considerably declined since 1966 as well. This decline is seen at all ages and, particularly, as was noted for general fertility, in the 15-19 and 20-24 age brackets (see Table 8.3.) This is explained by an increase in the interval between first marriage and first birth. A study of the recent evolution of nuptiality in Tunisia from 1965 to 1970 has shown that there has been an increase in the relative frequency of the youngest age groups entering marriage, both for men and women.[2]

DIFFERENTIAL FERTILITY

CBRs vary considerably among Tunisian provinces. The governorates of the south and center--the least economically developed and the least urbanized--have the highest rates. The governorates of the north and eastern coast have lower rates and, as

TABLE 8.1: Population, Births, and Crude Birth Rates in Tunisia, 1960–74

Year	Population on June 30	Registered Births	Adjusted Births	Observed Birth Rate (per 1,000)	Adjusted Birth Rate
1960	4,185,000	182,221	191,810	43.5	45.7
1961	4,259,000	184,396	194,100	43.2	45.4
1962	4,329,000	181,861	191,430	42.0	44.2
1963	4,417,000	187,395	197,260	42.4	44.6
1964	4,519,000	206,046	206,046	46.2	46.2
1965	4,665,000	193,220	203,390	41.4	43.5
1966	4,717,000	206,730	206,730	43.8	43.8
1967	4,825,000	187,320	197,180	38.8	40.8
1968	4,928,000	188,940	198,880	38.3	40.3
1969	5,027,000	194,940	205,200	38.7	40.7
1970	5,126,000	186,360	196,170	36.3	38.2
1971	5,228,000	183,311	192,960	35.0	36.8
1972	5,332,000	199,121	209,600	37.3	39.8
1973	5,444,000	194,764	205,010	35.7	39.3
1974	5,616,000	191,049	201,100	34.0	35.7

Note: Registered births were increased by 5 percent. For 1964 and 1966, the births have not been adjusted: the National Institute of Statistics estimates the collection rate at 100 percent for these years (these two birth rates become 47.9 per 1,000 and 46.1 per 1,000, respectively, if the births are increased by 5 percent).

Sources: Tunisia, Ministry of the Plan, National Institute of Statistics, various sources, notably, the "Statistiques de l'I.N.S.," Demographic Series no. 5 (Tunis: INS, December 1974).

TABLE 8.2: General Fertility Rates of Female Population of Reproductive Age, in Tunisia, 1966-74

Year	Female Population 15 to 54 on June 30	Female Population 15 to 49 on June 30	General Fertility for Women 15 to 54 (per 1,000)	General Fertility for Women 15 to 49 (per 1,000)
1966	1,071,300	983,800	193	210
1967	1,103,700	1,015,400	179	194
1968	1,135,200	1,056,300	175	188
1969	1,165,100	1,075,800	176	191
1970	1,194,300	1,104,600	164	178
1971	1,299,300	1,138,900	157	169
1972	1,268,200	1,176,800	165	178
1973	1,308,700	1,216,500	157	169
1974	1,350,000	1,257,000	149	160

Source: Tunisia, Ministry of the Plan, National Institute of Statistics, "Statistiques de l'I.N.S.," Demographic Series no. 5 (Tunis: INS, December 1974).

expected, Tunis, the capital, has the lowest CBR. These results, based on vital statistics, correspond closely with the results of the 1968-69 National Demographic Survey, which showed completed fertility at 7.6 children in rural areas and 6.1 in urban areas. In addition, fertility rates were consistently higher among women in all age groups in rural areas. (See Table 8.4.)

TABLE 8.3: Marital Fertility Rates, by Age Group, in Tunisia, 1966, 1968-69, and 1971 (per 1,000)

Mother's Age	1966	1968-69*	1971
15-19	416	345	319
20-24	415	384	351
25-29	391	349	344
30-34	340	274	293
35-39	262	193	215
40-44	137	74	107
45-49	43	20	30
50-54	17	14	11
Total	278	229	223

*National Demographic Survey, 1968-69.

Source: Tunisia, Ministry of the Plan, National Institute of Statistics.

TABLE 8.4: General Fertility Rates, by Age Group, in Urban and Rural Settings, in Tunisia, 1968-69* (per 1,000)

Mother's Age	Urban Setting	Rural Setting
15-19	32.8	39.0
20-24	249.1	297.1
25-29	333.3	349.9
30-34	290.8	344.7
35-39	192.2	271.0
40-44	97.3	159.7
45-49	33.4	48.3
50-54	1.3	20.0
Final number of children	6.1	7.6

*First round--National Demographic Survey, 1968-69.

Source: Tunisia, Ministry of the Plan, National Institute of Statistics.

Two additional surveys have provided information on differential fertility in Tunisia. The first, undertaken in Tunis, drew on household cards from the 1966 census. It showed that the wives of high-level administrators and men employed in the professions had the lowest fertility rates (103.4 per 1,000). Wives of day laborers and workers had an intermediate rate (216 per 1,000)--between that of artisans' and merchants' wives (268.5 per 1,000) and that of wives of low-level white collar employees and middle-level administrators (167.2 per 1,000).[3]

The second study, carried out in 1970-71, provided data on the fertility of 1,031 women from five regions of Tunisia who belonged to five different social categories.[4] The fertility of these women (by age group, marriage duration, and probability of family enlargement) was analyzed in relation to their use of contraceptives, level of education, socioeconomic status, and social mobility. As expected, women in the wealthiest social categories and living in an urban setting have lower fertility than women in the less-favored social categories. The fertility rate hierarchy (lowest to highest fertility) by duration of marriage was as follows: (1) El Menzah-Mutuelleville (wealthy residential neighborhoods with a modern-type population); (2) Sfax (white-collar employees and low-level administrators); (3) Djebel Lahmar (neighborhood on the periphery of Tunis, urban fringe population of rural origin); (4) Korba (rural center, tree cultivation); and (5) Sers (rural center, grain farming).

SOCIAL AND ECONOMIC FACTORS
AFFECTING FERTILITY

Since independence in 1956, Tunisia has been in the vanguard of Arab and African countries in regard to progressive legislation and governmental efforts to modernize traditional family patterns, provide equal rights for women, and help in the development of its people (by dramatically increasing access to education and health facilities). Tunisia was the first Arab state to develop a population policy and to put into effective operation a national family planning program. Numerous observers have discussed the impact of these measures, so we will not review them again here.[5] However, we wish to note that a systematic study of the determinants of Tunisian population trends could be of potentially great importance to policy makers in developing countries. This is because Tunisia provides a case of rapid fertility decline, probably caused primarily by investment and efforts in social and cultural development. Tunisia's economic development has so far provided meager results and, consequently, does not seem to be the major determinant of fertility reduction.

Tunisia's first Decade of Development Planning (1962-71) aimed at economic takeoff through heavy investment in infrastructure, education, and the development of agriculture. Considerable austerity was involved: savings more than doubled in the ten years while the mean per capita consumption nearly stagnated. According to official figures, the national income increased at a rate of only 2.4 percent per annum at constant 1966 prices, compared to the 4 percent forecast.[6]

It appears well established, therefore, that the decline in natality has been independent of the rise in the standard of living, at least for most of the population. It is also significant that the distribution of income and wealth, already distinctly unequal before independence, has only been slightly improved. The reduction of the distance between social categories, which in other countries occurred at the beginning of the decline in fertility, has not been very pronounced in Tunisia. Several studies have shown that the overall growth of 2.4 percent per annum has particularly benefited the middle class: its mean revenue increased about 20 percent in real terms during the decade, while a very high proportion of the population (40 percent according to official sources) still remains below the threshold of poverty and shares 10 percent of the national income.[7]

MEASURING EFFECTS OF VARIOUS FACTORS ON DECLINE OF FERTILITY

If it is difficult to evaluate the impact of social and economic changes in the recent decline in Tunisian fertility, it is nevertheless easy to measure statistically the effects of such factors as changes in age structure, marital status, and family planning activity. In order to determine these effects, 1966--a census year and a year when fertility remained very close to natural fertility--will be taken as the basic reference point. Official data from the National Institute of Statistics will be used for the following measures: (1) the total number of women in the 15 to 54 year age group from 1966 to 1974; (2) registered and adjusted births; (3) the GFRs and age-specific fertility rates relative to 1966; and (4) legitimate fertility rates (15-54) and legitimate fertility rates by age group relative to 1966.

If the overall fertility rate for 1966 is applied to the female population of 15 to 54 from 1967 to 1974, this gives us a measure of the potential live births from 1967 to 1974--as if the fertility rate had remained that of 1966. Horizontal column c of Table 8.5 gives the results of the calculations. Thus, in 1974, for example, the

TABLE 8.5: Theoretical and Real Births Avoided from 1967 to 1975, in Tunisia

Age Group	General Fertility Rate 1966	Theoretical Births								
		1967	1968	1969	1970	1971	1972	1973	1974	
15-19	73	15,950	17,400	18,850	20,260	21,300	21,300	22,710	23,460	
20-24	296	47,210	49,110	50,970	52,690	56,330	61,830	67,490	73,530	
25-29	350	52,500	51,590	50,650	49,700	50,330	52,360	54,570	56,730	
30-34	316	46,480	46,420	46,290	46,170	45,760	45,030	44,370	43,510	
35-39	236	31,550	32,070	32,500	32,970	33,280	33,250	33,250	33,130	
40-44	114	12,540	13,040	13,510	13,990	14,380	14,610	14,860	15,300	
45-49	31	2,990	3,020	3,040	3,060	3,130	3,270	3,400	3,470	
50-54	10	880	890	890	900	900	910	920	930	
Total	193	210,100	213,540	216,700	219,740	225,410	233,250	241,570	250,150	(a)
Registered and adjusted births		197,180	198,880	205,200	196,170	192,960	209,600	205,010	201,100	(b)
Theoretical births with the 1966 rate of 193 per 1,000		213,010	219,090	224,860	230,500	237,250	244,760	252,580	260,550	(c)
Births avoided by all the effects (c-b):										
Number		15,830	20,210	19,660	34,330	44,290	35,160	47,570	59,450	(d)
Percent		8.0	10.0	9.5	18.0	23.0	17.0	23.0	30.0	
Births avoided by the structural effects (c-a)		2,910	5,500	8,160	10,760	11,840	11,510	11,010	10,400	(e)
Births avoided by family planning		6,000	7,680	10,170	11,660	13,330	15,510	17,290	23,110	(f)
e/d in percent		18.4	27.2	41.5	31.3	26.7	32.7	23.1	17.5	(g)
f/d in percent		37.9	38.0	51.7	33.9	30.1	44.1	36.3	38.9	(h)

Source: Compiled by the author.

159

theoretical births would have been 260,550 if the overall fertility
rate of 193 per 1,000 of 1966 were applied to the 15- to 54-year-old
female population of 1974, estimated at 1,350,000 (see Table 8.2).
The births registered for 1974 in the official vital statistics, and
adjusted by 5 percent, amounted to 201,100. The difference between
260,550 and 201,100 equals the total number of births avoided by
all effects, or 59,450. (See Table 8.5, horizontal column d, for
the period 1967-74.)

The births avoided by various factors compared to the registered and adjusted births represent, from 1967 to 1974, the following percentages:

Year	Percent
1967	8.0
1968	10.0
1969	9.5
1970	18.0
1971	23.0
1972	17.0
1973	23.0
1974	30.0

An important increase in births avoided for the years 1971-73
and 1974 may be noted.

Age Structure Effect

By applying 1966 age-specific fertility rates to the total number of women in each age group from 1967 to 1974, we obtain a
measure of theoretical births for each year by age group. The difference between the births calculated with the GFR for 1966 and the
sum of the births obtained with the GFRs by age group for 1966
gives the births avoided through the structural effect.

Thus, for 1974, we would have the following: (1) theoretical
births obtained with the 1966 GFR, 260,550; (2) sum of the theoretical births obtained with the age-specific fertility rates, 250,150;
and (3) difference between (1) and (2), which represents the births
avoided through the structural effect, 10,400, or 17 percent of the
sum of births avoided by all the factors reducing fertility.

Epidemics and food restrictions during World War II produced
smaller than normal cohorts, and this explains, in large part, the
births avoided by the age structure effect. Without this smaller
cohort of women between 25 and 29 in 1971, one could estimate an
additional 20,000 women who would have given birth to 6,400 children.

This is clear if we apply to the total of 20,000, the GFR observed for the 25 to 29 year age group in 1971, 320 per 1,000.

It should be noted that the effect of a smaller cohort of women who were at their maximum fertility between 1969 and 1973 is circumstantial. The 25 to 29 year age group will be formed beginning in 1975 by the large cohort of women who were born right after World War II. At the present time, we see a number of births avoided through structural effects: 11,840 in 1971; 11,010 in 1973, and 10,400 in 1974.

Marital Status Effect

We will limit ourselves to the year 1974 in evaluating the effect of this factor. Age-specific fertility rates of married women in 1966 will be used as the basic reference. By applying the rate of each age group to the total number of married women corresponding to this age group in 1974,[8] we obtain the births that women married in 1974 would theoretically have given birth to, if the legitimate fertility by age had been maintained at the 1966 level. Thus, the difference between the sum of theoretical births for 1974, calculated on the basis of general fertility by age in 1966, and the sum of theoretical births for 1974, calculated on the basis of marital age-specific fertility rate of 1966, gives the births avoided by the marital status effect, or 250,150 minus 236,280 equals 13,870.

This represents 23.3 percent of the total number of births avoided by all effects. More than two-thirds of the births avoided by the marital status effect are concentrated in the 15 to 19 year age group. This explains, on the one hand, the delay in the age at marriage of the following group and, on the other hand, the increasing interval between age at first marriage and the first birth.

Family Planning Effect

The births prevented by the Tunisian family planning program (data presented in this chapter) were calculated by the Population Division of the National Office of Family Planning and Population. They are official data and they are very close to the estimations made by foreign researchers at the office.*

---

*The contraceptive continuation rates used by the National Office of Family Planning and Population for the calculation of

The total number of births avoided by the family planning program has doubled once from 1967 to 1971 and a second time from 1971 to 1974 (see Table 8.5). This program is responsible for more than a third of the fertility decline in Tunisia. In the years to come, and particularly from 1975 to 1980, the program must double its efforts in order to avoid the births (reduced in the past by the smaller cohorts due to wartime conditions) that will be born by the large female cohorts born after World War II.   These, of course, must be added to the births avoided through the family planning effect itself. Given current and continuing improvements in the program, we can reasonably hope that the program will be successful in its efforts.

---

women protected by the intrauterine device (IUD) were calculated before the rates given by the Tunisian contraceptive continuation survey of 1973. The earlier rates are lower, as the following table shows:

Mean Length in Months	Rates Used by the Office	Survey Rates
0	100	100.0
6	80	88.3
18	60	73.3
30	45	62.1
42	30	52.5

If we hypothesize that the births avoided by other methods have been overestimated by the Population Division of the National Office of Family Planning and Population, then the births avoided by all the methods are not overestimated, given that births avoided by the IUD have been underestimated. R. J. Lapham, 1970, has estimated the births avoided by family planning activity to be 8,800. Tunisia, Ministry of the Plan, National Institute of Statistics, 1974, estimated the births avoided by family planning in 1971 at 12,000. Seklani, M., 1974, estimated the births avoided by family planning in 1971, 1972, and 1973, at 12,297, 14,400, and 17,990, respectively. Finally, the National Office of Family Planning and Population gives for the years 1968, 1971, 1972, and 1973 the following figures, which are very close to those advanced above: 1968, 7,680; 1971, 13,330; 1972, 15,515; and 1973, 17,288.

CONCLUSION

Fertility in Tunisia has experienced a significant decline, beginning in 1970. Fertility is now in transition. In the future, and especially beginning in the 1990s, Tunisian fertility will experience a decline, which will bring it fairly close to the fertility levels of certain European Mediterranean countries during the 1960s.

Economic and social development (improvement in the standard of living, reduction of unemployment, greater access to education by girls up to the secondary and university levels), legislative efforts in favor of family planning, the flexible position of Islam concerning family planning, and a vigorous population policy are the guarantees of a considerable reduction of fertility in Tunisia. It remains to reduce the gap between rural and urban fertility. In order to do this, improvement in family planning activity in rural areas and, above all, a policy of long-term rural development will be required. If these considerations are taken into account, it will not be impossible to reach the demographic objectives that have been fixed in the Fourth Plan 1973-76, including attaining an overall fertility rate of 66 per 1,000 by the end of the century.

NOTES

1. Tunisia, Ministry of the Plan, National Institute of Statistics, 1973.

2. Behar, L., 1975.

3. Seklani, M., Rouissi, M., and Bchir, M., 1969.

4. Bchir, M., Bouraoui, A., Rouissi, M., and Zghal, A., 1973.

5. See Chapter 2 of this book.

6. Tunisia, Ministry of the Plan, 1973-76.

7. Tunisia, Ministry of the Plan, National Institute of Statistics, 1970.

8. Marcoux, A. J., 1972; the percentages of women married in 1974 were estimated from the censuses of 1956 and 1966.

PART II

Changing Family Patterns and Women's Status

9

Family Structures and Adaptations in the Iranian City of Isfahan

JOHN GULICK
MARGARET E. GULICK

INTRODUCTION

This chapter presents and discusses some of the findings of a study of families in the city of Isfahan that was conducted in 1970-71. Iran has a national family planning program that is intended to help the mass of the Iranian people lower their birth rate and, thereby, improve the quality of their lives. Our study was intended to explore the evidence for various degrees of readiness for family planning among working-class people in the city. In focusing upon working-class people, we wished to bring to light aspects of family life to which little attention has been paid as far as Middle Eastern cities are concerned. Popular generalizations and mass media images of

We acknowledge the financial assistance of the National Science Foundation (grant number GS-3108) and the Carolina Population Center, which made possible the research that produced the data presented in this chapter. The field research was carried out under the auspices of the University of Isfahan's Center for Population Studies, whose director is Mahmoud Sarram. We are very grateful to him for his many kinds of assistance. We also wish to thank Ghassem Motamedi, chancellor of the University of Isfahan, for his support of our project.

We are particularly grateful to those people without whose direct contribution this project would not have been carried out. Our special thanks go to Elaine Maleki. She helped us recruit and train our research team and was invaluable as our staff manager, assisted by Farideh Bassiri Malek and Fereshteh Sarram. Farajollah

Middle Eastern cities exaggerate the "modern," Western-style, professional upper-middle-class components of those cities' populations. As a result, one can easily jump to the conclusion that life for all or most city dwellers is a rapid, unidirectional transformation into Western-style middle-class patterns (including "rational" reduction of fertility in the interests of maximizing resources for the benefit of the children and freeing the mothers for nondomestic careers). In much of the urban literature, there seems to be a persistent tendency to ignore the social and cultural heterogeneity of cities, and therefore, they overgeneralize about supposedly uniform urban characteristics. Modern, Western-style, professional middle-class culture is only one of the cultures that occurs in Middle Eastern cities, and it is not necessarily the only culture that is functionally adapted to the urban environment. Indeed, there are traditional, non-Western patterns of life among Middle Eastern city dwellers. These include patterns of sex segregation, female seclusion, and high fertility. Our study was intended to reach Isfahan people whose lives were characterized by these patterns in order to see what their adaptations to innovations (such as systematic family planning and schools for girls) actually are. What we found was that while there is no doubt that many of them are changing, most of them are not being radically transformed--contrary to the predictions so often facilely made.

Our guess is that our findings from Isfahan are far more representative of Middle Eastern urban populations generally than are the Western-style middle-class transformation cases. A recent study of Kuwait increases our confidence in this regard. Kuwait is a city-state whose population has been exposed more intensively to more "modern" influences than has probably any other comparable population in the Middle East. This is due to the enormous petroleum revenues of this small nation and consequent high per capita income and extensive capital improvements by the government. Yet, among

Afrasiabi and Pauline Afrasiabi were very helpful to the project in a wide variety of ways. The field interviewers were (in alphabetical order): Naser Badami, Eshrat Darab, Mashid Emami, Ginous Hakimi, Sedigheh Karimpour, Asghar Kelishadi, Ali Langroudy, Mehdi Mansouri, Heshmatollah Nosrati, Parvaneh Rafe'i, Shaheen Shadzi, and Mahnaz Tashakkor.

The case numbers used in this paper are code numbers assigned for the purpose of analysis. They are not the same as the code numbers that many of the women in our sample had been given by the family planning clinic.

the native population of Kuwait, fertility levels remain very high and continue to be associated with cultural patterns that restrict female nondomestic social life.[1] These, along with various demographic and economic factors that do result from recent changes, characterize the native population of the city and, so far at any rate, constitute part of a variegated (not transformed) adaptational reality. If this is true in Kuwait, it should not be very surprising that it is true in other cities where the modern influences have been less intense.

We have described our research procedures elsewhere.[2] Briefly, we trained, supervised, and worked closely with a team of men and women university students who, during slightly more than one year, repeatedly interviewed the husbands and wives in 174 Isfahan households. More than half of the sample consisted of recent family planning clinic patients whose home addresses we could find. It was our hope that the study would extend over several years, so that there could be feedback between the families--with their ongoing experiences, decisions, and problems--and the institution. Hence, the clinic-patient subsample. We supplemented it with people clustered in two contrasting residential areas, which will be described later, who were mostly not family planning clinic users. In the long-term study, we hoped to do network and neighborhood analyses among them. Although our hopes were disappointed, we were able to obtain one-year longitudinal data on many of the families, and these make a considerable contribution to our perception of these families as adaptational systems.

ISFAHAN AS AN ENVIRONMENT

The families that are the subject of this chapter live in one of the major provincial capitals of Iran. With a population of about half a million people, it is the second largest city in the country, and it is growing steadily, due to inmigration (mostly of people from its own provincial hinterland) and to the natural increase of its resident population. Earlier in the twentieth century, migrants were attracted by the opportunities for employment in the several large new textile factories that were built on the southern outskirts of the city. The most recent major job attraction (in the 1960s and early 1970s) has been the construction of a large steel mill (and a new employees' town to go with it) a number of miles southwest of the city. Though Isfahan has its share of modern institutions that depend upon literacy-based skills (banks, hospitals, hotels, over 200 schools, a university, and so forth), it is primarily a manual workers', tradesmen's, and craftsmen's city. It lacks the glamorous and lucrative reputation of Tehran, the national capital. Though Isfahan is the second largest city in Iran, it is a very distant second to Tehran, which has about eight times the population.

The city has (or had in 1971 when last we saw it) a number of important livable features. The residential areas (whether in the old sections of courtyard houses on narrow and crooked alleys or in newer sections with straighter and wider streets) are either within moderate walking distance of shops, institutions, and places of work or are reasonably well served by inexpensive taxis and buses. There are almost no high-rise buildings of any kind, and so there is less congestion of traffic and people than there might otherwise be. Yet the city is compact, with little "sprawl," and it is densely populated. The main thoroughfares are indeed crowded with people and traffic but less massively and seemingly inescapably than in Tehran.

Among foreign scholars and tourists, Isfahan is famous for its architectural and artistic monuments, which have been preserved mostly from the Safavid period, during the latter part of which (1598-1722), Isfahan was the imperial capital. The Maydan (a great rectangular plaza most unusual for a Middle Eastern city), the Shah and Shaykh Lutfullah mosques, various royal pavilions, the Madresseh Chahar Bagh, and the great covered bazaar are among the better known of these monuments. Though they make Isfahan famous and provide aesthetic stimulus for the visitor, we do not know whether they are (except for the nontourist shop portions of the bazaar) of any particular interest to residents of the city such as those depicted in this chapter. One of the husbands in our sample worked in the laundry of the then most expensive tourist hotel in the city, but this is the only obvious instance of a possible direct link between the people we studied and Isfahan as it appears to most foreign outsiders. This man's home was in the squatter settlement that adjoins the air-port where most foreign visitors arrive and depart, though few of them may take any notice of the dusty, buff-colored, brick-walled enclosures of the houses there.

The architecture of this squatter settlement (unlike that of the bidonvilles of North Africa) is not notably different from that of other new residential areas of the city. But the houses are smaller, and the population is denser than in more affluent areas. The houses were built on land to which the builders did not have title, hence the name, Moftabad, meaning "free habitation site."

It is perhaps some indication of the accessibility of public transportation in Isfahan that the clinic-patient group that constitutes most of our sample came from homes scattered over most of the city. None lived in Jolfa, the Armenian Christian quarter (whose inhabitants prefer their own clinics and doctors), and only one came from one of the newer sections of the city, which is notable for the homes of the wealthy and prosperous middle-class people, who would

not be likely to patronize public clinics. With these exceptions, the
clinic sample members came from all over the city. (We do not
know anything about residential distribution of the patients of the
other family planning clinics in Isfahan.) This sample was aug-
mented, as we explained earlier, by a residential cluster in Moftabad
and another, for contrast, in Mahalleh Pa-Manar ("Foot-of-the-
Minaret Quarter"), which is between the shrine of Darb-e Imam and
the Friday Mosque.

HOUSES AND HOUSEHOLDS

Moftabad and Pa-Manar illustrate some of the general characteristics and new-old variations in domestic architecture and arrangements in the non-Westernized, nontourist-oriented parts of the city.
In Pa-Manar, the typical house consists of rooms arranged around
a rectangular courtyard. A crooked or curtained doorway (with a
very heavy door) connects the interior courtyard with the street or
alley; other houses are attached to the nonstreet sides. There are
few, if any, windows, except those that open onto the interior courtyard. This type of house is designed to protect the privacy of its
inhabitants from the potentially hostile exterior; at the same time,
it allows for variegated sociability (for instance, among neighbors)
within. This is the typical traditional or old-style house.
     The newer type of house occurs in Moftabad and in all the
newer sections of Isfahan, which means, for the most part, around
the outer edges of the older parts. Though smaller, shabbier, less
well built, and less well appointed, the Moftabad house is, in principle, the same as the others: a rectangular house (often two-story)
to which is attached a wall that encloses a yard, to which, in turn,
are attached other houses, except on the street side. These, along
with more sumptuous new-style houses, such as some of those along
Abbasabad Street, contrast with old-style houses. However, rich or
poor, new or old, all these Isfahan houses achieve the same effect:
a protected, private-walled enclosure. It is very striking that low-
level aerial photographs, showing contiguous new and old residential
sections of the city, reveal virtually the same texture throughout of
rectangular open spaces interspersed with walls and roofs.[3]
     Most of the houses in our sample were occupied by more than
one household, and therefore we refer to the houses, new and old,
as household compounds. While these compounds provide maximum
protection from the exterior (in sharp contrast to the American
suburban house, with its picture windows opening onto an unfenced
lawn), they allow for great sociability within. The old-style compound, with its separate rooms all opening onto the same courtyard,

can accommodate almost as many households as there are rooms--
those households consisting, normally, of nuclear families. One of
the reasons why Isfahan, which increased 60 percent in population
between 1956 and 1966, did not grow proportionately in its built-up
area is that many of the in-migrants moved into rented quarters in
already occupied compounds.

The old-style house lends itself to greater multiple occupancy
than the new-style house, where two households, one on each floor,
is the most usual multiple arrangement. These tendencies are suggested, in a very crude way, by the fact that in our Pa-Manar subsample, the range of number of households per compound was 1 to 5
and the average per household was 3.2, whereas in Moftabad, the
range was 1 to 3, and the average was 1.5. Yet the overall population density of the Moftabad area was even higher (more than 240
persons per hectare) than it was in the Pa-Manar area. [4]

FAMILIES AND COMPOUNDS

The 174 husband-wife pairs that constitute the core of our
sample live in a total of 140 compounds. Living in many of these
compounds were other people whom we did not interview. However,
we did determine the household composition of all of the people living in these compounds, and therefore, we can describe the compounds' structure. At the outset, we wish to emphasize that this
aggregation of domestic arrangements represents dynamic, changing
processes of interpersonal adjustments. We much prefer this view
to one that presumes fixed "household types," variations from which
are interpreted as being deviations from supposed norms. We are
highly skeptical of the many presumptions that there is an urban-
specific type of family, as opposed to a nonurban family type.

The total population of the 140 compounds is 1,395, giving a
mean compound size of 9.96 persons. The range is from 3 to 31
persons. The mean number of households per compound is 2.05
(range: 1 to 5), and the mean number of persons per household is
4.86 (range: 1 to 19). Further information on the distribution of
households in compounds is found in Table 9.1. [5]

Multiple-household compounds are somewhat more frequent in
our sample than they are in Isfahan as a whole, according to the
1966 census, and the mean number of persons per compound is somewhat higher, but the mean number of persons per household is virtually the same. Later, we will discuss the larger size of the one-
household compounds. We will also discuss the fact that in the one
year that we observed these people, there were changes in 47 of the
140 compounds, involving the moving in and out of individuals, families, and households.

TABLE 9.1: Household and Compound Size, in Isfahan, Iran, 1970-71

| | Number of Households per Compound | | | | | |
	1	2	3	4	5	Total
Frequency of compounds	55	49	18	10	8	140
Percent of compounds	39.29	35.00	12.86	7.14	5.71	100.00
Population of compounds	380	455	221	172	167	1,395
Mean number of persons per household	6.91	4.64	4.09	4.30	4.18	4.86
Mean number of persons per compound	6.91	9.29	12.77	17.20	20.88	9.96

Source: Compiled by the authors.

Following the usage of the Iranian census, with which we wished to have comparable data, we used the definition of a household as "a group of people, presumably relatives, who customarily eat together-- a commensal group." This definition posed problems in a number of cases, such as the case of women who prepare their food together but eat it separately with their respective families, women who eat together when their husbands are absent but not otherwise, and other behavioral patterns that complicate the conception of a domestic commensal group. We had to make some arbitrary decisions in regard to the classification of household arrangements in the compounds that possibly resulted in less emphasis on commensality than it should receive. Our findings also make us aware of the probable existence of women's domestic social systems that have been ignored by earlier research and need to be studied as such.

Of the 85 compounds that contain more than one household, only 32 contain households of which none are related to each other. Most of these are in the compounds with only two households, whereas all of the five-household compounds contain at least two who are related, and in three of them, all five are related. The most common kinship linkage is, as might be expected in this culture--and this approximates a general norm--virilateral. These include married brothers both with and without parents and with and without unmarried siblings of both sexes. However, there are a substantial number of cases that do not fit this general norm. For example, of the 26 two-household compounds where both households are related, nine are uxorilaterally related: married sisters, married daughters and their parents, unmarried siblings, and one case of two married female cousins. In addition, there are a few cases where the compound includes married brothers and married sisters with their respective spouses.[6] Somewhat more indirect linkages that blur the virilateral emphasis are the cousin marriages (41 percent of the core sample couples), which result in other persons in the compound being related to both the husband and the wife. Inheritance of property by women and various arrangements of convenience, necessity, and compatibility account for the considerable divergences from the stereotypic Middle Eastern "norm" of patrilocal extended family residence.

A few examples of moves into and out of these compounds, thus changing their composition, are as follows:

1. In the compound were a husband, his wife and children, and his parents. In the same compound were the husband's mother's sister and her children, who subsequently moved away. The emphasis is matrilateral, because the building was jointly owned by three sisters.

2. In the compound were two married brothers, a married sister, their spouses and children, their parents, and a cousin of the father with his wife and children. One of the married brothers and his wife and children moved out. The women had quarreled continuously (accusations from all sides were recorded), and before the move, the wife had returned to her own parents' house. This move left intact the married brother/married sister combination, which fits neither of the conventional models, that is, the matrilocal or patrilocal extended family.

3. Nuclear family moved out because they had been told to by the owner. They moved into a compound where their daughter's fiance was a tenant.

4. Compound contained four related nuclear families, including married brothers and their noncommensal mother, described by her daughters-in-law as being a troublemaker. One nuclear family moved out, the daughter of another got married and moved away, and an absent brother was expected to return in the near future.

5. A house contained three resident co-owners (all married and with children)--two brothers and an unrelated man. Two other unrelated families were also tenants. One of the brothers sold his share and moved away. The father of the wife of the unrelated co-owner moved in.

6. Compound contained two unrelated nuclear families. One, the tenant, moved out and was replaced by another unrelated family. The structure of this compound remained the same, but the family who departed moved in with the husband's parents and unmarried siblings, thus moving from an independent nuclear family situation to a stem-family situation.

7. Two married brothers and their wives, children, and mother were tenants in a house whose owner also lived in it with

his wife, two unmarried daughters, and a married daughter with her husband and two children. This was a compound in which there was both virilocal and uxorilocal residence. One of the tenant's daughters married and moved away. Then later, all of the tenants moved to a nearby building, which they were apparently buying--thus maintaining the virilocal extended family in a different location. The owners of the original compound were considering accepting some of their own relatives to replace the tenants who had left. [7]

We assume that compounds experience moves and changes of this kind over even longer periods of time. The moves and changes are themselves adaptations, and their occurrence means that individual family members are continually adapting to new and different conditions in their domestic social environments. This is one of the reasons why attempts to relate women's rates of fertility with the types of family in which they are residing at one particular time are based on incorrect premises. Each of their children could well have been conceived under conditions that were different from each other and from conditions at the time of observation. "Family type" is only a relative constant.

HOUSEHOLDS AND FAMILIES

We have already mentioned that most of the compounds contain households that are related to other households in them. The households themselves vary in structure. Further discussion of these varied arrangements, and their concomitance with family adaptations, will be presented later.

The frequencies of the household arrangements among the 174 families that we studied intensively are shown in Table 9.2.

In order to visualize a little more clearly the extent to which the husband-wife pairs live in the same compound with other relatives besides their own children, these categories can be recombined, as shown in Table 9.3.

The great majority of the simple-household married pairs that do not live in the same compound with other relatives, do have daily, frequent, or regular contact with the husband's and/or wife's parents and/or siblings. [8]

Further comments on these people's contacts with relatives will be made later, but here we will mention some of the indications of the intensity of social life with relatives and neighbors in these compounds that were picked up even by the method of periodic interviews (which we used) and which would probably be far more evident in data obtained by protracted participant observation. One woman,

TABLE 9.2: Frequency of Household Arrangements,
in Isfahan, Iran, 1970-71

Household Arrangement	Number	Percent
Simple alone	37	21.3
Simple with nonrelatives	41	23.6
Simple plus noncommensal relatives	47	27.0
Simple plus noncommensal relatives plus nonrelatives	11	6.3
Complex	20	11.5
Complex plus nonrelatives	8	4.6
Complex plus noncommensal relatives	7	4.0
Complex plus noncommensal relatives plus nonrelatives	3	1.7
Total	174	100.0

Source: Compiled by the authors.

TABLE 9.3: Compound Arrangements: Simple Households
without Other Relatives and Households with
Other Relatives, in Isfahan, Iran, 1970-71

Household Arrangement	Number	Percent
Simple alone and simple with nonrelatives	78	44.8
Simple with noncommensal relatives plus complex	96	55.2

Source: Compiled by the authors.

when asked if another woman living in the same compound had become pregnant recently, answered that she did not know because
they had had a quarrel and were not currently on speaking terms,
implying that ordinarily she would have known. A teen-aged daughter, in her mother's presence, denied her mother's statement that
she (the mother) was currently abstaining from intercourse in order
not to become pregnant again. A woman, commenting on her sister-
in-law's fertility, remarked that the other woman and her husband
"go to hammam (the bath) every morning," meaning that they have
intercourse every night. In one of the compounds of five households,

the wives earned some money by shelling pistachio nuts together in
the courtyard, and the only one of them who was practicing contraception was continually being teased by the others on this account.
Frank and bawdy repartee among Middle Eastern women in regard
to sexual behavior has been reported (but not extensively published
as far as we know) by women who have been accepted into informal
groups of them. This kind of behavior undoubtedly is frequent in
household compounds and is an indication of the kinds of family adaptations that take place in them (for example, adaptations to innovations, such as modern contraception, and to interpersonal problems,
such as jealousies between the wives of brothers).

FAMILIES: JOBS AND SCHOOLS

The occupations and educational attainments of the men and
women in our sample reflect some of the change occurring in Isfahan.
About one-third of the men have unskilled, semiskilled, or skilled
work of a sort that was not available a generation or two earlier--
in transportation as drivers, in construction as electricians or weld-
ers, or in modern factories. One-tenth of the women took advantage, after their marriage, of adult literacy classes, which have
only recently become available.

The occupations of the men range from unskilled day laborer
to physician, with the great majority in skilled and semiskilled occupations. They do not fit neatly into a division between "traditional" and "modern," but in Table 9.4, certain "traditional crafts,"
such as weaving, samovar making, and repair, and blockprinting of
cloth (kalamkar) are lumped with tailors, cobblers, and hammam
workers, under the heading "traditional skills," while the new occupations mentioned above are under the heading "factory and modern
skills." The heading "shops" includes those who work in fruit shops,
groceries, bakeries, restaurants, and cloth and china shops. The
sizable portion of illiterate men (41.3 percent) who are employed in
factories and modern skills is noteworthy. Also of interest is the
small percentage (14.3 percent) of illiterate compared to literate
men who are in traditional skills. There are seven men listed as
"professional": secondary school teacher and supervisor, medical
student, physician, and engineer. These are also the only men with
college or professional educations. The "white-collar" jobs include
clerk, typist, and primary school teacher. The first category of
"unskilled and semiskilled" is a catchall, including daily laborers,
cart drivers, and garden farmers.

About a quarter (24.8 percent) of the women earn money, but
most of these (20.2 percent) do so in their own or others' homes,

TABLE 9.4: Men's Occupations, by Education, in Isfahan, Iran, 1970–71

Occupations	None		Little to Six Years		More than Six Years		Total	
	Number	Percent	Number	Percent	Number	Percent	Number	Percent
Unskilled and semiskilled	13	20.6	11	14.3	1	3.3	25	14.7
Traditional skills	9	14.3	19	24.7	1	3.3	29	17.1
Shops	15	23.8	15	19.5	4	13.3	34	20.0
Factory and modern skills	26	41.3	27	35.1	9	30.0	62	36.5
White collar	0	0.0	5	6.5	8	26.7	13	7.6
Professional	0	0.0	0	0.0	7	23.3	7	4.1
Total	63	37.1	77	45.3	30	17.6	170	100.0

Source: Compiled by the authors.

and by far the most frequently reported home occupation is carpet weaving. The eight women (4. 6 percent) whose income-bringing occupations are nondomestic include hospital servant, nurse, and teacher. The remaining three-quarters of the women are occupied with the unpaid work of keeping house and caring for children; some of them sew or knit for their families. There are few exceptions to this total domestic involvement among the nonincome earners. However, one woman speaks of helping her 18-year-old son from time to time in his grocery store; ten women are finding time for adult literacy classes; and two of the 9.3 percent with more than primary school education are continuing their education.

As might be expected with the recent governmental effort to extend educational opportunities, younger men and younger women in our sample are less likely to be illiterate than the older ones. But despite increasing numbers of schools for girls as well as for boys, the discrepancy between the men's and women's rate of illiteracy is still marked, as is evident in Table 9.5.

TABLE 9. 5: Men's and Women's Education, in Isfahan, Iran, 1970-71

Education	Men		Women	
	Number	Percent	Number	Percent
None	65	37. 8	91	52. 6
Little to six years	77	44. 8	66	38. 2
More than six years	30	17. 4	16	9. 2
Total	172	100. 0	173	100. 0

Source: Compiled by the authors.

FERTILITY

Demographic Information

The average number of living children for the couples in our sample is 3.38, with a range from 0 to 9. Breaking the sample into three cohorts according to number of years married, Table 9.6 gives more detail on average ages, number of pregnancies, living children, and ideal number of children. Those married less than 18 years have lived their married years coincidental with the intensification of reforms after the overthrow of Mossadegh. Those

TABLE 9.6: Years Married, by Age, Pregnancies, Living Children, and Ideal Number of Children, in Isfahan, Iran, 1970-71

Years-Married Cohorts		Women's Age		Pregnancies		Living Children		Ideal Number of Children		
Years Married	Number	Mean	Standard Deviation	Mean	Standard Deviation	Mean	Standard Deviation	Number	Mean	Standard Deviation
1-7	64	20.7	3.9	2.4	1.2	1.6	0.8	57	3.2	1.4
8-17	74	26.3	3.6	5.3	2.0	3.6	1.4	64	3.9	1.4
18-31	36	36.4	4.8	9.1	2.7	6.1	1.7	29	3.5	1.4
Total sample	174	26.4	7.0	5.0	3.1	3.4	2.1	150	3.5	1.4

Source: Compiled by the authors.

TABLE 9.7: Household Type, by Years-Married Cohort, in Isfahan, Iran, 1970-71

Years Married	Simple Alone		Simple with Unrelated		Simple with Relatives		Complex		Total	
	Number	Percent	Number	Percent	Number	Percent	Number	Percent	Number	Percent
1-7	8	12.5	15	23.4	22	34.4	19	29.7	64	36.8
8-17	18	24.3	20	27.0	28	37.8	8	10.8	74	42.5
18-31	11	30.6	6	16.7	8	22.2	11	30.6	36	20.7
Total sample	37	21.3	41	23.6	58	33.3	38	21.8	174	100.0

Note: Reject the null hypothesis at .05 level; chi-square = 14.9; df = 6.
Source: Compiled by the authors.

married less than 8 years have had their marriages coincide with
land reform and then the governmental family planning program.

There is a sizable "excess" of children (ideal number minus
actual number) for the oldest cohort, and indeed, little correspondence has been found in much of the world between ideal and actual
number of children at the end of child-rearing years. However, for
contraception to be tried, ideas of spacing and limitation must be
present. We learned that "few" children usually means four or five
rather than more, which, when considering that the women's mean
ideal is 3.5 and the modal choice is four (usually two boys and two
girls), suggests that in their perception they want "few" children.
The frequently expressed ideal of two boys and two girls is given
explicit rationale by some of our respondents: a boy should have a
brother and a girl should have a sister. In cultures where sex segregation is marked, intrasex companionship and support are apparently considered particularly important.

One case that exemplifies parental influence (which will be
discussed further in the next section) and some of the processes of
adjustment in thinking about ideal number of children over the period
of our study, is that of Mrs. 319. She married at 14 and had been
married seven years at the beginning of our study. She had one 5-
year-old son, and condom and pill had been successfully used to delay the second pregnancy, which coincided with our study. She and
her husband and son lived and ate with her parents-in-law (a complex household) with others in the compound. Her mother-in-law
(who had had 11 pregnancies but had only two living children) was
urging her to have many children for fear of losing some. The
mother-in-law was somewhat ambivalent about large numbers of
children, however, because the daughter she had married off at the
age of 9 had given birth every year for five years since she was 12.
Mrs. 319's father-in-law recommended two boys and two girls, so
that each sex would have a sibling of the same sex. Mrs. 319's
ideal number at the second interview was four children, two boys
and two girls. She said that if she should have three sons in a row,
she would not get pregnant any more because the fourth child might
be a girl, and if that happened, she would have to get pregnant a
fifth time in the hopes of providing the girl with a sister. Mrs. 319
had four married sisters, all with children and all using some kind
of contraception.

By the third interview, Mrs. 319 had given birth to a girl.
With a boy and a girl, she now had mixed feelings; her husband
would like another boy and another girl (for the reasons already
mentioned), but she herself felt two children were enough. Her
mother, whom she saw every month, advised her to stop at two.
By the fourth interview (five months later), Mrs. 319 said that her

husband still wanted a male sibling for his son but was not insisting
on a sister for his daughter.

Domestic Social Organization

The living arrangements reflect, to some extent, the number
of years married and the number of living children, as shown in
Table 9.7. Those married less than eight years and having less
than three children are more likely than the next cohort to be living
in "complex households," that is, living and regularly eating with
one or more relatives or related nuclear families. Usually, but not
always, these are the husband's parents and his unmarried siblings.
Those married from 18 to 31 years, on the other hand, are at the
other end of this life-cycle pattern and may have a son's or daughter's spouse living commensally with them. However, families of
this cohort are also likely to be nuclear families, what we call
simple households, living alone in the walled compounds.

Almost four-fifths of the couples live in simple households,
but more than 40 percent of these live in the same compound with
relatives; combined with those in complex households, more than
half of the whole sample live in the same compound with relatives,
as was mentioned earlier.

Most of the relationships within complex households and in
compounds are through the husband, but links to the wife are important too: for 10 percent in complex households, for nearly 25 percent of the households sharing a compound with relatives, and for
15 percent more households where there are relatives of both husband and wife.

Table 9.7 also shows another category of living arrangement:
those in simple households living in the same compound with other,
but unrelated, individuals or families. This is a matter of economic necessity rather than choice--our respondents being either
the tenants or landlords in such arrangements.

Whether, and how much, living arrangements influence fertility, or vice versa, is a matter of considerable interest, and speculation can follow a number of directions. What are the effects of
living in close association with relatives, consanguineal and affinal?
What are the effects, if any, on fertility of feelings of crowdedness
and lack of privacy? Are these feelings more affected by sheer
space and numbers or by personal compatibility? We have no definite answers to these questions, but we can say that more women
than men feel they have too little living space, possibly because the
women are much more confined to the compound than the men and
because they and their children cannot avoid interaction with others

in the compound.[9] Women tend to be least satisfied with their living space when in simple households in compounds with others, whether related, unrelated, or both. This suggests, once again, that such close quarters with relatives, as well as with nonrelatives, are a matter of economic necessity rather than preference. Men also expressed dissatisfaction when in compounds with relatives, but less when the others in the compound were unrelated, suggesting that when husbands are home, they can ignore incompatible nonrelatives, but not incompatible relatives. In a detailed analysis of a subsample of 69 families, we did not find any relationship between feelings of crowdedness and desired fertility, nor is this apparent in the sample as a whole.[10]

Influence of Relatives

What we did find in the subsample was a large presence of relatives, regardless of living arrangements, with daily to weekly contact with one or more relatives of husband or wife, even when they were not living in the same compound. A similar web of kinship, affinal and consanguineal, characterizes the whole sample, as is evident by the fact that two-thirds of the women report frequent, often daily, contact with their own consanguineal relatives. Husbands' mothers, wives' mothers, husbands' brothers' wives, and wives' sisters are the adult relatives the wives see most frequently, judging from living arrangements and from reported contacts. In the more deeply examined subsample of 69, we found examples of both mothers and mothers-in-law whose influences on a wife were in the direction of reduced fertility, as well as the opposite. A number of women report that their mothers want them to have "few" children, while their mothers-in-law want them to have "many." What they do not often report is mothers or mothers-in-law who express no opinion on the subject, and given the living arrangements and frequent contacts, these opinions are part of the ongoing socialization influencing young married women's attitudes about desired fertility. Since the average age at marriage for the whole sample is 15.1 years (standard deviation [sd], 3.5), illiteracy more common than literacy (as reported in Table 9.5), and most young wives' premarital experiences limited to the protected domestic social environment, their chances are slight of becoming acquainted with alternative attitudes, except when there are differences among their relatives. These differences, such as between the mothers and mothers-in-law mentioned above, provide diversity in influences, which may be missing when a woman reports that both her mother and her mother-in-law think "the more children the better."

However, having no more children than can be disciplined
properly is also a frequently expressed preference, a normative
value that was used in a provincewide governmental campaign that
emphasized a limit of two or three children and promoted the pill
and intrauterine device (IUD). The campaign did not, in our opinion,
adequately take notice of these very present relatives, although our
impression is that their opinions with regard to contraceptives are
at least as evident to their daughters and daughters-in-law as are
their opinions with regard to the number of grandchildren they want.

CONTRACEPTION

Most of the men and women in our sample want to limit the
number of children they have. However, they must cope with various serious conflicts about it. One type of conflict has to do with
contraceptives (especially the pill and the IUD), owing to actual difficulties experienced with them and to general fears about their use.
Some give way to their fears and do not continue to use contraceptives of this sort, while others persist in their use in spite of difficulties. The pressures against using contraceptives include generalized pronatalist sentiments, which reinforce the reality that most
women have nothing to do except be mothers and grandmothers at
home. These sentiments are further reinforced by specific rewards,
such as the attention that new mothers receive, the notion that pregnancy cures ills, and the rivalry between women (especially wives
of brothers) in producing children, which is both an assertion and
an insurance of the husband's devotion. In spite of these elements
in their lives, there are, nevertheless, constant struggles and decisions with regard to reproduction.

We have discussed the probable influence of relatives on the
wife's ideal number of children. This influence is also apparent
with regard to contraceptive use and is both positive and negative in
its overall effects. On the one hand, are reports and rumors of
problems and serious illness resulting from the use of the pill and
the IUD, or there is a mother-in-law or mother who thinks prevent-
ing pregnancy is a sin. Some mothers are reported to want their
daughters not to have any more children but are also reported to believe contraception is sinful. On the other hand, there are female
relatives, including mothers and mothers-in-law, who are themselves reported to be successfully practicing contraception.

Although 74 (of 165) of the women, with an average of 2.14
living children, feel their families are incomplete, all but 20 (of 159)
have tried to prevent pregnancy, most reporting that they first tried
some method of prevention for the purpose of delaying the next

pregnancy. The desired space between children is often "until this baby is in school." In the subsample of 69, Mrs. 319 is a rare example of success in achieving a longer spacing between children, which most women want but few have actually achieved. At the fourth and last interview, Mrs. 319 reported that she was using an IUD for contraception, an IUD that she had had inserted shortly after the birth of her second child. The five years between the first and second children had been achieved through the use of condom and pill, so apparently her husband was also willing to take responsibility for contraception, unlike Mr. 319's sister's husband, who was reported to be too selfish to use the condom. Mrs. 319's mother-in-law was reported to be negative about contraceptive use but was ignorant of Mrs. 319's contraception, a fact that caused Mrs. 319 to keep the interviewer at the outer door during the last visit lest her mother-in-law guess her secret.

Multiple Methods and Communication

In this case, a husband and wife were cooperating to control their fertility and to resist the pronatalistic, anticontraception influences of his parents, with whom they lived. The fact that they had tried three different methods of contraception was not unusual, even though their success was. It may be that lack of communication in private, between husband and wife, prevents effective family planning. Certainly, a wife who stops taking the pill because of side effects but does not feel free to ask her husband to be responsible for contraception is likely to find herself pregnant again before she wishes to be.

Another aspect of communication that is important concerns the husband's and wife's desired number of children. In a part of the subsample of 69, husbands' statements agreed with wives' perceptions of husbands' wishes in 35 cases and disagree in 10. How much of the agreement is accidental and how much due to communication, we do not know. We do not have comparable information for the whole sample. We do find that although the average men's ideal number of children is about the same as the women's, the individual correspondence between husbands' and wives' ideals is not very high--a fact that could be accounted for by open disagreement as well as by lack of communication.

Ineffective Use or Method

There are undoubtedly innumerable other reasons besides lack of communication for ineffectiveness in use of contraceptive methods that some can use effectively. Withdrawal, the condom, the pill, and the IUD are all used effectively by some in our sample. For example, Mr. and Mrs. 302 successfully used the condom for many years, limited their children to three, and provided all of them with secondary school educations. Withdrawal has the advantage of being viewed with favor by al-Ghazzali, the Muslim theologian, and of costing nothing. Its effectiveness "has been traditionally underestimated by the medical profession."[11] Nevertheless, there are people in our sample who seem to be ignorant of it, and others who are ineffective in its use. There are also unwanted pregnancies, which are attributed to failure with condom, pill, and IUD. Reuse of condoms and monthly alternation of pill and condom are two kinds of misuse of method reported by respondents.

     Reliance on lactation as a method of contraception is reported by quite a number of women, although one-third of the sample (63) indicate that they do not think nursing is an effective way to prevent pregnancy. Table 9.8 indicates only those who seriously seem to rely on lactation as a means of preventing pregnancy. Since the possibility of its effectiveness, at least for some, is an open question, we have included it as a bona fide method. In addition to the methods of contraception listed in Table 9.8, abortion had been successfully used by 14 women and unsuccessfully by 7 women, with an additional 5 women for whom the information on miscarriage was ambiguous and suggested the possibility, if not the probability, of abortion.

TABLE 9.8:   Contraception: Percentages of Women, by Method of Contraception, in Isfahan, Iran, 1970-71

Method of Contraception	Ever-Used		Using at Last Interview	
	Number	Percent	Number	Percent
Condom	49	28.16	17	9.77
Withdrawal	33	18.97	31	17.82
Nursing*	35	20.11	14	8.05
Abstinence	11	6.32	3	1.72
Pill	60	34.48	50	28.74
IUD	21	12.07	23	13.22
Rhythm	0	0.00	1	0.57

*Excluding 63 women who did not think it effective.
Source: Compiled by the authors.

Initial Use

The information in Table 9.9 shows that a majority of the women first thought about contraception as a means of spacing their children rather than as a means of not having any more. Educational level is related to time of initial contraception: a larger proportion of the literate than the illiterate first tried to prevent pregnancy for the purpose of spacing. Inversely, a larger proportion of the illiterate than the literate waited until they had as many children (or until they had more children than) they thought ideal before first trying to use a method of contraception.

TABLE 9.9: Initial Effort to Practice Contraception, by Number of Children, in Isfahan, Iran, 1971

	Number of Women	Percent of Women	Mean Number of Children	Standard Deviation-- Number of Children
Never tried	20	12.6	2.5	2.1
Before first pregnancy	7	4.4	1.7	0.5
For spacing	82	51.6	2.8	1.5
When actual number equals ideal number	24	15.1	3.7	1.6
When actual number is greater than ideal number	26	16.4	6.0	1.8
Total	159	100.1	3.4	2.1

Source: Compiled by the authors.

AMBIVALENCE AND FAMILY PLANNING

In 1970-71, the Family Planning Program of the Iranian Ministry of Health was providing contraceptive services, largely through the agency of public health out-patient clinics. Publicity, emphasizing greater serenity and well-being in the family with two or three children, rather than more, was widespread. The idea of there being a population problem was presented in some of the textbooks in some secondary school programs. Most of the men and women in our sample were probably at least partly inclined toward such innovations because, as we have said, most of them felt the need to limit the number of their children. However, we have emphasized that on the whole, their actual performance was such that in most cases it failed to meet this particular need.

There are many reasons for this failure, the most inclusive one being that this whole area of life is full of ambivalence, doubt, fear, and conflict. These emotions are, in turn, enmeshed in individuals' adaptations within their families, in families' adaptations to each other, and in families' adaptations to other institutions in the culture. For example, as we have said, individual men and women must cope with the opinions of, and pressures from, various close kinsmen with whom they often have mutually dependent relationships. Sometimes, as we have seen, these influences are contradictory, making the ambivalence and conflict even worse. Families must adapt to pressures from other families to marry their girls as early as possible.

The sources of these pressures are many. One is the deep-seated fear of girls' premarital loss of virginity (or even the slightest indecorousness that might be grounds for rumor), at the root of which may be a heavy dependence on female seclusion for emotional security rather than an excessive concern about sexuality per se. Other reasons have been adduced, and their cumulative effect is such that serious students of the subject doubt that raising the Iranian legal minimum marriage age of females from 15 to 18 would, under present social and economic conditions, be effective in quickly raising the average age at marriage and, correspondingly, reducing high fertility.[12]

The uncertainty of some dependency relationships, which may accentuate emotional security needs, probably has ambivalent effects, as, for example, in pressures to have many children so that at least a few will survive to support their parents in their old age. None of our informants expressed this sequence of motives (widely accepted by population specialists), although many expressed the hope that their children--especially their sons--could and would support them in their old age. Several informants, however, were not hopeful in this regard, and the motivational relevance of the matter must, therefore, be in some doubt. A number of the household arrangements in compounds, and a number of the changes in these arrangements over the period of one year, suggest a variety of ad hoc adaptations in the matter of caring for elderly parents. Our point here--as elsewhere--is to question the reality of logical or consistent norms that seem to be dear to the hearts of policy makers. Even where motivations are explicitly stated, prediction is difficult. For example, Mrs. 204 is unusual in our sample in that she completed her secondary school education (leaving her young son and daughter with her mother-in-law, whom her husband supports in their house) and in that she wants to be a teacher so as not to be dependent on her children in the future. With two children, Mr. and Mrs. 204 nevertheless still want four, two of each sex. But when? At first, Mrs. 204 said not for another ten years, but later, she developed doubts about such a long period between children. Her own parents encourage her to have however many children she wants, but her mother-in-law (who has already taken care of the ones she has) is a maximum pronatalist. Mr. and Mrs. 204 have experimented alternately with the pill and the condom. Will they have more children soon, and if they do, will she be able to absent herself from home to be a teacher?

In their relationships with an institution like the family planning clinic, the families in our sample are faced with a situation in which they are expected to adapt themselves primarily to one contraceptive method (the pill), with secondary interest and help in regard to the IUD and the condom. The often desperate experiments of some of our informants with a wider variety of methods, in order to find an effective one, suggests a considerable deficiency in this aspect of family adaptation. High levels of education are not a guarantee of easy adaptation (as is sometimes assumed on the basis of studies correlating lower parity with higher education). Mr. and Mrs. 110 are both working at middle-class jobs, both having had secondary educations. They have two sons three years apart (not the seven to ten years that they consider preferable). For contraception, they have tried the condom, the pill, the IUD, and coitus interruptus, and she is not happy with any of these methods. Help and guidance of a quality that might be effective is apparently not available to this couple, which is presumably one of the most capable in the entire sample of finding and utilizing such help and guidance.

Success in contraception can be due to a concatenation of essentially unpredictable circumstances. Mr. and Mrs. 428 are both uneducated, and he has the lowly job of shoemaker's assistant. They have the number of children they want (two) after having lost three. She is having no problems with the pill, and all her relatives, as well as her husband, are strongly supportive of her using it. In this case, for reasons that we do not know, the pronatalist pressures are not in evidence. However, in other cases, they may not only be in evidence but also be in force, even where there is an already unusually large number of children. For example, Mrs. 120 has been taking the pill for two and one-half years, experimenting with different kinds because of continued disagreeable side effects. She has nine children, yet her relatives and neighbors are against the pill for various reasons, which reinforce her difficulties with it, at the same time as they recognize her excessive number of children.

In other words, they (including her mother-in-law) are not supportive of her in her contraceptive method and cannot help her in finding a better one. There are other cases like this one that also illustrate the commonly encountered situation where persistence at contraception is begun only long after a large number of children have been produced.

Given the conflicting values, norms, and pressures in the situation, this variety of responses and adaptations is not surprising. Amid the confusing evidence, we do think that it might be demonstrable that the attainment of a certain level of education (at least into secondary school) may increase the probability that the people concerned will have more general competence and confidence and, therefore, may more probably be able to adapt themselves to achieve contraceptive control. We think that cumulative effects may be especially important. This is suggested in the case of Mr. and Mrs. 233. Though married at 15, she finished primary school, and he finished ninth grade (both above the median for women and men in the sample). They live with his parents and unmarried siblings. Though uneducated, Mr. 233's parents saw to it that all four of their children received at least some secondary school education, and one of them is an unmarried woman of 22 who is a nurse. Mr. and Mrs. 233 themselves have four children; they have had some problems with some contraceptives, but have cooperated in experimenting for more satisfactory results, especially with the condom. Neither wants more children, and all of their relatives support them in this. Their high educational aspirations for their children and awareness of the high cost of education are, in this case, linked to their desire to have no more children.

Does the general situation of Mrs. and Mrs. 233 exemplify new norms or a dominant norm for the future? We do not know, but if it does, the factors in it certainly have to be related to changing elements in the culture as experienced by these people in the Isfahan city environment.

ADAPTATIONS TO CHANGE

The members of our sample have experienced two general kinds of change in the Isfahan environment. One of these consists of changes in the city itself, some of these being reflections of changes in the national culture as a whole. The other consists of the changes to which the migrants (mostly of rural origins) have had to adapt in moving to the city.

Changes in Isfahan

A widespread assumption is that in cities like Isfahan, which are undergoing industrialization and "modernization," the environmental changes mean drastic changes for urban residents, as well as for rural migrants to the city. These changes are assumed to involve traumatic adaptations for them. The members of our sample do not, on the whole, seem to have had such extreme experiences, because, we believe, the reality is not as extreme as this kind of reality is generally assumed to be.

In 1940, when many of our informants were yet to be born, Isfahan had an estimated population of 180,000. By 1966, it had grown two and a half times, to 425,000. In the process, the city expanded on the edges, but the center city remained densely populated; no "suburban sprawl" was involved. Throughout this growth period, the textile mills were the major modern industries of the city. New vehicular streets were cut into the old residential areas, but these remained basically intact. In other words, growth did not, as far as we know, mean major dislocation of existing patterns. One major change that did occur was the great increase in the number of schools and a decrease in illiteracy--part of a national policy, of course, and not peculiar to Isfahan. During the latter part of this period, when all of our informants had been born and some were still being raised (namely, between 1956 and 1966), the percentage of literate females in the city increased from 17.4 to 32.9, and the percentage of females over age ten in the city's labor force rose from 7.8 to 9.2.[13]

These are discernible changes, to be sure, but they nevertheless bear out the fact that in the "modernizing" city of Isfahan, the majority of females are still illiterate and their lives are mostly still circumscribed by domestic activities--these reflecting continuing, though modified, traditional norms. Most of the women's access to the mass media of communication is limited to the radio.[14] There may be some changes in internal domestic routines in regard to more children going to and coming from school and more husbands taking buses to work (rather than walking), but these changes do not necessarily mean any modification in the women's seclusion.

Between 1956 and 1966, a "modernization scale score" of Isfahan Province increased from 9.8 to 10.2, this being a measure of factors like males in nonagricultural and manufacturing occupations, proportion of population living in urban places (more than 5,000 population), and percentages of literate males and females over ten years of age.[15] The city of Isfahan, which is the major city of the province, is certainly reflected to a large degree in these provincial figures.

Paydarfar's hypothesis was that as the Iranian provinces' modernization scores increased, their average household sizes would decrease. This hypothesis was based on the widely held idea that modernization causes "the family" to become an isolated nuclear family, with fewer children than families had in the past. His findings did not bear out this hypothesis. The average household size in Isfahan Province (as in most of the others) actually increased, from 4.5 to 4.8. Paydarfar suggests that maybe this was due to the increased fertility ratio, to the rural quality of many city dwellers, to servants being counted as members of households, and to the possibility that modernization in most of the provinces was only in an incipient stage. [16]

We have already shown that the average household size of all of the households in all of the compounds that we studied was also 4.8 (not counting any servants), as was that of the city of Isfahan in 1966. We have also shown what the structural and size components of this figure actually were, in the case of our sample. There is a preponderance of nuclear families, but they are not isolated; indeed, most of them are immersed in complex networks of close-living relatives. This is the continuing basic adaptational family structure in the modernizing city of Isfahan.

The most clear-cut indication of cultural change in Isfahan, as far as our sample is concerned, is the fact that illiteracy is significantly less frequent among the younger people than among the older: 38.2 percent of the women native to Isfahan aged 15 to 24 are illiterate, as opposed to 78.6 percent of the 35- to 47-year-old city natives. Conversely, larger proportions of the younger women have been to elementary school, though very few of them have gone beyond that. A similar trend is present among the men, although it is less marked: 22.6 percent of the 20- to 29-year-old Isfahan-born men are illiterate, as opposed to 31.8 percent of the 30- to 39-year-olds, and 44.4 percent of the 40- to 49-year-olds, and 50 percent of the 50- to 70-year-olds.

Has the independent nuclear family household become increasingly frequent in Isfahan as Isfahan has become modernized? We do not know, but our data do not suggest such a trend among the members of our sample. Dividing the Isfahan-born women into two approximately equal age cohorts (15-24 and 25-47), we found that a substantial majority of the younger cohort (39 out of 55) live either in complex households or in simple households that share the same compound with other relatives. If there is a general trend toward a greater frequency of independent nuclear households, it does not show up among the younger people in our sample. In our sample, it is the older people (who generally have more children) among whom independent nuclear family households are the more frequent.

We think that these findings indicate various stages in household life cycles, wherein many newlyweds live and remain for some years with the extended family of one or the other member of the couple, while independent nuclear households become more frequent with length of marriage, until the first-married children's turn comes to remain, in many cases, with their parents. The variations in household type by age in our sample are, we believe, evidence of cyclic change within the family normative system. They do not, we believe, represent any systemic change through time. If there is any familistic systemic change in Isfahan, we expect that it is incipient and probably limited to upper- and upper-middle-class people, and we did not perceive it in our sample.

Migrants' Adaptations

In assessing the changes to which migrants to Isfahan may have had to adapt, we are hampered by not knowing whether the migrant men and women have any special characteristics that differentiate them from the people they left. A comparison of the migrant men in our sample with census data on the rural areas of an Isfahan shahrestan ("subprovince") suggests that these men in our sample may be better educated than the others. However, the basis of our comparison is dubious, owing to the fact that there were some migrant men who came from outside the shahrestan and others who came from technically "urban" places (more than 5,000 population) in the shahrestan. We have no reason to believe that the migrant wives have any special characteristics as migrants, for they came to Isfahan either as girls with their parents or as wives with their husbands, mostly the latter.

On the whole, we believe that the similarities between the migrants and the city natives in our sample are due to corresponding similarities between the urban and rural subcultures of people of the same general educational and occupational levels. The differences that we do discern between Isfahan natives and the migrants are, we think, reflections of rural-urban differences, the migrants retaining certain tendencies from their premigration lives. However, these differences are matters of degree only. We do not discern any distinctively urban as opposed to distinctively rural patterns, and this lack of polarized distinctions is to be expected in the Middle East,[17] although it contradicts conventional wisdom.

Comparisons between the city natives and the migrants are facilitated by the fact that their average length of marriage is the same (11 years). Further, the average ages of the men and the women are virtually the same: migrant women, 27.68 years (sd, 6.93) and native women, 25.82 years (sd, 7.09); among the migrants, the men are 8.79 years (sd, 3.89) older than their wives, while among the city natives they are 9.95 years (sd, 5.19) older.

With these basic similarities in mind, we have a standard perspective from which to view the other important similarities and the differences in degree.

Similarities between Migrants and Natives

One of the most popular generalizations about urbanization and modernization is that people (especially females) tend to marry later under their influence. Our data do not bear out this generalization. The average age at first marriage of the migrant women was 15.45 years (sd, 2.86), while the average age at first marriage of the city natives was even younger, 14.29 years (sd, 2.61). Whether the difference is significant is a moot question. The standard deviations are such that there is a clear overlap between the two averages. However, examination of marriage age cohorts within each sub-sample shows that the younger marriage age (9-15) is proportion-ately more frequent among the migrants (40.3 percent, as opposed to 25.8 percent). We think that among these people, pressures for the early marriage of females may be greater than among village dwellers, but we certainly could not prove it by means of these figures. What these figures do strongly suggest is that pressures for early marriage are at least as strong among these city dwellers as they are among village and small town dwellers (as represented by the migrants in our sample, most of whom were married before their move to Isfahan). The point is that early marriage of females is part of the culture complex of sex segregation and domestic female seclusion that typifies Middle Eastern culture, rural and urban. Modernization has affected some people in this system (as, for example, our women interviewers, who were all in their 20s, still unmarried, and all university students), but they are a small minority of city dwellers in general.

Considering the fact that they have been married the same length of time, it is noteworthy that the migrant women have had an average of 5.51 pregnancies and the city natives, 4.85. However, the standard deviations are large (3.53 and 2.82, respectively), and the medians are very close: 4.67 and 4.45, respectively. The average prenatal and stillbirth losses are the same (0.82 per mi-grant mother and 0.81 per native mother), and the average live births are, respectively, 4.62 (sd, 2.9) and 3.95 (sd, 2.5) and the medians 4.09 and 3.55. More of the migrant mothers (46 percent, contrasted with 34.3 percent) experienced more infant deaths (0.84

per migrant mother, as opposed to 0.52 per native mother). However, the difference is attributed largely to infant deaths experienced by the migrant mothers before their moves to the city. The ratio of infant deaths to births in the city is virtually the same for migrant and native mothers (0.14 and 0.13, respectively). If stress is a factor in prenatal loss and infant death, and if migrant adaptations in the city are stressful, we would expect those conditions to be reflected in our figures. They do not seem to be, and we believe one reason is that the migrant women have moved from protected domestic environments elsewhere to protected domestic environments in the city.

Differences between Migrants and Natives

The migrant women have somewhat more living children: average 3.57 (sd, 2.05) and median 3.54 versus an average of 3.33 (sd, 2.10) and a median of 2.93. Will they have substantially more by the time they and the city natives cease bearing children? (Migrants married 18 to 31 years have an average of 6.25 living children, as opposed to 6.09 among the city natives.) We do not know for the younger cohorts; the youngest migrant couples (married one to seven years) have an average of 1.50 living children, and the city natives of the same years-married cohort have a very similar average (1.68). There are some small differences between the two sub-samples that may signal future differences in completed family size. The migrant women (and men) are definitely less educated than the city natives.[18] These differences may simply be reflections of the fact that there are more schools for both sexes (but more for males than females) in Iranian cities than in rural areas. The number of schools in rural areas has been increasing, and this is reflected by the fact that more of the younger migrants have some schooling than the older ones. However, the number of migrant women who have tried to continue their educations in the city after marriage is slightly less than that of the city natives who have done likewise (12.7 percent, compared to 13.8 percent). Correlations have been shown in other studies between amount of education and lower fertility, but it seems to be not primary but secondary (or higher) education that really makes the difference, and that is of little consequence as far as our sample is concerned.

The educational statuses of, and the valuation of education by, the migrant and native parents seem to be reflected in the educational activities of their children. For example, of the 7- to 12-year-old sons, 81.4 percent of the migrants' sons are in school, as opposed to 93.6 percent of the natives' sons. There is more

difference among the daughters, with 59 percent of the migrants'
daughters in school and 92.7 percent of the natives' daughters. Of
the 13- to 18-year-old children, 29.4 percent of the migrants' children are still in school, as opposed to 47.3 percent of the natives'
children. Correspondingly more of the migrants' children, boys
and girls, are working, although more of the natives' 13- to 18-year-
old daughters are married.

     Neither the migrants nor the natives, for the most part, are
in a position to capitalize fully on the city's educational opportunities, especially the higher ones, but the natives and their children
seem to have a slight edge, in this regard, over the migrants.
Furthermore, more of the natives express high status aspirations
for their children (for example, 63 percent of natives with regard
to their sons as compared with 50 percent of migrants with regard
to their sons). And while more of the migrants' daughters are actually working (almost entirely at domestic crafts, principally carpet weaving), fewer of the migrant mothers express high-status,
nondomestic occupational aspirations for their daughters: 35 percent, compared to 53.4 percent of the native mothers.

     What precise connections there are between this and fertility
rates, contraceptive practices, and desire for more children we do
not know, but there are some differences between the migrants and
the natives in these matters also. Although the migrants and natives
have very similar average numbers of children, fewer of the migrant couples (63.9 percent) had tried, or were currently using, the
pill and/or IUD, as opposed to 78.4 percent of the native couples.
Fewer of the migrant couples (47.5 percent) had ever used, or were
currently using, the condom and/or coitus interruptus, as compared
with 69.8 percent of the natives. Differences in efforts to practice
contraception also showed up among the women having two to four
children: 20.7 percent of 29 migrant women had never tried contraception, while all 59 of Isfahan native women with two to four
children had tried. Of 20 migrant women with more than four children, 70 percent wanted no more children, as contrasted with 90.5
percent of the same type of women among the natives. The ideal
numbers of children expressed by the migrants was 3.93 and by the
city natives, 3.37. However, the modal preference expressed by
both groups was four children. This is not a statistical abstraction;
as was mentioned earlier, an explicitly stated reason for it as a
preference is that one should have two boys and two girls, for a boy
should have a brother and a girl should have a sister.

     These differences may indicate that there is, in fact, as con-
ventional wisdom takes for granted, something in the urban environment that inclines city dwellers toward "modernity" (that is, more
education, fewer children, and more lucrative jobs). However, we

repeat that the differences between the migrants and the natives are
not very great, and the distinctively "urban" influence of contact
with many different behaviors and values is minimized when women's
lives remain secluded and their education and access to media limited. In any case, an important intervening variable is wealth--it
costs money to become "modern" (Western style), money that almost no one in our sample had. The idea that it is "only a matter
of time" before people in general in cities like Isfahan become
"modern" is, we believe, open to serious question. Even where
wealth en masse is abundant, domestic modernization for many
people does not automatically ensue, as is shown by the case of the
city-state of Kuwait (mentioned at the beginning of this chapter).

We have already discussed the sample as a whole in regard to
its members' involvement with kinsmen. The differences between
the migrants and the natives are generally what one would expect,
and they do not weaken our observations about the whole sample.

Of the eight household-compound arrangements of the whole
sample (see Table 9.2), both the migrants and the city natives are
involved in all, except the one in which complex households live in
the same compound with noncommensal relatives but no unrelated
people (the seventh arrangement listed in Table 9.2). More migrants
(33 percent) are living in simple households with unrelated people in
the compound (the second arrangement listed) than are city natives
(17.6 percent), and this may be due to more migrants than natives
renting their quarters rather than owning them. The obverse of
this (more natives who own their living quarters) may be reflected
in the fact that virilateral links between native nuclear families and
other relatives living in the same compound are slightly more frequent among the natives than among the migrants. Somewhat more
native simple and complex households live with other relatives, and
it is not surprising that natives have more relatives in the city than
migrants do. Twelve migrant households (19 percent) have no relatives in Isfahan, as opposed to only one native (an isolate). Nevertheless, both migrants and natives are immersed in relatives wher-
ever they live: 65 percent of the migrant women and 76.5 percent
of the native women have daily or regular contact with relatives living in the city, and 31.7 percent of the migrant women (as opposed
to 13.7 percent of the natives) have regular contact with relatives
not living in the city. More migrants than natives (45.9 percent
and 35.3 percent, respectively) are married to relatives. Of those
women in our sample who have daughters and about whose preferences we have information, more migrants than natives express the
hope that their daughters will marry relatives (51.2 percent, as opposed to 19.6 percent) and that their sons will do likewise (40.4
percent, as opposed to 20.3 percent).

The attitudes of members in our sample toward the famous Middle Eastern practice of cousin-marriage are highly ambivalent. It may be that the migrants, somewhat less immersed in relatives and possibly somewhat less secure, tend to come down on the positive side (marrying relatives is safe), whereas the natives tend to come down on the negative side (cousin-marriages exacerbate quarrels among relatives because husband-wife quarrels tend to ramify).

CONCLUSION

The adaptational structure of both migrants and the natives remains primarily one of nuclear families that are immersed in complex networks of relatives and in which the roles of women are, for the most part, restricted to the domestic sphere. Whatever variations from these norms there may be, stimulated and facilitated by various modern influences, they are minor in extent. While we cannot predict that they will continue indefinitely to be minor, our findings suggest caution in assuming that urban people, in this culture, are all destined to be transformed by modernization. One macrosystemic change that may take place fairly soon is a great increase in the number of girls attending and graduating from secondary school. This would be made possible by the government's announced plans for providing free secondary education for all. Of course, a massive school-building and teacher training program would have to accompany this plan if it were to attract significant numbers of teen-aged girls and divert them, even temporarily, from the traditional path of early marriage and an early start on the predominant life-style of domestic seclusion.

NOTES

1. Hill, A. G., 1975, pp. 545-47.
2. Gulick, J., and Gulick, M. E., 1974 and 1975.
3. Gulick, J., 1974.
4. Gulick and Gulick, op. cit.
5. Ibid., pp. 445-46.
6. Ibid., pp. 448-50.
7. Ibid., pp. 452-54.
8. Ibid., p. 462.
9. Gulick, J., and Gulick, M. E., forthcoming.
10. Gulick and Gulick, 1974.
11. Segal, S. J., and Tietze, C., 1971, p. 2.

12. Momeni, D. A., 1972.

13. Touba, J. R., 1972, pp. 32-33.

14. Lieberman, S. S., Gillespie, R., and Loghmani, M., 1973, pp. 80-81.

15. Paydarfar, A. A., 1975, pp. 448-51.

16. Ibid., pp. 450-51.

17. Gulick, J., 1969.

18. Gulick, J., and Gulick, M. E., 1976.

10

Parents' Aspirations for Children and Family Planning in Iran

MARY-JO DELVECCHIO GOOD

This chapter argues that the patterns of social stratification and the culture of social status that currently exist in Iranian provincial towns influence parents' aspirations for children and attitudes toward family planning. Recent studies on the economic theory of fertility decline[1] propose that

> populations are divided into social status groups that have different tastes, who may to some degree have different desires for children (but not simply because of an income difference), and who especially see the whole cost structure of their expenditures including expenditures for children, from the viewpoint of vastly different preference structures.[2]

These studies, as well as others,[3] suggest that given the variation in preference structures, children "cost" more for families of higher-status groups, in part because of status-related expenditures on children, such as advanced education. Expenditures on children are linked to status values and to status behavior. Leibenstein feels that the cost of status-related expenditures is one factor that leads to a decline in fertility among higher-status families.[4]

The author would like to thank the Foreign Area Fellowship Program for a field research grant that supported my stay in Iran, 1972-74, and the Pathfinder Fund of Boston for financing the survey. I would also like to thank all those in the Ministry of Health who cooperated in this project.

In countries such as Iran, economic development and the modernization of the occupational structure has led to a burgeoning of positions in the "new middle class" and, thus, to new forms of status hierarchy and status values. As is frequently the case for families of new middle classes in developing societies,[5] Iranian families of the new middle class or status groups express a preference for fewer children than do more traditional or lower class families. Educational and occupational aspirations for children are among the complex factors that lead to a desire for smaller families (as compared to traditional norms) and, increasingly, to concerted efforts at birth control. These aspirations for children may be viewed as status-related values. In Iranian provincial communities, upwardly mobile "modern" families frequently describe their desire for small families in terms of the current financial cost and emotional commitment it takes to raise children for roles in modern Iranian society.[6] Such families are concerned with maximizing their children's opportunities in Iran's changing educational and occupational structure. Acceptable roles for women are also expanding as Iranian society modernizes. Thus, parental aspirations for daughters, which are also status related, have begun to reflect these structural and value changes as well. While parents' aspirations for children are high for all social groups in Iran, differences between status groups of various social ranks do exist.

The following discussion is based on data collected in the provincial town of Maragheh, in East Azarbaijan Iran, during 1972-74.* Field research included participant observation, in-depth interviews, family studies, and a survey on health and family planning. The survey was administered in November 1973. The sample of town women included 313 married respondents of childbearing age chosen from a stratified random household sample. The male sample included 221 married men with wives of childbearing age. The men were interviewed in their place of work rather than at home, where they seldom receive strangers. Three social groups were selected for the male sample--civil servants, including teachers, bazaaris ("shopkeepers, craftsmen, small merchants,"),

---

*In addition to the town sample, 154 women and 84 men were interviewed in three villages in the environs of Maragheh. The village material will not be presented in most of the tables, but it is interesting to note here that the mean income of villagers was higher than that of workers in the town. And on a number of other measures, villagers appeared on the average to have higher social positions than did urban workers.

and workers.* Although the male sample does not represent all the social groups of Maragheh, it does represent the three major occupational and status groups of the town. The social categories presented in the tables are culturally distinctive status groups that are recognized by the town's inhabitants. [7]

Orientations toward family life and family goals in provincial Iranian towns have been influenced in their formulation by the emergence of a dual pattern of stratification. This dualistic hierarchical system has emerged in provincial Iranian communities in the twentieth century and is a result of the imposition of a new class and status system upon the traditional patrimonial and Islamic hierarchical system that prevailed in the previous century. [8] The development of this new system of class and status has been linked to transformations in the economic, political, and cultural spheres, which have been closely related to the changing relationship between local provincial towns and the central government.

Among these changes are (1) the development of a modernized economic system that is a mixture of state and private capitalism; (2) the increasing centralization of authority through the expansion and modernization of the state civilian and military bureaucracies; and (3) the differentiation, and in the spheres of education and law, the secularization, of cultural institutions. The emergence of the new class and status hierarchical system has not destroyed or replaced the traditional pattern of class and status in provincial Iranian towns, such as Maragheh. Rather, each hierarchical system appears to penetrate the other, and due to the creation of a new class and status system, the character of the traditional pattern of stratification has taken on new cultural meanings and new structural roles in the contemporary era.

The implications of these changes in the pattern of stratification, particularly those changes in the occupational and mobility structures, are reflected in the aspirations that parents hold for their children, and less directly, in orientations of attitudes and practices related to family planning. This chapter explores these aspects of aspirations for children and orientations toward family planning in the context of the broader patterns of social stratification in a community in northwestern Iran.

Maragheh, once the Mongolian capital (thirteenth century), is located in northwest Iran. Its population, predominantly Azarbaijani

---

*In spite of the small numbers of males who fall into the category of lower civil servant, the distinction has been maintained for comparability with the women's sample.

Turkish, numbers approximately 64,000. The town is a provincial capital and has long been an administrative and agricultural center. Although Maragheh is located in a geographic cul-de-sac, which has limited its industrial development and isolated it from some of the modern influences of the capital of Tehran and other metropolitan industrial centers, the patterns of social stratification and family life do not differ greatly from other provincial towns of similar size. The structure of the stratification hierarchy in Maragheh can be envisioned as a pyramid, with vertical as well as horizontal divisions. (See Figure 10.1.)

FIGURE 10.1: Stratification in Maragheh, Iran

	OLD		NEW
Outside		=	
Maragheh	Old Aristocracy	=	Industrialists
(Tehran,	Elite Families	=	Top-Level Industrial-
Tabriz)		=	Bureaucratic Managers
		=	Top Professionals
		=	Intellectuals
Within		=	
Maragheh		=	
		=	
UPPER CLASS	ELITE FAMILIES	=	Professional/
	Ex-landlords	=	Managerial Families
	Large Merchants in	=	
	Wholesale Trade	=	
		=	
	Families of	=	White Collar Families
MIDDLE	Bazaaris (full range)	=	Teachers
CLASS	Most Religious Functionaries	=	Bureaucrats
		=	Clerks
		=	Security Services
LOWER	Lower Craftspeople, Service	=	
CLASS	Workers, Porters, Domestics,	=	Unskilled Factory
	Construction Laborers	=	Workers (only outside
		=	Maragheh)

Class distinctions are vertical. Status group distinctions are vertical and horizontal.

The vertical line divides the pyramid between "old" and "new" status groups. The older groups have had a long historical existence that predates the Pahlavi dynasty. The newer status groups have emerged with, and are linked to, the development of occupational changes in the society, as well as to changes in the cultural systems that have continued through the reigns of the two Pahlavi shahs (1925 to present). The horizontal lines divide the pyramid according to class or to relative inequality. At the top of the hierarchy are the "old" upper classes, the ex-landlord and merchant families who represent a status group of long standing. The bazaar craftsmen and shopkeepers and the religious functionaries are next in the hierarchy, followed by lower craftspeople and laborers. Of the newer status groups, the professional-managerial group is at the top, followed by bureaucrats, teachers, and lower civil servants. Life-style distinctions in Maragheh tend to follow these broad status group lines, especially for the men of the town. The pyramid, as presented here and as described by members of the community, is a result of inequalities in wealth, power, influence, and prestige. The distinction between the "old" and "new" status groups refer to differences in the cultural mode of these groups, in their use of status symbols in the presentation of the self or one's family, and in their place within the occupational hierarchy, which is in a state of flux and change. (See Tables 10.1 and 10.2 for data on income and education.)

PARENTS' ASPIRATIONS FOR CHILDREN AND CHANGES IN SOCIAL STRATIFICATION

Governmental policies of rationalization and modernization under the Pahlavi shahs have played a considerable role in the creation of the "new" status groups in the social hierarchy in provincial Iran. At the most general level, the expansion of "modern" bureaucratic, industrial, and financial institutions has led to the emergence of new occupational roles, which include middle-level and professional positions. These roles require an educated population; thus, the educational system, which has been under the control of the central government, provided the primary channels for mobility into modern occupations and, therefore, into the new status groups. Clearly, governmental policies concerning educational access affect the opportunities for mobility into the modern sector, as do the policies that result in the expansion of government-related positions in the bureaucracies and state-owned or -financed industries. New occupational roles tend to be more highly valued than traditional positions of similar economic rank due to the financial

TABLE 10.1: Income Distribution, by Social Group, in Maragheh, Iran, 1972-73[a] (in U.S. dollars)

Social Group	Mean Family Income	Mean per Capita Income[b]
Traditional elite (women only)	$7,300	$1,180
Professionals (women only)	5,750	1,100
High bazaar	3,100	500
High civil servants, teachers	2,920	565
Middle bazaar	1,630	270
Low civil servants, low military	1,600	280
Low bazaar	620	103
Workers	570	102

[a]Wealth is not included and would greatly inflate the differences between the traditional elite and the rest of the sample. High bazaar, professionals, and some civil servants also have additional sources of income from garden and urban properties. There is a tendency for respondents engaged in business to underreport income.

[b]The per capita income figure for Iran in 1972 was $571. In 1974, due to vast increases in oil revenues, per capita income increased to $1,258. In 1975, there was a decrease due to loss of oil revenues (down $2 billion).

Source: Compiled by the author.

TABLE 10.2: Mean Years of Education, by Social Group and Sex, in Maragheh, Iran, 1972-74

Social Group	Women		Men	
	Self	Spouse	Self	Spouse
Professional, high civil servant	7.8	12.6	11.9	6.6
Merchant, high bazaar	2.9	5.5	5.3	2.4
Lower civil servant, military	2.9	7.0	7.4	3.1
Middle and low bazaar	1.9	3.2	2.5	0.9
Workers	0.2	1.1	0.7	0.1

Source: Compiled by the author.

security of salaried bureaucratic positions, as well as the additional
prestige that accompanies modern educational attainment and employment in institutions of state authority. Thus, at this most general level, governmental policy influences families' orientations to
the occupational hierarchy, as well as their social class-status positions and the potential opportunities for their children's social
mobility. Thus, a family's aspirations for its children are reflections of changes in the social hierarchy, as well as reflections of
opportunity and mobility channels. It is also evident that occupational and educational aspirations are often inappropriately optimistic and must be evaluated as desirable rather than as realizable goals.

While the impact of long-term and general governmental policies on the stratification system indirectly contribute to the formulation of parents' aspirations for children, governmental policies in
the area of family planning contribute in a more specific way to the
formulation of attitudes and practices affecting family size and birth
control. But broader changes in patterns of stratification provide
the background within which orientations toward family planning are
structured.

Aspirations for Children

The very high aspirations that parents from all social groups
hold for their children is a reflection of the changes in the educational system and occupational hierarchy, as well as in the prestige
rankings of modern and traditional occupations. (See Tables 10.3-
10.6.)

In the survey, questions on parents' occupational aspirations
for children were open ended; they were later coded so that no occupation would inadvertently be left out. The survey responses were
remarkable in that the traditional high-prestige occupations, such as
wholesale merchants (tajirs), religious scholars (alam), and landlords (arbabs) were never mentioned as occupational options for sons.
And few respondents mentioned the traditional middle-class occupations in trade, crafts, or agriculture as occupational aspirations for
sons (of male respondents, 3 percent of teachers and civil servants,
7 percent of bazaaris, and 20 percent of the workers mentioned a
traditional middle-class occupation; women mentioned these occupations even less often). Yet, there is variation in occupational aspirations across social groups and sex. Each groups' aspirations for
their children appears to be modified by the social position of the
respondents' families. Thus, the majority of teachers and civil
servants (males) hoped to see their sons enter professional occupations (62 percent), whereas workers would be pleased if their sons

TABLE 10.3: Mothers' Occupational Aspirations for Sons, in Maragheh, Iran, 1972–74 (percent)

Occupational Aspirations	Social Group						
	Professional, High Civil Servants	Merchants, High Bazaar	Low Civil Servants	Middle and Low Bazaar	Workers	Total	Number
Professional*	86	73	60	45	24	52	145
Teacher	4	15	14	31	41	25	68
Civil servant	2	--	14	14	8	9	25
Military	2	8	9	6	11	7	20
Bazaar (crafts, trade)	--	--	5	--	6	2	6
Laborer	--	--	--	--	--	--	--
Don't know	6	4	--	4	10	5	14
Total	100	100	102	100	100	100	278
Number	49	26	44	96	63	278	--

χ^2 significance = < .001.

*Professional occupations mentioned most often by parents of both sexes for sons and daughters were doctors and engineers, followed by judges.

†Column 3 slightly over 100 due to rounding.

Source: Compiled by the author.

TABLE 10.4: Fathers' Occupational Aspirations for Sons, in Maragheh, Iran, 1972-74 (percent)

Occupational Aspirations	Social Group						
	High Civil Servant*	High Bazaar	Low Civil Servant	Middle and Low Bazaar	Workers	Total	Number
Professional	62	50	33	34	17	37	79
Teacher	2	6	33	32	35	23	48
Civil servant	12	25	33	21	27	21	45
Military	3	--	--	--	--	1	2
Bazaar (crafts, trade)	3	6	--	7	18	9	20
Laborer	--	--	--	--	1	.5	1
Don't know	18	13	--	5	1	8	17
Total	100	100	99	99	99	100	212
Number	60	16	9	56	71	212	--

χ^2 significance = $<.001$.

*Most teachers in this civil servant group did not want their sons to be teachers. The profession is often viewed as a step to the higher professions.

Source: Compiled by the author.

TABLE 10.5: Mothers' Occupational Aspirations for Daughters, in Maragheh, Iran, 1972-74 (percent)

Occupational Aspirations	Social Group						
	Professional, High Civil Servants	Merchants, High Bazaar	Low Civil Servant	Middle and Low Bazaar	Workers	Total	Number
Professional	46	16	29	9	3	18	48
Teacher, trained midwife	38	52	48	49	36	44	116
Civil servant	4	--	5	6	3	4	11
Crafts (seamstress, and so forth)	--	4	5	9	29	11	28
Housewife	10	28	14	26	26	21	56
Don't know	2	--	--	2	2	2	4
Total	100	100	101*	101*	99*	100	263
Number	48	25	42	90	58	263	--

χ^2 significance = $< .001$.

*Columns 3, 4, and 5 slightly different from 100 due to rounding.

Source: Compiled by the author.

TABLE 10.6: Fathers' Occupational Aspirations for Daughters, in Maragheh, Iran, 1972-74 (percent)

Occupational Aspirations	Social Group						
	High Civil Servants	High Bazaar	Low Civil Servant	Middle and Low Bazaar	Workers	Total	Number
Professional	32	29	33	9	--	16	31
Teacher, trained midwife	20	14	22	28	22	23	44
Civil servant	8	7	22	17	10	12	23
Crafts (seamstress, and so forth)	3	--	--	4	10	5	10
Housewife	20	43	22	38	54	37	72
Don't know	17	7	--	4	3	8	15
Total	100	100	99	100	99	101	195
Number	60	14	9	53	59	195	--

x^2 significance = $< .001$.
Source: Compiled by the author.

entered the salaried occupations as teachers or civil servants (62 percent). Few men viewed the military or security occupations as desirable options in spite of the high salaries (higher than equivalent ranks in the civilian bureaucracy) that accompany these positions. Women were even more hopeful that their sons would attain professional careers than were the male respondents of similar social groups.* But as with the men, the majority of working-class women (60 percent) had hopes that their sons would enter their salaried occupations or the civilian or military bureaucracy. The middle-level social groups also aspired to the salaried or professional occupations. Women from these groups expressed higher hopes for their sons' occupational attainments than did male respondents from similar social backgrounds.

These aspirations for sons are optimistic "hopes," and perhaps the male respondents tend to be more "realistic" than the female counterparts. Yet, these occupational aspirations do reflect patterns of social mobility that occur within the society as a whole (albeit with less frequency than the aspiring parents would wish). Among our respondents from the town sample, 32 percent had higher-ranking occupations (personally or their spouses) than did their fathers. And of those, 68 percent had entered modern occupations. Further, the majority of teachers and civil servants in the sample came from middle-class bazaar families (58 percent civil servants and 63 percent low civil servants), whereas professionals came primarily from the traditional elite. Thus, the change in occupational opportunities and structure is part of the direct and indirect experiences of the sampled population.

The changing role of women in the occupational structure of provincial Iranian towns is also reflected in our respondents' occupational aspirations for daughters. Of our total town sample, only 25 (4.7 percent) women, either respondents or spouses, were employed outside the home in a modern occupation, such as teaching or midwifery. Although opportunities for employment in the modern occupational sector have expanded much less rapidly for women than for men in provincial Iran, women are beginning to take on roles in education and health, and, to a lesser extent, in clerical

---

*The percentage differences for professional and high civil service women were negligible; thus, we have combined these two categories in the tables where there was no significant difference; women from the traditional elite (tajirs-merchants) and high bazaar were also combined. Thus, the professional group of women numbers 12; for tajirs, it numbers 6.

positions in the state bureaucracy, which bring them into the modern sphere. And women have begun to note the benefits of financial
independence that accompany employment in the bureaucracy or
professions.* This may be one of the reasons why a much higher
percentage of women hope to see their daughters in one of the
salaried occupations than do the male respondents of similar social
positions. (See Tables 10.5 and 10.6.) In the total town sample,
only 21 percent of the women, as compared to 37 percent of the
men, wanted their daughters to be primarily housewives. However,
there was a preference of women in the town to see their daughters
in those occupations that kept them away from extensive interaction
in the male public sphere (teachers in girls' schools, midwives),
whereas the male respondents were almost equally split in regard
to this issue: 44 percent of the town women wanted their daughters
to be teachers or midwives, whereas 23 percent of the town men
chose teaching or midwifery, as compared to 28 percent who chose
professional or civil service occupations, which would bring their
daughters more directly into contact with the public and predominantly male/occupational world.

The variation between occupational aspirations for sons and
for daughters is indicative of the limitations in "acceptable" occupational roles for females in provincial Iranian society. Even
among the most-educated and most modern respondents (professional
and high civil servant status groups), stated aspirations for professional occupations for daughters was approximately half that for
sons.† Regardless of class or status position, teaching and midwifery appear to be the most acceptable roles for women in the
modern occupational sector. Attitudes also differ between "modern"

---

*Women often worry about their financial dependency on hus-
bands, fathers, and sons. Discussions about marriage contracts,
divorce compensation, and sources of income is common. Women
also look upon their "freer" working sisters as gaining independence
from men because of their own personal income. One old woman who
was dependent upon her son for funds and livelihood enviously ex-
claimed to a working friend that she had become "independent," like
a "man." Separate incomes from property or jobs are jealously
guarded by women.

†Of all those in our sample who mentioned an occupation in the
public sphere for their daughters (67 percent women, 50 percent
men), 73 percent of the women and 68 percent of the men mentioned
the middle-level occupations; whereas 55 percent of the town women
chose a professional occupation for their sons, as did 48 percent of
the town men.

and "traditional" status groups of similar class positions. When
middle-class respondents are grouped by "modern" (civil servants,
teachers) and "traditional" (bazaar) categories, we find that a
higher percentage of the more modern status group of women (89
percent), and to a lesser extent men (60 percent), hope to see their
daughters in modern roles than do the more traditional status group
of bazaaris (64 percent women, 54 percent men). Yet, as previously noted, few men and women from either the modern or traditional middle class hoped their sons would fulfill traditional occupational roles. However, as in the case of aspirations for sons, a
higher percentage of women and men from the more modern status
groups hoped to see their daughters in professional occupations
than did women and men from the bazaar groups of similar class
position.

Educational aspirations for sons and daughters similarly illustrate the tendency for men and women of all social groups to
desire higher attainments for sons than for daughters. University
education is more highly valued for sons, whereas a high school
education or less is more acceptable for daughters. As with
parents' occupational aspirations, the degree of desired educational
attainment varies with class and status position of the respondents.
However, whereas more women than men expressed desires to see
their daughters in higher-status and modern occupational roles,
there was less difference across sex in expressions of educational
aspirations for daughters. And among the high bazaar and lower
civil servant status groups, a higher percentage of men wanted
their daughters to acquire a university education than did women
from the sample groups: 62 percent of the high bazaar men, as
opposed to 52 percent of the women, wanted their daughters to have
university education; 55 percent of the lower civil servant men, as
compared to 35 percent of the lower civil servant women, wanted
their daughters to have some university training. Men from the
middle bazaar group tend to be the most conservative in their attitudes toward the "proper" role for women. Few wanted their
daughters to have university training.

Education is the primary channel of mobility into the modern
occupational hierarchy and into higher class and status positions.
The parents' educational aspirations for sons and daughters reflect
their recognition of the importance of education as a mobility channel. Of course, the stated educational aspirations are similar to
the stated occupational aspirations in their excessive optimism.
Although institutions of higher education are rapidly expanding in
Iran, the percentage of high school graduates admitted to these
institutions, especially to the prestigious four-year universities,

remains small.* Yet, it is not unrealistic for the provincial urban
middle classes to expect their children to have high school training,
although for the working class, the cost of high school in direct out-
lays for books and tuition and in lost family income often proves
prohibitive to further education. However, a high school education
is sufficient to channel students into the middle-level bureaucratic
positions, including teaching in the literacy corps village schools
and, eventually, in urban primary schools.† Special night school
courses at the university enable such graduates to earn diplomas
in education, which qualifies them for higher positions. Thus,
families' aspirations for children that go beyond their social position
of origin are not altogether unreasonable. And as in the case of
occupational aspirations, our respondents' expressed educational
aspirations for children are influenced by changes in educational
opportunities due to the expansion of local and regional institutions.

"Why Have Two or Three Children? To Raise and Educate Them Better"

Although there is a considerable gap between expressed aspirations for the future of one's children and a family's behavior with
regard to securing that future, the central government does attempt
to play on those aspirations to further its family planning goals.
Many families, especially the urban, the young, and the educated,
are quite cognizant of the relationship between smaller families and
educational and occupational attainments of their children. It is not
only the educated and often more modern social groups who are
aware of this relationship; a large proportion of our entire sample
(68 percent men and women from all social groups) remarked that
couples who have only two or three children do so to "better raise
and educate their children," or "to secure a better future for their
children" (15 percent). And 39 percent noted that fewer children
would also allow a family to have a more comfortable material life.[9]

---

*Although institutions of higher education have been rapidly
expanding since the 1960s, only 17 percent of all applicants were
admitted in 1971.

†Numerous teachers in the high schools have only teaching
diplomas. But there has been a tendency to upgrade requirements
for high school teachers (to get either associate or university degrees). In Maragheh, 30 percent of high school teachers have university degrees.

The central government's family planning communication programs attempt to appeal to, and to foster, such attitudes and sentiments among families in the hope that it will reduce family size and population growth. The program is also geared to encourage families to associate the image of a family that has "made it" into the modern occupational sector and into modern status groups with the ideal of a successful family. Films and posters which advertise that "two to three children [and, more recently, only two children] are better" contrast large and small families. The large families are shown eating on the floor, in barren surroundings of shanty mud houses, dressed in ragged and traditional-style pajamas.* The mothers are veiled; the fathers unshaven—clearly, poor laborers. In contrast, the small families with two children each are portrayed as living in modern houses, with TVs, telephones, and refrigerators. The family eats at a modern table; the children, mother, and father are dressed in bright Western clothing (although the mother may be modestly scarved). The father sets off to work in the modern sector, often in his own car. The message may not be directly influential, but it is clearly made. And such films and posters reflect the aspirations, fanciful or not, of many Iranian families—to attain through one's children entrance into the modern occupational sector, into the social hierarchy of the educated and the salaried.

However, the general cultural and social milieu of provincial town life within which families bear and raise children also encourages large families of four or more children. Thus, there is considerable ambivalence over ideal or desirable family size, the use of family planning, and the "real" relationship between one's children's success and small families. And while many people feel that children in small families could have greater opportunities for mobility, they are also aware that the old, rich families of merchants and landlords had numerous children, many of whom became "successful" professionals—and even famous men.

These findings correspond to the "KAP-gap" between ideal family size stated in Knowledge, Attitude, and Practice surveys and actual birth control practices and real family size, which continues to bedevil researchers working in developing countries.[10] Yet, the

---

*Most families of all social classes eat on the floor around the sofra ("oilcloth"). But status seekers and upper class families do eat around tables, at least when they have guests. Similarly, the urban middle class continues to relax in pajamas (though not ragged ones) while at home. It is ironic that these films should present these two forms of behavior as "backward" or lower class.

persistence of differences between stated ideals, real live births, and family planning behavior that appears in most KAP studies does not render the studies totally invalid. Rather, a continuing gap between ideal and real norms for family size must be expected for most social groups in developing societies. Berelson finds the KAP instruments of administrative value in planning family programs. Although standard KAP instruments are limited in their ability to predict behavior, KAP data can convey general information about changing trends in attitudes toward family formation and contraception, especially when interpreted within the cultural context of a particular society under study.[11]

The ambivalence over desired family size, which is illustrated in our own data (see Table 10.7) is indicative of the KAP-gap problem. The various mean numbers of desirable children presented in the tables reflect several conflicting cultural trends. The traditional family size norms in Iran are quite high. The Iranian government is trying to alter these norms through its family planning communications campaign. In addition to the government's efforts, the lower family-size norms of younger "modern" upper- and upper-middle-class families have a trickle effect on the attitudes of the majority of the urban population. Thus, our middle- and lower-class respondents were frequently aware that the preferred family size norm of "modern" families and of the government was two or three children. This awareness was expressed in some of the responses given to interviewers. Thus, the gap between reported "ideal" family size and real desired or completed family size in part reflects these influences, which are external to the traditional situation of many middle- and lower-class families. Similarly, reported usage of contraceptive methods may be inflated, particularly of the women in the sample, because of the popularization of family planning practices.[12]

There was considerable variation in responses to several questions that attempted to elicit desirable family size norms for different status groups (see Table 10.7). In Table 10.7, the mean for each social group is given for the number of live children, additional children desired, and a summation of the two to reach a "realistic" ideal. The mean on three measures of attitudes on ideal family size are also included, and the highest mean for ideal number of children will be used as the basis of discussion and comparison.*

_____

*The first question on ideal family size came early in the interview; respondents were asked how many children they would want if they were newly married and planning a family. The second

TABLE 10.7: Desired Family Size: Social Groups, by Mean Number of Children in Real and Ideal Categories, in Maragheh, Iran, 1972-74

Social Group	Number in Each Social Group	Mean Number of Children					
		Live Children	More Desired	Real Desired	Ideal if All Live	Ideal if Start Anew	Ideal for Daughter
Town Women							
Professional, high civil servants*	57	2.2	.8	3.0	2.7	2.4	2.2
Merchant, high bazaar	16	4.0	.2	4.2	3.5	2.9	2.7
Low civil servant, military	49	3.2	.8	4.0	3.1	3.0	2.7
Middle bazaar	107	3.6	.6	4.2	3.4	2.9	2.5
Workers	74	3.4	1.0	4.4	3.8	3.4	3.0
Town Men							
High civil servant	62	2.6	.8	3.4	3.1	2.9	2.3
High bazaar	16	3.1	.6	3.7	2.9	2.6	2.3
Low civil servant	9	3.7	.7	4.4	3.6	3.9	2.6
Middle bazaar	60	3.1	1.0	4.1	3.6	3.1	3.0
Worker	74	2.9	1.2	4.1	4.3	3.6	3.7

*The inclusion of women from professional families (12) does not alter the overall means of this group.

Source: Compiled by the author.

Among town women, desired family size (number of children) varies with the class and status position of the respondents. Whereas the economic position of the traditional status groups is somewhat higher than that of the modern status groups of similar class position, the more modern status groups have lower means for "ideal" and "real" desired numbers of children. Thus, status, as well as class position, is an important factor affecting desired family size. Age is also a factor in the variation; women from the high bazaar social group tended to be older (mean age equaled 34) than the rest of the town women (mean age equaled 30), and they also had a higher ideal mean than women from the middle bazaar. The pattern for town men similarly varied with class position. Due to the small number of lower civil servants, it is difficult to interpret the variation within class due to status differences. But Table 10.7 does suggest that class differences are more important factors in affecting desired family size for men than women. In expressions of "ideal" number of desired children, men claim to want more children than do women from similar social groups, with the exception of the high bazaaris. However, differences in the mean "real" number of desired children are less clear cut, as men from the bazaar and working groups claim to want fewer children than do women of similar social groups.

The ambivalence regarding family size in the tables reflects the ambivalence that many of our acquaintances, friends, and informants (from participant observation and case data) felt about family size. While most of the younger, upwardly mobile professional and teachers' families were fairly clear about their desire to limit their children to two or three, and took measures to insure that such would be the case,* people who were less well educated, of lower social positions, less mobile, or a bit older had mixed feelings over the number of children they wanted. While many felt that they should not have "too many" because of the financial and emotional burdens, "too many" was defined within a social and

----

question came much later within socioeconomic status and cultural practice questions. We asked respondents how many children they would like if all were to live. This response tended to be a bit higher than the first one. For the third measure, we asked people with daughters how many children they would like their daughters to have after marriage.

*Abortion was a fairly popular method among the well educated and well-to-do. Most of these women were highly distrustful of the pill, but were less fearful of abortion. Although it is technically illegal, many are performed.

cultural context that legitimated rather large families. Thus, the
"ideal" number of children for many informants was often an expression of a newly popularized attitude (due to governmental propaganda and changing attitudes among the upper middle classes) and
not an expression of ideal behavior or norms. It is possible to interpret statements of ideal family size as illustrative of nascent
changes in attitudes toward the family unit. The clearest example
of this in the table, which is also supported by case data, is the
response to how many children one desires for one's daughter. The
means for each social group are all less than what the respondents
expressed for themselves. In the case studies (as in the comments
of interviewees), many people speculated that their daughters would
be living quite different lives from their own, in different social circumstances that would be more conducive to having smaller families.

The social milieu within which attitudes toward family size
are formed today is not as supportive of small families as our informants feel the future will be. In the total sample, a mean of
4.8 children was considered to be "too many" for a couple, yet
women perceived the average number of children born to women in
their own neighborhood as between 4.7, for higher civil servants,
and 5.8 for wives of workers. Men had a lower perception of
children born to their neighbors. High civil servant men felt that
the average was 3.6 children per family, and workers speculated
that the average was 5.0 per family. But the men were also less
involved in the neighborhood information networks.

Mothers and mothers-in-law are also seen as encouraging
fairly large families. The mean number of children desired by the
mothers of our female respondents for the respondents ranged from
3.2 for high civil servants' wives to 4.6 for wives of workers.
Mothers-in-law were perceived as wanting their daughters-in-law
to have even more children, with a range of 3.7 children for high
civil servant wives to 4.9 for wives of workers. The mothers of
our respondents had high numbers of children as well. For the
entire sample, the mothers bore an average of 6.6 children, of
whom 4.9 were still alive; mothers-in-law were reported as having a mean number of 6.7 births, of which 4.8 were still alive.

An additional complication for families concerned with limiting the number of children is the need for sons to support parents,
especially widowed mothers, in old age. The state has no social
welfare program for the aged, and this responsibility has traditionally fallen on the sons in the family. Seventy-eight percent of
town men and women felt that sons were necessary for parents in
their older years; the mean for each social group (except for professional and high civil servant and high bazaar women) was over
two, although for each social group the mean "ideal number of boys"
was considerably less than the mean number of sons necessary for

old age support. An even greater number of respondents (90 percent women, 84 percent men) readily admitted that they expected
their children to support them in old age, although the most modern
group of civil servants and professionals (60 percent women and 50
percent men) were less inclined to express that need.

The factors that encourage large families (as well as numerous others that we do not have space to discuss), contribute to the
formation of attitudes and behavior with regard to family planning
and cannot be completely balanced by governmental programs nor
by educational and occupational aspirations for children, which many
families realize are unrealistically high.

VARIATIONS IN FAMILY PLANNING USAGE
AND SOCIAL POSITION

The practice of family planning, when it does occur, takes
place within this milieu of ambivalence, with social and cultural
factors encouraging and discouraging its use. As with other attitudes that we discussed above, the use of contraceptives or birth
control techniques varies with social class and status (see Table
10.8). In our discussions with informants, we found that men,
particularly those from more traditional social groups, were reluctant to discuss contraceptive practices in public, especially with
other men. The table (Table 10.8) on family planning practice reflects this reluctance, and women, who talk about contraception
continuously in female company, are more reliable reporters of
usage behavior (although there may be some inflation in their
answers due to interviewer affects). Nevertheless, even when the
variation in reporting by sex is considered, we find that 57 percent
of the town women and 35 percent of the town men claimed to be
using some form of contraception at the time of the interview (pills,
condoms, withdrawal). Of these users, 52 percent of the women
and 57 percent of the men claimed to be using "the pill" (some
used several methods); 41 percent of the women and 12 percent of
the men claimed to use withdrawal (much underreported for men),*

_____

*Gillespie had similar difficulties with his respondents in the
Isfahan Province survey. Only 39 percent of the males in provincial
towns other than Isfahan and only 23 percent of the village men admitted knowledge of coitus interruptus. In contrast, 56 percent
of the women in provincial towns claimed to know of the practice
(S. S. Leiberman, R. Gillespie, and M. Loghmani, 1973).

Our findings were similarly skewed due to interviewer effect.
Although our interviewers were of the same sex as the respondents,

TABLE 10.8: Family Planning: Social Groups, by Contraceptive Usage, by Sex, in Maragheh, Iran, 1972-74

Present Usage of Contraceptive Method	Social Group					
	Professional	High Civil Servant	High Bazaar	Low Civil Servant	Middle and Low Bazaar	Worker
Town Women						
Percent no	8	36	45	39	36	65
Percent yes	92	64	55	61	64	35
Total number	12	45	20	49	107	74
Town Men						
Percent no	--	42	69	44	77	70
Percent yes	--	58	31	56	23	30
Total number	--	62	16	9	60	74

Significant under .001.

Source: Compiled by the author.

7 percent of the women and 14 percent of the men claimed to use condoms; and 2 percent of the women and 15 percent of the men claimed to use "safe days" or rhythm. Additional contraceptives used were intrauterine devices (IUDs) (four), tubal ligations (four), and contraceptive creams (ten). It was not unusual for people to use several methods at once or in alternation.

The practice of contraception among upper class women was reported as very high (92 percent of the wives of professionals), and the majority of middle class women, regardless of status group, also claimed to practice contraception. Women from the low bazaar and working classes were least likely to use contraceptives. Even when we account for a probable inflation of reported usage, class position appears to be associated with contraceptive use. However, other characteristics are also associated with use. Women who reported using a contraceptive device or technique at the time of the interview had a higher mean number of live children than did nonusers (3.6, as compared to 3.0). And both men and women who

---

men were very reluctant to even admit knowledge of coitus interruptus as a method of contraception, although it is the oldest method used in the Middle East. One of our interviewers also had difficulty with the question due to his own embarrassment. The fact that women were not reluctant to admit to knowing about, or using, coitus interruptus suggests that men associate withdrawal with a practice that questions their virile image. It is also possible that the high number of men who claimed that they used safe days, as compared to women, may be a euphemism for coitus interruptus. The practice of rhythm is not widespread, and most women were unaware of the method. Prior to the survey, however, all civil servants and teachers were invited to family planning conferences, during which various methods, including rhythm, were explained. Several people told us they learned of the method and started to use it after the conference.

Our findings on contraceptive practices and family size ideals in Maragheh in 1973-74 are similar to the findings of the UNESCO KAP survey of women administered in Tehran in 1971. In Tehran, the range in ideal family size was 2.9 children for literate women to 3.2 children for illiterate women. Of the respondents, 57.7 percent claimed to be using some form of contraception, with coitus interruptus the preferred method for 46 percent of the users (J. Friesen and R. V. Moore, 1972).

were users claimed to desire fewer children than did nonusers. The
mean number of ideal children for female users was 3.1 children
and for female nonusers, 3.3 children. The mean number of desired children for male users was 2.8 children and for nonusers,
3.7 children. Users were also less inclined to want any additional
children. Only 27 percent of contraceptive users wanted any additional children, as compared to 52 percent of the nonusers. The
social milieu for family planning users also suggests the importance
of peer support. Both female and male respondents who reported
current practice of contraception were more likely to have friends
and family who were also contraceptive users than did nonusers.

However, the major contributing factor to changes in attitudes
and practices regarding family size are, and will continue to be,
those changes that alter the social hierarchy and the patterns of
inequality. Iran is not unique in that the better-educated, wealthier,
more modern families have lower fertility rates and more positive
attitudes toward birth control and family planning. Numerous
studies suggest that economic development accompanied by changes
in the occupational and educational structure, by concomitant
changes in the status and income hierarchy, and by increased
modernism will lead to eventual fertility decline.[13]

Therefore, one may expect that as the Iranian middle class,
particularly the modern middle class, expands, social pressures
for large families will decrease while the socioeconomic impetus
for smaller families will increase. Families concerned with maintaining or elevating the social position of their children will be
more inclined to limit the size of their families.

This tendency is already noticeable among younger families
of the modern middle class and status groups. Families of the
lower and more traditional social groups are far less likely to
change their practices with regard to family size until opportunities
for upward social mobility are more obvious to them. At present,
we find that families from the lower bazaar and working class have
fairly high aspirations for their children and often identify potential
for social mobility with smaller families. Yet, while these attitudes
have trickled down to members of the lower social groups, they
continue to have little impact on their behavior. Again, the opportunity structure is viewed as not offering realistic chances for
mobility for lower-class children. Lower-class children are much
less likely to do well in school or to complete either the first or
second cycle of secondary education, which is a prerequisite for
most government jobs. And only 8 percent of the students enrolled
in institutions of higher education were from village or working-
class families in 1970.

The culture of poverty that has been the experience for many of the provincial working class presents major obstacles in socio-economic mobility and, thus, to changes in status-related behavior and values, which are central to the practice of family planning and fertility decline. Social mobility for members of working-class families, while not impossible, is not great. Of the respondents in our sample who had working-class fathers (108), only 5 were in the high civil servant status group, 8 in the low civil servant status group, and 19 in the middle bazaar. The remaining 70 percent of the respondents were of low bazaar or worker status.

The expansion of educational opportunities and the increase in literacy, which are part of the overall changes in patterns of social stratification, will also increasingly contribute to revisions in the notions about the family and family planning practices. Women who have more education consistently desire smaller families than those who are illiterate. At present, however, few married women of childbearing age in provincial and rural Iran have attained much more than a primary school education. Of the town sample of women, 59 percent had no schooling, 24 percent had some primary schooling, and only 17 percent had some high school or above. Similarly, changes in the occupational opportunities for women, which depend upon changes in educational and cultural patterns, will contribute to reductions in family size. Even though the percentage of working women in provincial towns remains small, we are beginning to see changes in employment patterns. More young, educated women from the modern middle class want to work and do so, to increase their own economic independence and to elevate the socioeconomic position of their families. These working women, upon marriage, are anxious to establish their fertility and their position as wife and mother. But after the first child, they often use contraceptive devices to space their families. And most try very hard to have only two or three children. As this group grows in size, with the expansion of middle-level and modern occupational opportunities and the increase in the participation of women in these roles, the practice of family planning will increase, as notions about the "ideal" number of children and proper mothers' roles are altered.

However, the magnitude of the changes in educational and occupational patterns that are necessary for this to occur is vast. As previously noted, only 4.7 percent of the women in the town sample (interviewees and spouses) were working in the modern sector, and of these, all were wives of teachers, higher civil servants, or professionals. In addition, when we examine educational attainments, we find that none of the women from the bazaar or working classes, and only 2 percent of the women from the lower

civil servant group, have the high school training or above that
would prepare them for occupational roles as teachers, trained
midwives, or health workers. The problem for the working class
is of even greater magnitude, as the vast majority are illiterate
(97 percent of workers' wives). Employment for these working-
class women means menial, poor-paying, and sporadic work in
traditional fruit-packing shops or as household servants. Clearly,
major changes in educational attainment for the working class will
have to occur before changes in attitudes and practices concerning
family planning can be expected.

When it is recognized that only 20 percent of the town's population belongs to the modern upper or middle status groups, in
which major reorientations of values and attitudes toward the family
are occurring, then it becomes clear that this process of reorientation (including notions of family size, child-related expenditures,
proper roles for women, and aspirations for children) will be a slow
one. Yet, it is also evident that changes in the pattern of social
stratification, especially the expansion of the modern middle class,
will greatly contribute to this reorientation and to eventual fertility
decline. The aspirations that parents hold for their children in
the areas of family size, educational attainment, and occupational
roles are indicative of the directions in which change is occurring.

NOTES

1. See Edlefsen, L., and Lieberman, S. S., 1974;
Leibenstein, H., 1975.
2. Leibenstein, op. cit., p. 3.
3. Robinson, W. C., and Horlacher, D. E., 1971.
4. Leibenstein, op. cit.
5. Synder, D. W., 1974; Paydarfar, A. A., 1974.
6. Lieberman, S. S., Gillespie, R., and Loghmani, M.,
1973.
7. See Good, M.-J. D., 1975a, 1976 for further elaboration
of methodology and discussion of stratification in Maragheh and in
Iran.
8. Bill, J., 1972; Good, M.-J. D., 1976.
9. In Gillespie's 1970 survey of population attitudes among
960 respondents in Isfahan Province, he found that

> most respondents very readily associated the notion of
> declining fertility on their part with improvements in
> their life style. . . . Ninety-five percent agreed that
> two or three children could get a better up-bringing,

and that a few educated children could provide better support for their parents' old age than four or five uneducated children" (Lieberman, Gillespie, and Loghmani, op. cit., p. 79).

10. Fawcett, J. T., ed., 1970; George, E. I., 1973; Berelson, B., 1969.

11. Berelson, op. cit.

12. Lieberman, Gillespie, and Loghmani, op. cit.

13. See Leibenstein, op. cit.; Guest, A. M., 1974; Synder, J., op. cit.; Schnaiberg, A., 1970; Fawcett, J. T., and Bornstein, M. H., 1973; and Williamson, J. B., 1970.

11

Determinants of Family
Structure in Turkey

SERIM TIMUR

In Turkey, there has been increasing interest over the last ten years in the social demographic factors affecting family size and the composition of families and households. Since three large nationwide demographic surveys have already been conducted (in 1963, 1968, and 1973, respectively), a very rich source of data exists to investigate the interrelationship between family structure and demographic change.

Based on some of these data, this chapter attempts to analyze some of the processes that underline structural change within the Turkish family, specifically, what factors and forces change family types and how these family types, in turn, affect other areas of individual behavior and social action.

METHODOLOGY

The data for this chapter are taken from the "1968 Survey on Family Structure and Population Problems in Turkey," conducted by the staff of Hacettepe Institute of Population Studies. The main objective of this survey was to empirically examine the applicability to Turkey of some of the current theories on family structure and population dynamics. Data were collected on family type, the process of family formation, and marital relations; fertility level;

This is a revised version of a paper originally presented at the UNESCO Workshop on Family Adjustment to Social Change in the Middle East and North Africa, Beirut, Lebanon, July 1-5, 1974.

knowledge, attitude, and practice of family planning; and the process
of migration. Stress was laid on the socioeconomic and rural-urban
correlates of these variables, as well as on regional and rural-
urban differentials.

The survey was based on a nationwide multistage probability
sample of 4,500 households. Turkey displays large urban-rural and
regional differences in several social and economic characteristics.
In view of these variations among regions and urban-rural residential units, cross stratification was done by five geographic regions
and by community size. The five geographic regions and stratified
urban-rural communities were:

Geographic Regions	Size of Communities
Central Anatolia	Metropolitan centers (Ankara, Istanbul, Izmir)
Black Sea coast	Cities (population, 50,000 and over)
Western Turkey	Cities (population, 15,000–50,000)
Mediterranean region	Towns (population, 2,000–15,000)
Eastern Turkey	Rural areas (less than 2,000)

FAMILY TYPES

Almost all the world's population live in family units, but the
types and structures vary not only from one society to another but,
also, from one class to another within the same society. The simplest type of family is a unit consisting of a married man and woman
with their offspring. This unit is referred to as the conjugal family,
when the accent is on the husband-wife relationship, and the nuclear
family, when it is viewed as the basic unit of all more complex
forms. The head of a nuclear family is independent, neither subject to the authority of any of his relatives nor economically dependent upon them.

Different criteria can be used to distinguish more complex or
extended families from simple nuclear families: number of mates
(monogamy, polygamy, polyandry); residence after marriage (patrilocal, matrilocal, neolocal); degree of authority (equalitarian,
patriarchal, matriarchal); generational prolification (vertical versus
horizontal);and so forth.

A crucial factor in the study of family types should be to determine the nature of the immediate family. The relation of the
family of procreation (conjugal or nuclear family) to husband's and

wife's families of orientation (their parents) is very important. This is clearly seen when we look at the explanations given about the nature of the two polar family types: the patriarchal extended family and the independent nuclear family.

Patriarchal Extended Family

Social scientists have characterized the patriarchal extended family as one in which the nuclear family is controlled by the head of the patrilineal extended family. The father has great power over his sons, and the husband over his wife. Relationships are not egalitarian. Marital choice is determined by the parents, and age at marriage tends to be quite young. To facilitate parental control, the newly married couple usually live with the parents. There are economic exchanges in connection with marriage. Sons generally follow their father's occupation; thus, social and geographical mobility is limited. This type of family is seen as being best suited to an agrarian society with little mobility and simple specialization.[1]

Independent Nuclear Family

In an independent nuclear family, neither parents nor the couple have many rights or reciprocal obligations in regard to each other. Parents do not choose the new couple's residence location-- it is neolocal. Mate choice is done by the people involved. Age at marriage is determined by the fact that youngsters have to be old enough to provide for themselves.[2] The husband's occupation, rather than that of the patriarchal father, determines the family's status. Occupation is no longer hereditary due to an increase in social and geographical mobility related to industrialization. The independent nuclear family is thus seen as a function of industrialization and urbanization.[3]

Most theoretical explanations of changes in family structure view industrialization and urbanization as the primary determinants. The emergence of the small nuclear family is generally seen in sociological theory as a consequence of the urban-industrial revolution. In fact, the structural-functional approach postulates a functional interdependence and implied causality between the urban-industrial complex and the small nuclear family.[4] Over time and through the processes of social change, industrialization, and urbanization, the extended family will be superseded by the independent nuclear family. Since extended families were thought to be prevalent in rural preindustrial societies, it was assumed that the typical residential family in these societies was the extended family, containing representatives of three or more generations and, perhaps, several collateral relatives.[5] This generalization was sustained by a few superficial observations, such as that extended families were more prevalent in rural than in urban areas, and cross-culturally, that extended families were more prevalent in underdeveloped agricultural societies than in developed industrial societies.

Recently, however, several arguments have challenged those generally accepted ideas. Considerable statistical evidence from underdeveloped countries, as well as historical research dealing with preindustrial societies, show that a large majority of people live, and have lived, in nuclear families. The extended family is not predominant in actual practice, except for the wealthy minority.

On the basis of empirical research, many demographers and family sociologists now agree that the extended or joint family is an ideal, polar type.[6] Bogue observed that while the extended family (where three or four generations live together under one roof or within one compound) is a part of the cultural standard of many countries, it occurs in fact primarily among the upper classes.[7] Thus, the extended family as described and discussed in the literature of family sociology and cultural anthropology appears to be more a sociological tradition than a statistical reality.[8]

The extended family was considered to be the modal form in rural areas of Turkey until quite recently. It was commonly believed that change toward the nuclear family would occur with industrialization, urbanization, and modernization. Based on the data from the 1968 nationwide survey, let us look specifically at the socioeconomic factors associated with Turkish family types.

FAMILY TYPES IN TURKEY

The term family, as used in this study, refers to the domestic family; the definitions of family types given below refer to a set of related persons who share a dwelling unit. * In any society, a detailed classification of who lives with whom would require a rather

---

*In other contexts, the term family is sometimes used in a wider sense to include persons tied to each other by kinship but residing in different households. This study adopts the UN definition, stating that "a family cannot comprise more than one household" (United Nations, "Principles and Recommendations for the 1970 Population Censuses," 1969).

long list of definitions. Here, we will classify family types that differ structurally and systematically, ignoring random variations.

Four basic types emerge when members of the household are classified according to their status with respect to the household head: (1) a nuclear family, composed of husband, wife, and their unmarried children; (2) a patriarchal (lineal) extended family, composed of a man and his wife and their married sons and wives with their children; (3) a transient extended family, in which the male, who is the head of the household, his wife, and his unmarried children live together with either the man's or his wife's widowed parents and/or with their unmarried siblings; and (4) a dissolved family or nonfamily household, in which one spouse is missing due to separation, divorce, death, and so forth.

This classification was not done mechanically, according to the number of generations or number of married couples and so forth, but was based on who was the head of the household. Although both patriarchal extended and transient families are three-generation families, in distinguishing these two types of families, the emphasis was placed on who was the head of the family, the father or the son. We classified a family as being a patriarchal extended one when the patriarch owned the property and controlled the labor of all under his roof, whereas in the transient extended family, the son was the household head and chief breadwinner.

It was observed that 60 percent of all families lived in nuclear households, 19 percent were patriarchal extended, 13 percent transient extended, and 8 percent were either dissolved families or nonfamily households. As expected, the proportion of nuclear families decreased from 68 percent in the metropolitan areas to 55 percent in the villages. In spite of this pattern, however, patriarchal extended households were clearly the minority in rural areas, comprising one-fifth of the households in small towns and only one-fourth in villages with less than 2,000 population. The national estimate of transient extended families (13 percent) did not vary by community size, this family type comprised virtually the same proportion in both urban and rural areas (see Table 11.1). Let us now turn to the factors that produce and maintain certain family types.

SOCIOECONOMIC CORRELATES OF FAMILY TYPES

Our survey data yield results similar to studies carried out in other countries, showing that the extended household can stay together only so long as its land or other wealth can support it and it can offer adequate opportunities to the younger generation. Evidence of the relationship between amount of property and type of family is provided by data on occupation and family type.

TABLE 11.1: Family Types, by Place of Residence, in Turkey, 1968 (percent)

Family Type	Place of Residence					
	Metropolitan	Large City	City	Town	Village	Turkey
Nuclear	67.9	65.8	63.3	61.5	55.4	59.7
Patriarchal extended:	4.6	9.7	9.5	20.0	25.4	19.0
Household head plus married sons	0.5	1.6	0.5	4.0	5.6	3.9
Household head plus married son and unmarried children	2.2	4.0	3.6	8.6	10.5	7.9
Household head plus one married son	1.0	2.5	3.9	5.1	6.7	5.0
Joint (household head plus married brother)	0.1	0.1	0.7	1.2	1.9	1.3
Household head plus married daughter	0.8	1.5	0.8	1.1	0.7	0.9
Transient extended:	12.4	11.6	15.0	12.7	13.3	13.1
Household head's mother	3.8	4.4	6.3	5.4	6.5	5.7
Household head's father	0.0	0.5	0.7	0.4	0.9	0.7
Household head's unmarried siblings	1.4	1.1	0.9	0.6	0.9	1.0
Household head's mother and/or father, and/or unmarried sibling, and/or other relatives	2.8	3.9	4.8	4.0	4.1	3.9
Household head's wife's relatives	4.4	1.7	2.4	2.2	0.9	1.3
Dissolved or nonfamily household:	15.0	12.9	11.9	5.7	5.9	8.3
One parent, children	8.9	7.8	7.7	3.3	3.8	5.1
Unrelated household	6.1	5.1	4.2	2.4	2.1	3.2
Total:						
Percent	100.0	100.0	100.0	100.0	100.0	100.0
Number	545	1,012	743	461	1,715	4,476

Note: Totals slightly different from 100 due to rounding.
Source: 1968 Survey on Family Structure and Population Problems in Turkey (Ankara, Turkey: Hacettepe Institute of Population Studies, 1968).

Classification of families by male occupation shows, surprisingly, that the highest and lowest proportions of nuclear families are found in rural areas. In rural areas, the farmers--especially those who own the most land--generally live in extended families, whereas the landless farm workers have the largest proportion of nuclear families. The proportion of nuclear families is less than half (44 percent) among farmers, rises to 64 percent among sharecroppers, and is extremely high among farm workers, rising to 79 percent. In urban areas, the proportion of nuclear families is highest (77 percent) among the professionals. Their economic independence from the parental household gives them freedom to form nuclear families at the time of marriage. The proportion of nuclear families is also high among workers (74 percent), decreasing to 69 percent among artisans and craftsmen. The relationship of property to family type can also be observed among businessmen, who have the highest proportion of extended families in urban areas. Among businessmen and industrial entrepreneurs, who are highly concentrated in the largest cities, only 64 percent live in nuclear households. There is clearly a tendency for families owning more property to have an extended family system, whether or not industrialization and urbanization are involved. (See Table 11.2.)

TABLE 11.2: Family Types, by Occupational Groups, in Turkey, 1968 (percent)

	Family Type			Total	
Occupation	Nuclear	Transient Extended	Patriarchal Extended	Percent	Number
Commerce and businessmen	64.1	25.9	10.1	100.0	45
Professionals and administrators	76.9	8.5	14.2	100.0	51
Clerical	73.6	18.8	9.7	100.0	338
Artisans and craftsmen	68.7	17.8	18.6	100.0	630
Workers	72.3	11.0	16.7	100.0	522
Farmers	43.8	16.8	39.4	100.0	903
Sharecroppers	63.6	20.2	16.3	100.0	47
Agricultural workers	79.3	4.4	16.2	100.0	73
Unemployed, other	70.9	9.5	19.7	100.0	49
Total number	1,619	450	589	--	2,658

Source: 1968 Survey on Family Structure and Population Problems in Turkey (Ankara, Turkey: Hacettepe Institute of Population Studies, 1968).

The survey data also show that extended families entail larger landholdings. The average size of a farm is 30 decares for nuclear families, whereas it rises to 127 decares among patriarchal extended families. Among families owning less than 10 decares of land, 59 percent live in nuclear households and only 22 percent live in patriarchal extended families, whereas among those owning more than 100 decares of land, this relationship is completely reversed, with 58 percent living in patriarchal extended families and 23 percent living in nuclear families. This overall correlation between size of land owned and size of family is also observed within each geographic region. (See Table 11.3.)

TABLE 11.3: Family Types, by Amount of Land Owned, in Turkey,[a] 1968 (percent)

Amount of Land (decares)[b]	Family Type			Total	
	Nuclear	Transient Extended	Patriarchal Extended	Percent	Number
1-10	58.6	18.2	23.3	100.0	250
11-24	45.9	19.6	34.5	100.0	222
25-50	42.0	12.5	45.5	100.0	256
51-100	36.3	12.2	51.3	100.0	128
More than 100	22.6	19.2	58.1	100.0	83

$X^2 = 61$; df = 15; $P < .01$.
[a]Landless agricultural families are excluded.
[b]One decare = 1,000 square meters.
Source: 1968 Survey on Family Structure and Population Problems in Turkey (Ankara, Turkey: Hacettepe Institute of Population Studies, 1968).

Other socioeconomic variables, such as education and income level, do not show any consistent relationship with family type. The proportion of nuclear families is highest among illiterates and the highest educational group, whereas it is lowest among those with a middle-level education. Similarly, per capita family income, considered by itself, does not reveal any association with differences in family type. In towns and cities, no relationship is observed between income level and family types. In rural areas, high per capita family income is associated with the extended family form, whereas in metropolitan areas, families in high income brackets are usually nuclear. Thus, the association between variables, such as education and family income with family type, can only be understood with reference to the occupational groups, with their distinct characteristics of educational attainment and income level. For example, nuclear families predominate among farm workers and small farmers in rural areas and among unskilled laborers in urban areas, all of whom are mostly illiterate. The family type characteristic of professionals and civil servants in urban areas who have university education is also nuclear. On the other hand, extended families are prevalent among large landowners and those who own middle-sized farms in rural areas and among artisans, retailers, and so forth in the urban areas who have medium levels of education.

Most people, especially in rural areas, place a high value on the extended family. A very high proportion of peasants (75 percent), by their own admission, aspire to live in an extended family, which they see as an indication of prosperity and prestige. This apparent social emphasis on large families appears inconsistent with the vast number of nuclear families. But it is not, when we consider that only the wealthy landlords can afford large families; for the poor, lack of land makes the ideal difficult to achieve.

Rules of Residence and Family Cycle

Cross-sectionally, at any given point in time, a majority of Turkish families live in nuclear households. A very large majority live in extended households at the time of their marriage. However, during the lifetime of most couples, they live in different family types. A cross tabulation of current family type by the family type at marriage shows that a high percentage of families were at one time part of an extended family. Sixty-two percent of all families were patriarchal extended, and 14 percent were transient extended, at the time of their marriage; only 24 percent were formed as independent, neolocal nuclear families. Even among families that were nuclear at the time of the survey, only 37 percent were formed as nuclear households when they were first married. Our data show that newly married couples break away from the extended household and become independent nuclear families shortly after marriage. More than half of the families that were patriarchal extended at marriage became nuclear in less than four years; three-fourths did so in less than ten years time. Although demographic factors, such as death (16 percent) and migration (25 percent) are important in dissolution of the extended family, the most important reason given for the breakup was financial difficulties (42 percent) and internal family conflicts (17 percent).

In Turkey, especially in the villages, couples usually experience a cycle of family types. Patrilocality is the rule at marriage, and the young couple is expected to reside in the groom's parental home, thus becoming a part of the patriarchal extended family. Soon after marriage, however, the young man breaks away from his father's household to form his own nuclear family. After separation, when the man's own sons grow up and get married, they also reside at their father's household, for a time, forming a patriarchal extended family. This pattern is very clear and consistent, especially in rural areas. We observe a cyclic development of the extended family, in which a married man passes through three stages of family life: within his father's household, in his own independent nuclear family, and as the patriarch household head of an extended family.

The major cause for leaving the parental household shortly after marriage appears to be the poverty of the family. If the father is landless or without other productive means, sons leave out of necessity; each son must find means to support his own nuclear family. If the father has a little land, married sons have to work for someone else as hired laborers or sharecroppers in the same village or in surrounding towns. When the family ceases to be the unit of production and when there are other ways to earn an income besides depending on family resources, the patriarchal extended family breaks down. Economic limitations prevent all but the fairly well-to-do from maintaining such extended households. It is not surprising then that extended households, functioning as common production and consumption units, form a small percentage of village households.

One might wonder why more couples do not establish a neolocal nuclear household at marriage rather than beginning as part of a patriarchal extended family and separating shortly thereafter. The answer lies in the traditional marriage customs, requiring expensive wedding ceremonies and the payment of bride-price. Traditional marriage rules and the extended family form are a series of functionally related phenomena. It is the father's duty to arrange the marriage of each of his sons, for it is very rare that the amount of money needed can be secured by the groom without the cooperation of his family. Since the marriage of the son is financed by the family--using the father's property and the labor of the other members of the household--the groom and his wife are obliged to stay and work in the father's house for some time after marriage. The married son is expected to support his father, at least until all his brothers get married. [9]

Economic necessities are reflected in the area of attitudes and norms. A newly married couple is expected to follow the usual patrilocal pattern. Although in actual practice most families live in nuclear households, norms and values seem to idealize extended families. When the respondents were asked if they would like to live with their married sons in the future, 73 percent of men and 79 percent of women said yes. As would be expected, the proportion of affirmative responses varies by place of residence: 90 percent of men in rural areas, 66 percent of those in towns, 53 percent of those in cities, and 31 percent of men residing in the metropolitan areas of Ankara, Istanbul, and Izmir expressed this wish.

Formation of Marriage

Since the family plays an important role in marrying their off-spring, it is not surprising that it also exerts a great influence in selecting marriage partners for their children. The extended family is not only the most important social unit but it is also the unit of economic production in agricultural areas. Marriage takes place by parental arrangement, since it involves not only the husband-wife relationship but the integration of the bride into the extended family. Consequently, it is expected that the choice of a spouse for the son or daughter will be made by the head of the family. If marriages are arranged by parents, then we can expect that they will also limit the possibilities for male-female acquaintance and will try to block opportunities for youngsters to meet future spouses.

Parents arrange a large majority of marriages in Turkey. Over two-thirds of the women in our sample in all places of residence and in all types of families said that their marriages had been arranged, with or without their consent (67 percent and 11 percent, respectively). Only 13 percent of the women said that they made their own choice, with their family's consent; 9 percent said that they had to "elope," since they could not convince their parents to agree to their own choice.

When men in the sample were asked about who made the final decision about their marriage, only half of them said that they had decided themselves. We also found that men who were able to open a new independent house at marriage were freer with regard to mate selection and marital decision than men who had to live in their father's house (see Table 11.4).

Since among extended families marriage is conceived as an alliance between two families and not simply as an agreement between two individuals, two other consequences emerge: economic transactions accompany marriage, and marriage among relatives is encouraged. The customs of bride-price payment and preferential marriage rules among certain relatives are means whereby the heads of families are able to control the marriage of their offspring. As can be seen from Tables 11.5 and 11.6, in half of the marriages, bride-price was paid, and one-third of all couples were relatives.

Among the couples who were related, 78 percent were married to first cousins.

Our data reveal that among patriarchal extended families, the payment of bride-price is quite common, and the amount paid is very high. On the other hand, in "always nuclear" families--currently nuclear families that were established neolocally--bride-price is paid only in few instances, and the amount is negligible. Apart from being highly associated with the patriarchal extended family system, bride-price is also found to be substantial where the economic contribution of the bride through labor is quite high.

TABLE 11.4: Final Decision Maker in Choice of Spouse for Men, by Family Type, in Turkey, 1968 (percent)

| Decision Maker | Family Type | | | | |
	Always Nuclear	Currently Nuclear	Transient Extended	Patriarchal Extended	All Types
Parents	12.0	37.6	43.2	50.3	38.3
Other relatives	21.8	8.4	5.3	6.6	8.1
Himself	64.3	51.9	49.5	41.4	51.6
Others	2.0	2.1	2.0	1.8	2.0
Total percent	100.0	100.0	100.0	100.0	100.0
Number	542	1,109	461	598	2,709

$x^2 = 113$; degrees of freedom (df) = 9; P < .01.

Source: 1968 Survey on Family Structure and Population Problems in Turkey (Ankara, Turkey: Hacettepe Institute of Population Studies, 1968).

TABLE 11.5: Proportion of Related Couples, by Family Type and by Place of Residence, in Turkey, 1968 (percent)

| Place of Residence | Family Type | | | | |
	Always Nuclear	Currently Nuclear	Transient Extended	Patriarchal Extended	All Types
Metropolitan	12.5	17.8	24.6	26.0	17.0
City	14.8	21.1	18.2	24.2	19.4
Town	11.4	27.3	22.4	17.6	21.3
Village	27.6	35.0	39.2	38.4	35.7
Turkey	20.2	29.0	31.9	34.3	29.2
Number	118	309	141	260	828

Source: 1968 Survey on Family Structure and Population Problems in Turkey (Ankara, Turkey: Hacettepe Institute of Population Studies, 1968).

TABLE 11.6: Proportion of Women for Whom Bride-Price Was Paid at Marriage, by Family Type and by Place of Residence, in Turkey, 1968 (percent)

	Family Type				
Place of Residence	Always Nuclear	Currently Nuclear	Transient Extended	Patriarchal Extended	All Types
Metropolitan	8.5	31.4	28.5	26.0	19.0
City	34.7	45.9	31.9	47.9	40.7
Town	44.6	47.6	45.6	50.1	47.5
Village	58.2	60.4	61.1	68.8	63.3
Turkey	41.4	52.3	50.5	63.8	53.1
Number	279	583	274	503	1,639

Source: 1968 Survey on Family Structure and Population Problems in Turkey (Ankara, Turkey: Hacettepe Institute of Population Studies, 1968).

This finding supports the view that sees bride-price as a compensation for the loss of work represented by the loss of a daughter. The custom of bride-price payment was most widespread in the rural areas of Eastern Turkey, the Black Sea coast, and Central Anatolia, where it is known that the economic contribution of women in agriculture is quite high. The importance of this marriage custom seems to have declined greatly in urban centers, as well as in the rural parts of the Mediterranean region and Western Turkey, where agriculture is highly mechanized. It can be concluded, then, that with urbanization and mechanized farming, bride-price will no longer be functional but will carry a symbolic meaning for some time and will soon disappear.

HOUSEHOLD TYPES AND INTRAFAMILY RELATIONS

Family types defined as always nuclear, currently nuclear, transient extended, and patriarchal extended not only denote the forms of household but cover the status and roles of the family members. It might be expected, therefore, that these different types of families will also differ significantly in authority pattern and role structure. This is indeed the case. In patriarchal families, inheritance, succession, economic resources, and social status are all concentrated in the hands of male heads of households, who, in turn, have absolute authority over the other members of the family. The responses to the question, "Who has the most say in your family?" well reflects the power structure in the family. Although 95 percent of male respondents in nuclear families stated that they were the chief decision makers in their families, this proportion decreased to 28 percent among patriarchal extended families. (See Table 11.7.)

TABLE 11.7: Who Has the Most "Say" in the Family, by Family Type, in Turkey, 1968 (percent)

| Has Most "Say" | Family Type | | | | |
	Always Nuclear	Currently Nuclear	Transient Extended	Patriarchal Extended	All Types
Husband (himself)	94.3	95.2	75.2	28.2	74.2
Wife	1.2	0.8	0.6	0.4	0.7
Husband's father	0.1	2.0	8.6	61.5	18.4
Husband's mother	0.7	0.4	10.1	4.1	2.9
Wife's parents	0.0	0.0	3.1	0.4	0.5
Others in the family	3.6	1.6	2.4	4.4	3.3
Total percent	99.9*	100.0	100.0	99.0*	100.0
Number	518	1,069	441	573	2,601

$X^2 = 1,524$; df = 24; P < .01.
*Columns 1 and 4 differ slightly from 100 due to rounding.

Source: 1968 Survey on Family Structure and Population Problems in Turkey (Ankara, Turkey: Hacettepe Institute of Population Studies, 1968).

In an attempt to measure intrafamily relations on three different dimensions of family life, a "family modernity scale" was formed, utilizing responses to a series of 16 questions. The three dimensions were classified as follows: (1) the decision-making process, (2) sex role ideologies and the degree of dominance patterns, and (3) husband-wife companionship--joint participation or segregation of conjugal roles.[10] In both urban and rural areas, the patriarchal extended families were the most traditional and nuclear families the least traditional, as measured by this scale. Due to the conventional association between economic resources and authority, power and social status are concentrated in the hands of the male heads of households. In the patriarchal extended family, all members are under the authority of the patriarch. All the monetary and other decisions concerning the family are made by him. (See Table 11.8.)

In the nuclear family, however, husband-wife relations are relatively more egalitarian, and the wife may participate in decision making. However, the most universal characteristic of all types of

Turkish families seem to be the subordination of women. This is especially true for patriarchal extended families in rural areas, where bride-price is paid at marriage and the amount of it is substantial. Despite the substantial economic contribution and hard work of the bride, her status is low, since she had no control over the produce of her labor and receives no retribution.

TABLE 11.8: Scores on Family Modernity Scale, by Family Type, in Turkey, 1968 (percent)

| Scale Score | Family Type | | | | |
	Always Nuclear	Currently Nuclear	Transient Extended	Patriarchal Extended	All Types
Modern (21–34)	28.5	16.9	14.9	3.6	15.1
Transitional (35–42)	28.3	37.8	31.4	16.3	28.7
Traditional (43–64)	43.2	45.2	53.8	80.1	56.2
Total percent	100.0	100.0	100.0	100.0	100.0
Number	680	1,183	554	798	3,215

$x^2 = 382$; df = 6; P < .01.

Source: 1968 Survey on Family Structure and Population Problems in Turkey (Ankara, Turkey: Hacettepe Institute of Population Studies, 1968).

Even when urban rural residence is held constant, power structure in the family and family modernity are highly associated with family type.

CONCLUSION

Our data show that the creation and maintenance of certain types of families are usually shaped by the primary property and work relations. When income and occupation come to depend on factors not controlled by the extended family, as when wage labor becomes common, this creates the possibility of change in the extended family. Independent nuclear families become more prevalent, whether or not urbanization, industrialization, or modernization are involved. However, industrialization and urbanization increase the proportion of nuclear families in the sense that these processes necessarily increase the proportion of people who earn their livelihood from wage labor.

Our data also reveal that once certain family types are formed, they, in turn, influence, and to a great degree even determine, the intrafamily relations and individual behavior of family members with respect to marriage patterns, formation of marriage, age at marriage, family authority patterns, and husband-wife relationship.

The connection between family structure and fertility are not very clear. Although it is commonly believed that the extended family, which features large households and encourages high fertility, is the premodern form, while the nuclear form, with small households and low fertility, is the family of modern industrial society, there exists little sociological evidence to support this belief.[11]

In Turkey, fertility is high among the nuclear families of agricultural laborers and unskilled industrial workers, whereas it is much lower among the urban extended families of men in commerce and business. Both the decline in fertility and the existence and prevalence of certain family types are closely related to the overall process of social and economic development. But the interrelationships and the interaction between family structure and demographic changes are not yet well understood. Further research directed toward the mechanisms involved in changes in which the family is thought to be acting as an intermediate agent is needed.

NOTES

1. Davis, K., 1949, pp. 415-17.
2. Goode, W. J., 1963.
3. Parsons, T., 1959.
4. Greenfield, S. M., 1961.
5. United Nations, 1973.
6. Goode, op. cit.
7. Bogue, D. J., 1969.
8. For further statistical evidence on an international basis, see United Nations, op. cit., vol. 1, pp. 335-64. For a more detailed analysis on the incidence, prevalence, and further traits of different types of extended families in a number of societies, see Timur, S., 1971, chaps. 1 and 2.
9. Rosenfeld, H., 1958.
10. Timur, op. cit.
11. Westoff, C. F., 1974.

12

Demographic Determinants of Gender Role Structure: The Case of Age at Marriage in Turkey

GREER LITTON FOX

INTRODUCTION

The central purpose of this chapter is to ascertain the meaning of age at marriage by examining its impact on the enactment of the wife role in Turkish marriage. This problem can be placed in a broader context, namely, the investigation of demographic factors as large-scale determinants of gender role structures. Before moving to an analysis of one specific demographic variable, age at marriage, I will consider some other sources of demographic influence on gender roles.

Demographic variables generally pertain to the size and composition of a population and its placement in space. Factors such as fertility, mortality, migration, and social mobility, which are involved in changes in the three dimensions of a population are also demographic variables. What distinguishes these variables from others in the sociologists' analytic armamentarium is not so much their content as their level of analysis. That is, demographic variables, while derived from characteristics or acts of individuals, are concerned only with aggregates of individuals, and it is only through aggregation that specific demographic variables emerge. Put another way, a population has an age-sex structure; an individual does not. A population has the capacity for simultaneous movement of its component parts in space (migration streams); an individual does not. Demographic variables are useful

Presented at the International Workshop on Changing Sex Roles in Family and Society, Dubrovnik, Yugoslavia, June 16-21, 1975.

in the analysis of gender roles, in part, simply because they force us to work on the supraindividual level of analysis. That they are relevant in still other ways will be discussed below.

Gender role structures have been much less clearly defined than demographic variables. Many persons working in the area of sex roles research have been content to use the terms gender roles, sex role structures, and so forth rather loosely, confident that all were talking more or less about the same thing. For the most part, it would seem that this approach has not been unreasonable.

Nevertheless, there have been some attempts at conceptual clarity. Angrist, for example, has suggested that "sex role" can be analyzed in terms of four components: label, behavior, expectations, and social locus. She proposes that "role constellation," the combination of roles that one occupies concurrently, and "role flexibility," or the degrees of freedom for enactment of given roles, are both more useful ways of analyzing the operation of sex in social structure than is a focus on sex role alone.[1]

Ridley makes a useful distinction between "gender status" and "gender role," defining the former as a comparison of the relative ranking of women and men at a given point in time and defining the latter in functional terms, that is, in terms of what men and women do.[2] Holter distinguishes between sex differentiation, or the institutionalization of differences between the sexes (which varies from a high degree of segregation on the basis of sex to a low degree of sex-based social separation), and sex stratification, or the different evaluation of men and women on such status hierarchies as power, prestige, and privilege.[3]

In this chapter, "gender role structures" means the kinds of positions and the content of those positions that are available to men and women in given social settings. I am interested to know what kinds of positions are available and in which institutional spheres. Are men and women constrained to fill only a limited set of roles, and if so, what are the sources of constraint? Under what conditions does the organization of roles by sex begin to change, and in what directions? Operationally, in this chapter, this has meant primarily a focus on the content of roles and a focus on the roles of women rather than of both sexes.

The connection between demographic variables and gender role structures can be seen through the use of an elementary theoretical proposition in human ecological theory, namely, that elements of social organization, in this case gender role structures, are a function of, or a response to, external situational elements, such as the nature of the population base that is available to staff the organizational structure. In other words, more pithily, ways of life are a function of conditions of life.

But the links between social organization and population base are reciprocal. That is, one can expect the flow of influence to be two-way; the structure of gender roles in a society will have both immediate and long-term effects on the nature of the population base, as well as vice versa. Further, if one utilizes Duncan's model of the ecological complex, one can postulate that the links between organization and population are not only reciprocal but that their mutual effects are mediated as well through elements of technology and the external environment.[4] As an example, Boserup's analysis of "male" and "female" farming systems is an excellent illustration of the interaction of population base, technological level, and environment as joint determinants of the organization of economic activity, in this case, along sex-linked lines.[5]

The relevance of the ecological model to the study of changing sex roles in family and society lies in its suggestion that in our consideration of the causes and consequences of alterations in sex roles we not lose sight of large-scale factors that influence sex role structures and which, at first glance, seem only remotely connected to such measures of sex role change as reconceptualization of the housewife role or the institutionalization of nonreproductive sex. The ecological complex model is also useful because it suggests some sources of variation in sex role structure: for example, the organization of sex roles can be expected to vary across levels of economic or technological development; gender role structures should vary along a rural-urban continuum; they may vary according to the degree of direct reliance upon the external environment, and so forth.

To illustrate the utility of this large-scale analytic posture, I will review briefly some work that has already been done on the impact of various demographic variables on the structure of sex roles. We can consider, in turn, the factors of sex and age composition, mortality levels, and fertility patterns of a population as they affect the availability and content of gender roles.

AGE-SEX COMPOSITION

The age-sex composition of a population can affect the structure of sex roles in a number of ways. For example, the availability of marital roles for each sex can be dramatically affected by the relative numbers of men and women at various ages. Where women tend to marry men older than themselves and where mortality declines have been rapid or where birth rates have tended frequently to fluctuate in response to changing socioeconomic conditions, imbalances in the ratio of women to men in the marriageable ages are not uncommon.[6] The imbalance can, of course, work in two ways: there can be a shortage of marriageable women relative to the numbers of available men or a shortage of men relative to marriageable women. Either way, one can expect the entry of men and women into marriage roles to be affected. The latter situation characterized marriage patterns in the United States, for example, during the late 1950s and throughout the 1960s. Described by demographers as the "marriage squeeze,"[7] the imbalance in the sex ratio at the marriageable ages meant an excess of close to 1 million women at its peak during 1967.[8] The demographic responses to this imbalance are familiar: an increase in the age at marriage of young women, a reduction in the age gap between husband and wife, as women begin to marry men of their same or contiguous birth cohorts, an increase in the proportions of women remaining single, and higher rates of remarriage among men.[9] Secondary effects of the circumscribed opportunities for entry into marriage roles have been to push the "extra" women into higher levels of education or job training or directly into the labor force in order to support themselves. It was during this period of the 1960s that we saw the contemporary renascence of the women's movement in America. It would be interesting to explore to what extent the secondary responses to the marriage squeeze were generative of, rather than a response to, the ideology of liberation.

Ridley, drawing upon Hajnal's work on nuptiality in eighteenth- and nineteenth-century Western Europe, describes a similar change in sex role structure in Western countries, that is, the institutionalization of educational and occupational roles for women in response to the decline in role opportunities for women in the familial sphere during the long-term demographic deficit of marriageable males in the nineteenth century.[10] Additionally, she speculates that we might expect a marriage squeeze to emerge in developing countries, though resulting from a different mechanism--declining mortality rather than fluctuations in fertility. In turn, this marriage squeeze should generate a similar shift in the organization of sex roles in those countries in the future.[11]

Thus far, we have been discussing imbalances in the sex ratio at marriageable ages. While altering the availability of marital roles for large blocs of young persons is probably the most critical effect of an imbalance in the sex ratio in terms of the direct and indirect effects on sex roles, an imbalance in the number of men and women can occur in other ways, again with implications for the structure of sex roles. Two brief examples can suffice.

Migration Streams

Migration streams that are differentially selective by sex have implications for the organization of sex roles in both community of origin and destination. For instance, in parts of southern Africa where heavy out-migration of men from rural areas to industrialized areas in search of work is a common practice, the demographic makeup of rural areas undergoes a periodic change, with a subsequent impact on the activities of the women who are left behind. Essentially, the woman's role expands to carry the full weight of responsibility for domestic, economic, and civic affairs. As Dixon suggests, this may increase the status of women by increasing their power and giving them experience in leadership and decision making. But at the same time, it entails the cost of "a double burden for the women left behind and an increased competition for the attention of the remaining males."[12] In those communities that are the end-points of migration streams, one often finds a very high sex ratio, with consequent disruption of marital patterns and curtailment of the domestic role for a large segment of men. Such a pattern has been noted in African "male towns"[13] and in frontier towns of the American West.[14]

Differential Rates of Mortality at Older Ages

Differential rates of mortality at older ages also affect the sex ratio. Currently, in the United States, widows outnumber widowers by a factor of four to one after age 65. This suggests that most American women can expect a fairly substantial period of widowhood toward the end of their lives, and thus, they will face a dramatic shift in role at the very time in the life cycle when they are supposedly least receptive to radical change. The effect on the organization of sex roles is not dissimilar to that noted above in the female-dominant villages. Women will take on additional activities and will move into spheres previously considered the province of men. And as noted above, while this can be seen as an opportunity to develop new competencies, at the same time, it does represent a real increase in workload and responsibility. But, and this is the main point, it also suggests that the organization of sex roles varies in response to the availability of persons to staff the roles. The limits to the interchangeability of men and women become highlighted in those instances in which one finds them in unequal numbers.

MORTALITY

Let us turn to an examination of mortality levels as a factor affecting the organization of sex roles. We have just looked at how mortality affects the sex ratio at older ages. Ridley and Sullerot have each cataloged other ways in which mortality levels impinge upon the roles of women.[15] Declines in mortality increase the average expectation of life, which implies that women will have a longer period of life remaining after childbearing and the intensive child-rearing period. A corollary is that a smaller proportion of a woman's total life will need to be spent in purely maternal functions.[16]

Declines in high rates of infant mortality also reduce the time and health burden of childbearing by reducing pregnancy wastage, defined as "the losses of time, human effort, and human life incurred by inefficient childbearing under conditions of high infant mortality." The same number of surviving children can be produced with smaller time and life costs under conditions of low infant mortality. By allowing for alterations in fertility patterns, changing mortality conditions can have an impact on women's roles.

Ridley suggests that longer life expectancy for men and women will lessen the threat of marital disruption through death of one of the spouses. Under conditions of low mortality, marital duration becomes extended into postchild-rearing years, a situation that Ridley suggests will foster the development of greater companionship and equalitarianism within the marital relationship.[17]

Both Sullerot and Ridley are suggesting that as life becomes less mean, the prospect of a lengthy life less precarious, then the focus of women's and men's lives can be shifted from mere survival and procreation to alternative activities. Both suggest implicitly that as the prospect for survival beyond childbearing becomes a reality for large segments of women, the process of investment in, and preparation for, additional roles becomes institutionalized. Investment in educational facilities for women and provision for economic and civic roles for women are resisted less when there is a likelihood of return on the investment. While the shift from high to low mortality cannot be seen as a sufficient condition for alterations in the organization of sex roles, the mortality shift may be a necessary condition for such change.

FERTILITY

The demographic variable that is tied most closely to sex roles may well be fertility, that is, the patterns of childbearing within a population. In a paper prepared for the UN World Population Conference of 1974, Dixon analyzed the status of women as both a consequence and a determinant of fertility patterns. She examined the consequences of different levels of childbearing and patterns of child spacing as they impinged upon women's education, occupational participation, marital patterns, and the participation of women in public life. Her conclusions were cautious: the relationship between fertility patterns and women's status is reciprocal, the directionality of effect hard to ascertain. Moreover, she suggested that the precise nature of the relationship between fertility and the position of women within a society is very much contingent upon operative cultural norms and values. Finally, she suggested that demographic variables, such as fertility patterns, may be of only minor importance to the status of women when compared to such factors as level of economic and technological development, political climate, the organization of family and kinship, cultural beliefs, and governmental policies.[18]

Nevertheless, although we risk oversimplification, we can suggest a few ways in which sex roles are affected by fertility variables. We can start with the interaction of overall level of childbearing with timing and spacing-of-birth patterns. Within the context of low mortality conditions, a decline in the number of children ever-born per woman, in combination with earlier starts and earlier finishes of the childbearing period, has meant that a decreasing portion of women's lives is spent in childbearing. This sets the stage for women's participation in nonmaternal spheres, and it also allows for a change in the ideological association of womanhood with motherhood. It should be noted, however, that this generalization may be relevant primarily where the family system is conjugal. As Ware points out, among some African women, individual high fertility is no barrier to intensive economic activity outside the home because of the ability to rely upon members of the extended family for assistance in child care.[19]

Low levels of childbearing per woman are not at all automatic indicators of improved status for women. Where mortality is high, one can expect great value to be attached to high levels of childbearing. In such settings, women with low fertility performance are likely to be devalued and to have low status within their community.[20] To illustrate the strength of high fertility values, consider Ware, who writes:

> Throughout Africa prestige is associated with parenthood and the plight of the childless woman is both emotionally and economically desperate. In many African societies to die childless is regarded as being equivalent to

committing suicide. There is no burial, no immortal-
ity for the childless. [21]

Moreover, it is likely to be the case that where mortality conditions
are unfavorable, morbidity is also high, so that subfecundity, or
impaired ability to bear children, is fairly common among women.
Thus, the process of producing "sufficient" numbers of surviving
children may come to occupy nearly all of a female's adult life.
       Finally, we can consider the situation of countries that are
passing through the "demographic transition" (where mortality
levels have fallen but where fertility levels remain high) in terms
of the effect of fertility on women's roles. Under these conditions,
more of the children conceived are likely to survive the stages of
gestation, parturition, and infancy. Without a change in fertility
values, the outcome is more children per woman and high levels of
completed fertility. Within the context of high-fertility cultural
values, this may be interpreted as a blessing. Objectively, however, it may translate into malnourishment, selective neglect of
children, [22] and greater time and energy expenditures in child-
rearing tasks. On an aggregate basis, this phenomenon results in
very rapid population growth, which itself can alter the opportunity
structure for women, both positively and negatively. [23]
       Another "fertility" variable that has implications for the
structure of sex roles is contraceptive technology. The development
of technologically sophisticated contraceptives has encouraged their
widespread adoption in some cultures. Contraception is significant,
not just because of its demographic effect in lowering fertility but
because it permits the separation of coitus from conception. Technologically, at least, the timing and extent of parenthood has been
made a matter of choice for both men and women. Perhaps equally
important in terms of male-female roles, the use of contraception
gives a woman the power to control her fertility with or without the
permission, or even the knowledge, of her husband. Indeed, it is
precisely this potential for disruption of traditional patterns of
power that has fostered male resistance to contraception in some
areas. [24] A correlate of the separation of coitus from conception is
the ability to separate sexual activity from marriage. Contraception
allows for nonreproductive sex premaritally, postmaritally, and
extramaritally. This, in essence, provides a foundation for the
development of a structure of male-female roles that is totally distinct from the traditional gender role structure located within the
familial sphere. Thus, as a technological innovation, contraception
can influence the organization of sex roles--indirectly, through its
impact on fertility and, directly, by allowing for control of female
sexuality by individual women themselves.

In summary, the analysis of sex roles in a particular society
and cross-culturally can be aided by an examination of demographic
variables as factors that influence directly and indirectly the organization of sex roles. This brief look at the effect of age-sex
composition, mortality, and fertility on the availability and content
of roles for women and for men was intended primarily to suggest
the utility of sex role research at this level of analysis. Only a
few demographic factors have been examined here. Additional examples of research efforts utilizing demographic variables are
Oppenheimer's analysis of the entry of women in the U.S. labor
market as a response to demand factors in the job market paired
with a particular demographic situation in the supply of available
women,[25] Ridley's analysis of women's roles as a function of the
education and economic composition of the female population,[26] and
the analyses of Gross and Singelmann of the content of economic
roles of women as a function of the occupational[27] or industrial
structure[28] of the labor force.

THE CASE OF AGE AT MARRIAGE IN TURKEY

With the foregoing general review as background, let us turn
now to a more intensive examination of one specific demographic
variable, age at marriage. While age at marriage is certainly
amenable to analysis at the aggregate level, in this next section, I
am more concerned with it as a factor in the determination of behavior at the individual level. Thus, let us shift from a concern
with the impact of demographic variables in general on the structure of sex roles to a look at the impact of different ages at marriage on the enactment of one particular role, that of wife within
the context of contemporary Turkish society.

It can be argued that age at marriage has meaning in the individual life cycle as a pivotal variable. It truncates life experiences
by cutting off or cutting short some experiences and opening up
other, different ones. We assume that single status allows exposure
to experiences in ways that married status does not and/or that the
same event is experienced differentially by marital status. I have
argued elsewhere that age at marriage has implications both for
the kind of person a woman is upon entering marriage and also for
the kind of wife she will be after marriage.[29] In modernizing
societies, age at marriage can determine how much exposure to
nontraditional attitudes and roles a young woman has prior to marriage. It is assumed that these opportunities for exposure to nontraditional influences and chances for self-development independent
of a husband, which are allowed (though not guaranteed) by late age

at marriage, will have an impact on how the wife-mother role is
handled. It is this assumption in particular that I want to examine,
using sample survey data from Ankara, Turkey. First, however,
let me suggest some additional meanings of age at marriage, particularly as it has become a focus of governmental policy in the
area of family-forming behavior.

Goode has argued succinctly and well that the community has a
stake in marriage, and his arguments need not be repeated here.[30]
The community's interest in marital liaisons are manifest in the
sanctification and institutionalization of marriage through ceremony
and contract. The interest of the community in marriage has carried over to the nation-state, which continues to regulate marriage.
Although the marriage regulations vary within and across nations,
they tend to revolve around such matters as who shall marry whom
(by sex, race, ethnicity, religion, health) and when (age, economic
preparedness).

Because of the intimate connection between age at marriage
and total length of exposure to risk of marital conception, population
policy planners have noted the possibility of using the power of the
state to foster an increase in the legal minimum age at marriage.
In other words, postponement of marriage is seen as one way to in-
hibit rapid population growth: simply remove whole blocs of young
fertile women from the risk of marital conception by disallowing
early marriage.*

The demographic outcome of slower growth rates occurs
through two related effects: an immediate effect of reduction in
marital fertility and a time-lagged effect of increasing the length of
a generation. These effects of marital postponement have spawned
much interest in nuptiality and the "nuptiality transition," the shift
from early to later ages at marriage, currently being experienced
in several developing areas.

In a recent paper that reviews much of the relevant literature,
Duza and Baldwin propose what amounts to a role-competition theory
of marital postponement.[31] That is, Duza and Baldwin attempt to
account for marital age in terms of the availability of attractive

---

*An obvious side effect of this policy is to lengthen the amount
of time a young woman is exposed to risk of pre- or nonmarital conception. This may not be so problematic in "confinement" cultures,
in which the opportunity for mixed sex interaction among young
people is low and where premarital pregnancy is severely sanctioned.
But it is a problem that is not yet fully faced up to in such "open"
cultures as the contemporary United States (see G. L. Fox, 1973b).

options to marriage. In so doing, they echo the earlier work of Bernard and Rossi, who suggest that in the absence of alternative options, women tend to marry.[32] As options increase and compete effectively with marriage as a "career," women tend to postpone marriage. In policy terms, Duza and Baldwin recommend governmental programs that will enhance the educational and occupational opportunities for women, since they see these two institutional arenas as the major source of nonfamilial role alternatives for women. They see social programming as a complement to governmental legislation in increasing age at marriage, which, in turn, fosters lower population growth rates.

While I think the work of Duza, Baldwin, and others on determinants of nuptiality is important and timely, I think it is incomplete. It seems to me that we need to carry the analysis further down the causal chain and ask whether age at marriage per se has any impact on individual marriage behavior. Knowing that greater opportunities for women are associated with higher median ages at marriage--which, in turn, are associated with lower aggregate levels of fertility--is not basis enough to suggest policy intervention with the nuptiality variables. The demographer's explanation of the latter link in the chain seems too facile, too mechanistic. It is true that the time a woman is not married is time she is not having babies, but what is to prevent her from making up for lost time once she is married through shorter interparity intervals and the extension of childbearing into later ages?

Social scientists need to seek some explanations for how postponed marriage versus early marriage tends to operate within the marriage relationship itself. There is little reason to be concerned with age at marriage and to attempt to manipulate it unless we can determine whether and how age at marriage makes a difference in marital behavior. A central policy issue then is to investigate the impact of age at marriage on family behavior. This leads back in some obvious ways to the assumptions discussed earlier about the operation of age at marriage, that is, whether age at marriage can cut off or open up opportunities for self-development prior to marriage and can determine the nature of role enactment in the wife-mother role set.

SOURCE OF DATA

I want to examine within a limited context the meaning of differential marriage age for marital behavior by using data from

the Ankara segment of the Ankara Family Study.* Interviews for
this study were conducted with 803 married women living with their
husbands at the time of the survey. The sample design represents
a virtually complete response (response rate equals 99 percent)
from a two-stage area-probability sample (systematic, stratified,
and clustered) derived from a sampling frame of dwelling-unit lists
prepared by the Turkish State Institute of Statistics for the 1965
census.

Since 1923, when Ankara became the national capital of Turkey,
the city has grown rapidly, so that today, Ankara is one of the
largest cities in Turkey, with a population of over 1 million inhabitants. A large portion of this growth is attributable to the sizable
influx of migrants from the surrounding villages of the central
Anatolian Plain.[33] The heterogeneity of the city population is reflected in the differentials in background characteristics exhibited
by respondents in the study sample. For example, 40 percent of
the respondents were born in villages; just under 25 percent were
married at age 15 or younger; almost 50 percent have had no formal
schooling; and 75 percent of the marriages represented by this
sample were arranged marriages. Thus, although the data are
taken from an "urban" sample, nevertheless, the sample represents the wide range of background experiences that one can find in
a modernizing country like Turkey.

VARIABLES IN THE ANALYSIS

The variables used as independent and control variables in the
contingency analyses that follow are straightforward. Community
background refers to the type of community--city, town, or village
--in which the respondent spent the bulk of her life prior to her
migration to Ankara. Of the sample, 45 percent are from city
backgrounds, 20 percent from towns, and 35 percent from villages.
Education is "trichotomized" into less than primary (illiterate or
literate, but with no formal schooling), primary, and more than
primary education categories. Of the sample, 48 percent have had
less than primary education, 32 percent have had some primary

------

*The Ankara Family Study was conducted in 1966 in Ankara,
Turkey, and in four outlying villages under the direction of David
Goldberg of the Population Studies Center of the University of
Michigan. The author acknowledges with thanks his kindness in
making these data available.

level education, while 20 percent have had more than primary level
education. Age at marriage has been "trichotomized" into 15 years
old or less (24 percent of the sample), 16 to 19 years of age (48 percent of the sample), and marriage age of 20 or older (28 percent of
the sample).

In the analyses that follow, three dimensions are used to sum-
marize the role relationships and behavior patterns of the Turkish
marriage: the distribution and exercise of power within the conjugal
relationship, the degree of segregation by sex of tasks and activities,
and the degree of confinement of the wife's physical and mental
worlds. Despite empirical overlaps, the dimensions can be separated analytically. The power dimension assesses the superordinance
of the husband over the wife and, inferentially, provides a measure
of the Islamic tradition of male dominance within the family. The
segregation dimension indicates the distance between male and female in their roles of husband and wife and taps the strength of traditional norms calling for segregation of the sexes. The confinement dimension is an indicator of the openness, or lack of it, of the
wife's world; this dimension, by inference, taps the degree to which
traditional female seclusion is adhered to.[34]

Within the framework set by these three dimensions, the traditional marriage pattern can be defined as one in which the husband
is superordinantly powerful, in which there is a high degree of segregation by sex, and in which the wife is confined physically and
mentally within the home. The modern marriage pattern, on the
other hand, is said to be one in which tasks and activities are
shared and/or assigned and carried out according to the abilities of
the partners and in which the wife has access to the world beyond
her home. As ideal-typical polarities on a continuum, the above
patterns leave room for a range of marriage patterns in between.

Six composite measures are used to indicate the dimensions of
power, segregation, and confinement in marital behavior. Each
variable has been dichotomized into "modern" and "traditional"
categories in order to facilitate the presentation of data.

Two variables pertain to the distribution of power. The "index of forbidden activities" is the number (up to eight) of activities
that some husbands forbid their wives to pursue (see the Appendix
at the end of the chapter for a full list of items comprising this and
the remaining measures of marital behavior); a "modern" response
is considered to be two or fewer forbidden activities. The "husband's power in decision-making" index is a measure of the husband's relative power in making final decisions about a series of
five family-linked matters. Low husband power, the "modern" response, is indicated by his making final decisions in three or fewer
matters.

Two variables are used to measure sex segregation in the marriage. The "segregation of decision-making" index ascertains the extent to which final decisions on the five family-linked matters are made jointly by both spouses or separately by either spouse alone. Joint decisions on three or more matters is the "modern" response. The second variable is a measure of the extent to which the respondent agrees with five statements about proper sex-segregated roles for women and men. Agreement with three or fewer statements was considered a "modern" response.

The final two variables indicate the dimension of confinement and attempt to measure the radius of the respondent's world-- whether her world is small and focused inward or large and open to ideas and activities beyond the boundaries of her home. The first variable is the respondent's estimate of the country located farthest from Turkey, with responses coded into "small" "medium," and "large" worlds. "Large" world is considered a "modern" viewpoint. The second measure of confinement is an index of how frequently the respondent goes out to restaurants, movies, and parties. Again, the aim is to get an indication of the nature of the wife's world and her activities in it. Frequent attendance at two or more of the three activities was considered as less confined, and thus more modern, than participation in only one or none of the three activities outside the home.

IMPACT OF AGE AT MARRIAGE
ON MARITAL BEHAVIOR

Essentially, the form of the question that is posed relative to the effect of age at marriage on marriage behavior is, Does postponement of marriage lead to different behavior than not postponing marriage? Obviously, we cannot measure this for the individual, since what we are asking is, "Would I be a different kind of wife at age 30 had I married at age 25 rather than at 16?" There is no way to answer this question for the individual, since the change of marital status is irreversible in terms of experience; doing one precludes the other. In the aggregate, the situation is confused by the selectivity effect. Perhaps the wifely behavior of child brides is different from that of mature brides, because the women were different to begin with and not because of the different age at marriage. The only way to deal with this problem is to match women on relevant variables and then look at the impact of age at marriage. This is done in Table 12.1.

Table 12.1 presents the relationships between age at marriage and marriage behavior within categories of community background

TABLE 12.1: Percent of Respondents with Modern Marriage Behavior, by Age at Marriage, Controlling for Community Background and Education, in Ankara, Turkey, 1966

Age at Marriage	Number	With Low Husband's Power	With Zero to Two Forbidden Activities	With Low Segregation in Decision Making	With Low Support for Traditional Sex Roles	With Large World	With Two or More Activities Out
Community Background							
City:							
15 years	54	68.5	27.8	70.4	57.4	13.0	16.7
16–19 years	175	80.0	37.1	74.3	55.4	25.7	25.1
20+ years	134	88.8	45.5	86.6	75.4	38.8	38.8
Town:							
15 years	40	60.0	15.0	60.0	50.0	22.5	12.5
16–19 years	80	65.0	17.5	63.8	56.2	15.0	13.8
20+ years	38	86.8	28.9	81.6	57.9	23.7	18.5
Village:							
15 years	101	44.6	2.0	37.6	24.8	3.0	5.9
16–19 years	131	50.4	3.8	49.6	32.1	5.3	3.8
20+ years	50	38.0	4.0	44.0	32.0	2.0	6.0
Education at Marriage							
More than primary:							
15 years	7	*	*	*	*	*	*
16–19 years	65	96.9	53.8	89.2	73.9	44.6	9.2
20+ years	92	92.4	51.1	93.5	84.8	53.3	6.5
Primary:							
15 years	55	72.7	14.5	67.3	52.7	14.6	20.0
16–19 years	142	79.6	25.6	75.4	54.2	17.6	33.7
20+ years	56	85.7	28.6	80.4	60.7	23.2	32.1
Less than primary:							
15 years	133	45.1	3.8	42.9	30.1	6.0	69.2
16–19 years	179	45.8	7.3	45.3	31.3	6.7	66.5
20+ years	74	51.4	14.9	51.4	36.5	6.8	64.9

*Number 20 cases.

Source: Compiled by the author.

and education. There are three points to be made from this table.
First, one can note the interrelationship between age at marriage
and community background and between age at marriage and education. It should not be surprising to find correlations here. Early
marriage is normative in villages but not in the cities; the opposite
is the case for late marriage. Thus we find that 36 percent of villagers marry at 15 or less; only 15 percent of city girls do.
Thirty-seven percent of city girls marry at age 20 or older, as
contrasted with 18 percent of the villagers.

There is also a positive correlation between age at marriage
and educational attainment. Women with less than a primary education are more frequently married at the younger ages and less
frequently at older ages than women with greater amounts of education. It was suggested earlier that age at marriage could operate
as a pivotal variable to truncate life experiences. It can be seen to
do that here: women marrying at 15 or less are typically cut off
from any further education (68 percent of the women marrying at
less than 15 have less than primary school education), while a later
age at marriage makes higher educational attainment much more
feasible (61 percent of those marrying at 20 and over have more
than primary school education).

The correlations of age at marriage with community background and education, respectively, can serve to emphasize that
whatever impact age at marriage has on marriage behavior, it derives in part from its correlations with the two background variables. We need to ask whether age at marriage has any impact of
its own on marriage behavior apart from its correlation with community background and education. Table 12.1 suggests, first, that
the effects of community background and education on marriage
behavior are each stronger than the effect of age at marriage. At
the same time, however, one can note, with a few minor exceptions
and one major exception, a consistent monotonic trend in modernism in marriage behavior across the three age-at-marriage categories when the effects of community background and education are
controlled. For example, among respondents with a city background,
68 percent of those married at 15 or less report a low degree of
husband's power in decision making. This compares with 80 percent
among the 16- to 19-year-old brides and 89 percent among women
married at age 20 or over. In short, then, age at marriage does
seem to have an impact, however slight, on marriage behavior, and
thus, it seems worth pursuing this relationship: Why or how does it
operate?

The third point to be made from Table 12.1 concerns the
major exception to the monotonic trend in modernism across age at

marriage noted above. When women with village background are considered, it is clear that age at marriage has no consistent effect on marriage behavior. This inconsistency is most peculiar, in light of the argument that late age at marriage should indicate an increased maturity and stronger self-development (or self-concept), which would then be reflected in a more "modern" marriage pattern. Indeed, one could expect that this kind of effect should be even more pronounced for village than for urban women, since village areas are generally "opportunity poor," and thus, there should be no competing variable (such as education) that would dilute the "pure" effect of the age at marriage differential. The data suggest otherwise, however. This inconsistency will be pursued at a later point in the analysis, and an explanation will be proffered then.

Before leaving Table 12.1, let me report that a similar analysis was made with age of respondent as a control. This seemed appropriate, given previous research which suggests that the kind of marriage behavior variables used in this chapter are affected by marital duration. Controlling for age of respondent is equivalent to controlling for marital duration. Within age categories, age at marriage was consistently related to marriage behavior in the expected directions. Age itself, however, was not consistently related to modernism in marriage behavior. Correlational analysis was performed with the variables, using the full range of scores rather than the collapsed-category coding scheme used in the contingency analysis. Zero-order correlations between age at marriage and marriage behavior were significant at the .001 level or better. When the effect of age was partialed out, the relationships retained their significance at the .001 level or better. The zero-order relationships between age and marriage behavior approached standard levels of significance on the power items. Given these results, I have not included age as a critical variable in any of the remaining analyses.

Table 12.2 looks more closely at the operation of age at marriage by translating later age at marriage into two kinds of experiences that are possible after age 15 and prior to marriage, namely, being in school and living in or visiting an urban area. Obviously, going to school and being in an urban area are possible prior to age 15 and after marriage. But it is the time period of single, young adulthood that I wanted to focus on, as it is this kind of time that is gained through postponement of marriage. What happens, if anything, to women during this time period? In other words, experientially, what are we talking about when we refer to increased age at marriage? What can postponement of marriage mean?

TABLE 12.2: Percent of Respondents with Modern Marriage Behavior, by Urban and School Experience between Age 15 and Age at Marriage, Controlling for Age at Marriage, in Ankara, Turkey, 1966

Urban and School Experience by Age at Marriage	Number	With Low Husband's Power	With Zero to Two Forbidden Activities	With Low Segregation in Decision Making	With Low Support for Traditional Sex Roles	With Large World	With Two or More Activities Out
Marriage at 16 to 19:							
Urban experience:							
(1) School experience	26	100.0	61.5	92.3	84.6	50.0	45.2
(2) No school experience	261	69.0	25.3	66.7	48.7	17.2	17.6
No urban experience:							
(3) School experience	1	*	*	*	*	*	*
(4) No school experience	98	52.0	1.0	48.0	31.6	6.1	1.0
Marriage at 20 and over:							
Urban experience:							
(5) School experience	57	95.0	56.1	96.5	91.2	54.4	54.4
(6) No school experience	132	80.3	31.1	76.5	59.1	23.5	22.7
No urban experience:							
(7) School experience	2	*	*	*	*	*	*
(8) No school experience	31	32.3	3.2	38.7	22.6	0.0	0.0

*Number 20 cases.

Source: Compiled by the author.

In an attempt to answer this question, a determination was made for each respondent as to whether she had indeed been in school or in an urban area after reaching age 15 and prior to the time she married. For those who married at 15 or younger, by definition, neither experience was possible. Among those who married between 16 and 19, 7 percent had been in school after 15 and prior to marriage; 74 percent had had an urban experience during that period. This compares with a school experience for 27 percent of those marrying at age 20 or later and an urban experience for 85 percent of the late marriers. Given the rural-urban differential in Turkey in the availability of postprimary education, being in school during the period we are focusing on is tantamount to being in an urban area; that is, practically all of the respondents with a school experience also were in an urban area between age 15 and marriage.

Table 12.2 presents differentials in marital behavior, simultaneously controlling for age at marriage and urban and school experiences. There are several points to be made from these data about the translation of marriage postponement into experience. We can get an estimate of the "costs" of a lack of postpubertal school experience for marital behavior by comparison of percents in rows 1 and 2 and rows 5 and 6. Thus, we are controlling for urban experience and age at marriage and allowing school experience to vary. The differences in these rows are labeled "School Effect" and are shown in Table 12.3. The differences are large, which suggests that the effect of schooling during the years gained by marital postponement is strong. But we can also note that in general, among these women, the effect of having or not having had a school experience is greater for the 16- to 19-year-old brides than for those 20 and over. I suggest what we see here is that the older brides (20 and over) have a longer opportunity for exposure to urban influences, the "modern world of modern ideas," independent of a husband than do the 16- to 19-year-olds, and this longer exposure to the urban milieu can offset the costs of the lack of educational experience.

Second, by comparing rows 2 and 4 and rows 6 and 8, we can control for school experience (at the level of no experience) and age at marriage and allow the urban experience to vary. The differences in percent of modern responses on the marital behavior items are presented in Table 12.3, labeled "Urban Effect." Again, we note that within each age-at-marriage group, there is a "cost" associated with the lack of an urban experience during the period between age 15 and marriage. In this instance, however, the "cost" in modernism is greater for the older (20 and over) than for the younger (16-19) brides.

TABLE 12.3: Comparison of Differences in Percentages (Δ)
for Selected Rows of Table 12.2

Marriage Behavior	School Effect		Urban Effect		Age at Marriage Effect	
	Rows (1)-(2) 16-19	Rows (5)-(6) 20+	Rows (2)-(4) 16-19	Rows (6)-(8) 20+	Rows (6)-(2) No School	Rows (5)-(1) School
Power	31.0	14.7	17.0	48.0	11.3	-5.0
Forbids	36.2	25.0	24.3	27.9	5.8	-5.4
Segregation	25.6	20.0	18.7	37.8	9.8	4.2
Sex roles	39.9	32.1	17.1	36.5	10.4	6.6
World	32.8	30.9	11.1	23.5	6.3	4.4
Activities	28.6	31.7	16.6	22.7	5.1	8.2

Source: Compiled by the author.

Part of what we are seeing here is attributable to the fact that
the women with no school experience and no urban experience in the
period between age 15 and marriage are former villagers. Indeed,
if we compare row 4 with row 8, that is, compare the 16- to 19-year-
old brides to whom nothing has happened (in our terms) with the
20-and-over-year-old brides to whom nothing has happened, we see
the same reversal of the relationship between later age at marriage
and modernism that was first observed in Table 12.1. We find
larger proportions of modern responses from 16- to the 19-year-
old group than from those 20 and older.

I suggest that we can account for this effect in two ways. I
think, in part, we are looking at what happens (or fails to happen)
to those village women who sit at home as unmarried "children" for
several years beyond childhood. Because opportunities for self-
development in the villages are either poor or nonexistent, women
who marry late are unable to take advantage of the "extra" years
between 15 and marriage as a time to grow experientially and to
develop skills that can be translated into independence as a wife.
The effect seems to be a not unreasonable one: the longer they stay
at home in the village out of range of countermanding influences,
the more ensconced and trained they become in traditional culture
patterns and practices. The older the unmarried women become,
the more they come to participate as adults in traditional family
roles; and this traditional adult behavior is carried over into their
own marital patterns when at last they do marry.

In addition to this "adult socialization into traditional roles" explanation for the greater modernism among the younger brides, I would like to suggest a "marriage market" explanation. The traditional marriage market places a high value on youth, beauty, and virginity. Moreover, to remain single is to face a life of shame. The valuation of youth and the degradation of single status combine to put older candidates for marriage in a relatively poor bargaining situation. In such a setting, conformity with traditional values may be one price of late marriage. Because the market value of an older bride is low, she may have to relinquish claims to power within the home and participation outside it.

A third set of observations to be made from Table 12.2 involves the comparison of rows 6 and 2 and rows 5 and 1. In these comparisons, we are holding urban and school experience constant and allowing age at marriage to vary, so as to obtain an "Age at Marriage" effect (see Table 12.3). First, the overall magnitude of the differences here is much smaller than for either of the two experiences, school or urban. Second, for those women who have had an urban experience but not a school experience, the 20 and over brides are more modern (rows 6 and 2). Although gained from a different vantage point, this is essentially the same information we obtained from the examination of the "School Effects"; and so the explanation should be the same. That is, among the older brides, a lengthier exposure to the urban milieu can offset the lack of educational experience.

But when we compare women who have had both the urban and the school experience (rows 5 and 1), we find that the brides who are 20 and older are only slightly more modern than the 16- to 19-year-old brides, and in the case of the power measures, they are less so. In other words, we see that age at marriage per se makes the least difference when both experiences are present. This suggests that we have succeeded in meaningfully translating marriage postponement into experience. That is, the effect of age at marriage on marital behavior has been "washed out," or "captured," by the two experience variables. Analytically, this brings us much closer to an understanding of the operation of differential age at marriage on some components of marriage behavior.

DISCUSSION

The purpose of the foregoing analysis was to seek a meaning for age at marriage and to see whether and how different ages at marriage affect marital behavior. What has been seen most clearly is that the "meaning" of age at marriage differs by social context.

In city and town areas, where opportunities for exposure to, and participation in, nontraditional or nonfamilial roles are available, late age at marriage can be translated into "developmental" activities. That is, the years gained through marriage postponement can be used for active, experiential maturation. In these settings, age at marriage is positively correlated with modernism in the enactment of marital roles. However, as was seen in Table 12.2, a good deal of this effect can be understood as resulting from the different exposures to school and urban experience between age 15 and marriage for the older versus younger brides.

In villages, however, the meaning of age at marriage is not so clear. On the one hand, we saw in Table 12.1 a positive relationship between age of marriage and modernism in marriage behavior when we compared the child brides (15) to the 16- to 19-year-old brides. Very early age at marriage catches a girl as a child and places her in dependent or subordinate roles in marriage. This effect is mitigated somewhat if marriage is postponed a few years. On the other hand, village women who marry late (20+) are more traditional than the 16- to 19-year-old brides. In village areas, the years gained through late age at marriage cannot be translated into developmental experience, because the opportunities for it are nonexistent in the villages.

In effect, then, the usefulness of age at marriage as an analytic variable derives primarily from its significance as an indicator of behavior, which varies according to social context rather than from any intrinsic meaning attached to chronological age itself. The impact of age at marriage depends in large part on active experiential maturation rather than on the accretion of years. In other words, to the extent that something happens to a woman during her postpubertal years when single, then marriage postponement has a payoff in nontraditional marital behavior. How little that "something" needs to be is seen by one of the two experience variables we used. Mere exposure to an urban area sometime after age 15 and prior to marriage is not the kind of developmental experience that calls for elaborate policy interventions; yet, mere exposure appeared in Table 12.2 to have a rather strong impact on marriage behavior. The second experience variable, postpubertal education, is a different matter. Elsewhere, I have indicated the significance of postpubertal education with relation to the maintenance of traditional values and behavior patterns among Turkish women.[35] Making secondary and postsecondary educational facilities more available and acceptable to women does call for a concerted policy effort; but the impact on women's behavior in a variety of role contexts, familial and nonfamilial alike, should be enormous.

CONCLUSION

Let me conclude with some comments about conceptual schemes and population policy in the area of family formation behavior. Earlier, I mentioned the interest of population planners in age at marriage because of the inverse association between median marriage age and fertility and because of the relative ease of governmental intercession with the age at marriage variable. The conceptual scheme looks something like this:

$$AM \; \text{---------------} \quad \text{Fertility} \tag{1}$$

The policy implication of the conceptual scheme above is as follows: if the goal is a decrease in fertility, then efforts should be made to inflate age at marriage through legislation or decree.

Duza and Baldwin's work suggests an additional link in the chain, namely, that the availability of nonfamilial role alternatives will inflate age at marriage. Conceptually, this looks like:

$$\text{Availability of NF Role Alt.} \; \overset{+}{--} \; AM \; \overset{-}{--} \; \text{Fertility} \tag{2}$$

The policy implication is: facilitate the availability and attractiveness of nonfamilial role alternatives if the goal is lower fertility.

The analyses in this chapter suggest three additions to the conceptual scheme. First, age at marriage is interpretable as an indicator of experience. Second, taking a step back, age at marriage (and, therefore, experience) is influenced by community background. Third, age at marriage (and, therefore, experience) influences the enactment of marital roles. Schematically, this looks like:

$$\text{Type of Community} \; -- \; AM= \text{Experience} \; -- \; \text{Marital} \atop \text{Behavior} \tag{3}$$

The next step is to combine the two conceptual schemes. The missing link between modernism or traditionalism in marital behavior and fertility is provided in a series of papers by Goldberg.[36] Using variables similar to those used in this chapter to measure marital behavior, Goldberg finds that the degree of modernism in the wife's role is predictive of expected births and of contraceptive use in two cultural settings (Turkey and Mexico).

A second step toward combining the two chains is to assess the differential availability of nonfamilial role alternatives by community type. Although there is some argument about the greater opportunity for role diversity for women in towns as opposed to

villages,[37] opportunities for participation in the modern sector of
various institutions are clearly greater in the centers of modernization, the cities, and, to a lesser extent, in the towns.[38] Indeed,
that is the picture obtained from the marginal distributions in Table
12.2. In sum, then, I would argue that at the present time, nonfamilial role alternatives are more readily available in urban areas
than in rural areas in developing countries like Turkey. Thus, to
complete the conceptual scheme, we can add (3) to (2), as follows:

Type of Comm-- Avail of NF Role Alt-- AM=Exp--
    Marital Behavior-- Fertility   (4)

Conceptually, I am suggesting a clarification of the mechanism
through which age at marriage translates into fertility. I suggest
that rather than (or in addition to) affecting the length of time a
woman is exposed to risk of marital childbearing, age at marriage
has an impact (inherited through experience) on her enactment of
her marital roles; and marital role behavior itself is predictive of
fertility.[39]
    With respect to policy in the area of family formation, I would
urge some caution, particularly on the point of specific legislative
attempts to increase age at marriage. Manipulating the age at
marriage variable is risky policy for two reasons. Where there
are "developmental" opportunities for young women during the postpubertal period, young versus older age at marriage does not seem
to differentiate among subsequent marital behavior. This suggests
that legislation to increase the minimum age at marriage may be
neither necessary nor worth the trouble. And in those areas where
there are no opportunities for meaningful experience during the
extra years gained by marital postponement, legislation to increase
age at marriage could actually produce the opposite (of the desired)
effect. Marriage postponement would merely provide to those who
marry late an opportunity to learn and to participate in traditional
adult attitudes and behaviors. And this could offset whatever gains
in fertility reduction that accrue from postponed marriage.
    A final point I want to make relative to conceptual schemes is
related to our notions of role alternatives, role competition, and
the substitution of one role for another. Theories of role competition and role compatibility predominate in the current literature on
fertility. For example, it is argued that occupations or professional
careers will provide alternatives to the wife-mother roles; that the
"opportunity-costs" of children are greater for employed women
and, thus, can account for their lower fertility; that work and
mothering roles compete; that career success can substitute for
childbearing; and so on. All these notions argue that one route to

lowered fertility is to increase role competition between the wife-mother role and other attractive alternative roles. If the competition is severe and the alternative to mothering sufficiently attractive, women will opt for an alternative role and thereby reduce their own childbearing, which, in the aggregate, will decrease total levels of fertility. As I suggested earlier, Duza and Baldwin, among others, propose a similar explanation of marital postponement (indeed, they recommend a social policy to hasten the nuptiality transition that is based upon a role substitution model).

There are reasons to be skeptical of such theories as a basis for policy. First, the work of Ware in Africa suggests, for example, the ease with which, in some settings, mothering can be combined with "substitute" roles. Moreover, others have pointed out the possibility that widely available day-care centers could foster an increase in childbearing, by making child care less burdensome and less competitive with other activities. All of this suggests that even with its problems, the difficulties of role combination are not so great as to make role substitution a likely choice for many women. Second, even in "developed" countries, like it or not, family and marriage are the arenas that are of central importance to the majority of women. To expect wholesale defection from familial roles (implied by the role competition and role substitution models) is sheer folly. Less drastic and more realistic would be a shift in research focus away from substitutions for marriage and mother-hood and toward study of how changes in behavior within those roles might be enacted and with what implications for other dimensions of those same roles.

APPENDIX

Items Included in the Indexes of Marriage Behavior

Index of Forbidden Activities

1. Husband forbids wearing of short-sleeved dresses
2. Husband forbids sitting with male visitors in the home
3. Husband forbids shopping alone
4. Husband forbids going out without a scarf or head covering
5. Husband forbids going to a matinee at the movies alone
6. Husband forbids talking to men not known by the husband
7. Husband forbids visiting with women not known by the husband
8. Husband forbids going to parties alone

Index of Husband's Power in Decision Making

1. Husband makes final decision about choice of couples to visit
2. Husband makes final decision about choice of relatives to see
3. Husband makes final decision about purchase of major household goods
4. Husband makes final decision about budget for food
5. Husband makes final decision about uses of savings and earnings

Index of Segregation in Decision Making

1. Husband or wife alone makes final decision about choice of couples to visit
2. Husband or wife alone makes final decision about choice of relatives to see
3. Husband or wife alone makes final decision about purchase of major household goods
4. Husband or wife alone makes final decision about budget for food
5. Husband or wife alone makes final decision about uses of savings and earnings

Index of Respondent's Attitudes toward
Traditional Sex Roles

1. Agrees that it is all right for men to go out alone whenever they wish
2. Agrees that women cannot be trusted and are irresponsible
3. Agrees that men should make the important decisions in the life of the family
4. Agrees that men should not be expected to do housework
5. Agrees that there is men's work and women's work and that men and women should not be doing each other's work

Respondent's Estimate of Country
Located Farthest from Turkey

Question: What country do you think is the farthest place in the world from Turkey?

Response codes: 1. Small world: Turkey, Near East, Eastern Europe, close segments of Western Europe, ambiguous answers, don't know.
2. Medium world: Distant segments of Western Europe, Russia, India, Africa, Central Asia, United States.
3. Large world: Southeast Asia, Pacific, Latin America, the poles, western United States.

NOTES

1. Angrist, S., 1969, pp. 215-32.
2. Ridley, J. C., 1969, pp. 199-250.
3. Holter, H., 1970.
4. Duncan, O. D., 1959.
5. Boserup, E., 1970, pp. 15-36.
6. Ridley, J. C., 1968, pp. 15-25.
7. Akers, D., 1967, pp. 907-24; Glick, P. C., Heer, D. M., and Beresford, J. C., 1963; Goldberg, D., 1965, and 1967, pp. 255-64.
8. Goldberg, 1967, p. 258.
9. Ibid.; Ridley, 1968.
10. Hajnal, J., 1953, pp. 80-101, and 1965; and Ridley, op. cit.
11. Ridley, 1968, pp. 22-25.
12. Dixon, R. B., 1975, pp. 1-20.
13. Boserup, op. cit.; Southhall, A., 1961.
14. Peterson, W., 1970.
15. Ridley, 1969; Sullerot, E., 1971.
16. Sullerot, op. cit.
17. Ridley, 1969.
18. Dixon, op. cit.
19. Ware, H., 1975.
20. Dixon, op. cit.
21. Ware, op. cit.
22. Adlakha, A., 1970; Dixon, op. cit.
23. Dixon, op. cit.
24. Ware, op. cit.
25. Oppenheimer, V. K., 1970, and 1973, pp. 946-61.
26. Ridley, 1969.
27. Gross, E., 1968, pp. 198-208.
28. Singelmann, J., 1975.
29. Fox, G. L., 1973b, pp. 523-24.
30. Goode, W. J., 1963.
31. Duza, M. B., and Baldwin, C. S., 1975.
32. Bernard, J., 1971, p. 171; Rossi, A., 1965.
33. Schnaiberg, A., 1971.
34. Goode, op. cit.; Berger, M., 1964.
35. Fox, G. L., 1975.
36. Goldberg, D., 1974 and 1975.
37. Boserup, op. cit., pp. 157-93 passim.
38. Peterson, op. cit.; Schnaiberg, op. cit.
39. Goldberg, op. cit.

13

Changing Roles in
Five Beirut Households

CYNTHIA L. MYNTTI

Beirut is regarded by Arabs and Westerners alike as a cosmopolitan, modern city. Yet one who knows its inhabitants is quick
to add that while "modern" in comparison to other parts of the Middle
East, family organization and the roles of women have been some of
the slowest aspects of society to change. This chapter will examine
the roles of members of five Beirut households.

The term role is used as a constallation of rights and obligations held by one person vis-a-vis the other members of his or her
household. The basis of such rights and obligations is thought to be
religious law. One could ask, for example, what are the legally
prescribed rights of a Muslim wife? Emphasis here, rather than
on theoretical questions of Islamic Shari's or Christian canons, is
on practical and perceived roles. One could argue that there is a
very fine line between customary rights and duties and those thought
to be legal dictates.

My choice of the five households does not claim to be a representative sample, although it does represent the spectrum of socioeconomic levels and several of the religious sects in Lebanon. Intensive case study research, the field methodology utilized, has
merit if only to delineate common patterns that traverse sect and
class boundaries. These patterns are those concerning the behavior
of Arab women--their common goals and common restrictions.

This chapter is based on research carried out in Beirut, in
spring 1974. Data were gathered during interviews with the five
women and through intensive household observation. Emphasis
here is on the women's perceptions. It is deliberately one-sided,
since in much Middle Eastern ethnography, women are either in-
articulate or inaccessible. Names have been changed.

SOCIAL ENVIRONMENT OF EACH HOUSEHOLD

Research on settlement patterns in the city of Beirut has described several trends that have held true in this study.[1] People tend to settle in neighborhoods where there are connections, such as land owned, extended kin already resident, other migrants from their original village, or the same sectarian composition. Unlike many Western cities, Beirut does not have social class differentiation by neighborhood as much as by particular buildings within an area. It would be possible, for example, to have Christian migrants from the same mountain village, of differing income levels, living in one Beirut neighborhood.

Such settlement patterns suggest that in an urban situation like Beirut, traditional attachments and loyalties could certainly be maintained. Khalaf and Kongstad state that "despite a mounting population density, an increasing scale of urbanization, and changing land use patterns, the social structure of the city has not displayed any substantial change in the traditional basis of social solidarity."[2]

Following are brief descriptions of the five households and their physical and social environments:

Muhammad al-As'ad, a deputy in the Lebanese Parliament, is a lawyer by education and a businessman by trade. Najla al-As'ad is a member of the al-As'ad family. They believe themselves to be the only wealthy Shi'a Muslim family native to Beirut. They live in Ashrafiyyé, where land has been owned by their kin for several generations. They own the deluxe apartment building in which they live and in which other al-As'ad families live, and they own adjacent buildings. Muhammad, who works long, erratic hours and travels away from Beirut a good deal, is not at home much of the time. Najla assists her husband in political and social affairs, and has cooking, cleaning, and child-care help. They have five children, aged 4 to 16.

The Haddads are Protestants, originating from southern Lebanon. Emile Haddad has lived in Australia; after they were married, the Haddads lived in Saudi Arabia on an American oil company compound. Nuha Haddad is a schoolteacher working a full day, Monday through Friday. It is important to note that she is the only woman of the five who is engaged in salaried work. The Haddads moved to Beirut six years ago from Saudi Arabia and live in Ras Beirut, where a good number of people from their village live. They socialize with many neighbors, and Nuha's kin live nearby. Their residence is close to both the Haddads' work. They have two daughters and one son, all in school.

The al-Hajj family, a native Sunni Muslim family, moved to their present house in Tariq Jadidé six years ago. Their family has lived for generations in Tariq Jadidé. They also own mountain property. Nabil al-Hajj's father, who lives with them, made the choices as to residence and property and all the buildings are still in his name. The family is a respected middle-class one, and their apartment building is the elite one of the neighborhood. They socialize with extended kin and with those in their apartment building but not with the other neighbors. Mr. al-Hajj has two supervisory jobs, one at the Arab University and the other in a hospital. He married at age 24, which is young for an Arab man; his wife (Mounira) is one year his junior. This household is different from the others in two respects: (1) it is farther along the development cycle, that is, the children are older--they have a son who is still in school and four daughters, two of whom are married--and (2) Nabil al-Hajj's parents live with them and have a considerable influence in household decision making.

Samir Hijazi ("Abu Samir") and his wife Fatma ("Ūm Samir") are Sunni Muslim Palestinian Arabs who met and married in a refugee camp on the outskirts of Beirut. He is now working as a concierge in an apartment building situated in Ras Beirut, and his wife and seven children live with him in the one-room apartment belonging to the concierge. Six of the seven children are in UNWRA schools (UN schools for Palestinian children), and the youngest son is still at home. Fatma Hijazi spends most of her day working in the apartment--making bread, cooking, cleaning, washing clothes, and caring for the children. Ūm Samir has a few appliances to facilitate her work, including a large refrigerator and a washing machine. Many people call on them from the building, as do relatives passing through Ras Beirut. No extended kin live nearby. During a regular working day, Mr. Hijazi often returns to the apartment for coffee with friends.

The Khourys are Christians; he (Joseph) is a Maronite and she (Aida) is a Greek Catholic. They originate from different villages but have lived in Beirut since they were married 18 years ago. He is a businessman and hotel owner (in the mountains) and would be considered among the newly emerging upper middle class of Beirut. They chose to live in 'Ain ar-Roumainé, largely, they say, because it is a Christian neighborhood. In addition, Joseph Khoury's work is easily accessible, and family and former village friends are near. They live in one of the two high-rent buildings in the area. Extensive visiting takes place during the daytime among the women of the two buildings, to the extent that Aida Khoury feels she knows everything about her neighbors.

Several generalizations can be drawn from these data. The native Beirut families, namely, the al-As'ads and the al-Hajjes, live in sections of the city that have been inhabited for generations by their kin. Upon moving to Beirut, the Haddads and the Khourys chose to live where kin and friends from their villages had settled. The Khourys further specified their preference for a Christian neighborhood. The four Lebanese households are in conformity with Beirut patterns of settlement as Khuri defined them. The Hijazis, refugees from Palestine, live where work is available for Abu Samir.

All of the families socialize with neighbors of similar socio-economic status, usually within their own apartment building. Khalaf and Kongstad report that social intimacy in Beirut is directly related to length of residence in one neighborhood. Their data show that residents who have lived longer than 11 years in Hamra, for example, displayed a noticeable degree of neighborliness and knowledge of their neighbors.[3]

This information suggests that the maintenance of a semi-intimate environment is possible, and indeed probable, in Beirut. All five families have a fierce sense of honor, as well as a strong fear of gossip. All feel that their behavior is constantly being scrutinized, particularly that of their women.

Visiting has been cited as an important form of social exchange among circum-Mediterranean peoples. It entails subtle and unspecified obligations not only to entertain visitors but to pay visits. Visiting, therefore, embodies and reflects a whole structure of social duties to kin and friends.[4]

On the surface, visiting in Beirut is most obviously a form of relaxation and entertainment in leisure time. In addition, when visiting is sexually differentiated, it may tend to maintain segregated spheres of social interaction by sex. Bott developed a theory of husband-wife separation, based on a study of London working-class families, showing that the more a husband and wife are linked to their respective kindred and friends of the same sex, communication and counsel are to a large extent gratified outside the conjugal bond.[5] This means that the husband remains attached to the public, male world, while the social world of the wife is female and household oriented. Sexually differentiated visiting patterns are the basis of these divisions. It is quite true in Beirut that as males socialize with males in Bourje coffeehouses or Hamra sidewalk cafes and females visit one another regularly at home, rigid spatial and social unisex spheres are perpetuated.

As a third function, visiting is also the vehicle by which the commonest and most dreaded form of social sanction--gossip--is

passed. This will be discussed below in its connection to the behavior control of women.

    The frequency of visiting within the extended families of the
five Beirut households is regular and extensive. The women, with
the exception of Fatma Hijazi, are in contact with their own kin at
least once a day, but they make no quantitative distinction between
visits with the khwāl ("wife's kin of orientation") and the 'amūm
("husband's kin of orientation"). [6]

    Basically, the four Lebanese women have no restrictions on
their visiting. Fatma Hijazi, however, is quite restricted from
socializing outside her home. Unlike the other women, she has no
domestic help, and her household work schedule is a demanding one.
So in fact, she is quite tied by duties to her home. She does not
think it proper to go out alone, but often on Sundays, she goes for
walks at Raouché or visits family members near the Bourje with
her children. All five women have female friends, but for the most
part, these have not been carried over from school or premarriage
days. "Visitors" would most often be affinal relatives of their own
kin.

    While in all five cases, visiting and socializing are sexually
differentiated, no concise conclusions concerning Bott's theory of
conjugal role segregation can be drawn. Granted that five households are indeed a small sample for any generalizations, but it is
interesting to point out that in the Haddad case, where conjugal roles
are not strictly segregated nor division of labor rigid, the visiting
pattern does not differ from the other families.

    It has been shown that visiting serves an important function in
Arab society. It provides the stage for transmission of gossip.
This has a direct impact on the household, since all behavior by its
members that is not considered respectable is talked about, and
precarious family honor can be destroyed. In a face-to-face, personal society, such as that in Beirut, maintenance and protection of
this honor is of utmost importance.

CHILD-PARENT RELATIONSHIPS

    It may seem a truism, but all five women explicitly stated
that it is the duty of children to love, respect, and obey their parents
while growing up. Daughters have the added responsibility to behave
properly so as to maintain family honor and not bring shame upon
members of the family. Fathers and brothers are obliged to assist
in safeguarding the chaste reputations of their female kin, since
Arab girls and women are not generally regarded as being able to
protect themselves. An important part of the Arab definition of

masculinity is connected with this role of guardian of the virtues of women kin.

When children are grown and supporting themselves, they are expected to support their parents financially. There is disagreement as to whether this regulation is as definite as religious law and whether it can be enforced by civil law. The four Lebanese women believe that whichever child is best able to support his or her parents should, though usually only sons do. Fatma Hijazi, however, feels that once a daughter is married, her responsibility to her parents ceases--"she belongs to her husband's house."[7]

Children are thus regarded as a form of social security. There is tremendous criticism when children disregard their parents in their old age. Two anecdotes illustrate this subject:

> A widow from Sidon had three very famous sons, all doctors, and one daughter. They refused to take their mother in and put her in a home for old people. She died soon after. A short time later, the daughter was killed in a car accident. People said this happened because the children had been so cruel to their mother.

> One time a woman was forced to work and could not take care of her widowed mother, who had had a stroke and was in a coma. She was worried that people would say she had no heart if she put her mother in an old age home. After three months of publicly noticed weeping and deliberation, she put her mother in a home.

Although it appears that there is no official pronouncement about obligatory support of parents, there is great social pressure to make children conform. There seems to be no forgiveness for stingy children.

The foremost legal right the children have vis-a-vis their parents is that of inheritance. On this issue, it seems that the relationship between specific religious rules, civil code, and what actually happens is obscure. The three Muslim families believe that the Koranic prescriptions concerning inheritance should be followed, whether or not there is a will. Daughters are usually given money rather than property. Often daughters relinquish all shares of their inheritance to their brothers, particularly those who feel that they are adequately provided for by their husbands. It is commonly held that if a woman gives her inheritance to her male siblings, she would expect reciprocal favors from them in time of need.[8]

Generally, "it is against the Arab mentality" to write wills, Aida Khoury believes. A will makes social relationships rigid. The possibility of a will set in a particular child's favor keeps parent-child relationships fluid; children, in effect, are kept guessing as to how the patrimony will be divided. This is to the advantage of parents, since the possibility of favor in the will keeps their children attentive to their desires in old age.

Parental duties toward children are differentiated by sex into distinctly male and female spheres. A father owes his children financial support until their education is completed and they are able to be financially self-sufficient. A mother regards her first duty toward her children as providing them with the love and affection they need in their home.

Jokingly, Mounira al-Hajj referred to herself as the "wazira dakhliyyé," or minister of the interior, and to her husband as the "wazir kharijiyyé," or foreign minister. She was referring to the division of responsibilities concerning the functions of the household and the supervision of the children. For example, her children would have to have permission from their father to leave the house in the evening. The extrahousehold decisions are in his sphere of influence. Najla al-As'ad and Aida Khoury do not see these divisions as being so rigid, because often their husbands are not at home, and out of necessity, their duties and supervision of the children branch out into the kharijiyyé, or foreign sphere.

In any case, final and serious discipline of all the children rests with the father in all households. All families have a sense of appropriate behavior (primarily for the daughters), which must be judged in the end by the fathers. Day-to-day discipline, however, varies among the families.

The women agree that few mothers in the Middle East treat their sons and daughters in an equal fashion. Sons are given obvious preferential care. Mounira al-Hajj charges that some mothers serve as "agents" for their sons, bargaining with the father on the son's behalf or even taking money for him. In these respects, they say, women are not rational, and have a subconscious desire to keep their sons attached. The principle of reciprocity is evident here; an obligation for repayment of favors is subtly established between mother and son. Yet it was observed that mothers tend to become selfish with all their children in an attempt to keep them dependent and near. The five women expressed a deep vocation in motherhood. "Children are everything, a reason for existence," said Mounira al-Hajj.

In the Hijazi household, the children fear their father. Abu Samir is its undisputed patriarch. Trends are, however, away from the Abu Samir type. The idea of a harsh paterfamilias is in transition, and the strict father-affectionate mother dichotomy is changing

with the current generation. Najla al-As'ad believes that her husband and his contemporaries are much less tyrannical than her
father's generation. Friendship is now possible between a son and
his father; it was not in the past. A trend toward earlier financial
and emotional independence of children seems to foster this.

General care for the children obviously falls into the sphere
of the mother's domestic responsibility. In all families, the children generally entertain themselves during off-school hours, but
children are incorporated gracefully into parlor discussions, and
weekend outings are planned on their behalf. Occasionally, sons
are allowed to stay with relatives or accompany their fathers to work.
Thus, none of the mothers felt that entertaining the children was
specifically her task, but such tasks as feeding and caring for the
children were.

The parent with the most education is supposedly obligated to
assist the children with their lessons. This would be the father in
all cases. Often, the fathers are too busy or too tired to render
this help, so the mother does.

In summary, divisions of responsibility of the parents with
respect to their children are differentiated by sex, with the mother
predominantly in the dakhiliyyé (or interior) sphere and the father
in the kharijiyyé (or foreign) sphere. The father is considered responsible for the financial support of the children, while the mother
offers the emotional support. Parental roles do overlap, since the
father is the ultimate disciplinarian and decision maker for all
household affairs and since the mother is called on often to make
essential day-to-day decisions regarding her children and the functioning of the household.

HUSBAND-WIFE RIGHTS AND RESPONSIBILITIES

None of the five couples were married by civil marriage.
Strictly speaking, Christian marriage is a sacrament, while Muslim
marriage is considered a contract. If contracts can be assumed to
stipulate the rights and duties of the parties involved, can it likewise
be assumed that roles of the husband and wife in an Islamic marriage
would be more clearly stated and understood than in the Christian
marriage? None of the couples, whether Christian or Muslim, re-
calls marital duties spelled out as part of the marriage ceremony.
Vague reference was made only of the wife's duty to obey her husband and the husband's duty to provide adequate support for his wife.

A tactical observation in the Sunni Muslim marriage contract
ceremony, the katabé al-kitab, shows that it is often concluded at
the home of the groom, with only males in attendance. The bride's

male representatives sign for her. Any specification that the bride might wish to add to the contract could well be disregarded if not considered socially proper by her male kin. This custom exists, among other places, in the orthodox Beirut Sunni Muslim community. Distinctive marital obligations do not seem, therefore, to result from promises at the time of the marriage ceremony, whether Christian or Muslim.

For each of the five couples, this was a first marriage. Rights to divorce not only vary with religious sect but with the sex of the spouse. Theoretically, divorce is forbidden among the Catholics and Maronites in Lebanon; traditionally in Islam, women have no right to initiate divorce proceedings. Yet, each of the five Beirut women could cite instances where religious rules regarding divorce were manipulated. Aida Khoury gave an example of this from the Maronite community. "A Maronite man wanted a divorce, so he told the priest that the mother of his young wife had been, in fact, his mistress. His wife was actually his daughter. His marriage was annulled immediately." While marriage is theoretically indissoluble, annulment is possible "with a little money." These means to a divorce are not only used by Maronite husbands but by their wives as well. A wife has equal access to divorce, or at least annulment and separation, by manipulating the rules. Khuri states that Maronites in a Beirut suburb who wished divorce either separated for a time or converted to the Greek Orthodox Church. [9]

Under numerous circumstances, Orthodox and Protestant communities grant divorces, and women can initiate the procedures, as well as men. Divorces take place in the religious courts, and women have the right to collect alimony, which is enforceable in civil courts. *

In Islamic law, women may specify their right to initiate divorce in their marriage contract. Given the situation at the katabé al-kitab, this prerogative is rare. It is generally not considered socially correct for a woman to act in an assertive manner at the time of her marriage. An exception is made if a woman has been divorced and is remarrying; it is often written into her second marriage contract that she can initiate divorce. Clearly, in these matters, custom prevails more than does actual Shari'a law.

At the time of divorce, a Muslim woman does have certain financial rights (those that have been specified at the time of her

---

*Such cases occur "often," I learned from Civil Judge Issam Baroudi, president of the Chambre à la Cour d'Appel of Beirut.

marriage). Theoretically, the second part of the bride-price, mahr mu'akhar, is paid to the bride should she be divorced by her husband. In the past, this was always a considerable sum, and it was said to act as a deterrent to impulsive divorce on the part of the husband. In addition, the husband is obliged to pay alimony, nafaga. And as with Christian divorces, alimony payments are enforceable in civil courts.

In recent years, changes in Beirut society have actually diminished the rights of women in respect of divorces. In the increasing number of marriages "for love," it is fashionable to essentially disregard the second part of the bride-price by setting it at a minimum of five piasters. Assuming that a high mahr mu'akhar is a deterrent to divorce, a small amount substantially lessens the husband's inhibitions to divorce. This point is often made, though it is open to question. Lower bride-price and marriages for love are only two aspects in the complex of changing attitudes toward marriage and divorce.

The three Muslim women referred to a type of Islamic divorce believed to be common now, where dissolution of the marriage comes about by mutual consent of the spouses and renders the "divorce surety" aspect of the mahr mu'akhar nil. This divorce, called the mukhala'ah, often takes place on the initiative of the wife, who, in return, abandons her monetary rights to mahr mu'akhar and nafaga. Thus, when this occurs, the woman does obtain a divorce but forfeits her financial compensation.[10]

Concerning succession and inheritance, Christian and Islamic norms differ slightly but, in practice, are nearly the same. Christian women can inherit from their husbands and can become de jure heads of households should their husband die. In practice, religious courts usually appoint a guardian from the 'amum to be responsible for the children and domestic finances. It is commonly believed that because he is an "insider," or part of the deceased's patrilineage, he will administer his brother's affairs justly, while the wife, or the khwāl, if appointed guardian, may not. Similar patterns in the Islamic community are defined in the Koran by the malzoum al-'amm ("obligations of the husband's brother").

It would seem that since the Islamic system is more contractual, social relationships (based on such legalities) would be better defined in the Islamic than in the Christian system. My empirical data suggest that a good deal of similar manipulation of rules and regulations occurs in both groups, Christian and Muslim, and that marital roles are not a function of sectarian regulation.

In summary, husbands and wives in these households generally have duties and amusements differentiated by sex. Yet, without exception, the relationships showed a great deal of mutual respect and, in the Haddad and al-Hajj households, a sharing attitude toward household management. The women, without question, take pride in their roles as wife and mother and are respected for the good performance of such roles. Husbands gain esteem as adequate providers, their most important role, vis-a-vis dependent wives and children.

ROLES OF THE EXTENDED KIN

Members of the extended family have a structural and organizational effect on the household, that is, an ideological and functional one. This section will discuss the rights and obligations of grandparents and uncles. Theories have been advanced concerning the effects of deference relations in a strongly patriarchal system; relations with the husband's kin are formal and cold, while those with the wife's kin are warm. [11]

In patrilineal, patriarchal Beirut society, it is believed that the oldest male of an extended kin group is the ultimate authority and is responsible legally and financially for the women and children. In both the al-Hajj and Khoury families, the husband's father is alive and has, in fact, a good deal of influence. Grandfather Khoury, who encouraged Joseph and Aida to have more children, now shoulders many of the children's expenses, particularly with regard to education. Visiting is regular and reciprocal between Beirut and the mountain village where he lives. Grandfather al-Hajj is not only the most respected male of the household but is its chief decision maker and de facto head. The husband's mother does not have any apparent influence in any of the cases where she is alive.

As mentioned earlier, Islamic Shari'a and Christian custom dictate that the 'amūm are legally responsible for the wife and children should the husband die or be disabled. The Christian custom is called mas'uliyyé adabiyyé, or the moral obligations of the husband's kin.

Just as the 'amūm have legal responsibilities, so, too, do they have rights. In Sunni Islam, the 'amūm can inherit from their brother should that brother have no sons. This is not the case in the Shi'a community or with the Christians. Universally, in the Arab world, it is the right of the ibn 'amm ("father's brother's son") to take the bint 'amm ("father's brother's daughter") in marriage. Ethnographic literature on the Middle East often cites this matrilateral parallel cousin marriage preference. [12] All religious sects have the proverb: "Take the girls to marry from the breasts of the 'ammat," or the husband's kin group.

In addition to the legal and customary responsibilities that may formalize social relations with the 'amūm, a psychological explanation was often given. Nuha Haddad believes that images of formality and respect which are attributed to the father of the household are also extended to his brothers and sisters. This argument equates the siblings of the father with the father, all receiving similar deferential treatment. Conversely, children associate the warmth of their mother with the khwāl. A common Arab proverb reflects this affectionate feeling: "relations of the womb are stronger than any other."

Aida Khoury feels that khwāl relations are warm and informal: her own kin do not feel like strangers in her home where they might in the home of a brother's wife. Thus, the wife sets the tone for extrahousehold relations. Good relations with the in-laws depend on the wife's initiative. Fatma Hijazi had made it a practice to be generous with her mother-in-law and husband's kin. So, too, has Najla al-As'ad. She argues that if she treats her in-laws as she would her own kin, there would be no difference in affection between the 'amūm and the khwāl.

All five women agree that their own brothers have no legal responsibility to them and their children. (Some comments on brother-sister relations are in order here.) Before a girl's marriage, her brother is responsible for the maintenance of her chastity. While this could be a threatening situation, brother-sister relations tend to be warm ones. In the five case households, teenage siblings occasionally go out in the evenings together. And while not obliged to, often a brother will give his sister a hand in early years of married life. As previously mentioned, fraternal protection may be clearly established between a brother and his sister if she relinquishes her inheritance to him.

In sum, from the literature, one might hypothesize that a woman's influence and status in her household may be increased through a strong emotional identification by her children with their khwāl.[13] My data suggest that this represents a negative view of the situation. Instead, the wife's most effective role vis-a-vis extended kin is as a positive link between them and her household. There may be no difference in relations between the khwāl and the 'amūm, even given major variations in legal responsibilities. It is impossible to generalize on this issue from five cases, but this information at least suggests that more research must be done on the wife as a structural link, or perhaps barrier, between the household and the extended kin.

EXTRAHOUSEHOLD ROLES

Evidence shows that when women play important roles in
extrahousehold affairs, their status within their home is positively
affected. This section will describe some of these traditional and
nontraditional roles.

In societies in which the free mixing between the sexes and
marriage by choice are still restricted to a great extent, preliminary marriage inquiries are essentially and importantly a female
task.[14] It is the women who arrange formal introductions between
prospective spouses. During March 1974, 23-year-old Nawal al-
Hajj became engaged, after initial investigations and introductions
between her mother and her fiance's mother.

Arab women can play an integral part in the success of their
husband's work. During my residence with them, Fatma Hijazi, as
wife of the concierge, lent a sum of money to an ex-tenant, sent
bread and **manaquish** to building residents, and was called on to com-
fort a woman tenant. It was obvious that she was a popular and well-
regarded personality and that she assisted her husband greatly.
Najla al-As'ad made political visits in a dedicated and organized
fashion for her husband; almost every afternoon was spent calling
on families in her husband's electoral district. She has often been
asked to serve as an intermediary in a constituent's search for employment. While Abu Samir and Muhammad al-As'ad have greatly
dissimilar jobs, the social aspects of both men's jobs have been substantially enhanced by their wives.

Salaried work outside the home for females, whether married
or unmarried, is still met with considerable resistance. Ironically,
city life has restricted Arab women. It is important to remember
that Bedouin and peasant women have always contributed not only to
food production but also to cash acquisition, by engaging in cottage
industries, such as carpet making. In Cairo, for example, Nelson
feels that there are still barriers to female employment outside the
home, that it is considered 'aib ("shame") for a man not to be able
to support his family.[15] Thus, it is assumed that women work because the salary of the husband is not adequate.

Opposition, then, to extrahousehold work by women comes
from men, and it is directly related to the honor code regulating
female behavior. Some feel that the chaste reputation of women kin
can be protected adequately only within the confines of their father's
or husband's house. In Beirut, there are families who will allow
their daughters to work only after they have checked on the reputations of the male employees of the establishment. And generally,
the "safest" and most tolerated profession for a woman in Beirut
would be a schoolteacher.[16]

As an example of the traditional attitude toward female work, Aida Khoury said that she had promised her husband that she would never work outside the home before they were married. He had given her several reasons why she should not: "People will gossip, wondering why a well-to-do man would have his wife work. It is 'aib." In addition, a working woman might have the chance to meet other men while at work. Most men, argues Aida Khoury, would not stand for such a precarious marital situation. This is a conventional view still held by many Lebanese men, though it is changing with the current generation.

One might suspect that even among the elite group of university-educated women in Beirut, there are many who are not engaged in extrahousehold work. Most women who do work outside the home do so primarily because they need the additional income. With the rise in the cost of living in Beirut, especially for educational expenses, more and more households are having to compromise with respect to traditional ideas on the shame of extrahousehold work for women. Nuha Haddad works to meet the high cost of educating their children in private schools. The al-Hajj daughters also work to augment family finances, but in university-related work, which is considered respectable.

Given the unique sharing relationship between Emile and Nuha Haddad, one wonders if she plays a considerable part in home management, since she contributes substantially to the household income. It is often said that the Beirut father still has ultimate power in the household, because he controls the household money. Perhaps this will change when the mother is also providing and controlling part of the monthly income.

INFLUENCE OF WOMEN IN THE HOME

Power in the Middle East and Mediterranean region is culturally defined in favor of the household patriarch. Deference to the male head, however, must be considered apart from actual power. Indeed, Friedl feels that it is the women in Greece who hold the power.[17] Yet, others have argued that when a strict, authoritarian father exists, a compassionate mother serves as a balance (for emotional compensation with the children). This is difficult to systematize empirically. If, in fact, women do gain power from emotional compensation in a rigid patriarchy, perhaps it is now lessening, as fathers of the new generation are tending to be less dictatorial. Yet, even with the traditional power arrangement in the Hijazi household, there was no great emotional balance in favor of Ūm Samir, however loved and respected she was.

As in other patrilineal societies, Arab society has traditionally kept children dependent on both parents. A reciprocal arrangement of favors seems to be established between parents and their
children during their youth. Asad calls this pattern that of generalized exchange, where a repayment obligation is definitely established, with the time of reimbursement by the offspring indefinite.[18]

Decision making is usually studied as an index to power, and
setting aside the cultural definition of power for a moment, a look at
the decision-making patterns in the five Beirut households is instruc-
tive. The women were asked how decisions were made on a number
of issues: place of residence, naming and schooling of the children,
holidays, and other expenditures, such as clothes, food, and furniture. On a comparative scale, decision making varied among the
five households. It must be remembered that decision making is a
multiphasic process though, and all five women felt that when there
was a decision to be made or a disagreement, the points were dis-
cussable and their advice often heeded in the ultimate decision.
Rather than direct confrontation, indirect tactics are often used.

The Haddad and Hijazi extremes in decision making are noteworthy. Decisions in the Haddad household are, for the most part,
mutual. In the Hijazi home, Abu Samir makes all the decisions:
where the children study, the children's names, food purchased,
and even clothes for Fatma. Abu Samir, says Fatma, supplies "the
money and the house, therefore he has the right to choose everything. He is rab al-beit," or the person responsible for the household. Yet, Fatma sees herself as definitely having an influence on
his decisions, and he seems to recognize her powers as well. He
described his wife to me as qawiyyé, of strong character, and that
he was the weak one, da'if.

Najla al-As'ad is the chief decision maker in their household
by default. As a parliamentary deputy, Muhammad is home so seldom that it is essential that she take full charge of the management
of the household. As with many Beirut husbands who work long and
irregular hours or spend time with male companions in their leisure,
this information suggests that decision making by default by wives is
common. Gans showed this to be the case among North American
urban working-class families.[19]

In addition to the cultural definitions of power and power by
decision making, Blood and Wolfe proposed a theory that women
gain influence because of certain "resources," such as legal rights;
wealth and prestige of their kin group; personal attributes, such as
personality and attractiveness; education; salaried employment; and
community activities.[20]

A previous section on roles demonstrated that married women
do have rights specified in religious codes in Lebanon. The data do

not, however, adequately suggest that women gain or lose power because of jural norms, since these codes are rather unclear and extremely malleable in practice.

Concerning the "resource" of the wealth and prestige of a
wife's family of orientation, my evidence shows that all five couples
married within a stratum of families equal in wealth and prestige.
They believe that marriages across class boundaries are rare and
were adamant that it is especially not proper for a woman to belong
to a more prestigious, wealthier family than the one she marries
into. If she does, they say, she will not be satisfied and will attempt
to run the household.

All husbands have more education than their wives. There is,
however, a positive correlation between educational levels of both
husband and wife and the sharing of household power. That is, the
more educated both husband and wife are, the more a husband will
entrust his wife with the details of household management.

A strong case can be made for the additional power base a
woman has if she is working and earning a salary. With the Haddads
as an example, her actual financial independence is a salient factor
in her unparalleled influence in her household. It would be naive to
suggest that this is the only factor affecting this particular power
balance; much depends upon the personalities of the spouses, their
education, and past residence abroad.

If a woman is not working, participation in community activities
has been named a factor affecting her influence and prestige within
the bounds of her home. This aspect of the Blood and Wolfe resource
theory is designed to explain situations where women participate in
various social, political, and religious groups, but it does not seem
broadly applicable to the Middle East. The five Beirut women had
no contact with such organizations. Women's cultural and educational organizations do exist in Beirut, but their membership is
small. A woman might gain power in a community as a gossip, but
that is not what Blood and Wolfe had in mind.

It also has been asserted that a woman can affect her status
and power by personal attributes, such as personality and physical
attractiveness. In the Middle East, a more essential and superior
female quality is that of modesty. Living up to this ideal--indeed,
the culturally defined ideal of womanhood--would give a woman an
honorable status.[21] The five women mentioned that "success in
life" was to be the mother of sons, another aspect of culturally defined honorable status.[22]

Personal attributes, education, and extrahousehold employment tend to have a positive correlation with a wife's household influence. Women are said to rule their husbands in later years,
after they have proven themselves by producing children and living

within the honor code of behavior. As one husband said, "In this
world, the wife is the boss and the husband only her shadow."

BEHAVIOR CONTROLS ON WOMEN

Data have suggested that it is not generally acceptable for a
mother, and in many cases for daughters as well, to leave the household domain for the external world of men. Arab women are not consciously aware that there are other options in life, because rather
homogeneous norms mold their self-identity and definitions of success. It is by being a wife and mother that a woman defines herself
as a success, not by a career in the working world of men. Many
in the elite class of women who have been university educated, including Najla al-As'ad, subscribe to this norm.

Anthropologists have dealt with the honor system as a behavior-
sanctioning phenomenon present in Middle Eastern and Mediterranean
societies. Being honorable means conformity to culturally defined
ideals, and intertwined in these are definitions of Arab masculinity
and Arab femininity. [23]

Levantine Arabic differentiates between two types of honor,
'ird and sharaf. Sharaf is equivalent to the English meaning of
honor, while 'ird is sharaf al-bint, or the honor of the girl.

From the female point of view, maintaining 'ird is retaining
eligibility for marriage by a reputation of sexual purity, that is, virginity. If a girl loses her 'ird she loses her future, since the reputation of virginity is a prerequisite for suitability. In a social system where a single woman has no niche or cannot easily be financially independent and self-sufficient, she must marry or she will be a
burden on her kin. Daughters, thus, have traditionally been regarded as social, moral, and economic liabilities. It is in the interest of fathers and brothers to see that the girls remain in an honorable state so that they are marriageable. 'Ird has persisted because the tradition of premarital chastity is still strong; being financially dependent, Christian and Muslim women alike cannot risk a
bad name for themselves or their daughters. Marriage is at stake.

Maintenance of honor for a female is connected with modesty
in word and action. To the five women, this trait in their daughters
means that they are respectful, obedient, mild, quiet, and above all,
pure. 'Ird applies to married women too: fidelity is of greatest importance; the women are expected to be gentle and loving mothers
and not openly contradictory to their husbands.

Modesty can most obviously be interpreted by dress. This,
of course, is a relative evaluation, but it exists throughout the society nonetheless. All women in the households mentioned had

certain rules of dress laid down by their husbands. Fatma Hijazi was not allowed to wear trousers. The al-Hajj girls were not allowed to wear sleeveless tops or go swimming in public. On political calls, Najla al-As'ad covered her hair and wore long-sleeved black dresses.

Modest behavior dictates that none of the daughters in the five households may attend mixed social or cultural gatherings, whether school sponsored or not. The al-Hajj girls, older than the other daughters, must not meet young men out of the university classroom bounds. The other teen-age daughters are not allowed to go out without a guardian.

For married women, rules of modest action apply as well. It is a direct insult to her husband and his kin if a woman is reputedly immodest or unfaithful. Traditionally, if a married woman committed a crime against 'ird, her husband would have divorced her and sent her back to her own kin for punishment. This is changing now, with husbands taking the dominant role of protector and punisher. Most importantly, if a married woman is thought to behave improperly, her daughters' marriageability will be affected.

In Beirut, the most forceful mechanism of social sanction is gossip. Modesty and 'ird would hardly be such important issues if gossip were an unimportant factor. Gossip defines social obligations and prescribes suitable behavior. For the reputation of every household, talk is a weapon, and honor must be kept unviolated. As argued in preceding pages, Beirut is not anonymous, as most cities are, nor are social encounters random or unstructured in any sense.

SUMMARY

In the existing structure of Beirut society, women's roles predominate in the household. Within such a system, women are seen to have a good deal of manipulative, covert influence. Indeed, they perceive themselves in this way. Trends are away from a rigid patriarchy, partly due to increased education and earlier financial independence of the children. There is evidence pointing to more sharing attitudes between husband and wife concerning household organization, as well as relaxation of the modesty code permitting women to leave the household for salaried employment.[24] Extrahousehold work, of course, must be seen in the context of the total Lebanese economy and the extent that women can be absorbed into a nonindustrial economy.

NOTES

1. Khuri, F. I., 1975, p. 61.

2. Khalaf, S., and Kongstad, P., 1973, p. 3.

3. Ibid., p. 82.

4. Abu-Zahra, N. M., 1974, p. 122; the special issue of Anthropological Quarterly 47, no. 1 (January 1974), devoted to "Visiting Patterns and Social Dynamics in Eastern Mediterranean Communities."

5. Bott, E., 1971, pp. 60, 68–69.

6. See also Prothro, E. T., and Diab, L. N., 1974, p. 89, and Table 4-16, on visiting patterns of women.

7. Anthropological literature has long debated the extent to which women in a patrilineal system are legally incorporated into their husband's group. For an interesting discussion, see Lewis, I. M., 1962, last chapter.

8. Aswad, B., 1967, pp. 143-44; Mohsen, S., 1967, p. 166.

9. Khuri, op. cit., p. 151.

10. Ibid., p. 150; Prothro and Diab, op. cit., p. 176.

11. See Ammar, H., 1954, and Hamamsy, L., 1958.

12. Khuri, F., 1970.

13. Ammar, op. cit., p. 137; Hamamsy, op. cit., p. 594; Stirling, P., 1965, p. 144.

14. Khuri, 1975, p. 141; Lutfiyya, A., 1966, p. 130.

15. Nelson, C., 1968, p. 67.

16. For an illuminating article on another alternative, see Hamalian, A., 1974, on all-female Armenian savings cooperatives in Beirut.

17. Friedl, E., 1967.

18. Asad, T., 1970, p. 82.

19. Gans, H., 1962, p. 62.

20. Blood, R. O., and Wolfe, D., 1960, p. 36.

21. Antoun, R. T., 1968, p. 682.

22. Aswad, B. C., 1967, p. 150.

23. Abu Zahra, N. M., 1970; Antoun, op. cit.; Dodd, P., 1973.

24. Prothro and Diab, op. cit., p. 134.

14

Tunisian Attitudes toward
Women and Child Rearing

MARK A. TESSLER
JANET M. ROGERS
DANIEL R. SCHNEIDER

During its first decade of independence, Tunisia had a particularly coherent and explicit program of planned social transformation.[1]
In 1956, following independence, a personal status code replacing
Koranic law in the areas of marriage, divorce, and children's rights
was enacted. In 1958, a new educational program was instituted. It
offered a bilingual and bicultural curriculum and laid the basis for
gradual Arabization. In 1960, the country's president, Habib
Bourguiba, denounced the traditional observance of Ramadan, arguing that the customary fasting decreased productivity and increased
national economic woes. This desire to sweep away cultural barriers
to progress, which Bourguiba once referred to as "outmoded beliefs,"
was reflected in countless speeches by the president and other officials. In one address, Bourguiba stated that "a large majority of our
people are still entangled in a mass of prejudices and so called religious beliefs."[2] In another, he said, "Faith and spiritual values are
only effective to the extent they are based on reason."[3]

There were also concrete programs designed to persuade
people to accept reform. The National Union of Tunisian Women,
for example, organized numerous meetings to draw attention to problems of women, the family, health, and so forth. A more extensive
resocialization effort was undertaken by the Neo-Destour Party,

---

Some of the material in this chapter appears in Mark A.
Tessler, Janet M. Rogers, and Daniel R. Schneider, "Women's
Emancipation in Tunisia: Changing Policies and Popular Responses,"
in Nikki Keddie and Lois Peck, eds., <u>Beyond the Veil: Women in the
Middle East</u> (forthcoming).

Tunisia's ruling party, which became the Destourian Socialist Party (PSD) in 1964. The party's 1,250 territorial and professional cells met regularly to discuss national problems and acquaint the population with the need for change. Thus, as a leading student of Tunisia observed a few years ago, more than any other Arab state, Tunisia had developed a durable political organization that articulated and implemented its ideology.[4]

The object of these programs was not the erosion of all aspects of traditional life. As the president put it in a 1965 speech, the country's "modern civilization" was to be faithful, dynamic, and open: ". . . faithful because it respects permanent moral and spiritual values, dynamic because it is capable of evolving on an intellectual and scientific plane, and open to a constructive dialogue between civilizations and cultures."[5] On another occasion, he asserted that development would be accomplished "in accordance with the teachings of the Holy Book."[6] A determination to incorporate traditional elements into the social order under construction was noticeable in several domains. For example, Arabic was to be made the principal language of public life. Tunisia also asserted its Muslim identity. Islam became the official religion, and Islamic symbols were incorporated into the national ideology. Nevertheless, the dominant emphasis was on change, not on continuity with the past, and this was especially so with respect to the status of women, the rights of youth, and other attributes of personal status. Expressing his dedication to female emancipation, Bourguiba once explained that "my love for my mother has been the keystone of all the efforts I have made to promote women."[7] On one occasion, he personally intervened in a judicial process where he felt a woman had been mistreated. As he later explained, "In this country we intend to behave like civilized men. As a citizen, a wife and a mother, a woman has rights which no one is going to take away from her. Our judges are here to see to that."[8]

As important as official pressures for change during this period was the intensifying impact of unplanned agents of social transformation. The proportion of the population living in cities rose dramatically after independence. Estimates placed it as low as 15 percent in 1956 and as high as 45 percent 15 years later. Individuals moving to the cities were exposed to new ideas and had to develop new life-styles, both of which called into question traditional values. The advent of the radio also increased exposure to non-indigenous ideas, producing psychic mobility even where there was no physical movement. Perhaps the greatest stimulus for change was education. In the decade following independence, literacy climbed from 15 percent to 35-40 percent; the proportion of children attending primary school grew from 25 percent to 60-70 percent;

and the proportion of students completing high school increased from
3 percent to almost 30 percent. These and other agents of unplanned
change--extension of the cash economy and mechanized agriculture
in the countryside and new professional opportunities in cities--
placed many traditional values in doubt. In one small village, for
example, a team of sociologists reported that people were no longer
oriented exclusively toward local affairs. "Their personal center of
gravity is shifted to Tunis, the bright center of national life."[9]

By the mid-1960s, official and unplanned pressures for social
transformation had set in motion a psychological and cultural revolution. Empirical studies show that exposure to these agents of
change was associated with increased willingness to examine critically traditional values and to adopt nonindigenous social codes, including ones pertaining to women and child rearing.[10] Especially among
the growing professional and white-collar middle class, but to some
extent among the expanding proletariat too, support for the reform
of traditional society and the construction of a social order blending
new and old elements was rapidly increasing.

In the last seven or eight years, Tunisia's commitment to
planned change has diminished considerably. Initially, this was due
to disorientation, resulting from a number of domestic political
crises, most notably Bourguiba's recurring illnesses, the Ben Salah
affair, and the ensuing power struggle within the PSD. In 1969,
Ahmed Ben Salah, the dynamic minister of plan and finance and
architect of the country's socialist orientation, was removed from
office, eventually to be convicted of treason. After 1971, liberal
politicians who had been instrumental in ousting Ben Salah were removed from positions of importance by supporters of Bourguiba,
who by then was returning to active leadership. One result of these
developments was reduced popular political participation. Party
cells met less often, and party machinery began to decay. Another
was declining political trust and the emergence of an ideological
"counter culture."[11] More directly related to our present concerns
was a reduction in commitment to programs of resocialization and
social engineering. The revolutionary elan that characterized
Tunisia during the first decade of independence dissipated rapidly.
As one Tunisian social scientist put the matter, "The Tunisian elite
is in the process of losing its dynamizing and liberating powers . . .
the political system has lost its equilibrium."[12]

The regime that came to power following this period of confusion has had conservative economic policies and little concern for
planned social change. Bourguiba and Prime Minister Hedi Nouira,
former director of the National Bank, are comparatively uninterested
in restructuring traditional society. Apparently, they do not believe
such reforms are a necessary ingredient for social and economic

progress. As a respected Tunisian sociologist observed in 1972, the country is experiencing a "reactivation of tradition."[13] In 1969, Bourguiba gave a talk that signaled the change in his outlook. He discussed the need to put modernization "in perspective." Referring to female emancipation, formerly one of his most cherished goals, he warned that too much reform will lead to "a loosening of our morals." Freedom, he said, "must be coupled with religious and moral education in order to produce the respect for virtue that was formerly assured by long robes and heavy veils."[14] The net effect of changes in political organization, ideology, and leadership is that Tunisia has lost much of the revolutionary momentum that had been generated by the mid-1960s.

Though planned programs of resocialization and social transformation have diminished, the situation is different with respect to unplanned agents of modernization. School enrollments have leveled off or even declined slightly. The government places less emphasis on education, because of its high cost, an inability to provide appropriate jobs for all graduates, and a decline in standards accompanying mass enrollment. But the country still maintains an impressive educational system, and there is no question of going back to the pre-independence situation. Further, there has been an intensification of pressures for change in other areas. The economy has performed well in recent years due to several good harvests and increasing revenue from petroleum and tourism. Growing numbers of Tunisians are employed in Europe, and urbanization and media participation also continue to expand. Thus, on balance, unplanned pressures for social, structural, and economic transformation have remained intense since the late 1960s, despite the reduction in official programs of change.

This chapter examines popular Tunisian attitudes toward two important cultural issues--the status of women and child-rearing practices[15]--and attempts to determine whether and how these attitudes have changed as a result of recent political events in Tunisia. Toward this end, we shall present the results of a survey conducted in 1967 and replicated in 1973. The earlier survey was completed prior to the Six-Day War and the major demonstrations that also took place in June 1967. At that time, political participation and political trust were generally high, and official efforts to promote reform were still significant. By the time the latter survey was conducted, however, the political climate had changed markedly. By comparing findings from these points in time, we seek to accomplish two objectives. First, we shall determine how attitudes toward women and child rearing have changed and attempt to discover the causes of any variations observed. Our objective here is to develop propositions about the independent and combined impact on cultural values of

planned and unplanned social change.[16] Second, we shall assess the
degree of cultural conflict and/or consensus being generated in
Tunisia by recent political and ideological currents.

METHODOLOGY

The Data Base

Data for this analysis are from surveys conducted in 1967 and
1973. Information about the 1967 survey, as well as the principal
findings derived from the research, are described elsewhere in some
detail.[17] Briefly, stratified quota samples of literate and regularly
employed adults were drawn in Tunis and three smaller towns. Variables of sample stratification were education, income, and place of
residence; and quotas were established to assure that all empirically
existing combinations of these variables were included in the sample.
A total of 283 persons were interviewed. In 1973, a similar sample
was selected, using education and place of residence as variables of
sample stratification and substituting occupation for income to control for inflation between 1967 and 1973. A total of 349 persons were
interviewed, using the survey instrument employed in 1967. Table
14.1 presents the distribution of respondents in each sample across
categories of education, income, and place of residence. The table
shows that respondents in each year are drawn from a wide range of
social categories and, collectively, reflect much of the diversity of
the Tunisian middle class and working class.

The Matched Pairs

To assess change over time, individuals from the 1967 survey
were matched to those from the 1973 survey. To constitute a match,
respondents from the two samples had to be of the same sex and
highly similar with respect to age, educational level, income category, and place of residence. In cases where a respondent from one
year could be matched with equal accuracy to two or more respondents from the other year, selections were made on a random basis.
A total of 211 matched pairs were formed. Table 14.2 shows the
distribution of matched pairs with respect to age, education, sex,
and place of residence. As will be explained, these variables constitute the parameters of the factorial research design according to
which data will be analyzed. Income was not employed in this analysis because it correlates strongly with education, and additional findings of notable significance are not obtained by its inclusion. Matched

TABLE 14.1: Distribution of 1967[a] and 1973[b] Respondents along Dimensions of Sample Stratification, in Tunisia

| | Level of Education | | | | | | | |
| | Residents of Tunis | | | | Residents of Smaller Towns[c] | | | |
Income	University	High School	Intermediate	Primary	University	High School	Intermediate	Primary
				1967 Sample				
< 30 dinars	0	0	13	17	--	--	7	17
30–49 dinars	0	17	30	17	--	4	13	5
50–69 dinars	6	18	9	7	--	11	6	1
70–99 dinars	9	6	7	7	--	1	--	1
> 100 dinars	23	18	13	0	--	--	--	--
				1973 Sample				
< 30 dinars	1	6	10	20	--	--	4	12
30–49 dinars	3	8	40	24	--	--	12	14
50–69 dinars	5	10	35	12	--	1	7	1
70–99 dinars	21	10	20	7	--	2	4	5
> 100 dinars	29	6	6	14	--	1	1	--

[a]Number = 283.
[b]Number = 349.
[c]In 1967, interviewing was done in Grombalia, Mahdia, and Nefta. In 1973, it was done in Nabeul, Ksar Hillal, and Houmt Souk. All six towns had a population of less than 15,000 when surveyed. In each year, one town selected was from the northern part of the country near Tunis, one was from the Sahel, and one was from the southern part of the country.

Source: Compiled by the authors.

pairs include respondents from almost all sample categories and are diverse enough to indicate trends operating generally among literate and regularly employed Tunisians.

TABLE 14.2: Matched Pairs, by Age, Education, Sex, and Place of Residence, in Tunisia, 1967 and 1973

	Level of Education		
	High School or		
Age	University	Intermediate	Primary
Men from Tunis:			
Under 23	9	19	4
23-34	35	20	20
Over 34	11	16	16
Women from Tunis:			
Under 23	1	6	3
23-34	10	5	0
Over 34	0	0	1
Men from smaller towns:			
Under 23	0	6	4
23-34	1	8	5
Over 34	2	5	6

Source: Compiled by the authors.

Dependent Variables

The dependent variables in this analysis are six survey items dealing with the status of women and child-rearing practices. Information on procedures used to design and administer the 1967 survey instrument have been presented elsewhere and testify to item validity and reliability and the absence of interview bias and other forms of response set.[18] These procedures were generally used again in 1973, the only important difference being that a questionnaire rather than an interview methodology was favored. For purposes of parsimony, only three items dealing with each area will be discussed. These items, which serve as dependent variables in our analysis, are listed below. The response indicating support for reform is given in parentheses following each item.

1. Do you think it is more important for a boy to go to school than it is for a girl? (No)

2. Is it acceptable for a woman to direct a professional enterprise employing many men? (Yes)

3. Muslim women should have the same rights as Muslim men to marry foreigners. (Agree)

4. Children should be encouraged to think for themselves, even if this means they occasionally disobey their parents. (Agree)

5. Within a family, the mother should be more affectionate toward the children than the father. (Disagree)

6. A father should be both respected and loved by his children, but it is more important that he be respected. (Disagree)

Mode of Analysis: Independent and
Specification Variables

Variations over time in national political and ideological currents constitute the independent variable in this study. But it is unlikely that these currents have had the same effect on cultural attitudes among all categories of the Tunisian population. For this reason, data will be analyzed according to a multivariate factorial research design. Age, education, sex, and place of residence are the parameters of this design and serve as specification variables in our analysis of the relationship between political currents and changing attitudes toward women and child rearing. In presenting data, respondents are categorized on the basis of the four specification variables, taken in combination, * and the aggregate response of persons in each category on each dependent variable is given. The particular variables being used were selected because (1) many studies have shown them to be strongly related to cultural attitudes, such as those being considered; (2) they correlate with other potentially relevant specification variables--such as income, media consumption, professional status, and foreign travel--and, thus, may suggest how additional personal attributes affect the relationship between cultural preferences and social and political forces; and (3) they divide respondents into sufficiently diverse and important social categories to permit meaningful observations about the distribution of attitudes and attitude change throughout the sectors of society

---

*The one exception is the absence of women from smaller towns. Due to problems of access, no women were interviewed in smaller towns in 1967.

encompassed by the samples. Two points about the utility of the design should be noted. First, it enables us to assess the specification effects of any single variable with the others held constant. For example, to determine whether place of residence affects the way that attitudes changed between 1967 and 1973, the nature of attitude change among residents of Tunis and smaller towns who are comparable with respect to education, age, and sex may be contrasted. Second, the combined as well as independent effects of specification variables can be considered. To assess the joint impact of education and place of residence, for example, the relationship between education and attitude change in each milieu would be determined, and the observed relationships would then be compared.

ATTITUDE CHANGE BETWEEN 1967 AND 1973

Findings

Table 14.3 presents responses to the items about women and child rearing for the entire 1967 and 1973 samples and for the matched pairs drawn from each sample. Table 14.4 shows the degree to which attitudes toward cultural reform changed between 1967 and 1973 for subsets of matched pairs grouped according to residence, sex, age, and education. For each subset, the percentage of individuals favoring reform in 1967 has been subtracted from the percentage favoring it in 1973, and the result is shown in the table. Taken together, Tables 14.3 and 14.4 show the amount, direction, and distribution of attitude change during the period under consideration.

One set of conclusions to be drawn from the tables concerns the nature and direction of attitude change. In general, support for traditional cultural values increased between 1967 and 1973. Table 14.3 shows that support for reform dropped on four of the six items examined, and Table 14.5 shows that it dropped among a majority of respondent categories (55 percent), indicating that the decline was broadly based. Further, the magnitude of the decline was often substantial. Desires for reform did increase slightly on two items and among a significant minority of respondent categories (27 percent). But, overall, support for traditional values pertaining to women and child rearing increased substantially.

A second set of conclusions concerns differences in attitude change with respect to the two substantive focuses under consideration. Table 14.3 indicates that support for nontraditional child-rearing practices increased slightly on two items and declined by only 7 percent on the third. Further, Table 14.4 shows that support

TABLE 14.3: Responses to Items Dealing with Female
Emancipation and Child Rearing of 1967 and
1973 Samples and Matched Pairs, in Tunisia

| | Percent Favoring Cultural Reform | | | |
| | Samples | | Matched Pairs | |
Item	1967[a]	1973[b]	1967[c]	1973[c]
(1) Do you think schooling is more important for a boy than for a girl?	65	55	65	51
(2) Is it acceptable for a woman to direct a professional enterprise employing many men?	44	32	46	32
(3) Muslim women should have the same rights as Muslim men to marry foreigners.	37	26	39	27
(4) Children should be encouraged to think for themselves, even if this means they occasionally disobey their parents.	71	76	69	76
(5) Within a family, the mother should be more affectionate toward the children than the father.	24	27	22	29
(6) A father should be loved and respected by his children, but it is more important that he be respected.	35	28	36	27

[a]Number = 283.

[b]Number = 349.

[c]Number = 211.

Source: Compiled by the authors.

TABLE 14.4: Difference between Levels of Support for Cultural Reform in 1973 and 1967 among Matched Respondents, Grouped on the Basis of Sex, Residence, Age, and Education, in Tunisia

Age	Men in Tunis			Women in Tunis			Men in Smaller Towns		
	High[a]	Medium[b]	Low[c]	High[a]	Medium[b]	Low[c]	High[a]	Medium[b]	Low[c]
(1)Difference in Percent Believing Schooling Is as Important for a Girl as for a Boy									
Under 23	0	-30	-25	--	30	-30	--	-30	0
23-34	-18	0	2	-10	-38	--	--	0	-20
Over 34	0	-30	-50	--	--	--	--	-40	-30
(2)Difference in Percent Believing It Is Acceptable for a Woman to Direct a Professional Enterprise Employing Many Men									
Under 23	10	-40	-25	--	20	50	--	0	25
23-34	-16	9	-23	-36	-23	--	--	-75	-60
Over 34	-56	-30	-30	--	--	--	--	-40	-20
(3) Difference in Percent Believing Women Should Have the Same Rights as Men to Marry Foreigners									
Under 23	0	5	-30	--	-20	100	--	-60	-80
23-34	0	10	-40	-22	0	--	--	-25	0
Over 34	-27	-10	-40	--	--	--	--	-20	-50
(4) Difference in Percent Believing Children Should Be Encouraged to Think for Themselves, Even If They Occasionally Disobey Their Parents									
Under 23	-27	0	0	--	-20	0	--	0	30
23-34	8	17	25	-10	22	--	--	13	0
Over 34	15	-10	0	--	--	--	--	-40	50
(5) Difference in Percent Believing the Father Should Be as Affectionate toward the Children as the Mother									
Under 23	13	0	0	--	70	30	--	30	-25
23-34	12	43	-5	-19	62	--	--	-13	30
Over 34	-27	20	-20	--	--	--	--	0	-30
(6) Difference in Percent Believing It Is Not More Important That a Father Be Respected by His Children than that He Be Loved									
Under 23	-37	-30	0	--	0	-50	--	-20	0
23-34	-1	-1	10	-19	82	--	--	-45	-30
Over 34	0	-20	-50	--	--	--	--	-20	20
Average Difference in Percent Supporting Cultural Reform									
Under 23	-5	-16	-15	--	13	14	--	-12	-9
23-34	-2	13	-1	-19	18	--	--	-24	-13
Over 34	-16	-13	-31	--	--	--	--	-27	-12

[a]High = high school or university.
[b]Medium = intermediate.
[c]Low = primary or less.
Source: Compiled by the authors.

for cultural reform pertaining to child rearing increased and decreased in about the same number of respondent categories (40 percent and 38 percent). Attitudes toward women, on the other hand,
changed more substantially and consistently, and indeed they account
for most of the general decline previously noted. The proportion of
persons favoring women's liberation dropped on all three relevant
items and in a significant majority of respondent categories (71 percent). Thus, while total support for reform pertaining to child
rearing changed little between 1967 and 1973, total support for reform pertaining to the status of women declined noticeably.

A third and more complex set of conclusions concerns demographic correlates of variations in the extent and direction of attitude change. It will be recalled that changing governmental policies
are the independent variable in this analysis, and demographic factors are treated as specification variables, variables defining the
locus of different kinds of attitudinal responses to changing political
currents. Table 14.4 reveals that variations in attitude change are
not distributed randomly across respondent categories. A disproportionate decline in support for cultural reform occurred among
well-educated women of intermediate age levels, among older and
relatively well-educated men living in smaller towns, among older
men in Tunis, and among younger and poorly educated men in Tunis
and smaller towns. A disproportionate increase in support for cultural reform occurred among younger and/or relatively poorly educated women and among male residents of Tunis with intermediate
age and educational levels.

Discussion: Theoretical Implications

The period prior to 1967 was characterized by high levels of
planned and unplanned social transformation. The period between
1967 and 1973 witnessed a significant reduction in official programs
of development but saw continuing high levels of unplanned change.
By noting whether, how, and among which respondent categories
attitudes toward women and child rearing changed between 1967 and
1973, we may advance some propositions about the cultural consequences of both planned and unplanned change. Our research design is of course limited by the absence of data from a period characterized by intense planned and diminished unplanned social change
and one characterized by few pressures for social transformation of
either variety. Thus, a clear distinction needs to be made between
previously reported empirical findings and theoretical formulations
purporting to account for changes observed. If our methodology is
sound, the former are accurate. The latter, however, though

consistent with the data at hand, may not exhaust the universe of plausible explanations and should be understood as propositions open to discussion and in need of additional, independent empirical confirmation. Nevertheless, our findings suggest a number of potentially significant theoretical insights, which we shall now make explicit.

As a general rule, support for cultural reform declined between 1967 and 1973, suggesting that agents of unplanned social change are not sufficient to generate support for cultural reform. But there are instances where preferences for cultural reform did increase. One of these involved attitudes toward child rearing. While support for women's emancipation declined consistently, support for liberal child-rearing practices increased on two of the three relevant indicators and in a large number of respondent categories. Apparently, high levels of urbanization, education, media consumption, and economic growth tend to produce a rejection of authoritarianism in child rearing and a preference for warmth in father-child relations, even in the absence of official programs of resocialization. One possible explanation for this is that traditional attitudes toward child rearing are less firmly anchored in Tunisia's traditional belief system than are attitudes toward women and, hence, may be modified more easily. This possibility leads to the following general proposition: general proposition number one--agents of unplanned social change are sufficient to increase support for cultural reform in areas less firmly anchored in traditional belief systems and are not sufficient, though probably necessary, to increase support for cultural reform in areas more firmly anchored in traditional belief systems.

There are also certain respondent categories among which a disproportionate increase in support for reform was observed. These are women in general, and especially younger and relatively poorly educated women, and men in Tunis of intermediate age and educational levels. Several dynamic forces are probably at work in these cases. First, women, whose public role is traditionally limited, have an obvious interest in reform, especially if they believe social change is creating new opportunities for persons not prohibited from seizing them by traditional normative codes. Second, men in Tunis with intermediate age and educational levels are neither high enough in socioeconomic status to be satisfied with the status quo nor so poorly prepared for modern life that they are threatened by social change. Thus, not unlike women, they support cultural reform because it is part of the emergence of a social order offering them additional opportunities for personal development. In view of these suggestions, the following general proposition seems plausible: general proposition number two--agents of unplanned social change are sufficient to increase support for cultural reform among individuals

who are limited in their opportunities and/or socioeconomic status
and who believe their status would be enhanced by modernization.

Population categories among which a substantial decline in
support for cultural reform was observed include (1) well-educated
women of intermediate age, (2) older and relatively well-educated
men living in smaller towns, (3) older men living in Tunis, and (4)
poorly educated young men from Tunis. In the first two instances,
similar considerations may account for our findings. The fact that
opposition to cultural reform increased among well-educated women
may reflect a kind of "queen bee" syndrome. Women advantaged by
their education and/or professional status may reject reformist
ideologies because they believe advancement is possible within the
traditional system. They may also feel their privileged position is
threatened by women's liberation and, for reasons of self-interest,
become more conservative. A similar explanation for attitude
change among older and relatively well-educated men in smaller
towns suggests itself. Residing in comparatively traditional surroundings, these individuals have relatively little competition for
positions of high status within their communities. Thus, they may
consider the status quo satisfactory and reason that social and cultural change would increase their competitors for prestige and influence. Following this logic, we would also expect planned change
to diminish support for cultural reform. In any event, continuing
high levels of unplanned change are associated with increased opposition to reform in these instances and this suggests the following
proposition: general proposition number three--agents of unplanned
cultural social change are sufficient to increase opposition to reform
among individuals who are in comparatively privileged social positions and who believe competition for status and influence would increase with modernization.

The latter two categories, where opposition to cultural reform
increased between 1967 and 1973, also share certain characteristics.
Individuals in both categories are relatively unprepared to play meaningful roles in the sectors of society expanded by social change and,
thus, may feel threatened by modernization. Older men in dynamic
Tunis, especially if poorly educated, may believe their status will
decline and their marginality increase with modernization. For this
reason, they oppose an emphasis on education and youth and new
social codes that appear to favor others. Younger, poorly educated
men in Tunis and in smaller towns may have similar fears. Their
educational and professional opportunities are limited, and hence,
their levels of frustration and self-doubt are probably high. In such
a situation, they are likely to oppose women's liberation, because it
increases the number of persons with whom they must compete for
jobs and status, and to reject cultural reform generally, because it

symbolizes the forces responsible for their marginality. If these
explanations are correct, the advent of planned change would intensify fears and increase resistance to cultural reform. The following general proposition may be derived from this analysis: general proposition number four--agents of either unplanned or planned
social change are sufficient to increase opposition to cultural reform
among individuals who consider their social position precarious.

An alternative explanation for increased opposition to reform
in the latter two categories also suggests itself. Since these people
live in comparatively conservative milieus, where unplanned change
is not intense and where traditional opposition to reform is high, it
may be that without official programs of change, there is simply too
little pressure for change to produce support for cultural reform.
This explanation gives rise to another proposition, which is stated
below. If this explanation is correct, the advent of planned change
will decrease opposition to cultural reform, in contrast to what was
suggested above. It is also possible that both propositions numbers
four and five are correct, each applying in a different locale. The
present proposition seems most plausible when considered in relation to residents of smaller towns: general proposition number five--
agents of unplanned social change are not sufficient to increase or
maintain levels of support for cultural reform among individuals who
live in comparatively traditional milieus.

CHANGING PATTERNS OF CONSENSUS AND CLEAVAGE

Findings

The distribution of support for reforms pertaining to women
and child rearing was not the same in 1967 and 1973. Table 14.5
shows the percentage of persons favorable to reform in each year
for each respondent category and suggests several conclusions about
differences between cultural orientations in the years under consideration.

One set of conclusions pertains to attitude variations among
women and between women and men. First, the distribution of attitudes among women was not the same in 1967 and 1973. In 1967,
support for cultural reform among women was positively associated
with age and education, and the magnitude of these variations was
substantial, indicating the presence of a potentially important normative cleavage among women. In 1973, by contrast, differences
among categories of female respondents were much smaller, reflecting reduced support for cultural reform among well-educated
women of intermediate age and increased support among younger

TABLE 14.5: Levels of Support for Cultural Reform in 1967 and 1973 among Matched Respondents, Grouped on the Basis of Sex, Residence, Age, and Education, in Tunisia

	Men in Tunis						Women in Tunis						Men in Smaller Towns					
	High[a]		Medium[b]		Low[c]		High[a]		Medium[b]		Low[c]		High[a]		Medium[b]		Low[c]	
Age	1967	1973	1967	1973	1967	1973	1967	1973	1967	1973	1967	1973	1967	1973	1967	1973	1967	1973
(1) Percent Believing Schooling Is as Important for a Girl as for a Boy																		
Under 23	89	89	46	16	75	50	--	--	53	83	97	67	--	--	63	33	25	25
23–34	74	56	65	65	44	46	90	80	78	40	--	--	--	--	50	50	40	20
Over 34	55	55	74	44	94	44	--	--	--	--	--	--	--	--	80	40	80	50
(2) Percent Believing It Is Acceptable for a Woman to Direct a Professional Enterprise Employing Many Men																		
Under 23	12	22	51	11	50	25	--	--	30	50	0	33	--	--	33	33	80	0
23–34	55	39	46	55	52	29	86	50	84	61	--	--	--	--	75	0	0	0
Over 34	83	29	49	19	55	25	--	--	--	--	--	--	--	--	20	0	50	0
(3) Percent Believing Women Should Have the Same Rights as Men to Marry Foreigners																		
Under 23	75	75	16	21	30	0	--	--	37	17	0	100	--	--	60	0	80	0
23–34	46	46	35	45	21	11	89	67	50	50	--	--	--	--	37	12	0	0
Over 34	54	27	24	14	46	6	--	--	--	--	--	--	--	--	80	40	50	0

(4) Percent Believing Children Should Be Encouraged to Think for Themselves, Even If They Occasionally Disobey Their Parents

Under 23	100	73	76	76	50	50	—	97	100	100	—	60	60	70	100
23–34	81	89	72	89	39	64	90	78	—	—	—	50	63	25	25
Over 34	75	90	83	73	56	56	—	—	—	—	—	80	40	33	83

(5) Percent Believing the Father Should Be as Affectionate toward the Children as the Mother

Under 23	20	33	11	11	0	0	—	0	0	67	33	0	33	25	0
23–34	31	43	15	58	16	11	79	18	60	80	—	13	0	0	33
Over 34	54	27	13	33	26	6	60	—	—	—	—	60	60	30	0

(6) Percent Believing It Is Not More Important that a Father Be Respected by His Children than that He Be Loved

Under 23	62	25	47	17	0	0	—	17	17	50	0	20	0	25	25
23–34	36	35	41	40	18	28	59	0	80	—	—	60	15	63	33
Over 34	54	54	40	20	56	6	40	—	—	—	—	20	—	0	20

Average Percent Supporting Cultural Reform

Under 23	59	54	41	25	36	21	—	39	52	41	55	39	27	42	33
23–34	52	50	45	58	33	32	83	50	68	—	—	45	21	32	19
Over 34	63	47	46	33	55	24	—	—	—	—	—	57	30	47	35

[a]High = high school or university.
[b]Medium = intermediate.
[c]Low = primary or less.
Source: Compiled by the authors.

and/or less-well-educated women. Second, attitude differences between women and men changed between 1967 and 1973, increasing in
some instances and declining in others. Among the youngest respondents, support for cultural reform was about the same for women
and comparable men in 1967; but in 1973, due to the fact that support
for reform decreased among men and increased among women, the
latter were noticeably more supportive, particularly with respect to
female emancipation. Among respondents of intermediate age who
had not completed high school, women were slightly more supportive
of cultural reform in 1967, and the pattern was about the same in
1973. Among better-educated persons of intermediate age, women
were substantially more supportive of reform in 1967; but since their
levels of support declined thereafter while those of men changed little,
attitude differences between men and women in this category were
much smaller in 1973. The net result of these findings is that (1)
attitude differences among women diminished between 1967 and 1973
and (2) differences between women and men diminished among the
best-educated respondents and increased among the youngest and
least well-educated respondents.

Another set of conclusions concerns attitude variations among
men in smaller towns and between these individuals and comparable
residents of Tunis. First, attitude differences among men in smaller
towns declined between 1967 and 1973. In 1967, support for cultural
reform was positively associated with age and education; older and
better-educated respondents were more supportive of reform than
persons in other categories. In 1973, however, due to diminished
support for reform among older and better-educated individuals, the
magnitude of variations across respondent categories was substantially reduced. Second, attitude difference between men in smaller
towns and comparable residents of Tunis changed between 1967 and
1973. In 1967, attitude differences associated with residence were
small and in no consistent direction. In 1973, they were larger,
though only moderate, and still in no single direction. Among the
oldest and best-educated respondents, increased cultural distance
between city and town involved greater opposition to reform among
residents of Tunis. Among persons of intermediate age, regardless
of educational level, it involved greater opposition to reform among
residents of smaller towns. To sum up, from 1967 to 1973, there
was increased homogeneity in the cultural attitudes of men in smaller towns and increased cultural distance between town and city, with
town residents sometimes being more supportive and sometimes being less supportive of reform.

A third set of conclusions concerns the attitudes of men in
Tunis. In 1967, older and/or better-educated men in Tunis were
most supportive of cultural reform and younger and less-well-

educated men were least supportive. The difference between these
two groups was substantial but not extremely large. In 1973, by
contrast, age was related to support for reform in a curvilinear
way--with older as well as younger people opposing it most fre-
quently--and differences associated with education had increased.
Figure 14.1 illustrates these findings, depicting the locus of comparatively frequent and comparatively infrequent support for reform
in each year. It shows that from 1967 to 1973, (1) older and poorly
educated respondents joined the ranks of younger and less-well-
educated persons, increasing the number of respondent categories
in which opposition to cultural reform was strong, and (2) the cultural distance between this group of respondent categories and those
where support for reform was comparatively frequent was greater
in 1973 than in 1967.

FIGURE 14.1:   Demographic Locus of Support for Cultural
               Reform Among Men in Tunis in 1967 and 1973

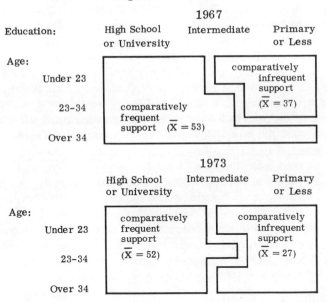

Discussion: Potential for Conflict

     Attitudes toward reform were more polarized in 1973 than in
1967, suggesting greater potential for social discord. For one
thing, attitudes in the latter year were more honogeneous among
women in Tunis and men in smaller towns, increasing the salience
of sex and residence as variables defining the locus of support for
cultural reform. Also, the cultural distance between these two

population categories increased substantially; women generally became more supportive of reform between 1967 and 1973, while support consistently declined among men in smaller towns. These observations reveal that normative cleavages and social divisions based
on sex and place of residence reinforced one another in 1973, and
this, following the logic of conflict theorists who argue that coincid-
ing cleavages produce instability, increases the potential for social
conflict.

We have already noted growing polarization in the attitudes of
men in Tunis. One group of respondents, composed of well-educated
persons and those of intermediate age and educational levels, is relatively supportive of cultural reform. Another, composed of poorly
educated individuals and younger and older persons with intermediate
levels of schooling, opposes reform. Thus, instead of bridging the
gap between urban women and men in smaller towns, divisions among
men in Tunis reinforce the aforementioned cleavage. Male supporters of reform in Tunis are joined by women from Tunis and constitute something of a bloc favoring cultural reform. Male opponents
of reform in Tunis are joined by residents of smaller towns (in those
respondent categories examined) and constitute a bloc with contradictory predispositions. Since the social composition of these blocs
was more clear-cut in 1973 and the cultural distance between them
greater, it appears that recent political trends in Tunisia have polarized cultural attitudes and increased the potential for discord.

It will be asked whether a continuing commitment to planned
change beyond the late 1960s would have produced different results,
and we must acknowledge that no definitive answer to this question
can be derived from the data at hand. As proposition number four
from the preceding section suggests, official programs of change
might have increased opposition to reform among disadvantaged elements of the population and decreased it among those better able to
compete for status in the modern sector, thereby adding to polarization and the potential for discord. Alternatively, as proposition
number five suggests, such policies might have mobilized and re-
socialized more traditional elements of the population and, given an
equal distribution of opportunities for personal advancement, served
to promote normative consensus. While these and other possibilities
remain speculative, the fact remains that growing polarization over
cultural questions is one important result of the policies followed
from 1967 to 1973.

Despite these considerations, there are also several factors
limiting polarization. First, a measure of disagreement exists
within the group of respondent categories where support for reform
is comparatively frequent. On many items, the position of the
majority is rejected by a substantial minority, and so this "bloc" is

not united in its opposition to those less supportive of reform.
Second, absolute support for reform declined between 1967 and 1973
among most respondent categories in this bloc. This is particularly
true among better-educated men and women in Tunis, persons whom
we would expect to have intense feelings about cultural issues. Without agitation and leadership from these individuals, and especially
in light of the reduction in programs of planned change, the saliency
of cultural issues underlying social cleavages has probably declined.
Third, an increased normative consensus among women, among well-
educated persons in Tunis, and among men in smaller towns con-
trasts with increased cultural distance at the overall societal level.
This suggests that within certain more limited social environments--
within which much day-to-day activity in fact takes place--disagree-
ment about cultural questions has actually diminished since 1967.
Thus, while attitudinal differences about women and child rearing
have increased overall, there are factors operating that may reduce
some of the tension that could result from this situation.

CONCLUSION

The research reported in this chapter suggests that recent
political and ideological trends in Tunisia are producing conserva-
tism insofar as cultural issues are concerned. During the late 1950s
and early 1960s, Tunisia was one of the most daring and radically
innovative Arab countries in the area of cultural policy. In the last
seven or eight years, however, the government has abandoned much
of its earlier commitment to planned social and cultural transformation, and an apparent result is diminished support for cultural reform at popular levels. Overall support for female emancipation
has declined noticeably, and opposition to cultural reform in general
has increased in two particularly important social categories. First,
persons old enough and sufficiently well educated to serve as opinion
leaders and models for personal development have become more
conservative, reducing pressure for cultural change from nongovernmental sources. Second, among persons low in personal and professional status, opposition to cultural reform has increased even
more, strengthening the coincidence of normative and socioeconomic
cleavages and expanding the sectors of society within which traditional social codes predominate. These developments are probably
not attributable entirely to changing governmental policies, but an
association of changing attitudes at the societal and individual level
is clear, and it is probable that the former are at least one important cause of the latter.

Nor is opposition to cultural reform likely to dissipate quickly
in Tunisia. In some sectors of society, programs of planned change
appear to be necessary to generate popular acceptance of cultural
reform. Yet there is no evidence that the kinds of programs that
characterized Tunisia during the first decade of its independence
are about to be reinstituted. The government seems, rather, to be
encouraging a resurgence of traditional values. Further, the frustration of persons marginally integrated into the modern sectors of
society appears to be stimulating opposition to reform; and with the
government's renunciation of socialist principles, economic disparities and personal frustration may well intensify. For the present,
Tunisia is still one of the Arab countries where traditional cultural
values have changed the most. But the country is no longer the
radical innovator it once was and, should present political and economic policies continue, in a few years, it may not even be among
those progressive Arab states where a new normative order is
emerging.

NOTES

1. See Micaud, C. A., 1974 and 1969, pp. 468-84. See also
Tessler, M. A., O'Barr, W. M., and Spain, D. H., eds., 1973,
pp. 193-303, on which part of this account is based. For additional
discussions of Tunisian political life during the first decade of independence, see Moore, C. H., 1965; Ashford, D., 1967; and Rudebeck,
L., 1969.
2. Bourguiba, H., "L'Enseignement, fonction sociale," a
speech given in 1965.
3. Bourguiba, H., "Dimensions du sousdeveloppement," a
speech given in 1963.
4. Moore, C. H., 1971, p. 106.
5. Bourguiba, 1965.
6. Bourguiba, H., "Discours prononcé à l'occasion du
Mouled," a speech given in 1966.
7. Bourguiba, 1965.
8. Bourguiba, H., "Edifier une societe saine et equilibrée,"
a speech given in 1966.
9. Duvignaud, J., 1970, p. 233. For comparable findings,
see Bardin, P., 1965; Louis, A., 1965, pp. 373-400; and Filali, M.,
1966, pp. 83-114. Similar findings based on urban milieus are summarized in Tessler, O'Barr, and Spain, eds., op. cit.
10. For a summary, see Tessler, M. A., 1971, pp. 290-308.
For a fuller discussion, including a summary of findings from other
research conducted in Tunisia and elsewhere, see Tessler, O'Barr,
and Spain, eds., op. cit.

11. See Entelis, J., 1974, pp. 543-68. See also Tessler, M. A., Rogers, J. M., and Schneider, D. R., 1975.

12. Hermassi, E., 1972, p. 215. For additional accounts of the changing character of Tunisian political life, see Schaar, S., 1970, pp. 43-46.

13. Zghal, A., 1972, pp. 225-38. Zghal presents an excellent discussion contrasting social and cultural policies of the Tunisian elite in the years immediately following independence and in the last few years.

14. Bourguiba, H., "Problemes de la jeunesse dans leur vraie perspective," a speech given in 1969.

15. A summary of traditional normative patterns in these areas should not be necessary for readers of this volume. For details pertaining to Tunisia, readers may consult Tessler, O'Barr, and Spain, eds., op. cit., pp. 242-47, for a discussion of female emancipation, and pp. 247-50, for a discussion of child rearing. For fuller introductions, readers may see Gordon, D., 1968, and Camilleri, C., 1973.

16. For evidence that attitudes toward these cultural focuses strongly covary with other cultural orientations, see Tessler, op. cit.

17. See Tessler, M. A., 1973, pp. 29-43, and Tessler, M. A., in Tessler, O'Barr, and Spain, eds., op. cit.

18. Ibid.

15

The Patriarch in the
Moroccan Family:
Myth or Reality?

FATIMA MERNISSI

INTRODUCTION: THE MODERN FAMILY AS A
RELIGIOUS INSTITUTION

Engaged as they are in a developing process, Arab countries
have expressed their will to transform their environment and introduce technology--and to import its latest creations and realizations.
But new means of production are bound to create new modes of relations, foster new institutions, and dismantle old ones. The desire
for change in the Arab world is apparently limited, since change
in some spheres is considered catastrophic and a crime against
Muslim identity. Such is the case of change within the institution of
the family. Some independent Muslim states have reaffirmed the
religious character of the family. By so doing, they stamped traditional sexual and generational relations, as well as authority patterns, with the seal of eternity.[1] To change religious prescriptions
is by definition a blasphemy, an outrageous insult to the religious
authority of Allah. His transcendental sight is beyond time; centuries do not matter; bid'a, innovation in religious institutions and
prescribed regulations, is condemned as dalalah, errance, departure from the right path. Therefore, a religious code for the
family (reproducing models and patterns of the seventh and eighth
centuries after Christ's death--the first centuries of Muslim cal-
endar--as ideals for modern interfamily relations) has tremendous
implications in a developing Muslim nation.

This chapter is a revised version of a report presented to the
Division of Applied Social Sciences, UNESCO, Paris, in December
1975, as part of a UNESCO-funded research project on the Moroccan
family.

Unlike Turkey, which integrated the religious family code into its civil code, some independent Muslim states, such as Morocco, have maintained a dual system, a secular civil code and a religious family code.[2] The family codes go back to the seventh century, when the first rules of the Muslim social order were laid down by supernatural divine forces. They draw their legitimacy and authority from their conformity with the original prescriptions. This chapter will discuss some implications of the religious character of the family code for the domestic unit in the developing Moroccan economy.

The reenactment of medieval Muslim family law in modern family codes has definite and direct bearings on the nature of the family structure and its stability or lack of stability, and therefore on the sexes' roles, not as they are defined in legal texts but as socioeconomic necessities shape them. One of the differences between the seventh-century Muslim family and the twentieth-century one is the importance of tribal network solidarity in the former and its absence in the latter. However, a certain point should be clarified at this point, namely, the relatively minor function of the conjugal unit in seventh-century Arabia and its increasingly decisive role in 1975 Morocco. A general effect of the industrializing process is the shrinking of the family size, the fragmentation of pre-existing extended family networks, and the atomization of the family into small nuclear-type units.[3] Morocco is no exception to the rule; statistical data show clearly this trend already in the 1960s. The 1960 census established that the most numerous kind of households are households of two or three persons in urban areas and four or five persons in rural areas.[4] The average family size is five persons in an urban setting and six in a rural one.[5] The number of urban households with one to six persons, which used to constitute 83 percent of households in 1960, does not constitute more than 69 percent in 1971.[6]

We will see throughout the text that a corollary of the disintegration of the large family is the loosening of solidarity networks between individuals related by blood or affinal ties. This is one of the main differences between the seventh-century Arab family and the present one. The whole concept of "honor" is based on this solidarity, honor being a two-sided phenomenon; there are two rights involved: one is the right to chastise the disobedient group member and the other right is the duty to protect him. The decisive function of group feeling and group solidarity is a vital mechanism in the functioning of the ideal Muslim order, as has been so eloquently argued by Ibn Khaldoun.[7] The absence of group feeling and solidarity networks set an entirely different setting for family interaction and family roles and functions. Predominance of tribal ties over the conjugal ones is an established feature of early Arab Islam.[8] In the twentieth century, the dismantling of tribal power and the destruction of the agricultural basis of the patriarchal family have undermined the family's solidarity mechanisms. Nationwide mobility of the peasant population in search for jobs, in and out of the country, and scarcity and insecurity of jobs and income set a specific frame for males, called upon by family law to claim, as well as to perform, their medieval rights and roles.

The first part of this chapter will analyze some implications of the character of the institution of the family, namely, instability and fragility of the conjugal unit. A second part will explore the gap between the legal privileges of the patriarch (according to the family code) and the harsh realities imposed by underdevelopment, especially immigration and unemployment. This part stresses the emergence of new forces within the family sphere, the collapse of the father's power, and the strengthening of the state power within domestic activities and its decision-making mechanisms. The conclusion briefly discusses the emergence of the mother from the midst of the collapsing patriarchal family, as an agent of continuity and the main agent in the dialogue between the welfare state and the domestic unit.

SEXUAL INEQUALITY AS A RELIGIOUS INSTITUTION: DESTRUCTIVE EFFECTS OF POLYGAMY AND REPUDIATION ON FAMILY'S STABILITY

After often bitter nationalist struggles, Arab nations, newly emerging from the humiliations of colonization, were eager to enter the international arena and make their existence known. Membership to the UN and the ratification of the Declaration of Human Rights were logical steps. Both the UN Charter and the Declaration condemn all forms of discrimination and claim equality as the basis of relations between the sexes. Morocco showed its will to enforce the principle of sexual equality by including it in its Constitution.* Morover, all cases in the family law where the man's

---

The Moroccan Constitution (March 10, 1972) states that "in order to make its actions consistent with the activities of international organizations to which it belongs, the kingdom of Morocco subscribes to the principles, laws, and obligations stated in the charters of these organizations." Bulletin Official no. 3098, p. 456. Articles 5, 8, and 13 guarantee the woman's economic and political rights.

sexual rights were not only utterly different from, but constituted limitations and violation of, the woman's rights were denied by the new legislation. For example, the Moroccan penal code grants a man who kills his adulterous wife circonstances attenuantes.[9] This is not the best way to either promote sexual civility within the conjugal unit or guarantee the woman's (elementary) right to live. This flagrant aspect of sexual inequality is even more striking when one knows that it is utterly alien to traditional Muslim law, which imposes equal punishment for both adulterous men and women. The punishment in the Koran is scourging and not death, and proof of adultery is almost impossible to realize, given the complicated combination of facts required.[10] Another example of an unequal restriction imposed by Moroccan family law is the wife's need to have the husband's authorization to leave the house. This is in flagrant contradiction to Article 9 of the Constitution, which recognizes that all citizens have the right to move (droit de circuler).[11] Another example is the male's right to choose a spouse with a different religion, while the woman's choice is limited to a Muslim spouse, and her marriage with a non-Muslim is considered null.[12] The list of unequal rights is a long one.

Rights and duties of husbands and wives have direct repercussions on the stability of the family. Given the upheavals of economic development, the reenforcement of medieval male sexual privileges, such as polygamy and repudiation, magnifies the structurally disintegrating effects of such phenomena as rural migration and male unemployment.

Polygamy's Destructive Socio-demographic Effects

Polygamy constitutes a flagrant violation of sexual equality, not only because it allows many sexual partners to males and condemns females to monogamy but also because it allows elderly men to marry women one or two generations younger. This aspect of polygamy has been strangely overlooked, although it has decisive effects on the couple's harmony and the children's personality structure.

Polygamy has been maintained in most Arab family codes, and Morocco is no exception.[13] Although it has been practiced for 14 centuries by Muslim males, it is one of the least-investigated phenomena by modern social scientists. Statistical data are scarce and not detailed. Data exist on the percentage of polygamous families, but very little on their size or behavior patterns. A brief review of Moroccan data suggests that polygamy is not the glamorous conjugal unit so much joked about at elegant dinners, but a monstrous institution, whose far-reaching destructive effects on wife and child go beyond its statistically minor importance. Surveys have established that only 3 percent of Moroccan families are polygamous.[14] However, a recent survey by the Centre d'Etudes et de Recherche Démographiques (CERED) revealed that there is a wide gap between the number of married women and married men. There are 9 percent more married women than men in rural areas, and 6 percent more married women than men in urban areas.[15] The 1971 census reveals similar discrepancies in the number of married men and women[16] and explains these differences by the number of Moroccan workers emigrating to Europe. It is important to remember that the average Moroccan emigrant worker is a young man and that men marry quite late in Morocco,[17] which leads us to think that the number of polygamous families is probably higher than public opinion wants it to be.

A 1955 survey in Casablanca established that polygamy has strong class aspects; the rate among the low-income group was 2 percent while it reached 21 percent among average-income strata.[18] The survey identifies two kinds of polygamous men: the polygame de luxe and the polygame utilitaire.[19] For the first, the motivation is masculine pride, "phallocratic" show-off. The men in this category are chronically polygamous. The second type is only temporarily polygamous; he reverts to monogamy when his aim is reached. His polygamy is instrumental, he has a specific goal to realize: either his wife is sick and he needs domestic and sexual services during this period, or his first wife is sterile, and he marries a second who will give him a child he will manage to keep after repudiating her.[20] These findings suggest the whimsical and unethical aspects of polygamy, which allows the manipulation of women for purposes alien to their own interests. But the most dangerous repercussion of polygamy is its impact on monogamous households. A CERED survey established that polygamy was invoked as grounds for divorce in 18.5 percent of the cases studied in urban areas and 12.2 percent in rural ones.[21] Women when threatened by the likelihood of a second wife prefer to ask for divorce, since this is the only alternative given to them by the current family code. The irony is that the legislator, in his zealous mission to limit polygamy (by allowing women to contest the man's previously sovereign right), did not make it possible for them to claim their right without increasing the family's instability. A less-chauvinistic legislator would have thought of making the second marriage null in case the first wife opposed it, not in leaving her only with the alternative of destroying her own marriage.* A wife who is threatened by a second wife, loses, if she chooses divorce, her very means of support, the husband. Her chances to remarry are very slim, especially if she has children (which is often the case) or if she is over 30. The peculiar structure of the marriage market in a Muslim community, where elderly men are equipped with legal and economic assets to marry multiple spouses in time and space, allows them also to marry women one or two generations younger. This hurts the marriageable value of women who are older. A survey established that the average polygamous man is 50 years old. The age difference between the man and his second wife is estimated to be 20 years for the average couple. The age gap widens when a man marries a third wife; she is usually 26 years younger than him.[22] This age discrepancy between spouses predisposes such families to early dissolution by death, with negative economical and psychological repercussions for the children's socioeconomic chances.

As for psychological aspects of polygamy, these are clearly illustrated in popular culture by sayings and jokes, which perceive it as a way to undermine women's value and demean them.† For example, the joke, "Why doesn't the economy take care of elderly wives like it does of used cars? Why not an institution where you bring your old wife, add a few dirhams, and get a new one like we do with cars?" Beyond the dynamics of the adults involved in a polygamous unit, one can imagine the impact on the children in general, and those of the first wife in particular, who usually has a specific status, that of Al-Mahjoura, the abandoned one. The Mahjoura cannot expect her husband to care about her children as he used to do.

_____

*"A woman has the right to divorce if she stipulates in her marriage contract that her husband does not have the right to marry another woman" (Family Law, La Muduwana: Dahir no. 1-57-343, November 22, 1957, art. 31).

†Sidi Abderahmane Al Majdoub's poems are famous about the use of rivalry between women as a way to undermine their value, such as the following:

> Tamou is a treasure chest
> Aicha is the key to it.

(in S. A. Al Majdoub, Les quatrains du Majdoub le sarcastique, poete Maghrebin du XVI siècle, J. Scelles Millie and B. Khalifa, trans. [Paris: Maisonneuve et Larousse, 1966]).

Repudiation: The Male's Sovereign Right
to Dissolve the Family

If statistically, polygamy is dying, as some maintain, it has
been widely replaced in Morocco by what Baron calls "polygamie
dans le temps," or serial marriages. These are the outcome of
another family institution maintained in modern codes: repudiation.

Morocco has one of the world's highest divorce rates, compared to either developed countries (four times the divorce rate of
the United States for married women aged between 20 and 24)[23] or
developing ones (eight times the rate of India for similar age
groups).[24] Even within Muslim countries, Morocco has an unusually
high divorce rate: seven times that of Pakistan and five times that
of Syria and Egypt.[25] According to the 1960 census, 32 percent of
the nonsingle women had married several times.[26] The divorce
rate seems to increase with women's age; from 15 percent for the
age group 15 to 19, it reaches a peak of 30 percent after the age of
29. A family planning survey undertaken in 1966–67 gave similar
rates.[27]

To blame the instability of the Moroccan family on modernity
(and the dissolution of ethics and morals) is to use an argument that
belongs more to demagogy than to a real assessment of the situation. This kind of argument, often supported by individuals and
groups who have vested interests in idealizing tradition, does not
hold up when confronted with statistics. The divorce rate among
generations born between 1895 and 1915 in a rural community relatively "unspoiled" by modernity was evaluated at 49 percent of all
marriages.[28]

Repudiation is essentially different from divorce in that it is
not under the state's (and its representative's--judges) control. It
is a perfect illustration of the archaic powers of the patriarch to
decide unilaterally the fate of the household members--among
other things, to dissolve the conjugal bond and dismiss his wife
without explanation, justification, or regular economic compensation.* The husband does not have to justify himself in front of any
higher authority. The court's role is limited to simply registering
his will. Moreover, the verbal dimension pertains to the realm of
magic: he just has to pronounce the fatal "I repudiate thee," and
the woman vanishes from his horizon, although he is obliged to

---

*The 'Idda, the woman's right to be supported economically
by husband after repudiation, does not last more than a few months;
see chap. v of Tunisia, Family Law, La Muduwana, Dahir no.
1-57-343, November 26, 1962.

leave the house and feed her for few 'Idda months, during which he is not supposed to interact with her in any meaningful way.* Most Arab codes of the family reenacted repudiation, with minor adaptations and changes, without altering its unilateral patriarchal essence. Before going into the effects of repudiation in Morocco, it is interesting to see if the elimination of repudiation as a legal institution has any effects at all on the stability of the family.

According to statistics, elimination of repudiation does seem to make a large difference in family disruption rates. Morocco's rate is almost three times that of Tunisia and four times that of Turkey, two Muslim countries that have eliminated repudiation.[29] However, this does not mean that repudiation alone is to be blamed for Morocco's high rate. Economic upheavals, which occur in the transition from an agrarian to an industrial economy, contribute to the intensification of repudiation's traditional effects. These effects are likely to more seriously affect those groups who experience the most disintegration and marginalization vis-à-vis modern sectors, namely, low-income groups. Unlike polygamy, repudiation hurts poor women more severely, the nascent industrialization process having liberated the husband from the social pressure network inherent in the traditional system.

Class Bias of Repudiation: No One Wants to Get Rid of a Rich Woman

A comparison between the 1960 and 1971 censuses establishes that repudiation is definitely a thriving institution. The number of divorced women is increasing.[30] But more than the statistical importance of this category, it is relevant to investigate the profile of the average repudiated women. There is no in-depth thorough study yet; however, fragmentary data reveal the main features.

Women as Heads of Households

One of the effects of generalized unemployment in the Moroccan countryside is emigration toward towns and unplanned urbanization. This results in dislocation of the family unit and erosion of its solidarity networks. Data reveal that the evolution of the size of the Moroccan family is toward smaller units; the extended family,

---

*The husband is not supposed to interact with his repudiated wife during the "Idda period. He can have her back if he wants to before the expiration of the 'Idda period.

especially in urban areas, seems to have broken down into smaller units.[31] More than 50 percent of urban households have no more than four persons.[32] The average household has five persons in the urban setting and six in the rural.[33] A corollary of the disintegration of the traditional extended family is the loosening, if not the disappearance, of solidarity networks. A genuine patriarchal family is, by definition, a family whose pride is the unconditional, everlasting, unfailing support of women by males.[34] The prestige of the patriarch rests with his capacity to protect and safeguard the interests of his womenfolk. Repudiated daughters, widowed daughters-in-law, once deprived of the affinal male support, come back to the house of the father or the brother, who is obliged to take care of them. A family whose repudiated or widowed daughters live in separate households is a family whose honor is tarnished. According to the rigid traditional honor code of patriarchy, one can say that presently, for many patriarchs, their prestige is more than jeopardized; the number of households headed by women have increased by 33 percent between 1960 and 1971, while the number of households headed by males have hardly increased.[35]

A classification of households according to the marital status of its heads reveals that while 91.25 percent of male households are headed by married men, only 13.63 percent of female households are headed by married women. Eighty-three percent of women household heads are either divorced or widowed.[36] Also, details of sizes of households according to sex of the head of the household show that there are 13 times more households of 1 person headed by women than those headed by males of the same size, and twice as many households of 15 persons headed by women than those of the same size headed by men.[37] The number of households between 6 and 8 persons constitute 23 percent of male-headed units and 37 percent of female-headed ones.

From the above, one can conclude that the disintegration of the extended family has, among other things, drastically changed sex roles. Although traditionally, women were supposed to be cared for by related or affinal males, they seem to be left, in many cases in the present, to care for themselves and their progeny. The woman, the only stable partner of the family, emerges as the only factor of continuity as well.

The instability of the family seems to increase with degree of industrialization. The breakup of families is more common in towns than in the countryside,[38] and more common in bigger towns than in smaller ones.[39] Moreover, women born in the countryside who emigrate to towns have a higher risk of being divorced than women who do not experience emigration.[40] Proximity was an important element in the traditional family system, where the

husband in the conjugal unit was not independent and free to decide
on such matters as repudiation.* Because the marriage itself was
a group affair, an engagement between families, so was the dissolution of the conjugal unit. With isolation of husbands from the
group, either for geographical or economic reasons, the wife's
family has no mechanisms to pressure their in-laws or to protect
their daughters. Before ending this exploration of the breakup of
the family, we ought to ask how these women, who before were
economically dependent on powerful patriarchs, manage to survive.

The Divorcees' and Widows' Economic Position

It seems there is a peculiar relation between work and divorce
in a Muslim woman's life. The divorce rate is higher among the
female active population than among nonactive women.[41] Also, the
divorcees constitute the bulk of the working women. Of the total
active female population, 53 percent are divorcees, while only 7
percent are married.[42] To get an idea of their condition, one has
to describe briefly the situation of women in the labor market.

Getting a job and working outside of the house is certainly not
the dream of the average Moroccan woman, not because she is
particularly happy with her traditional fate and roles and duties but
simply because there is very little variety in jobs open to her and
slim chances of promotion in those openings. The majority of
working women were in the lowest salary bracket, according to a
1963 survey.[43] This is hardly surprising; the illiteracy rate for
the active female population reaches 99 percent (a higher rate than
the national one, 86 percent).[44] Work for most women does not
constitute either a break in their routine or an opportunity to learn
new skills, even when they are supposed to be integrated into the
modern economic sector. They are either maids in the service
sector (17 percent of the female active population), or textile
workers (13 percent), or food industry workers. In all these cases,
they still perform tasks similar to domestic ones. As to their
contribution in the traditional agricultural sector, which accounts

---

*The famous preference among Arab societies for paternal
cousin's marriage is, among other things, a way for families to
make sure that they have some control over their daughter's husband and his behavior toward her. Traditionally, Moroccans,
either in rural or urban areas, prefer to give their daughters to
men who live in the same area, whose behavior or misbehavior can
be checked easily.

for 33 percent of the active women, it is hardly acknowledged as
an economic contribution. Most women have the status of aide
familiale, which, by definition, is a person working for relative
who lives in and does not receive a salary. [45]

The structural disintegration of the family in the developing
economy rather than the reenactment of the patriarch as the pillar
of the modern Moroccan conjugal unit ought to be investigated. We
argue in the next part that the Moroccan patriarch is being reduced
to a powerless individual vis-à-vis the state, which is gradually
emerging as the main force influencing the family.

THE BANKRUPT PATRIARCH AND THE EMERGENCE
OF THE STATE AS A RIVAL FORCE IN THE
MOROCCAN FAMILY

The Moroccan family code defines men as the only economic
agents in the family. They are the only providers and source of
income. Wives are defined as dependent and economically nonactive agents. One of the functions of marriage is to provide the
woman with a husband, whose duty is to ensure her food, clothing,
and shelter, the nafaqua. [46] We will not deal here with one of the
most explosive implications of this Muslim definition of the sex
roles: the nonmobilization of female labor for developmental purposes, a question Arab states have to decide upon very soon.
Feminist movements, offshoots of nationalist movements, clearly
stated the problem at the end of the nineteenth and beginning of the
twentieth century. [47] Taking the family law as a criterion for a
general policy toward women, it appears that Morocco does not
plan to include the female labor force in its developmental plans,
and thus, women will continue to be fed and provided for by fathers
and husbands. Let us look now at the actual economic situation of
these patriarchs, whose duty it is to feed wife, children, and other
dependent women.

Patriarchal Power and Class Disequilibrium

Present Moroccan society is the outcome of decades of violent
and bloody nationwide changes caused by colonization. [48] In spite
of a (suspiciously) strong idealization of tradition and the past, the
most evident features of this society are not continuity but change,
not equilibrium and harmony but imbalance and disharmony. Two
dimensions in which change and imbalance appear clearly are in
the formation of new classes and the widening gap between citizen

power and state power. Both dimensions have a direct impact on
the family.

A consequence of colonization and the postcolonization era is
the sharpening of class distinctions between a privileged minority
and an increasingly impoverished majority.[49] This class disequilibrium is seen in the purchasing power of households, for example.
The 1973-77 Plan de développement économique et social identifies
households according to their consumption capacity:

Households	Percent	Percent Consumption Capacity
Group 1	10.54	37.59
Group 2	39.17	55.66
Group 3	50.29	18.07

The first group, the high-income group, which does not constitute more than 10.54 percent of the Moroccan families, consumed
37.59 percent of all goods, while the third group, the low-income
one, which represents one-half of Moroccan families, cannot afford
more than 18.07 percent of available goods.[50]

This disequilibrium between classes in consumption power is
nothing but a reflection of widespread job insecurities and income
mediocrity for the average father, if we keep in mind that he is the
only family provider. Economic analysis of North African economies has established that while consumption of goods increased
after independence, production was stagnant until the early 1970s.[51]
Stagnant production means, among other things, unemployment,
and unemployment in a patriarchal setting means the bankruptcy of
the patriarch. The average patriarch is, in reality, an illiterate
man, either unemployed or an emigrant, and, therefore, absent
from the family unit, either physically or economically.

Illiteracy rate among the male population reaches 62.5 percent and constitutes in itself a good indicator of the Moroccan man's
inability to make the jump from a basically agricultural setting,
based on oral exchange, to a technological society, based on writing
and literacy and the skills acquired during formal schooling.
Forty-four percent of unemployed young men seeking jobs for the
first time in their lives have never had any modern formal education or training.[52] The official unemployment rate is 350,000,
mainly males (officially, women constitute only 15 percent of the
active population), that is, 9 percent of the total active population.[53]
As for disguised unemployment, statistics suggest it reaches
1,194,000 individuals. This means that 30 percent of all active
men are not employed to their full capacity.

A corollary of unemployment that has a decisive bearing on family life is migration, both within and without the country. The 1971 census estimated that a flow of 90,000 individuals emigrates every year toward towns in search of jobs they often do not find.[54] They represent 2.5 percent of the active population. As for external emigration, European sources have evaluated the number of Moroccans working in European countries at 405,000, which constitutes the equivalent of 10 percent of the total active population.[55]

One can conclude that one Moroccan man out of two runs a high risk of being either unemployed, barely employed, or obliged to emigrate within the national borders or go abroad to seek a job. Unemployment in all its forms puts tension on the everyday relations within the family, especially if we remember that the father is the only officially responsible breadwinner. Any shortage in supply for family needs is likely to be perceived as a weakness on his part. He cannot rely on his wife for help, for only 7 percent of married women work.* It is not surprising that a recent survey identified material problems as a chief reason for divorce invoked by women.[56]

The psychological repercussions of unemployment on the male's self-image are likely to be devastating in a patriarchal society, where male pride is constantly invoked, enhanced, and encouraged by a whole set of cultural mechanisms, now magnified by modern mass media. Ads on Moroccan television have the traditional patriarchal structure: a woman, for example, who wonders and touches with eyes flowing with love new-bought furniture her husband has just bought after receiving a loan from the Banque Populaire. Most shampoo ads feature a woman washing her hair in a hugh bathroom and then combing it while walking through a plush apartment, while in reality, 33 percent of Moroccan households do not have more than one room to live in.[57] A patriarchal male structure is known to be more fragile than a nonpatriarchal one, the male being highly susceptible to any questioning of his maleness. Boasting and continuous self-inflation are necessary and characteristic traits in such cultures.[58] Further, honor is not something acquired once and for all; it is a never-ending task of rebuilding, which can be destroyed by a minor event, such as the woman's rumored (not proven) infidelity.†

---

*Women prefer to quit working as soon as they can get married. Work for women in low-income strata, who have the worst opportunities, is considered a (low-status) stigma. See A. Adam, 1972.

†Honor is not a prescribed attribute earned once and for all. On the contrary, it is a set of principles that have to be materialized

Patriarchal structure has never been challenged in Morocco, as it was under Bourguiba's guidance in Tunisia. The actualization of masculinity, through successful power to acquire goods and lavish them on wife and child, carries over in present Morocco uncontested. Popular culture equates masculinity with money power:

Money, money, toward which women incline,
I would not like my dog to be in the situation of a man
    without money.[59]

In Al Majdoub's terms, money constitutes the man's only attribute to which women are sensitive, and a male without money is as worthless as a dog.

Self-depreciating mechanisms are likely to accompany unemployment and overall economic powerlessness, with direct repercussions on interfamily relations. Repudiation, which puts at the disposal of the humiliated, unemployed father an almost magical means to disengage himself from family responsibilities, is likely to assume a disastrous magnitude in low-income groups.

The Emergence of the Patriarchal State

In a society where the state takes over the father's previous duties and rights, without a change in sex roles, we find a continuity in the mother-wife's economic dependency together with an equally dependent father. The presence of an increasingly overwhelming state apparatus in Morocco is a result of colonization, when concentration of bureaucratic-based power became a necessity. Historically, the Moroccan state was a fragile one.[60] The central authority was constantly contested and efficiently contained by other institutional groupings, such as the tribes. Moreover, its task pertained more to security matters than to welfare; its role consisted of collecting taxes and insuring the towns' security.[61] The present Moroccan state, like most states in developing countries, is a huge machinery, lavishly expanded after colonization. It is also a state with a specific mission--to realize the hopes and welfare needs voiced during nationalist struggles, and admitted by all social groups,

---

every day in the subject's behavior and in that of those related to him by affinal or blood ties. The tragedy of the patriarch is that he is utterly at the mercy of his subjects, who can destroy his reputation by a simple misplaced look or gesture.

including ruling ones, as legitimate needs. The priority goals of
the development plans are education, work, and an overall amelio-
ration of the quality of life for everyone. The success of the word
socialism among those who do and do not practice it is revealing of
this consensus: Arab socialism, Muslim socialism, and African
socialism are expressions of the ruling groups' awareness that the
days of unjustified privileges are gone. In present Morocco, everyone takes it for granted that it is the state's duty to provide good
health services, a decent school system, and plentiful employment
opportunities. The development plan is a poetic recapitulation of
the masses needs and the state's attempts to meet them.[62] No
Moroccan would have dreamed in 1900 that the state would take
care of, besides security problems, the health of children and
mothers, which were considered intimate family matters. Most
Moroccan children are presently expected to be taken care of by
the state for health, schooling, and even feeding (in state canteens).
Thus, the state's new duties as welfare provider make it the most
influential force in the present Moroccan family.

The State as the Factual Father:
Education and Health

A comparison of the number of children in public and private
schools establishes the predominance of the state school system.[63]
(See Table 15.1.)

TABLE 15.1: Evolution of Primary and Secondary School Figures
between 1967 and 1972, in Morocco

Schools	1967–68		1971–72	
	Figures	Percent	Figures	Percent
	Primary Schools			
Public system	1,040,044	94.10	1,171,307	95.00
Private system	65,193	5.89	60,629	5.00
	Secondary Schools			
Public system	238,199	89.00	284,376	90.70
Private system	29,432	10.99	29,048	9.26

Source: Morocco, Plan de Développement économique et
social, 1973-77, vol. 2, pp. 690-91.

As for the health system, the number of private doctors is roughly equal to that of doctors in public health services (538 and 567, respectively). However, only public health doctors are available to the average Moroccan, who is, by definition, a low-income person, as the consumption studies of Moroccan families have revealed.* Private medical services are closed to the average low-income Moroccan, not only because they are too expensive but, also, because they are concentrated in towns, where only 17 percent of the Moroccan population lives.[64] Two-thirds of all doctors in private practice are concentrated in the main Moroccan towns.[65] Casablanca alone has 55 private doctors.[66] Many provinces (Al Hoceima, Beni-Mellal, Ksar souk, Tarfaya, and Taza) would have no chance to see a doctor at all if it were not for the presence of public health services, which forces doctors (most of them of foreign nationality) to settle in unglamorous parts of the country.

Besides health and education, the state has usurped another role that was the patriarch's: the capacity and duty to employ the son and integrate him into a production unit. The traditional family was an economic unit managed in order to consolidate assets exploited in common within a specific hierarchy.[67] Nowadays, only a few rich Casablanca families could afford to employ their own sons and daughters if they wanted to. The average youngster turns toward the state (its civil servants in charge of the administration and management of the nation's wealth). The state is the only important investor in the country. Private capital of the national bourgeoisie is not only tiny but often invested in speculative operations, which are not geared to creating jobs.[68]

The emergence of the state as a "domestic" force, which cares for children's health, education, and unemployment, has undermining effects on traditional sex roles. The women have ample occasion to witness the civil servant's power to decide and to provide. To become a civil servant is the dream of illiterate and semiliterate youngsters, who see in him a powerful modern role. He just has to sign the paper or the file and things get moving. If economic dependency is the stigma of females in traditional family structure, the patriarch now shows strong female traits, namely, powerlessness and economic dependency, vis-à-vis civil

---

*Low-income people often strive to save enough money to go to a private doctor whenever they can because of the better quality of care, compared to public services, where one of the most disliked features is the five- to six-hour wait just to see a nurse in the first stage.

servants. One can venture to say that a side effect of the transition from an agricultural to a technological economy in Morocco is the collapse of previous sexual roles and authority patterns, the leveling of the father's status to that of his dependent wife vis-à-vis the state, and the emergence of a new family authority to whom wife and husband bow equally, the civil servant, the <u>bureaucratarche</u>.

The State as the Factual Husband

The state, through employment and the guarantee of a salary to the husband, actually indirectly guarantees the wife's support. It is true that as long as the husband has a steady job and the salary is flowing regularly into the family budget, the traditional economic subordination of wife to husband is guaranteed and the husband's economic dependency successfully masked. But the problem arises when this flow is interrupted, for one reason or another, and the husband finds himself jobless. The unequal allocation of power between an insecure patriarch and a constantly powerful bureaucratarche is evident, and it is likely that influences male and female self-images and perceptions of each other. We will illustrate this rivalry between state and patriarch through the very legislation that enthroned the father as patriarch in the midst of economic upheavals. The state attitude toward this legally enthroned patriarchy is far from coherent. At the same time that the legislator showers privileges upon the patriarch in the family code, in other texts, he attacks his privileges and undermines them. One of the most important legal texts is certainly the Constitution, [69] which affirms sexual equality as one of the basic principles underlying the country's structure and grants identical economic and political rights to both sexes.* The fact that Morocco has ratified the Declaration of Human Rights, which condemns sexual inequality "within the family," constitutes a serious challenge to the basis of the traditional Muslim family. The woman's newly gained right to work outside of the home, which constitutes in itself a symbolical denial of traditional domestic labor division, is an outcome of this legislation. The text regulating access to public functions condemns sexual

---

*Article 16 of the Declaration of Human Rights specifies that "beginning at physical maturity, men and women, without restriction based on race, nationality, or religion, have the right to marry and establish a family. They have equal rights when a family is established during marriage and at its dissolution."

inequality and states that public jobs are open to both sexes.* Labor legislation grants women maternity rights and similar benefits.

The number of female civil servants is estimated at 27,000. This ought to be weighed not statistically but culturally, since a few decades ago, the idea that women could manage the state's affairs was an absurdity. Today, a woman working in a governmental service is considered a casual happening. Women who are discriminated against make protests to their bosses; although they might be unconvinced of women's claims, they still have to put on a show in order to conform with legal injunctions.

What is relevant here is not the quality of work women are doing, or the conditions in which they perform their new duties, but the fact that the allegiance to their husband is challenged by their allegiance to their boss. The fact that a woman's right to work outside the home is still debated in court cases reveals the prevailing traditional seclusion patterns. But what is more important is that some women are claiming their rights. Patriarchal authority is more symbolic than real, as are all hierarchies. Theater (conventional gestures and attitudes) is an important part of it. Women who claim the right to work say explicitly that they want to put themselves in a subordinate position toward an employer, who is likely to be a man. A husband whose wife works outside is a husband who shares the wife's allegiance with another male, and this is precisely the negation of patriarchal pride. Patriarchal allegiance of women is indivisible. No wonder Arab countries until now have showed strong resistance to women working in nonagricultural traditional activities. Regardless of their degree of industrial development, they have the lowest rate of female employment of the developing countries.[70] But it is precisely because patriarchal pride is still so alive that any token number of working women ought to be considered as the incarnation of the system's failure. A growing number of women are stepping out of their houses every day and into the labor market. They are increasingly in contact with public services.

---

*Dahir No. 1-58-008, February 24, 1958, Portant Statut de la Fonction Publique, Article 1: "Every Moroccan has equal rights to consideration for public employment . . . no distinction . . . should be made based on sex in the application of this statute." Articles 46, 59, and 6 organize maternity leave and grant the mother other rights and privileges.

CONCLUSION: EMERGENCE OF MOTHER AS MAIN DIALOGIST WITH PUBLIC SERVICES ON BEHALF OF THE FAMILY

There is a nascent dialogue between the mother, as the main person responsible for child rearing and child care, and the public services. It is the mother who takes the sick child to routine hospital checkups, not the father. He only intervenes for serious decisions, such as hospitalization or major surgery. The child is perceived as an integral part of the domestic sphere, and any interference in domestic spheres is demeaning for the patriarch's pride. It is common for an unemployed father to spend the day playing cards and sipping tea in the neighborhood meeting place (it can be the cafe or the butcher's or barber's shop) while his wife is trying to combine cooking and waiting in hospital lines. A look at dispensaire clinic registers reveals that most of the public service users are women. The novelty in this is that the mother is taking responsibilities believed to be patriarchal prerogatives, such as the dialogue with public services. That this dialogue is impeded and difficult, given the fact that the mother is often illiterate and the public services built on bureaucracy and use of writing, is one of the problems developing Muslim nations have to deal with.

Studies of the modern Muslim family, fascinated by the patriarch and his legendary power, have until now failed to account for a highly changing reality. New hierarchical relations have emerged, new allegiance systems have appeared, with drastic changes in traditional sex roles and status. No serious development plan can neglect the emerging force in the domestic sphere, especially the mother, who is assuming heavier responsibilities without being equipped for them. Nor can those development plans be efficiently implemented if they continue to think that the patriarch is as strong as in the ancestral myths.

NOTES

1. Vesey-Fitzgerald, S. G., 1955, vol. 1, p. 104.
2. Chehata, C., 1970, pp. 56, 91, 92.
3. Goode, W. J., 1970, p. xv (Paperback edition).
4. Resultats de l'enquete à objectifs multiples, 1961-1963, n.d., p. 52 (hereafter cited as EOM).
5. Morocco, Recensement, 1971, vol. 4, series S, p. 6.
6. Ibid., p. 32.
7. Ibn Khaldun, 1967, p. 97.
8. Ibid.

9. Morocco, Code Penal, art. 418, Dahir no. 1-59-413, November 26, 1962.

10. Koran, Surate 24, "Light."

11. Morocco, Constitution, "The Constitution guarantees freedom of movement to all citizens," and so forth.

12. Morocco, Family Law, La Muduwana, Dahir no. 1-57-343, November 22, 1957 (hereafter cited as Muduwana).

13. Muduwana, art. 30.

14. Committee for International Coordination of National Research in Demography, La Population du Maroc, 1974, p. 30.

15. Centre d'Etudes et de Recherches Démographiques, La Nuptialité, 1975, p. 3.

16. Morocco, Recensement, 1971, vol. 1, p. 5.

17. Ibid.

18. Baron, A. J.; Pirot, H., 1955, p. 31.

19. Ibid., p. 35.

20. Ibid.

21. Centre d'Etudes et de Recherches Démographiques, op. cit., Table 17.

22. EOM, p. 43.

23. Centre d'Etudes et de Recherches Démographiques, op. cit., Table 1.

24. Ibid.

25. Youssef, N. H., 1972.

26. EOM, p. 44.

27. Morocco, Enquete d'opinion sur la Planification Familiale.

28. Maher, V., 1975.

29. Chehata, op. cit., p. 91.

30. Morocco, Recensement, 1960, vol. 3, p. 528; Morocco, Recensement, 1970, vol. 1, series S, Table 02-D, p. 25.

31. EOM, p. 52; Morocco, Recensement, 1971, vol. 4, pp. 6, 32.

32. Morocco, Recensement, 1971, vol. 4, p. 7.

33. Ibid.

34. See Ibn Khaldun, op. cit., and Abu Zeid, A., in Peristiany, J. G., 1970.

35. A comparison between the 1960 census, vol. 4, p. 947, and the 1971 census, vol. 1, p. 90.

36. Morocco, Recensement, 1960, vol. 4, Table 56, p. 963.

37. Ibid., Table 54, p. 946.

38. Ibid., vol. 3, pp. 529, 547.

39. Ibid., p. 542.

40. Ibid., pp. 535-36.

41. Morocco, Recensement, 1960, vol. 3, p. 545.

42. Morocco, Recensement, 1970, vol. 2, Tables 1-5, p. 27.

43. EOM, Table 2, p. 104.

44. Morocco, Recensement, 1960, vol. 3, pp. 582-94.

45. Morocco, Recensement, 1971, vol. 2, series S, p. 135. Boserup's study on women in developing economies establishes that industrialization and technology have, until now, worked against women; see Boserup, E., 1970.

46. Muduwana, art. 35.

47. Amin, K., Tahrir Al Mar'a [The liberation of women], 1870, and Al Mar'a Al Jadida [The new woman], 1928.

48. The violence of twentieth-century Moroccan history appears in nationalist accounts, such as Al Fassi, A., 1970.

49. Amin, S., 1970, pp. 209-36.

50. Morocco, Plan de développement économique et social, 1973-77, vol. 1, p. 77.

51. Amin, op. cit., p. 215.

52. Morocco, Recensement, 1971, vol. 2, p. 13.

53. Ibid., p. 12.

54. Ibid., vol. 1, p. 18.

55. Migration and Transfer of Technology, Case Studies: Algeria, Morocco, Tunisia, and France, 1975, p. 18.

56. Centre d'Etudes et de Recherches Démographiques, op. cit., Table 17.

57. Morocco, Recensement, 1971, vol. 4, p. 13.

58. Slater, P., 1968, p. 410 and also p. 43.

59. Al Majdoub, S. A., 1966, p. 115.

60. Lahbabi, M., 1958.

61. Ibid.

62. Particularly Parts 2 and 3 of vol. 1, of Morocco, Plan de développement économique et social.

63. Ibid., vol. 2, pp. 690-91.

64. James, A. P., 1969, pp. 18-25.

65. Ibid.

66. Ibid.

67. Blisten, D., 1963, p. 190.

68. Morocco, Plan de développement économique et social, vol. 1, p. 51.

69. Morocco, Constitution.

70. Youssef, N., 1971.

16

Women and Social Change
in Urban North Yemen

CARLA MAKHLOUF
GERALD J. OBERMEYER

This chapter will focus on some of the changes taking place in North Yemen in women's roles and images, the conflicts that arise between traditional and modern roles and legitimations, the social institutions that both maintain and transform the social position of women, and more importantly, perhaps, how women perceive and react to the reality of change. In other words, both the subjective and objective aspects of change are the concern here. For political, economic, and religious reasons, Yemen has been historically one of the most isolated societies in the world. Consequently, it should provide abundant data and ideas for the study of modernization.

The main part of this study took place in the summer of 1974 in the city of San'a, which is considered--both by Yemenis and outsiders--as the most traditional urban center in the country. Such traditional practices as female seclusion and veiling remain strictly enforced in San'a, as compared to other cities and despite growing outside influences. The study focused on changes at two different levels of social structure.* On the one hand, data were collected

----

Data for this chapter were collected in the course of seven months of fieldwork in San'a, North Yemen: July-August 1974 and March-July 1976.

*We also analyzed, over a period of two months, the content of press articles about women and one of the radio programs specifically directed toward women over a period of two months. The aim was to evaluate the extent to which the mass media expressed and directed women's perception of the social world. Since September 26, 1975, television has been introduced in San'a, and it has

through the standard anthropological method of participant observation, by visiting women and taking part in their daily and ritual activities. In this way, we not only gained access to a number of female social networks in the city but also gained a good impression of the institutions that women perceived as significant agents of change. Hence, the other focus of the study--change at the institutional level--observed by interacting with women occupying posts in, and interacting with, such modern institutions as schools, hospitals, the Women's Association (Jam'iyat al Mar'a al Yamaniya), as well as the San'a University. (In 1970-71, the year the university opened, it had no Yemeni female students; in 1974-75, it had almost 200 Yemeni female students.[1] In 1976, one of the informants, a student herself, said there were over 200 Yemeni girls at the university.)

Of the women encountered, a sample of 40 were systematically interviewed, and 15 of these three or more times. During a subsequent stay in San'a in 1976, some of these women were interviewed again, in addition to a number of other women. Four of the 40 women can be considered "key informants," in that they were important links with others and provided entries into other people's houses and contacts with new friends. These four informants were generally our guides to their society and determined, to some extent, many of our contacts and impressions. Thus, circumstances of association, as well as chance factors, greatly influenced the nature of our sample. As a result, most of the women in the sample belong to the upper and middle social strata of San'a.

Age	Number
11-15	5
16-20	15
21-25	12
26-30	3
31-40	3
41+	2

Education	Number	Percent
None	10	25.0
Literate	5	12.5
Primary	8	20.0
Secondary	17	42.5

---

become indispensable to study its impact on women's perception of themselves vis-à-vis their own society and vis-à-vis other cultures' perceptions of women. But this would be a study in and of itself and is not dealt with here.

Marital Status	Number
Single	15
Married	16 (4 as second wives)
Divorced	6
Widowed	3

Occupation	Number	Percent
Housewife	20	50.0
Student	9	22.5
Employed	11	27.5

Marital Status of Employed Women	Number
Widowed	1
Never married	1
Unmarried	3
Married	3
Divorced	3

By selecting such a group for study, one cannot directly generalize to Yemeni women as a whole, or even to San'ani women. However, this can have several advantages. First, women in these groups have been most exposed to change, and their problems in confronting traditional patterns highlight the main areas of conflict between tradition and modernity in North Yemen. Second, as an elite group, their behavior is likely to be emulated by others. They are currently acting as brokers of ideas and patterns of behavior, an avant garde that is directly influencing the process of change in their society.

HISTORICAL BACKGROUND [2]

The severe isolation of Yemen has been due both to its relative lack of importance for colonial powers and to the closed-door policy of its Zaidi rulers. Imams Yahya (1904-48) and Ahmed (1948-62) had a policy of keeping out foreigners, as well as their modern innovations. The imams wished to keep the country free from foreign interference in order to preserve its independence and its traditional religious way of life. This policy, however, was not wholly feasible. Since Yemen was not economically self-sufficient and depended on other countries for a number of vital products, private contacts for commercial purposes were essential, and a number of Yemeni merchants established themselves outside the country. Moreover, the imams themselves began to establish relations with other countries. Even though their motive was primarily to bolster their traditional regime (buying arms and military equipment), they could not protect it from modernizing influences. For example, students sent to the military academies in other Arab countries, especially Iraq, as well as those whose families encouraged them to get an education abroad, encountered progressive ideas and became major advocates of change in the country. Thus, the imams contributed--however unwillingly--to fostering change. Under Imam Ahmed, agreements were signed with foreign countries (including the USSR and China) for the construction of roads connecting the major cities, agricultural projects, and a number of small industries. Medical missions (Russian, Chinese, Italian, and French) began working at that time, and a number of development projects were in operation.

Thus, although certain modernizing forces began to slowly transform the traditional culture before 1962, the revolution marked the beginning of concern for political change and progress away from autocracy toward a more representative type of government. The various regimes since the revolution have all couched their claims to power in an ideology of national development. Each has stated that the primary goal was to hasten the development of the country and compensate for the delays of the prerevolution "years of ignorance."

With substantial aid from international agencies and other countries, Yemen is now attempting to deal with the obstacles that hinder its development: an underdeveloped economy, poor communications, poor health conditions, and a traditional and very small educational system. All organizations that contribute to developing these sectors are encouraged.

Underlying all the problems of development in Yemen are two general needs: trained manpower and infrastructure. The pace of change seems at the same time rapid and slow: rapid, if we consider what has been accomplished in less than a decade, but extremely slow, if we consider all that remains to be done, as Tables 16.1, 16.2, and 16.3 suggest. As we can see from Table 16.1, the educational level is low and illiteracy a major problem, even in the capital. Similar inadequacies are found in other sectors as well, as Tables 16.2 and 16.3 suggest.

MODERNIZATION

This chapter attempts to examine societal changes from the point of view of the individual San'ani woman and to discuss those aspects of social change that seem most relevant to her and which have the most significant influence on her life. A number of women

TABLE 16.1: Population of San'a, Yemen Arab Republic,
by Educational Level, 1973

Educational Level	Number	Percent
Illiterate	61,705	67.22
Read and write	13,255	14.44
Primary	12,475	13.59
Preparatory	2,075	2.25
Secondary	1,790	1.95
University	495	0.54
Total	91,795	100.00

Source: Yemen Arab Republic, Central Planning Organization,
Statistical Yearbook, 1973.

TABLE 16.2: Development of Health Care Services in the
Yemen Arab Republic, 1973

	1968	1969	1970	1971	1972	1973
Physicians	150	176	184	199	203	265
Medical assistants	616	643	643	720	720	878
Hospitals	22	23	26	29	31	31
Beds	3,450	3,470	3,670	3,875	3,905	3,878
Dispensaries	5	5	5	7	9	13
Drugstores	108	109	118	128	129	130

Source: Yemen Arab Republic, Central Planning Organization,
Statistical Yearbook, 1973.

TABLE 16.3: Development of Health Care Services in San'a,
Yemen Arab Republic, 1968-73

	1968	1969	1970	1971	1972	1973
Physicians	80	80	80	82	83	83
Medical assistants	195	255	267	279	279	380
Hospitals	5	5	5	5	5	5
Dispensaries	3	3	3	5	5	9

Source: Yemen Arab Republic, Central Planning Organization,
Statistical Yearbook, 1973.

were asked their view of the major changes in the country since the revolution. Their replies were of two types: one perceived change as facilities and new objects to use within the home; the other concerned more general societal changes, such as roads, hospitals, and schools. In other words, some women saw change affecting the world of the household, while others looked beyond to the extra-familial.

The world of the household reflects the degree of surface change in the life of women and, perhaps, even a traditionalization of modern material culture. For instance, one notices in San'a that sitting rooms (majlis) are decorated across the city in much the same way as the traditional home. Modern electrical appliances are handled with care and in a conspicuous manner, as one would handle a foreign, fragile, perhaps even sacred object. This is perhaps a new status symbolization process. It may be that some of these objects are precious, and even sacred, because they represent what Gellner calls "the magic of industrial society," to which only a few can have access.

The practical and more obvious dimension of modernization is, for many women, that which caused their perception of change. Often when asked, "What has changed in Yemen?" women pointed to physical objects of a practical nature. For example, one woman replied, "Before they used pottery for cooking. Now, we use aluminum ware. Also, before they dressed differently. Now, some girls wear modern trousers under their dress." Another one said: "Before the bride used to wear the taj Yamani [traditional Yemeni head cover] on the day of her marriage, now many wear the taj masri [Egyptian-type head cover, close to the Western type and now worn in most Arab countries]." A number of other women said the higher cost of living had been a major change and gave examples of the increase in the price of the various goods. Thus, at the level of the household, what represents modernity is the more concrete, such as the cost of objects, and, more importantly, the availability of new objects for use. "Usefulness," says Berque about modern household items, "but also facticity, since they are the result of a modernization process that is passively accepted and borne, rather than actively exerted."[3] It is in part through the medium of such objects--however factitious--that women first relate and are "tuned" in to the rest of the world.

In general, the most uneducated women tended to perceive the material aspects of change as the most immediate, while the more educated tended to be aware of broader societal changes.

Beyond the household sphere, women are becoming critically aware of three aspects of change: health, education, and the mass media. The institutions that emerge in connection with the development of these three sectors come to constitute the basis for the

conflict between old and new and the conditions for the emergence of
an alternative world. In this chapter, two dimensions of the process
of change are examined: the first is expressed in changing patterns
of interpersonal relations, the second, in changing roles for women.*

The institutions that will be considered in our discussion of
change include the girls' primary and secondary schools, the postprimary teachers' training school and nursing school, and the hospitals and dispensaries established by the various medical missions.
To these we should add--even though they are not part of the three
sectors of change mentioned above--the San'a textile factory founded
by the Chinese in 1967, which employs 400 women, and the offices
of commercial companies, which sometimes hire women.[4] All
these institutions have certain characteristics in common: they are
situated outside the home; they are not defined by kinship criteria;
and therefore, the woman's role is not the traditional familial one,
and her status is not a mere reflection of her father's or husband's
status. Thus, the 400 women in the San'a textile factory work outside the home, and their status in the factory depends upon their
skills and capacities. They are able to enter into relationships with
other women co-workers, as well as with superiors and subordi-
nates, or with the foreign or Yemeni social workers who run the
nursery during working hours.

As in other Middle Eastern countries, many of the employed
women in the factory were divorced. At first glance, and according
to the standard view of modernization, this may suggest that these
women were obliged to seek work to support themselves and that
they had to have recourse to the factory's nursery because they
could not rely on their extended family to take care of their children
while they worked. Even though this may be true in some cases,
the contention here is that work is not necessarily something divorced women are forced into but an activity they can choose, because they are, to a certain extent, freed by their divorce from
some traditional constraints. A divorced woman is no longer completely under her father's authority and has been freed by divorce
from her husband's authority. Yet, according to shari'a, her father
has the legal duty to support her until she marries again--if she

---

*Other important dimensions of change--the perception of
women's roles and images at both the individual and the social level,
the significance of crises in individual biographies for decision
making about life planning, the emergence of the critical attitude--
are not included here. In other words, the focus is more on the
objective than on the subjective aspects of change. For a more
complete understanding, however, one would have to combine both.

wishes to do so--and to support her children until they reach the
legally specified age when they return to their father. Consequently,
one may argue that rather than having to work, a divorced woman
can, in fact, choose to take a job to supplement her and her family's
income--even though she does not have to do so. Moreover, in
many cases, she still can take advantage of her extended family and
leave her children with her mother or another older female relative.
Most of the informants who were divorced and had taken a job, in
fact, left their children with their mothers and only saw them outside working hours.

        The possibility for women in the textile factory to leave chil-
dren at the factory's nursery may actually be the preferred choice,
because of the advantages of the close supervision by foreign or
trained Yemeni personnel compared with the minimal supervision
that characterizes traditional Yemeni child-rearing practices. Thus,
taking a job and leaving one's children at a public nursery do not
necessarily constitute a pis aller, better-than-nothing attitude, but
can mean new options superimposed upon the traditional patterns
and among which the individual may choose.

        In the same way, medical facilities provide new alternatives
for knowledge, social interaction, and, of course, well being. They
bring women into contact with a wide range of people. Mothers
take their children to the clinic and there interact with specialists
(doctors and nurses), as well as with other women, some friends
and some strangers, who have similar problems. They acquire
knowledge, which they may share with other women. Women generally attempt to understand medical treatments and to follow innovations in that field. A number of times we heard women exchanging
information about new drugs and giving advice to one another or
trying to explain sickness in terms of their recently acquired knowledge. Along with a new body of "knowledge," social ties are
strengthened among those who share it.

        In the educational sector, also, schools (primary, secondary,
teachers', nurses') represent another common experience and seem
to strengthen bonds between individuals. The emergence of friendship between girls as a type of relation that is chosen by both
partners and does not depend upon ascribed kin roles is a new
phenomenon. The theme of freedom to forge bonds of friendship is
absent in traditional Yemeni culture, where girls grow up with
women of all ages rather than with peer groups.

        The school thus provides the context for new types of social
relations and the possibility for individuals to choose "friends" on
other than traditional grounds. Girls begin for the first time to
share ideas outside the context of kinship. They also begin to de-
rive pleasure from social relations that can only be described as an

individualistic and creative adaptation to a new situation. As some girls begin to be conscious of the other-than-kin world, they seek to expand their ties outside the family.

Modern institutions also influence the quality of relations between the sexes. Even though schools are not mixed, there may be a male teacher in a girls' school. This allows girls to encounter males not covered by the incest taboo and to discuss a variety of topics with them. The same is true of girls who work in an office, since this generally involves interaction with men.

The declining importance of the veil is involved in this process. In the context of the school, the hospital, and the office, men and women interact on a well-defined basis; the individual woman is not seen as a "generalized female" but as in a particular role, relatively independent of her sex role. In other words, in such situations, sex no longer permeates all male/female encounters but rather becomes one element in a relationship, and one that may-- temporarily, if not definitely--be bracketed and put aside. It becomes possible to separate the components of an individual's status and to base a social relationship upon those components that are directly relevant to the particular situation. Since part of the rationale of the veil is that it is a protective device separating "mankind" from "womankind," the emergence of role-specific relations between the sexes is bound to make it lose its importance. This seems to be happening; for instance, three out of the seven schoolgirls aged 13 and below who were interviewed did not wear the veil at all. According to the informants, a large proportion wore the veil outside the school but not in the classroom, even if the teacher was a male. One of the informants, who worked in a commercial company, said that she wore the lithma ("inner veil") in the office if there were men around but took it off when working alone. The head of the Woman's Association, who also worked in an office side by side with men, always wore a very transparent lithma. On the surface, this does not seem to depart from traditional practices in any way. However, the constant and frequent alternations of lithma/no lithma, according to the definition of the situation, is related to the dedramatization of the veiling "performance." If it is often repeated, there is a consequent decreasing significance of the veil. In fact, comparing veiling practices in 1974 and 1976, it became obvious that over two years, there had been a certain relaxation: an increasing number of girls and women walked in streets with the khunna ("outside veil") completely lifted, retaining the inner veil, which allowed one to see their eyes; there was more freedom in veil manipulation;[5] and also, a larger number of girls wore the balto (a deformation of the Russian word for coat) as an outer garment instead of the sharshaf or sitara. The balto

is a long-sleeved ankle-length coat worn over trousers, with a scarf
on the head. For an increasing number of males and females, this
type of dress is considered to be in conformity to the requirements
of modesty, as stated in the shari'a, and a few women have begun to
wear it. Some religious leaders have agreed that the balto is an
acceptable female dress.

The decreasing significance of the veil has been expressed by
one of the informants in terms that deserve special attention, because they uncover one of the mechanisms through which traditional
patterns are challenged and changed. That informant, a 13-year-
old schoolgirl, when asked whether she was veiled in class when the
teacher was a male, replied: "He is like my brother. Why should
I veil in his presence?" As happens frequently in the Middle East,
the idiom of kinship is used here to express the content of a nonkin
relationship. More importantly, here as in other cases, fictitious
kinship expresses how a role that in its modern form is foreign to
Yemeni culture comes to be incorporated in the traditional system.
A similar case was brought to our attention by the head of the nursing school, who said that most of the students called her "mother."
The teacher and the head of school, as cultural brokers, are thus
symbolically incorporated into the kinship sphere, and people may
relate to them in the traditional idiom, even though they consciously
challenge the bases of traditional culture.[6] This dual position is the
root of the broker's power. The successful broker is the one who
can manipulate traditional ties while being critical of tradition and
attempting to change it. He can, for instance, lead people into
accepting modern patterns of behavior that they would otherwise
have refused. Thus, the head of the nursing school obtained permission from the parents of one of her students to let their daughter
travel to Egypt. At first, the girl told us, her father was opposed
to the idea, because, he said, no unmarried girl travels by herself.
He was later convinced by the head of the school, who promised that
she would take care of the girl as if she were her own daughter.

Breaking the traditional segregation practices is not accepted
by everyone. For example, there have been attempts to discourage
parents from sending their daughters to school by circulating rumors
discrediting schoolgirls. One such rumor (apparently widespread,
since three informants who did not know one another reported it to
us) was that once girls start going to school, they become perverted
and begin to use contraceptives. One informant also said that the
opposition to girls' education was so strong--especially from such
groups as the Ikhwan al Muslimun ("Muslim Brothers")--that the
prime minister had, on an important occasion, devoted an entire
speech to refuting all rumors and encouraging parents to educate
their daughters.

Traditional attitudes are reflected in the relatively high dropout rate for girls. A number of girls did in fact complain that their parents had forced them to leave school before they even completed their primary education, even though they wished to pursue their studies. Such practices, however, have begun to change, and it is taken for granted by the younger generation--as well as by a substantial number of educated older people--that girls should go to school.

It is significant that many of the persons Yemeni women encounter in the course of their socialization into new institutions are foreigners. A government report indicates that in 1972-73, 92 of the 203 physicians working in Yemen, or 45 percent, are non-Yemenis. The number of foreign teachers is also high: 884 out of a total of 4,688, that is, about one-fifth.[7] There are also many foreigners in development projects, such as factories, experimental farms, and construction projects. These foreign specialists are related to traditional culture only insofar as they are experts in a certain field; they are not entangled in the web of primary relations in which Yemenis live. Interaction with them is restricted to the performance of those activities that are defined by their specialized role, especially since, as is often the case, they know just enough Arabic to go about their regular activities. Remaining to some extent outside the traditional complex of relations, they contribute to socializing the Yemenis with whom they come into contact in those institutions where interaction is structured according to well-defined role sets (rather than diffuse traditional ties). In other words, they promote the specialization of roles and relationships that characterizes a modern society.

In a modernizing situation, role opportunities are opened to the female that are relatively independent of the traditional definition of her as a woman. In other words, the traditional definition of the female comes to be confused by the opportunities to play roles in the newly emerging social groupings.

There has been some discussion in the social science literature on the use of the concepts "domestic/public sphere" in discussing women's roles.[8] Some might argue that modern institutions in Yemen allow women to assume new roles and, thus, step into the public sphere, which had previously been exclusively the male domain. With this process, women are no longer seen as belonging exclusively to the private, domestic sphere and needing the protection of the veil. This would not be accurate, however, for two reasons. First, it is not exact to say that in traditional society, women are confined to the private sphere: they do have access to some kind of public sphere (through visiting), and they may achieve some power over decision making in society.[9] Second, it is not completely accurate to maintain that in traditional society, the public sphere is the male domain.

The public sphere in a traditional society is not a sphere differentiated into suprafamilial institutions of "public interest" and to which all can--at least ideally--have access. Rather, there are only a few such institutions, and the access of both men and women to that "public" is determined not by the simple criterion of sex but by the more complex factor of stratification. The few "public" institutions that do exist in a traditional society are accessible to only the middle and upper strata. In a transitional situation, it is also the middle and upper strata that can best have access to, and take advantage of, the opportunities to participate in the emerging "public" institutions. As long as access to political roles and/or decision making about the public is not evenly distributed in a society, both lower class men and women are deprived of participation in the public sphere--though perhaps in different ways.

Thus, taking the concept of "public" within the context of a changing stratification system, one can argue that the existence of new role opportunities for women is part of a societal process that provides the individual with a wider basis for participating in public decision making. It then seems possible to maintain that what changes with modernization is not so much the relative position of the sexes as the status--in the broadest sense of the word--of the person as such, whether male or female, and, consequently, the status of the woman as a person.

One obvious result of the emergence of institutions outside the area of kinship is the loss of importance of traditional groupings. In traditional society, female groupings are structured around two main activities: housework and visiting. These networks are made up of female relatives, and occasionally neighbors, who have household tasks and visit one another in the morning, and those of relatives, neighbors, and friends who meet under the ritual conditions of afternoon visits (tafrita). It is within this context that the activities of all females, whatever their age and marital status, take place. Opportunities for involvement in other institutions, activities, and groups affect traditional networks in two interrelated ways: first, cleavages are produced within them; and second, those networks themselves are being gradually "deserted" by women who are becoming modernized.

In traditional society, unmarried girls are part of an intergenerational world in which their mother, aunts, and grandmothers partake and in which differences, such as age or education, are not the bases for internal segmentation. With the increase of education, girls become part of peer groups structured according to age and educational level--a phenomenon unknown before, since traditionally, at the age of ten, girls no longer played in the streets but became part of the "harem." Moreover, a schoolgirl subculture is now emerging from which older women are excluded. Whereas in traditional culture, the separation between age groups is de-emphasized, in the current transitional situation in North Yemen, it comes to be stressed, to the point of becoming the basis of a real cleavage.

Two observations help illustrate how the increase in girls' education emphasizes the social difference between girls and women and results in what we may refer to as a shift from kinship to friendship, that is, when girls of different kin groups come to have more in common than girls and women of related kin groups. During some afternoon visits, schoolgirls do not seem to like sitting in the main room where women are gathered, but prefer a smaller room, where they can chat and joke more freely. The cleavage between the two groups is here expressed, in Goffman's terms, in the opposition between the "frontstage" and the "backstage." It can also be expressed at other times by "code switching," to use another of Goffman's terms. Thus, the arrival of a married female visitor into a gathering of schoolgirls caused a considerable change in the atmosphere: laughter ceased, conversation became constrained and, after the preliminary greetings, none of the girls could find anything to talk about with the woman, who remained silent while some of the girls whispered to one another. This situation was unusual, since in traditional culture, women generally receive visits from other women unknown to the group without the disturbing stiffness and awkwardness that prevailed during the above visit.

These two instances suggest that the separation between age groups cannot be sufficiently explained by invoking the traditional pattern of respect of girls toward married women. In traditional culture, girls and women of all ages share most of their experiences. The point is that schoolgirls are aware that they cannot freely share their common experiences in the presence of uneducated married women. With the increase in school attendance, a new phenomenon is emerging in Yemen that is comparable to what has been called in the West the generation gap. The experience of a modern education accentuates the uneasiness that may everywhere characterize relations between age groups. It is not age per se but age as related to degree of education that is the basis of the cleavage.

Another implication of women's participation in new institutions is that a hierarchy of experts emerge, and people who do not share the same knowledge begin to inhabit different worlds. This is in contrast with traditional society, where every woman possesses all the skills necessary to take care of a house and children --in other words, the distribution of knowledge is homogeneous.

Now, discrepancies in knowledge and skills are emerging: not every woman knows, for instance, what students or nurses or doctors learn, and some may even have a very limited idea of what these roles are.

It may be that part of the prestige of modern "experts" is related to the ignorance of many people about exactly what these experts actually do. Parents sometimes completely ignore what their children do at school. For example, one informant was so impressed with her son's gradebook from school that she did not even realize that he had been required to repeat his class. The prestige of getting grades and going to school was such that the grades themselves became irrelevant; she gave her son a present and was proud to show the gradebook to her friends and relatives.

Closely related to the process whereby traditional groupings become characterized by various "cleavages" is another process whereby those very groupings, and the activities around which they center, come to be "deserted" by an increasing number of women. Since a transitional situation provides new activities in which women can participate and new groups in which they can associate, the traditional symbolic universe is being "relativized." The traditional world becomes only one among other possible worlds, and some women may participate in it in only a limited manner. Thus, those among my informants who were studying or working could not be at home when housework was generally done. Seven of them were housewives and had an occupation at the same time: they had to delegate their domestic responsibilities either to a female relative, if they lived in an extended household (four cases), or to a maid (three cases). Four of my unmarried informants were employed outside the home, and nine were students; none of them could help their mothers with housework, except on Fridays. It is obvious that in all such cases, the networks of female relatives that share housework are weakened or even cease to exist.

Moreover, the domestic sphere is no longer seen as an inevitable component of the woman's condition, but only one among other activities, sometimes even an obligation to be reduced to a minimum. Working women, who because they live in nuclear families cannot leave all the housework to a female relative, attempt to reduce the amount of time they spend on it; they do not often cook traditional, time-consuming dishes and sometimes altogether suppress the pattern of the midday meal as the central meal, because the evening is the only time they can be home with their husband and prepare food. In their daily schedule, domestic duties are only a part, sometimes a minor one, and one over which the school, the hospital, or the office takes precedence. Similarly, social duties, that is, visiting, become an obligation that cannot be completely avoided, a concession made to friends and relatives--and tradition. For women who are becoming modernized, the afternoon visit is no longer experienced as the most enjoyable and exciting part of the day:[10] the 11 women interviewed who were employed outside the home all said they rarely went to tafrita, and only on very special occasions, so as not to hurt people's feelings. Schoolgirls, too, try to avoid formal visits and prefer to be among themselves. Thus, an institution that was fundamental in maintaining the reality of the traditional universe can no longer keep its central place. The woman's separate sphere, of which tafrita was the symbol, no longer constitutes the context of social experience. And the woman's life, instead of being that integrated whole where work and leisure, domestic and extrafamilial activities alternated without rigid boundaries is now beginning to be compartmentalized into sectors that are relatively independent of one another.

NOTES

1. Yemen Arab Republic, Central Planning Organization, Statistical Yearbook, 1975, p. 159.
2. For further historical background, see Wenner, M. W., 1967, and Halliday, F., 1974.
3. Berque, J., 1964, p. 206.
4. For a detailed discussion of two institutions that explicitly define themselves as aiming to introduce changes in the lives of women, see the discussion of the Women's Association and of the women's radio program in Makhlouf, C., 1975.
5. See the discussion of how girls in traditional society manipulate their veil to make symbolic statements in Makhlouf, op. cit., chap. 2.
6. For an example of cultural brokers operating in Arab traditional political culture, see Obermeyer, G. J., in Nelson, C., ed., 1973.
7. From the Yemen Arab Republic, Central Planning Organization, Statistical Yearbook, 1973.
8. Nelson, ed., op. cit.
9. This is discussed in more detail in Makhlouf, op. cit.
10. See the description and discussion of tafrita in Makhlouf, op. cit.

Bibliography

Abu-Lughod, J. "The Emergence of Differential Fertility in Urban Egypt." Milbank Memorial Fund Quarterly 43, no. 2 (April 1965): 235-53.

_____. "Urban-Rural Differences as a Function of the Demographic Transition: Egyptian Data and an Analytical Model." American Journal of Sociology 69, no. 3 (March 1964): 476-91.

_____. "Migrant Adjustment to City Life: The Egyptian Case." American Journal of Sociology 67, no. 6 (July 1961): 22-32.

Abu-Zahra, N. M. "Material Power, Honour, Friendship and the Etiquette of Visiting." Anthropological Quarterly 47 (January 1974): 120-38.

_____. "On the Modesty of Women in Arab Muslim Villages: A Reply." American Anthropologist 72, no. 5 (October 1970): 1079-87.

Abu-Zeid, A. In Honor and Shame: The Value of Mediterranean Society, ed. J. G. Peristiany. London: Weidenfeld and Nelson, 1965; Chicago: University of Chicago Press, 1970: 243-60.

Adam, A. Casablanca. Paris: Presses Universitaires de France, 1972.

Adlakha, A. "A Study of Infant Mortality in Turkey." Ph.D. dissertation, University of Michigan, 1970.

Afghan Family Guidance Association. "Constitution of the AFGA." Mineographed. Kabul: AFGA, 1969.

Ahmad, R. "A Study of Social Differentials among Non Users and Users of Contraception in Lebanon." Master's thesis, American University of Beirut, 1974.

Akers, D. "On Measuring the Marriage Squeeze." Demography 4, no. 2 (May 1967): 907-24.

Al Fassi, A. The Independence Movements of Arab North Africa.
     New York: Octagon Books, 1970.

Allman, J., and Hill, A. G. "Fertility, Breastfeeding and Family
     Planning in the Yemen Arab Republic." Paper read at the
     Colloquium on Biology, Society and History in Islam, Sep-
     tember 1977, University of Pennsylvania.

_____. "Fertility, Mortality, Migration and Family Planning in
     the Yemen Arab Republic." Population Studies, forthcoming.

Allman, J., and Mathsson, B. "Social Science Research on Family
     Planning in Developing Countries." International Social
     Science Journal 27, no. 1 (1975): 174-82.

Allman, J.; Ben Achour, C.; and Stone, T. A Bibliography of Re-
     cent Social Science Research on the Family in the Arab States.
     Paris: UNESCO, 1974.

Al Majdoub, S. A. Les quatrains du Majdoub le sarcastique, poete
     Maghrebin du xvi siecle. Translated and collected by J.
     Scelles Millie and B. Khalifa. Paris: Maisonneuve et
     Larousse, 1966.

Al-Qazzaz, A. Women in the Arab World: An Annotated Bibliog-
     raphy. Detroit: Association of Arab-American University
     Graduates, 1975.

Amani, M. Report on the Study of the Impact of Literacy and Edu-
     cation on Fertility and Family Planning by KAP Method in
     City of Tehran and City of Ispahan. Tehran: Institute for
     Social Studies, University of Tehran, 1971.

Amin, K. Al Mar'a Al Jadida [The new woman]. Cairo: 1928.

_____. Tahrir Al Mar'a [The liberation of women]. Cairo: Dar
     Al Maarif, 1870.

Amin, S. Le Maghreb Moderne. Paris: Editions de Minuit, 1970.

Ammar, H. Growing Up in an Egyptian Village: Silwa, Province
     of Aswan. London: Routledge and Kegan Paul, 1954.

Angrist, S. "The Study of Sex Roles." Journal of Social Issues 25,
     no. 1 (1969): 215-32.

<u>Anthropological Quarterly</u> 47, no. 1 (January 1974) (special issue devoted to "Visiting Patterns and Social Dynamics in Eastern Mediterranean Communities").

Antoun, R., and Harik, I., eds. <u>Rural Politics and Social Change in the Middle East</u>. Bloomington: Indiana University Press, 1972.

Antoun, R. T. "On the Modesty of Women in Arab Muslim Villages." <u>American Anthropologist</u> 70 (1968): 671-97.

<u>Arab Culture and Society in Change</u>. Beirut: Dar El-Masrek, 1973.

<u>Arab Women</u>. Minority Rights Group, Report no. 27. London: 1975.

Arowolo, O. "Correlates of Fertility in Moslem Populations: An Empirical Analysis." Ph.D. dissertation, University of Pennsylvania, 1973.

Asad, T. <u>The Kababish Arabs</u>. New York: Praeger, 1970.

Ashford, D. <u>National Development and Local Reform: Political Participation in Morocco, Tunisia and Pakistan</u>. Princeton, N.J.: Princeton University Press, 1967.

Association Algérienne pour la Recherche Démographique. Economique et Social. <u>Enquete socio-démographique</u>. 8 vols. Algiers: Secrétariat au Plan, 1972.

Aswad, B. C. "Key and Peripheral Roles of Noble Women in a Middle East Plains Village." <u>Anthropological Quarterly</u> 40, no. 3 (July 1967): 139-53.

Audroing, J. F., et al. "Recherche des corrélations entre des variables démographiques, sociologiques et économiques dans les pays arabes." <u>Population</u> 30, no. 1 (January-February 1975).

Bardin, P. <u>La Vie d'un Douar</u>. Paris: Mouton, 1965.

Baron, A. J., and Pirot, H. "La Famille prolétarienne." <u>Le Cahier des faits et idées</u>, no. 1 (1955).

Bchir, J.; Bouraoui, A.; Rouissi, M.; and Zghal, A. "L'Influence sur le taux de fécondité du statut et du role de la femme dans

la société Tunisienne." Revue Tunisienne des Sciences
Sociales, nos. 32-35 (1973).

Beaver, S. E. Demographic Transition Theory Reinterpreted.
Lexington, Mass.: Lexington Books, 1975.

Behar, L. "Evolution récente de la nuptialité en Tunisie." Mimeographed. Tunis: National Office of Family Planning and
Population, 1975.

Berelson, B. "KAP Studies on Fertility." In Family Planning and
Population Programs, ed. B. Berelson, pp. 655-68. Chicago:
University of Chicago Press, 1969.

Berger, M. The Arab World Today. New York: Doubleday, 1964.

Berksan, S. "Marriage Patterns and Their Effect on Fertility in
Turkey." In Turkish Demography, ed. F. C. Shorter and
B. Guvenc, pp. 147-65. Institute of Population Studies, Pub-
lication no. 7. Ankara: Institute of Population Studies,
Hacettepe University, 1969.

Bernard, J. Women and the Public Interest. Chicago: Aldine-
Atherton, 1971.

Berque, J. The Arabs. New York: Praeger, 1964.

Bill, J. The Politics of Iran. Columbus, Ohio: Merrill, 1972.

Bindary, A. "Egypt Studies a New Plan of Action." Studies in
Family Planning 3, no. 8 (August 1972): 193-94.

Biraben, J. N. "Essai d'estimation des naissances de la population
algérienne depuis 1891." Population (Paris) no. 4 (1969):
711-34.

Blisten, D. World of the Family. New York: Random House, 1963.

Blood, R. O., and Wolfe, D. Husbands and Wives. New York:
The Free Press, 1960.

Bogue, D. J. Principles of Demography. New York: John Wiley,
1969.

Boserup, E. Woman's Role in Economic Development. London:
George Allen & Unwin, 1970.

Bott, E. Family and Social Network. 2d ed. London: Tavistock Publications, 1971.

Bourgiba, H. "Problemes de la jeunesse dans leur vraie perspective." Speech given in 1969, Ministry of Information, Tunisia.

_____. "Discours prononcé à l'occasion du Mouled." Speech given in 1966, Ministry of Information, Tunisia.

_____. "Edifier une societe saine et equilibrée." Speech given in 1966, Ministry of Information, Tunisia.

_____. "L'Enseignement, fonction sociale." Speech given in 1965, Ministry of Information, Tunisia.

_____. "Dimensions du sousdeveloppement." Speech given in 1963, Ministry of Information, Tunisia.

Breil, J. "Essai de détermination du niveau et des tendances de la fécondité des musulmans d'Algérie." In World Population Congress, pp. 795-808. Vol. 1. Rome: International Union for the Scientific Study of Population, 1954.

Breznik, D. "Fertility of the Yugoslav Population." In World Views of Population Problems, ed. E. Szabady et al., pp. 53-68. Budapest: Akademiai Kiado, 1968.

Brown, G. F. "Moroccan Family Planning Program: Progress and Problems." Demography 5, no. 2 (May 1968): 627-31.

Buchanan, C. Implications of Different Assumptions on the Nationality of the Shanty Dwellers. Kuwait: Planning Board, January 1976.

Cairo Demographic Center. Demographic Measures and Population Growth in the Arab Countries. Cairo: Cairo Demographic Center, 1970.

Camilleri, C. Jeunesse, famille, développement. Paris: Presses Universitaires de France, 1973.

Central Agency for Public Mobilization and Statistics. Population: Researchers and Studies 1, no. 1 (October 1971).

Centre d'Etudes et de Recherche Démographiques. La Nuptualité. Rabat: Direction de la Statistique, 1975.

_____. La Fécondité Marocaine. Rabat: Direction de la Statistique, 1974.

Chamie, J. "Religious Differentials in Fertility: Lebanon 1971." Paper read at the annual meeting of the Population Association of America, April 1976, Montreal.

Chehata, C. Droit Musulman. Paris: Dalloz, 1970.

Cho, L.-J., et al. Differential Current Fertility in the United States. Chicago: Community and Family Study Center, University of Chicago Press, 1970.

Clarke, J. I., and Fisher, W. B., eds. Population of the Middle East and North Africa. New York: Africana, 1972.

Cleland, W. W. The Population Problem in Egypt. Lancaster, Pa.: Scientific Press, 1936.

Coale, A. J. "The Demographic Transition Reconsidered." In International Population Conference, vol. 1, pp. 53-72. Liège: International Union for the Scientific Study of Population, 1973.

_____. "The Decline of Fertility in Europe from the French Revolution to World War II." In Fertility and Family Planning: A World View, ed. J. Behrman, L. Corsa, and R. Freedman. Ann Arbor: University of Michigan Press, 1969.

_____. "Birth Rates, Death Rates, and Rates of Growth in Human Population." In Public Health and Population Change, ed. M. C. Sheps and J. C. Ridley, pp. 242-65. Pittsburgh, Pa.: University of Pittsburgh Press, 1965.

_____; Hill, A. G.; and Trussell, T. J. "A New Method of Estimating Standard Fertility Measures from Incomplete Data." Population Index 41, no. 2 (April 1975): 182-210.

Committee for International Coordination of National Research in Demography. La Population de l'Algérie. Paris: National Institute of Demography, 1974.

_____. The Population of the Arab Republic of Egypt. Paris: National Institute of Demography, 1974.

_____. La Population de l'Iran. Paris: National Institute of Demography, 1974.

_____. La Population du Liban. Paris: National Institute of Demography, 1974.

_____. La Population du Maroc. Paris: National Institute of Demography, 1974.

_____. La Population de la Tunisie. Paris: National Institute of Demography, 1974.

_____. The Population of Turkey. Paris: National Institute of Demography, 1974.

Courbage, Y., and Fargues, P. "La Population des pays arabes d'Orient." Population 30, no. 6 (November–December 1975): 111–41.

Davis, K. "Population Policy: Will Current Programmes Succeed?" Science no. 158 (November 10, 1967): 730–39.

_____. Human Society. 19th ed. New York: Macmillan Co., 1965.

_____. The Population of India and Pakistan. Princeton, N.J.: Princeton University Press, 1951.

_____, and Blake, J. "Social Structure and Fertility: An Analysis Framework." Economic Development and Social Change 4 (April 1956): 211–35.

Declaration of Teheran. Promulgated at International Conference on Human Rights (convened by United Nations), Tehran, 1968.

Dixon, R. B. "Women's Rights and Fertility." Reports on Population/Family Planning, no. 17 (January 1975): 1–20.

Dodd, P. C. "Family Honor and the Forces of Change in Arab Society." International Journal of Middle East Studies 4 (January 1973): 40–54.

Duncan, O. D. "Human Ecology and Population Studies." In The Study of Population, ed. P. M. Hauser and O. D. Duncan. Chicago: University of Chicago Press, 1959.

Duvignaud, J. Change at Shebika. New York: Praeger, 1970.

Duza, M. B., and Baldwin, C. S. "Non-familial Female Roles as
    Determinants of Female Age at Marriage." Paper read at
    the annual meeting of the Population Association of America,
    Seattle, Washington, April 1975.

Edlefsen, L., and Lieberman, S. S. An Econometric Model of Dif-
    ferential Fertility in Iran. Research Paper no. 2. Cambridge,
    Mass.: Center for Population Studies, Harvard University,
    1974.

El-Badry, M. A. "Trends in the Components of Population Growth
    in the Arab Countries of the Middle East: A Survey of Present
    Information." Demography 2 (1965): 140-86.

El Biblawi, H. A. "Pattern and Trends of Fertility in Egypt."
    General Diploma paper, Cairo Demographic Center, Decem-
    ber 1974.

El-Sanabary, N. M. "A Comparative Study of the Disparities of
    Educational Opportunities for Girls in the Arab States."
    Ph.D. dissertation, University of California-Berkeley, 1974.

El-Sayegh, M. A. In Cairo Demographic Center, Fertility Trends
    and Differentials in Arab Countries. Cairo: Cairo Demo-
    graphic Center, 1971.

El Shafi, A. M. N. "Administrative and Other Problems of Data
    Collection in North African and West Asian Arabic Speaking
    Countries." In International Population Conference, pp. 286-
    93. Vol. 1. London: International Union for the Scientific
    Study of Population, 1969.

El Tay, O. A. "Country Statement--Sudan." Mimeographed.
    Addis Ababa, Economic Commission for Africa, working
    group on fertility levels and differentials in Africa and pros-
    pects for the future, December 18-22, 1972.

Entelis, J. "Ideological Change and an Emerging Counter-Culture
    in Tunisian Politics." Journal of Modern African Studies 12
    (1974): 543-68.

Fawcett, J. T., ed. Psychological Perspectives on Population.
    New York: Basic Books, 1973.

_____. Psychology and Population. New York: Population Council, 1970.

_____, and Bornstein, M. H. "Modernization, Individual Modernity, and Fertility." In Psychological Perspectives on Population, ed. J. T. Fawcett, pp. 106-31. New York: Basic Books, 1973.

Fernea, E., and Joseph, S. "A Brief Commentary and Report on the Round Table and Panels on Women's Roles Held at the 1975 MESA Meeting." Middle East Studies Association Bulletin 10, no. 2 (May 1976): 20-23.

Ffrench, G. E., and Hill, A. G. Kuwait, Urban and Medical Ecology. Berlin: Springer Verlag, 1971.

Filali, M. "Les Problèmes d'intégration posés par la sédentarisation des populations nomades et tribales." Revue Tunisienne des Sciences Sociales 3 (1966): 83-114.

Fox, G. L. "Love Match and Arranged Marriage in a Modernizing Nation: Mate Selection in Ankara, Turkey." Journal of Marriage and the Family 37, no. 1 (1975): 180-93.

_____. "Nice Girl: The Behavioral Legacy of a Value Construct." Paper read at the annual meeting of the National Council on Family Relations, London, Ontario, October 1973a.

_____. "Some Determinants of Modernism among Women in Ankara, Turkey." Journal of Marriage and the Family 35, no. 3 (1973b): 520-29.

Freedman, R. "The Sociology of Human Fertility: A Trend Report and Bibliography." Current Sociology 10-11 (1963): 35-119.

_____, and Berelson, B. "The Record of Family Planning Programs." Studies in Family Planning 7 (January 1, 1976): 1-40.

Frejka, T. The Future of Population Growth. New York: John Wiley, 1973.

Friedl, E. "The Position of Women: Appearance and Reality." Anthropological Quarterly 40 (1967): 97-108.

Friesen, J., and Moore, R. V. Iran: Country Profile. New York: Population Council, 1972.

Frisch, R. "Menstrual Cycles: Fatness as a Determinant of Minimum Weight for Height Necessary for Their Maintenance or
Onset." Science 185 (September 13, 1974): 949-51.

Gans, H. J. The Urban Villagers. New York: The Free Press,
1962.

George, E. I. "Research on Measures of Family Size Norms." In
Psychological Perspectives on Population, ed. J. T. Fawcett,
pp. 354-70. New York: Basic Books, 1973.

Glass, D. V. "Fertility Trends in Europe since the Second World
War." In Fertility and Family Planning: A World View, ed.
S. F. Behrman et al., pp. 25-74. Ann Arbor: University of
Michigan Press, 1969.

Glick, P. C.; Heer, D. M.; and Beresford, J. C. "Family Forma-
tion and Family Composition: Trends and Prospects." In
Sourcebook in Marriage and the Family, ed. M. B. Sussman.
Boston: Houghton-Mifflin, 1963.

Goldberg, D. "Socio-economic Theory and Differential Fertility:
The Case of the LDC's." Social Forces 53, no. 4 (1975).

_____. Modernism: The Extensiveness of Women's Roles and
Attitudes. Occasional Paper no. 14. London: World Fertility
Survey, 1974.

_____. "Some Observations on Recent Changes in American Fer-
tility Based on Sample Survey Data." Eugenics Quarterly 14,
no. 4 (1967): 255-64.

_____. "Fertility and Fertility Differentials: Some Observations
on Recent Changes in the United States." In Public Health and
Population Change: Current Research Issues, ed. M. C.
Sheps and J. C. Ridley. Pittsburgh: University of Pittsburgh
Press, 1965.

Gondreau, F., and Volle, M. Enquete démographie, Madagascar,
1966. Tananarive: Institut Nationale de Statistique et
Recherches Economiques (INSRE), 1967.

Good, M.-J. D. "Social Hierarchy and Social Change in a Provincial
Iranian Town." Ph.D. dissertation, Harvard University, 1976.

_____. "From Solidarity to Status: A Comparative Perspective on Women in Provincial Iran and Turkey." In Women in the Muslim World, ed. L. Beck and N. Keddie. Cambridge, Mass.: Harvard University Press, forthcoming.

Goode, W. J. World Revolution and Family Patterns. New York: The Free Press, 1963; paperback edition, 1970.

Gordon, D. Women of Algeria. Cambridge, Mass.: Harvard University Press, 1968.

Gray, A. W. Childhood, Children and Child Rearing in the Arab Middle East. Beirut: The Ford Foundation, 1973.

Greenfield, S. M. "Industrialization and the Family in Sociological Theory." American Journal of Sociology 67 (1961): 312-22.

Gross, E. "Plus ca change . . . ? The Sexual Structure of Occupations over Time." Social Problems 16, no. 2 (1968): 198-208.

Guest, A. M. "The Relationship of the Crude Birth Rate and Its Components to Social and Economic Development." Demography 11 (1974): 457-72.

Gulick, J. "Private Life and Public Face: Cultural Continuities in the Domestic Architecture of Isfahan." Iranian Studies 7, nos. 3-4 (1974): 629-51.

_____. "Village and City: Cultural Continuities in Twentieth Century Middle Eastern Cultures." In Middle Eastern Cities, ed. I. M. Lapidus, pp. 122-58. Berkeley and Los Angeles: University of California Press, 1969.

_____, and Gulick, M. E. "Migrant and Native Married Women in the Iranian City of Isfahan." Anthropological Quarterly 49, no. 1 (1976): 53-61.

_____. "Kinship, Contraception and Family Planning in the Iranian City of Isfahan." In Population and Social Organization, ed. M. Nag, pp. 241-93. The Hague: Mouton and Co., 1975.

_____. "Varieties of Domestic Social Organization in the Iranian City of Isfahan." In City and Peasant: A Study in Sociocultural Dynamics, ed. A. L. LaRuffa et al., pp. 441-69. Vol.

220, art. 6. New York: Annals of the New York Academy of Sciences, 1974.

_____. An Annotated Bibliography of Sources Concerned with Women in the Modern Muslim Middle East. Princeton Near East Paper no. 17. Princeton, N.J.: Princeton University, 1974.

_____. "The Domestic Social Environment of Women and Girls in Isfahan." In Women in the Muslim World, ed. L. Beck and N. Keddie. Cambridge, Mass.: Harvard University Press, forthcoming.

Hajnal, J. "European Marriage Patterns in Perspective." In Population in History, ed. D. V. Glass and D. E. C. Eversley. London: E. Arnold, 1965.

_____. "The Marriage Boom." Population Index 19, no. 2 (1953): 80-101.

Halliday, F. Arabia without Sultans. London: Penguin, 1974.

Hamalian, A. "The Shirkets: Visiting Pattern of Armenians in Lebanon." Anthropological Quarterly 47 (January 1974): 71-92.

Hamamsy, L. "The Changing Role of the Egyptian Woman." In Readings in Arab Middle Eastern Societies and Cultures, ed. A. Lutfiyya and C. Churchill, pp. 592-602. Paris: Mouton, 1958.

Harik, I. The Political Modernization of Peasants: A Study of an Egyptian Community. Bloomington: Indiana University Press, 1974.

Hathout, H. H., and El Din Selim, M. M. "A Menstrual Survey of Girls' Schools." Journal of the Kuwait Medical Association 6 (1972): 141-58.

Hawley, A. H. Human Ecology: A Theory of Community Structure. New York: Ronald Press, 1950.

Henin, R. A. "Nomadic Fertility as Compared with that of Rain Cultivators in Sudan." In International Population Conference. Vol. 1. London: International Union for the Scientific Study of Population, 1969.

Henry, L. "Some Data on Natural Fertility." Eugenics Quarterly 8, no. 2 (June 1961): 81-91.

Hermassi, E. Leadership and National Development in North Africa. Berkeley: University of California Press, 1972.

Hill, A. G. "The Demography of the Kuwaiti Population of Kuwait." Demography 12, no. 3 (August 1975): 537-48.

_____. "Population Growth in the Middle East and North Africa: Selected Policy Issues." In The Middle East: Oil, Conflict, and Hope, ed. A. L. Udovitch, pp. 7-56. Lexington, Mass.: Lexington Books, 1976.

Holter, H. Sex Roles and Social Structure. Oslo: Universitetsforlaget, 1970.

Ibu Khaldun. The Mugaddimah. London: Routledge and Kegan Paul, 1967.

International Planned Parenthood Federation. The History of Contraceptives. Santiago: 1967.

International Union for the Scientific Study of Population with the United Nations. Variables and Questionnaire for Comparative Fertility Survey. N.d.

Issawi, C. "Economic Change and Urbanization in the Middle East." In Middle Eastern Cities, ed. I. M. Lapidus. Berkeley and Los Angeles: University of California Press, 1969.

James, A. P. "L'Organisation de la santé et les médecins après l'independance." Lamalif (1969): 18-25.

Johnson, G. Z. "Differential Fertility in European Countries." In Demographic and Economic Change in Developed Countries, pp. 36-72. Princeton, N.J.: Princeton University Press, 1960.

Jordan. Statistics Department. "Final Draft Report: National Seminar on Population Policy in Relation to Development Strategy." Mimeographed. Amman: Statistics Department, 1972.

Khalaf, S. "Family Associations in Lebanon." Journal of Comparative Family Studies 2 (Autumn 1971): 235-50.

_____, and Kongstad, P. Hamra of Beirut: A Case of Rapid
Urbanization. Leiden: E. J. Brill, 1973.

Khalifa, A., and Khalifa, A. M. Status of Women in Relation to
Fertility and Family Planning in Egypt. Cairo: National Center for Social and Criminological Research, 1973.

Khalifa, A. M. The Population of the Arab Republic of Egypt.
Paris: National Institute of Demography, 1973a.

_____. "A Proposed Explanation of the Fertility Gap Differentials
by Socio-Economic Status and Modernity: The Case of Egypt."
Population Studies 27, no. 3 (November 1973b): 431-42.

Khalil, F. "Indigenous Midwifery in Selected Villages in the Second
Governorate of People's Democratic Republic of Yemen."
Master's thesis, American University of Beirut, 1972.

Khuri, F. I. From Village to Suburb: Order and Change in Greater
Beirut. Chicago: University of Chicago Press, 1975.

_____. "Parallel Cousin Marriage Reconsidered: A Middle East-
ern Practice that Nullifies the Effects of Marriage on the Intensity of Family Relationships." Man 5 (1970): 597-618.

Kirk, D. "Factors Affecting Moslem Natality." In Family Planning
and Population Programs, ed. B. Berelson et al. Chicago:
University of Chicago Press, 1966.

Kiser, C. V. "Social and Economic and Religious Factors in the
Differential Fertility of Low Fertility Countries." In World
Population Conference, pp. 219-22. Vol. 2. Publication nos.
66, 13, and 8. New York: United Nations, 1967.

Kjurciev, A., and Courbage, Y. "Alternative Population Projections
and Analysis of the Essential Data in Bahrain." Population
Bulletin of the UN Economic Commission for Western Asia
no. 6 (January 1974).

Kjurciev, A., et al. "Population Dynamics and Education in the Development Process of the Arab Countries." Paper read at the
Seminar of Experts on Population, Education and Development
in the Arab Countries, ASFEC, Sirs El Layyan, Egypt, February 1976.

Koran. Surate 24, "Light."

Krotki, K. J., and Beaujot, R. "La Population marocaine: recon-
stitution de l'évolution de 1950 à 1971." Population 30, no. 2
(March–April 1975).

Lahbabi, M. Le Gouvernement à l'Aube du vingtième siècle. Rabat:
Editions Techniques Nord Africaines, 1958.

Lapham, R. J. "Family Planning and Fertility in Tunisia."
Demography 7, no. 2 (May 1970): 241–53.

Leibenstein, H. The Economic Theory of Fertility Decline. Center
for Population Studies, Contribution no. 81. Cambridge,
Mass.: Harvard University Press, 1975.

Lestaeghe, R. "Nuptiality and Population Growth." Population
Studies 25, no. 3 (November 1971): 415–32.

Lewis, I. M. Marriage and the Family in Northern Somaliland.
African Studies no. 15. London: School of Oriental and African Studies, 1962.

Lieberman, S. S.; Gillespie, R.; and Loghmani, M. "The Isfahan
Communications Project." Studies in Family Planning 4
(April 4, 1973): 73–100.

Lorimer, J. G. Gazeteer of the Persian Gulf, Oman and Central
Arabia. Calcutta, 1908 and 1915. Reprint. Dublin: Irish
Universities Press, 1970.

Louis, A. "Greniers fortifiés et maisons troglodytes Kaar Djouama."
Institut des Belles Lettres Arabes, 28 (1965): 373–400.

Lutfiyya, A. M. Baytin: A Jordanian Village. The Hague: Mouton,
1966.

Maher, V. Women and Property in Morocco. New York: Cambridge
University Press, 1975.

Maklouf, C. "Changing Women, A Study of San'a North Yemen."
Master's thesis, American University of Beirut, 1975.

Marcoux, A. J. "Sur les facteurs de l'évolution passée et future des
naissances en Tunisie." Mimeographed. Tunis: Office Nationale de Planning Familiale et Population, 1972.

Micaud, C. A. "Leadership and Development: The Case of Tunisia." Comparative Politics (July 1969): 468-84.

_____; Brown, L. C.; and Moore, C. H. Tunisia: The Politics of Modernization. New York: Praeger, 1974.

Migration and Transfer of Technology, Case Studies: Algeria, Morocco, Tunisia, and France. Paris: OECD, 1975.

Mohsen, S. "Legal Status of Women among the Awlad Ali." Anthropological Quarterly 40, no. 3 (1967): 153-66.

Momeni, D. "Determinants of Female First Marriage in Shiraz, Iran." Paper read at meeting of the Population Association of America, 1975, Seattle, Washington.

Momeni, D. A. "The Difficulties of Changing the Age at Marriage in Iran." Journal of Marriage and the Family 34, no. 3 (August 1972): 545-51.

Montague, J. G., ed. "The Middle East and North Africa." Studies in Family Planning 6, no. 8 (August 1975): 302-19.

Moore, C. H. "On Theory and Practice among Arabs." World Politics 25 (October 1971): 106-26.

_____. Tunisia Since Independence. Berkeley: University of California Press, 1965.

Morocco. Plan de developpement économique et social. Vol. 1. 1973-77.

_____. Constitution, March 1972.

_____. Plan Quinquennal, 1968-72. Rabat: 1968.

_____. Code Penal, art. 418, Dahir no. 1-59-413, November 26, 1962.

_____. Recensement, 1960, vols. 3 and 4, 1970, vols. 1 and 2, and 1971, vols. 1, 2, and 4.

_____. Family Law, La Muduwana, Dahir no. 1-57-343, November 22, 1957.

_____. Enquete d'opinion sur la Planification Familiale.

Musallam, B. F. "The Islamic Sanction of Contraception." In Population and Its Problems, ed. H. B. Parry, pp. 300-10. Oxford: Clarendon Press, 1974.

Nadot, R. "Fécondité." In Afrique Noire, Madagascar, Comores. Démographie comparée INED, INSEE, ORSTOM. Paris: National Institute of Demography, 1966.

Nazer, I. R.; Karmi, H. S.; and Zayid, M. Y., eds. Islam and Family Planning. Originally published in Arabic. 2 vols. Beirut: International Planned Parenthood Federation Middle East and North Africa Region, 1974.

Nedjati, S. Etude bibliographique: La Famille et la dynamique de population en Turquie et en Iran. Paris: UNESCO, 1974.

Negadi, G., and Vallin, J. "La Fécondité des Algériennes: Niveau et tendances." Population no. 3 (1974): 491-516.

Nelson, C. "Changing Roles of Men and Women, Illustrations from Egypt." Anthropological Quarterly 41 (1968): 57-77.

Nortman, D. "Population and Family Planning Programs: A Fact Book." Reports on Population/Family Planning. No. 2. 6th ed. December 1974.

Noureldin, S. S. "Analysis of Data on Fertility, Mortality and Economic Activity of Urban Population in Libya Based on a Household Sample Survey." The Egyptian Population and Family Planning Review 4, no. 1 (June 1971).

Obermeyer, G. J., in The Desert and the Sown: Nomads in the Greater Society, ed. C. Nelson. Berkeley: Institute of International Studies, University of California, 1973.

Omran, A. R., ed. Egypt: Population Problems and Prospects. Chapel Hill: University of North Carolina, 1973.

Oppenheimer, V. K. "Demographic Influence on Female Employment and the Status of Women." American Journal of Sociology 78, no. 4 (1973): 946-61.

_____. The Female Labor Force in the United States: Demographic and Economic Factors Governing Its Growth and Changing Composition. Population Monograph Series, no. 5. Berkeley: University of California, 1970.

Ozankaya, O. Kö yde Toplumsal Yai ve Siyasal Kültür [Rural social structure and political culture]. Ankara: Siyasal Bilgiler Fakü ltesi Yayinlari, 1970.

Parsons, T. "The Social Structure of the Family." In The Family: Its Function and Destiny, ed. R. Anshem, pp. 241-74. 1959.

Paydarfar, A. A. "The Modernization Process and Household Size: A Provincial Comparison for Iran." Journal of Marriage and the Family 37 (1975): 446-52.

_____. "Sociocultural Correlates of Fertility among Tribal, Rural and Urban Populations in Iran." Social Biology 22, no. 2 (Summer 1975).

_____. "Differential Life-Style between Migrants and Non-Migrants of the City of Shiraz, Iran." Demography 11 (1974): 509-20.

Peristiany, J. G., ed. Honor and Shame: The Value of Mediterranean Society. London: Weidenfeld and Nelson, 1965; Chicago: University of Chicago Press, 1970.

Petersen, W. Population. New York: Macmillan Co., 1970.

Peterson, K. K. "Demographic Conditions and Extended Family Households: Egyptian Data." Social Forces 46 (June 4, 1968): 531-37.

Povey, W. G., and Brown, G. F. "Tunisia's Experience in Family Planning." Demography 5, no. 2 (1968): 620-26.

Prothro, E. T., and Diab, L. N. Changing Family Patterns in the Arab East. Beirut: American University of Beirut, 1974.

Rainwater, L. Family Design. Chicago: Aldine, 1965.

Rapid Population Growth. 2 vols. Baltimore: Johns Hopkins Press, 1971.

Republique Algerienne Democratique et Populaire. ENSP, Premiers résultats provisoires de l'enquete démographique. Algiers: Secrétariat d'Etat au Plan, 1971.

_____. Secretariat d'Etat au Plan, Direction des Statistiques. Etude Statistique Nationale de la Population, Résultats de l'enquete démographique. II Mouvement de la Population, Series 2, vol. 5. Oran: Centre Nationale de Recherches Economiques et Sociales (CNRES), 1974.

_____. Etude Statistique Nationale de la Population, Résultats de l'enquete fécondité, Series 2, vol. 2. Oran: CNRES, 1972.

Resultats de l'enquete à objectifs multiples, 1961-1963. Rabat: Service Central des Statistiques, n.d.

Ridley, J. C. "The Changing Position of American Women: Education, Labor Force Participation, and Fertility." In The Family in Transition, pp. 199-250. Fogarty International Center Proceedings, no. 3. 1969.

_____. "Demographic Change and the Roles and Status of Women." The Annals of the American Academy of Political and Social Science no. 375 (January 1968): 15-25.

Riesman, D. The Lonely Crowd. New Haven: Yale University Press, 1961.

Rizk, H. "Trends in Family Size, Attitudes and Practice of Family Planning in Jordan." Mimeographed. Bureau of Statistics, Amman, Jordan, 1975.

_____. "National Fertility Sample Survey for Jordan 1972: The Study and Some Findings." Population Bulletin of the United Nations Economic and Social Office in Beirut no. 5 (July 1973): 14-31.

Robinson, W. C., and Horlacher, D. E. Population Growth and Economic Welfare. Reports on Population/Family Planning. New York: Population Council, 1971.

Rosa, F. "Breast Feeding: A Motive for Family Planning." People 3, no. 1 (1976): 10-13.

Rosenfeld, H. "Process of Structural Change within the Arab Vil-
    lage Extended Family." American Anthropologist 60 (1958):
    1127-39.

Rossi, A. "Barriers to the Career Choice of Engineering, Medi-
    cine, or Science among American Women." In Women and the
    Scientific Professions, ed. J. A. Mattfeld and C. G. Van Aken.
    Cambridge, Mass.: The M.I.T. Press, 1965.

Roux, C. "Tendances récentes de l'activité féminine en France."
    Population. Special edition, February 1970, pp. 179-94.

Rudebeck, L. Party and People: A Survey of Political Change in
    Tunisia. New York: Praeger, 1967.

Ryder, N. B. "Fertility in Developed Countries during the Twen-
    tieth Century." In World Population Conference Proceedings,
    p. 20. Vol. 2, no. 66. New York: International Union for
    the Scientific Study of Population, 1967.

Sabagh, G. "The Demography of the Middle East." Middle East
    Studies Association Bulletin 4, no. 2 (May 1970): 1-9.

_____. "Analyse de l'influence du niveau d'instruction sur la
    fécondité au Maroc." Revue Tunisienne de Sciences Sociales
    nos. 17-18 (June-September 1969).

Sauvy, A. Théorie générale de la population. 2 vols. Paris:
    Presses Universitaires de France, 1966.

Schaar, S. "A New Look at Tunisia." Mid East (February 1970):
    43-46.

Schieffelin, O. Muslim Attitudes to Family Planning. New York:
    Population Council, 1972.

Schnaiberg, A. "The Modernizing Impact of Urbanization: A Causal
    Analysis." Economic Development and Cultural Change 20
    (October 1971): 80-104.

_____. "Rural-Urban Residence and Modernism: A Study of
    Ankara Province, Turkey." Demography 7 (1970): 71-85.

Schultz, T. P. "Fertility Patterns and Their Determinants in the Arab Middle East." In Economic Development and Population Growth in the Middle East, ed. C. A. Cooper and S. S. Alexander. New York: American Elsevier, 1972.

Segal, S., and Tietze, C. "Contraceptive Technology: Current and Prospective Methods." Reports on Population/Family Planning no. 1 (1971).

Seklani, M. "La Fécondité dans les pays arabes: donées numériques, attitudes et comportements." Population no. 5 (1960).

_____; Rouissi, M.; and Bchir, M. La Fécondité des ménages à Tunis, résultats de trois enquetes socio-démographiques. Série démographique no. 3. Tunis: Cahiers du CERES, 1969.

Shorter, F. C. "The Application of Development Hypotheses in Middle East Studies." Economic Development and Cultural Change 14, no. 3 (April 1966): 340-54.

Singelmann, J. "Women in the Labor Force: A Cross-National Perspective." Paper read at the annual meeting of the Population Association of America, Seattle, Washington, April 1975.

Slaber, E. J.; Feinlieb, M.; and Macmahon, B. "The Duration of Post-Partum Amenorrhoea." American Journal of Epidemiology 82, no. 3 (1966): 347-58.

Slater, P. The Glory of Hera. Boston: Beacon Press, 1968.

Southall, A., ed. Social Change in Modern Africa. London: Oxford University Press, 1961.

Stirling, P. Turkish Village. New York: John Wiley, 1965.

Stys, W. "The Influence of Economic Conditions on the Fertility of Peasant Women." Population Studies 2, no. 2 (1957): 136-48.

Sullerot, E. Women, Society and Change. New York: McGraw-Hill, 1971.

Synder, D. W. "Economic Determinants of Family Size in West Africa." Demography 11 (1974): 613-28.

Tabbarah, R. B. "Population Policy Issues in International Instruments: With Special Reference to the World Population Plan of Action." Journal of International Law and Economics 9, no. 3 (December 1974): 419-54.

_____. "Toward a Theory of Demographic Development." Economic Development and Cultural Change 19, no. 2 (January 1971).

_____. "Birth Control and Population Policy." Population Studies 18, no. 2 (November 1964): 187-96.

Tabutin, D. "La Mortalité infantile et juvénile en Algérie." Ph.D. dissertation, Ecole Pratique des Hautes Etudes (Paris), 1974.

_____. "Quelques données sur l'allaitement en Algérie du Nord." Population no. 6 (1973): 1177-86.

Tanas, R. S. "Family Planning in Tyre." Master's thesis, American University of Beirut, 1974.

Teitelbaum, M. S. "Relevance of Demographic Transition Theory for Developing Countries." Science 188 (May 2, 1975): 420-25.

Tessler, M. A. "Problems of Measurement in Comparative Research: Perspectives from an African Survey." Social Science Information 12 (1973): 29-43.

_____. "Response Set and Interview Bias." In Survey Research in Africa: Its Applications and Limits, ed. W. M. O'Barr, D. H. Spain, and M. A. Tessler. Evanston, Ill.: Northwestern University Press, 1973.

_____. "Cultural Modernity: Evidence from Tunisia." Social Science Quarterly 52 (September 1971): 290-308.

_____; O'Barr, W. M.; and Spain, D. H., eds. Tradition and Identity in Changing Africa. New York: 1973.

_____; Rogers, J. M.; and Schneider, D. R. "A Longitudinal Analysis of Political Attitude Change in Tunisia between 1967 and 1973." Paper read at the 1975 annual meeting of the African Studies Association.

Timur, S. Turkiye' de Aile Yapisis [Family structure in Turkey].
    Hacettepe University Publications, D-15. Ankara: Hacettepe
    University, 1971.

Touba, J. R. "The Relationship between Urbanization and the Chang-
    ing Status of Women in Iran, 1956-1966." Iranian Studies 5,
    no. 1 (1972): 25-36.

Tunisia. Ministry of the Plan. Fourth Plan for Economic and
    Social Development 1973-1976.

_____. National Institute of Statistics. Recensement général de la
    population et des logements du 3 mai 1966. Vol. 1. Tunis:
    1973.

_____. "Enquete sur la consommation et les dépenses des ménages
    en Tunisie 1965-1968." Etudes et Enquetes de l'Institut Na-
    tional de la Statistique no. 1 (December 1970).

Turkey. Ministry of Health and Social Welfare, School of Public
    Health. Statistics from the Turkish Demographic Survey
    1966-1967. In both English and Turkish. Ankara: Hacettepe
    University Press, 1970.

_____. Population Division. "1975 World Population Data Sheet."
    Mimeographed. Notes 2 and 3.

_____. Population Studies. No. 50. 1973b.

_____. "Principles and Recommendations for the 1970 Population
    Censuses." 1969.

United Nations. The Determinants and Consequences of Population
    Trends, ST/SOA/SER.A/50. Vol. 1. New York: UN, 1973a.

United Nations Economic and Social Office in Beirut. "Civil Regis-
    tration and Vital Statistics in Selected Countries in the Middle
    East." Population Bulletin of the United Nations Economic
    and Social Office in Beirut no. 2 (January 1972): 13-19.

United Nations Educational, Scientific and Cultural Organization.
    Project Proposal to UNFPA. "Comparative and Cross-
    Cultural Studies on the Relationship between Family Structure,
    Status of Women and Demographic Behavior." Mimeographed.
    Paris: UNESCO Population Division, 1975.

_____. Regional Office for Education in the Arab States. Popula-
tion Dynamics and Educational Development in Syria, Exhibit
1: Population Dynamics. Beirut: UNESCO, 1974.

United Nations Fund for Population Activities. "Status of Requests
Formally Submitted." UNFPA/FIN/73/PR/2. Mimeographed.
New York, 1973.

Valaoras, V. "Abortion in Greece." In Social Demography and
Medical Responsibility. London: International Planned
Parenthood Federation, 1970.

Valaoras, V. G. Population Analysis of Egypt (1935-1970). Occasional Paper no. 1. Cairo: Cairo Demographic Center, 1972.

Vallin, J. "Nouvelles donées sur la population algérienne."
Population no. 6 (1974): 1141-48.

_____. Facteurs socio-economiques de l'age moyen au mariage
des femmes algériennes." Population no. 6 (1973a): 1171-77.

_____. "Influence de divers facteurs économiques et sociaux sur
la fécondité en Algérie." Population nos. 4-5 (1973b): 817-42.

_____. "Rapport de masculinité à la naissance et qualité de
l'observation dans l'enquete fécondité algérienne 1970."
Paper presented at the International Union for the Scientific
Study of Population (IUSPP) Congress, Liège, August, 1973c.

_____. "L'Enquete nationale démographique tunisienne." Popula-
tion, Special Issue (March 1971), pp. 205-44.

_____. "Les Populations de l'Afrique au Nord du Sahara." Popula-
tion no. 6 (1970): 1212-36.

Van Dusen, R. A. "The Study of Women in the Middle East: Some
Thoughts." Middle East Studies Association Bulletin 10, no. 2
(May 1976): 1-19.

Van Nieuwenhuijze, C. A. O., ed. Commoners, Climbers and
Notables: A Sampler of Studies on Social Ranking in the
Middle East. Leiden: E. J. Brill, 1977.

Vesey-Fitzgerald, S. G. "Nature and Source of the Sharia." In Origin
and Development of Islamic Law, ed. M. Khaduri and H. J.
Liebesney. Washington, D. C.: Washington Institute, 1955.

Ware, H. "The Relevance of Changes in Women's Roles to Fertility Behavior: The African Evidence." Paper presented at the annual meeting of the Population Association of America, Seattle, Washington, April 1975.

Wargon, S. "The Study of Household Family Units in Demography." Journal of Marriage and the Family 36, no. 3 (1974): 560-64.

Watson, W. B., and Lapham, R. J., eds. "Family Planning Programs: World Review 1974." Studies in Family Planning 6, no. 8 (August 1975): 215-19.

Wenner, M. W. Modern Yemen. Baltimore: Johns Hopkins University Press, 1967.

Westoff, C. F. "Population and the Family: Overview." 1974 World Population Conference Background Paper. Mimeographed. E/CONF.60/CBP/8. New York: United Nations, 1974.

Williamson, J. B. "Subjective Efficacy and Ideal Family Size as Predictors of Favorability toward Birth Control." Demography 7 (1970): 329-39.

Wilson, A. T. The Persian Gulf: An Historical Sketch from the Earliest Times to the Beginning of the Twentieth Century. Oxford: 1928.

World Health Organization. Health Aspects of Family Planning. Technical Report Series, no. 442. Geneva: WHO, 1970.

World Population Data Sheet 1975. Washington, D.C.: Population Reference Bureau, 1975.

Wrong, D. H. "Trends in Class Fertility in Western Nations." Canadian Journal of Economics and Political Science 24 (1958): 216-29.

Yaukey, D. Fertility Differences in a Modernizing Country. Princeton, N.J.: Princeton University Press, 1961.

Yemen Arab Republic. Central Planning Organization. Statistical Yearbook 1975.

_____. Statistical Yearbook, 1973.

Youssef, N. Women and Work in Developing Countries. Population
    Monograph Series, no. 15. Berkeley: University of California
    Press, 1974.

_____. "Social Structure and the Female Labor Force: The Case
    of Women Workers in Muslim Middle Eastern Countries."
    Demography 8, no. 4 (1971): 427-39.

Youssef, N. H. "Differential Labor Force Participation of Women
    in Latin American and Middle Eastern Countries: The Influ-
    ence of Family Characteristics." Social Forces 51 (December
    1972): 135-53.

Yurtören, S. "Fertility and Related Attitudes among Two Social
    Classes in Ankara, Turkey." Master's thesis, Cornell Uni-
    versity, 1965.

Zachariah, K. C. In Cairo Demographic Center, Fertility Trends
    and Differentials in Arab Countries. Cairo: Cairo Demo-
    graphic Center, 1970.

Zeyoms, S. La Révolution des Femmes au Coeur de l'Asie
    Soviétique. Paris: Editions Sociales, 1971.

Zghal, A. "The Reactivation of Tradition in a Post Traditional
    Society." Daedelus 101, no. 1 (Winter 1973): 225-38.

About the Editor
and Contributors

JAMES ALLMAN is currently a research scientist for Battelle Institute's Population and Development Policy Program. He previously taught at the American University of Beirut, Harvard University, and the University of Tunis and was a consultant on projects in the Middle East for the Population Division of UNESCO, Paris. He has conducted research in Tunisia, Lebanon, Syria, Yemen Arab Republic, and recently was World Fertility Survey resident adviser in Haiti. He received a Ph.D. in sociology and Middle Eastern Studies from Harvard University and studied demography at the Harvard School of Public Health and the Institute of Demography, University of Paris. His publications include articles on social change and development, particularly in the areas of education and population, reports for UNESCO, the UNDP, the ILO, and the World Bank, and a forthcoming book, Social Mobility, Education and Development in Tunisia.

MOHAMED AYAD, on leave at the Harvard School of Public Health in 1976-77, is currently head of the Demographic Evaluation Unit, Office of Population and Family Planning, Tunisia. He has written on Islam and population, the measurement of contraceptive use and continuation, and fertility trends in Tunisia. He studied sociology at the University of Tunis and received the degree of "expert démographe" from the Institute of Demography, University of Paris.

GREER LITTON FOX is currently on the faculty of the Merrill-Palmer Institute, where she heads the research program in family sociology. She has taught at Bowling Green College, the University of Vermont, and conducted research in Turkey. She has written on modernization, marriage and family patterns, and fertility behavior. She has a Ph.D. in sociology from the University of Michigan.

MARY-JO DELVECCHIO GOOD currently holds an appointment at the School of Medicine, University of California, Davis. She taught previously at Wellesley College and Harvard University. She conducted research in Turkey and Iran, and has written on social stratification, ideological change, and family planning in the Middle East. She has a Ph.D. in sociology and Middle Eastern studies from Harvard University.

375

JOHN GULICK is currently professor and chairman of the Anthropology Department, University of North Carolina. His widely published research includes Tripoli: A Modern Arab City, The Middle East: An Anthropological Perspective, and numerous articles on urbanization, household and family structure, and social change in the Middle East. He has conducted field research in Iran and Lebanon.

MARGARET E. GULICK is currently with the Sociology Department, University of North Carolina. She has published articles and conducted research jointly with her husband, John Gulick, on various topics related to social change in the Middle East. Most recently, the Gulicks spent time in Isfahan, studying population dynamics from both anthropological and sociological perspectives.

ALLAN HILL is currently the regional representative for the Population Council's Demographic Division in Western Asia. His research interests are focused on the explanation of the high fertility levels in the Middle East, especially the Gulf states and Kuwait. From 1973 to 1975, he was a Harkness Fellow in the United States, where he studied at the Office of Population Research, Princeton University. Before that, he lectured in geography at the University of Aberdeen in Scotland and taught at the University of Kuwait. His Ph.D. research, done at Durham University, was on the population of Kuwait. He has written a book on Kuwait (with G. E. Ffrench) and has published a number of articles on the Middle East and on techniques of demographic estimation with inaccurate or incomplete data.

THE INTERNATIONAL PLANNED PARENTHOOD FEDERATION is a union of autonomous national family planning associations. In April 1970, a regional office was established in Beirut to administer activities in the Middle East and North Africa. The Middle East and North Africa region covers the countries from Afghanistan to Morocco, having member associations in the following countries: Afghanistan, Arab Republic of Egypt, Cyprus, Iraq, Jordan, Lebanon, Morocco, Sudan, Syria, Tunisia, and Yemen.

YOLANDE JEMAI is currently with the Demographic Evaluation Unit, Office of Population and Family Planning, Tunisia. She is interested in demographic models and the effects of population policy on fertility trends. She is an economist and received the degree of "expert demographe" from the Institute of Demography, University of Paris.

ATEF M. KHALIFA is currently UN statistical expert at the Office of Statistics in Amman, Jordan. He taught previously at Cairo University and the UN Cairo Demographic Center in Egypt and was director of the Demography Unit, Institute of Statistical Studies and Research, Cairo University. He received a Ph.D. in demography from the University of North Carolina, Chapel Hill, and degrees from Cairo University in statistics. He has published numerous articles on fertility trends, differentials, and determinants in Egypt.

CARLA MAKHLOUF is a research associate at the School of Public Health, American University of Beirut. She has an M.A. in anthropology and a B.A. in sociology from the American University of Beirut and is currently enrolled in the Ph.D. program in history. She conducted field research in the Yemen Arab Republic in 1974 and 1976.

FATIMA MERNISSI teaches sociology at Mohamed V University in Rabat. She has worked as a consultant for the UN Economic Commission for Africa and UNESCO on projects dealing with the impact of socioeconomic development on women and the family in Africa and the Arab countries. She has recently published a book on Islamic views of women, entitled Beyond the Veil. She studied at the University of Rabat, the University of Paris, and received a Ph.D. in the United States.

CYNTHIA L. MYNTTI received an M.A. in anthropology from the American University of Beirut in 1974 and is now a candidate for a Ph.D. in social anthropology at the London School of Economics. She has studied and worked in Iran, Tunisia, Lebanon, and Jordan and is currently conducting field research in the Yemen Arab Republic on population change and women's roles.

GERALD J. OBERMEYER is chairman and professor of anthropology in the Department of Social Sciences, American University of Beirut. He conducted research in North Yemen and Egypt, and received a Ph.D. in anthropology from Indiana University.

HANNA RIZK is currently demographic consultant for the World Fertility Survey, London. He was previously UN statistical expert at the Office of Statistics in Amman and taught for many years at the American University of Cairo. He has published numerous articles on fertility trends and population policy in the Middle East. He received demographic training at the Office of Population Research, Princeton University, where he earned a Ph.D. in economics.

JANET M. ROGERS and DANIEL R. SCHNEIDER are graduate students at the University of Wisconsin, Milwaukee.

MARK A. TESSLER is chairman of the Department of Political Science, University of Wisconsin, Milwaukee. He has conducted research in Tunisia, Morocco, and West Africa. He is co-author of Tradition and Identity in Changing Africa, co-editor of Survey Research in Africa and Arab Oil, and author of a forthcoming book, Three Nonassimilating Minorities: Jews in Tunisia and Morocco and Arabs in Israel. He studied at the University of Tunis and received a Ph.D. in political science from Northwestern University.

SERIM TIMUR, of the Population Division, Social Sciences Sector, UNESCO, is currently in charge of UNESCO's social science and population research program. She was formerly lecturer and senior research associate at the Institute of Population Studies, Hacettepe University, in Ankara (1967-74), and director of the Demographic Research Section, Turkish Ministry of Health and Social Assistance (1965-67). She is the author of Family Structure in Turkey (1972), Income Distribution in Turkey (1968) (with T. Bulutay and H. Ersel), and numerous articles on fertility trends, population action programs, migration patterns, and methodological aspects of demographic surveys. She received a Ph.D. in sociology-demography from Hacettepe University in 1971 and an M.A. in sociology from Cornell University in 1965.

JACQUES VALLIN is currently maitre de recherche at the Institut National d'Etude Démographique, Paris. He was formerly Population Council resident adviser in Tunisia and Algeria. His research interests focus on demographic change in the developing countries of Africa and Asia, as well as on the study of mortality in France and Europe. Publications include La Mortalité par génération en France depuis 1879 and numerous articles and contributions to collective works dealing with demographic change in Africa and Asia. He is an "expert démographe" (Institute of Demography, University of Paris) and received a doctorate in economics from the University of Paris.

Related Titles
Published by
Praeger Special Studies

EQUALITY OF OPPORTUNITY WITHIN AND AMONG NATIONS

edited by
Khadija Haq

THE FERTILITY OF WORKING WOMEN:
A Synthesis of International Research

edited by
Stanley Kupinsky

IMPACT OF FAMILY PLANNING PROGRAMS ON
FERTILITY: The U.S. Experience

Phillips Cutright
Frederick S. Jaffe

SEX AND CLASS IN LATIN AMERICA

edited by
June Nash
Helen Icken Safa

WOMEN AND WORLD DEVELOPMENT:
With an Annotated Bibliography

edited by
Irene Tinker
Michele BoBramsen
Mayra Buvinic